CAMBRIDGE LIBRARY

Books of enduring scholc

Classics

From the Renaissance to the nineteenth century, Latin and Greek were compulsory subjects in almost all European universities, and most early modern scholars published their research and conducted international correspondence in Latin. Latin had continued in use in Western Europe long after the fall of the Roman empire as the lingua franca of the educated classes and of law, diplomacy, religion and university teaching. The flight of Greek scholars to the West after the fall of Constantinople in 1453 gave impetus to the study of ancient Greek literature and the Greek New Testament. Eventually, just as nineteenth-century reforms of university curricula were beginning to erode this ascendancy, developments in textual criticism and linguistic analysis, and new ways of studying ancient societies, especially archaeology, led to renewed enthusiasm for the Classics. This collection offers works of criticism, interpretation and synthesis by the outstanding scholars of the nineteenth century.

Studies on Homer and the Homeric Age

Four-time prime minister William Ewart Gladstone (1809–98) was also a prolific author and enthusiastic scholar of the classics. Gladstone had spent almost two decades in politics prior to his writing the three-volume *Studies on Homer and the Homeric Age*. This work and the preceding 'On the place of Homer in classical education and in historical inquiry' (1857), reflect Gladstone's interest in the *Iliad* and the *Odyssey*, which he read with increasing frequency from the 1830s onward and which he viewed as particularly relevant to modern society. As he relates, he has two objects in the *Studies*: 'to promote and extend' the study of Homer's 'immortal poems' and 'to vindicate for them ... their just degree both of absolute and, more especially, of relative critical value'. Volume 1 establishes Homer's contemporary relevance and provides an extensive 'ethnography of Greek races' related to Homer's works.

Cambridge University Press has long been a pioneer in the reissuing of out-of-print titles from its own backlist, producing digital reprints of books that are still sought after by scholars and students but could not be reprinted economically using traditional technology. The Cambridge Library Collection extends this activity to a wider range of books which are still of importance to researchers and professionals, either for the source material they contain, or as landmarks in the history of their academic discipline.

Drawing from the world-renowned collections in the Cambridge University Library, and guided by the advice of experts in each subject area, Cambridge University Press is using state-of-the-art scanning machines in its own Printing House to capture the content of each book selected for inclusion. The files are processed to give a consistently clear, crisp image, and the books finished to the high quality standard for which the Press is recognised around the world. The latest print-on-demand technology ensures that the books will remain available indefinitely, and that orders for single or multiple copies can quickly be supplied.

The Cambridge Library Collection will bring back to life books of enduring scholarly value (including out-of-copyright works originally issued by other publishers) across a wide range of disciplines in the humanities and social sciences and in science and technology.

Studies on Homer and the Homeric Age

Volume 1:
I. Prolegomena; II. Achaeis; or,
The Ethnology of the Greek Races

William Ewart Gladstone

CAMBRIDGE UNIVERSITY PRESS

Cambridge, New York, Melbourne, Madrid, Cape Town, Singapore,
São Paolo, Delhi, Dubai, Tokyo

Published in the United States of America by Cambridge University Press, New York

www.cambridge.org
Information on this title: www.cambridge.org/9781108012041

© in this compilation Cambridge University Press 2010

This edition first published 1858
This digitally printed version 2010

ISBN 978-1-108-01204-1 Paperback

This book reproduces the text of the original edition. The content and language reflect
the beliefs, practices and terminology of their time, and have not been updated.

Cambridge University Press wishes to make clear that the book, unless originally published
by Cambridge, is not being republished by, in association or collaboration with, or
with the endorsement or approval of, the original publisher or its successors in title.

STUDIES ON HOMER

AND

THE HOMERIC AGE.

BY THE

RIGHT HON. W. E. GLADSTONE, D.C.L.

M. P. FOR THE UNIVERSITY OF OXFORD.

IN THREE VOLUMES.

VOL. I.

Plenius ac melius Chrysippo et Crantore.—HORACE.

OXFORD:
AT THE UNIVERSITY PRESS.
M.DCCC.LVIII.

[*The right of Translation is reserved.*]

STUDIES ON HOMER

AND

THE HOMERIC AGE.

I. PROLEGOMENA.

II. ACHÆIS:

OR,

THE ETHNOLOGY OF THE GREEK RACES.

BY THE

RIGHT HON. W. E. GLADSTONE, D.C.L.

M. P. FOR THE UNIVERSITY OF OXFORD.

Plenius ac melius Chrysippo et Crantore.—HORACE.

OXFORD:
AT THE UNIVERSITY PRESS.
M.DCCC.LVIII.

[*The right of Translation is reserved.*]

THE CONTENTS.

I. PROLEGOMENA.

SECT. I.
On the State of the Homeric Question.

Objects of this Work .... Page	1
Results thus far of the Homeric Controversy	2
Improved apparatus for the Study of Homer	4
Effect of the poems on Civilization.........................	5
They do not compete with the Holy Scriptures	6

SECT. II.
The Place of Homer in Classical Education.

Study of Homer in the English Universities.................	9
Homer should not be studied as a Poet only.................	11
His claims compared with those of other Poets	14
Study of Homer in the Public Schools	18

SECT. III.
On the Historic Aims of Homer.

High organization of the Poems...........................	21
The presumption is that the Poet had Historic aims	22
Positive signs of them	23
Pursued even at some cost of Poetical beauty	26
Minuter indications	28
General tone	28
Hypothesis of reproduction inadmissible	30
What is chiefly meant by his Historic aims	35

CONTENTS.

SECT. IV.
On the probable Date of Homer.

The main question: is he an original witness 36
Adverse arguments 37
Affirmative arguments 39

SECT. V.
The probable Trustworthiness of the Text of Homer.

The received text to be adopted as a basis 42
Failure of other methods 44
State of the Manuscripts 46
Complaints of interpolation 47
Testimonies concerning the early use of the Poems 49
Preservative power of the Recitations or matches 55
Pseudo-Homeric poems 56
Argument from the Cyclic poems 59
The Alexandrian period 60
Amount and quality of guarantees 64
Improbability of wilful falsification 67
Internal evidence of soundness in detail 69

SECT. VI.
Place and Authority of Homer in Historical Inquiry.

Homer paramount as a literary authority 71
He has suffered through credulity 73
And through incredulity 79
Proposed method of treatment 81
Instances of contrary method, (1) Hellen and his family 82
Authority of Hesiod 84
Instance (2), personality of Helen 87
Conclusion 89

II. ACHÆIS.

ETHNOLOGY OF THE GREEK RACES.

SECT. I.

Scope of the Inquiry.

Preliminary objection of Mr. Grote stated 93
Synopsis of national and tribal names to be examined 96

SECT. II.

On the Pelasgians, and cognate races.

The Pelasgians 100
Pelasgic Argos 101
Dodona 106
Thessaly and the Southern Islands 109
Epithets for Pelasgians 113
Use of this name in the singular 114
The Pelasgians and Larissa 115
The Arcadians Pelasgian 119
Why προσέληνοι 121
The Arcadians afterwards the Swiss of Greece 122
The Graians or Greeks 123
Ceres and the Pelasgians 124
The Iaones or Ionians 127
The Athenians in the Catalogue 129
The Catalogue, vv. 546-9 129
The same, vv. 550, 1 132
The same, vv. 553-5 135
Review of the Homeric evidence as to the Athenians 137
Their relations with Minerva 140
Post-Homeric evidence of the Pelasgianism of Attica 145

CONTENTS.

The Pelasgians related to Egypt 148
The Egyptians semi-fabulous to Homer 151
Their Pelasgian resemblances, in Homer and otherwise 153
The Greeks of the Iliad why never termed Pelasgian 156
The Θρῆκες and Θρῄκιοι 158
The Caucones and Leleges 161

SECT. III.

The Pelasgians: and certain States naturalized or akin to Greece.

Minos in Homer 166
His origin 167
His place in the nether world 168
The power of Crete 169
Two of the five races apparently Pelasgian 170
The tradition of Deucalion 172
The extent of the Minoan Empire 175
Evidence of Post-Homeric tradition 176
Circumstantial evidence 178
The Lycians 181
Their points of connection with Greece 183
Elements of the population 185
Cyprus 188
Inhabitants probably Pelasgian 190
No other name competes with the Pelasgian as designating the first inhabitants of Greece 193
The Pelasgians were the base or *substratum* of the Greek nation. 194
Post-Homeric testimony respecting them 195
K. O. Müller's Summary 200
The Pelasgian language 203
The Pelasgian route into Greece 205
Probably twofold 206
Route of the Helli 208
Peloponnesus the old centre of power 209
Derivation of the Pelasgian name 211

CONTENTS.

SECT. IV.
On the Phœnicians and the Outer Geography of the Odyssey.

Tokens of the Phœnicians in Greece 216
Limits of Homer's Inner or Greek Geography 217
And Greek Navigation 219
His Outer Geography Phœnician 221
The traditions connected therewith also Phœnician 223
Minos the 'Ολοόφρων 225
Commercial aptitude of the modern Greeks 227
The Homeric Mouth of Ocean 228
The two Geographical reports are blended into one 228
The Siceli and Sicania 229
Their site is probably on the Bruttian Coast 231
The Epirus of Homer 234
The Thesprotians in Homer 235
The Cadmeans in Homer 239
Period from which they date 240
Conclusions respecting them 244

SECT. V.
On the Catalogue.

The Greek Catalogue, properly an Array or Review 245
The Preface 246
The List 247
The principle of arrangement 249
The distribution in chief 250
The sub-distribution 251
Proofs of historic aim 255
Genealogies of the Catalogue 256
The Epilogue 259
The Trojan Catalogue 261

SECT. VI.
On the Hellenes of Homer.

The word Hellas the key to this inquiry 264
List of passages where used 265
Some of them admit the narrow sense 266

CONTENTS.

Some refuse it	268
None require it	272
Hellenes in Il. ii. 684	274
Panhellenes in Il. ii. 530	277
Cephallenes in Il. ii. 631 and elsewhere	278
The Helli or Selli	279
Selli of the Scholiast of Aristophanes	280

SECT. VII.

On the respective contributions of the Pelasgian and Hellenic factors to the compound of the Greek nation.

Contributions to Mythology	285
Correspondences with Rome and Troy	287
The Pelasgian religion less imaginative	289
Their ritual development fuller	290
Order of Priests in Homer not Hellenic	293
Contributions to language	294
Classes of words which agree	298
Classes which differ	301
Evidence from names of persons	307
General rules of discrimination	309
Names of the Pelasgian class	311
Names of the Hellenic class	317
Contributions to political ideas	320
To martial ideas	320
Corporal education and Games	322
Music and Song	329
Supposed Pelasgianism of the Troic age	331
The traditions of Hunting	332
The practice of Navigation	336
Summary of the case	338
States especially Hellic or Pelasgic	342

SECT. VIII.

On the three greater Homeric appellatives.

Modes of formation for names of peoples	346
The three greater appellatives not synonymous	348
Proofs of their distinctive use	350

CONTENTS.

The Argive Juno, Argive Helen 353
The Danaans of Homer 355
Epithets of the three appellatives 356
The Danaan name dynastic 359
Campared with the Cadmean name 361
Epoch of the dynasty 363
Post-Homeric tradition 366
Application of the name Argos 368
Achaic and Iasian Argos 373
The phrase μέσον Ἄργος 378
The Apian land 379
Summary of geographical conclusions 380
Etymology of the word Argos 381
Its connection with ἔργον 384
The etymology tested by kindred words 388
The Danaan Argeians of Od. viii. 578 391
The Argive Juno 392
Transition to Achæans 393
Relation of Argeian and Pelasgian names 396
The etymology illustrated 397
Different extent of Ἀργεῖοι and Ἄργος 401
Propositions as to the Achæan name 402
Particulars of its use 403
Signs of its leaning to the aristocracy 406
Mode of its application in Ithaca 411
Its local sense in Thessaly 416
In Crete 417
In Pylos 418
In Eastern Peloponnesus 419
Force of the name Παναχαιοὶ 420
The Æolid and Æolian names 423
The Heraclids in Homer 425
The descent of the Æolids 427
The earliest Hellenic thrones in Greece 429
The Danaan and Argive names used nationally in poetry only.. 431
Summary of the evidence 433
Later literary history of the three great appellatives 436
Their value as primitive History 437

SECT. IX.

On the Homeric title of ἄναξ ἀνδρῶν.

Difference between Epithets and Titles	440
Examples of Homeric titles	443
The Βασιλεὺς of Homer	445
Common interpretations of the ἄναξ ἀνδρῶν	443
Some particulars of its use in Homer	446
How far connected with metrical convenience	447
The κρείων and the ποιμὴν λαῶν	448
Arguments for a specific meaning in ἄναξ ἀνδρῶν	450
Persons to whom the title is applied	453
Persons to whom it might have been applied	455
Associations of reverence with it	456
It may indicate patriarchal chieftaincy	459
Presumptions of this in the case of Agamemnon	461
Propositions respecting his extraction and station	463
Arguments against his Hellenic descent considered	465
Connection of Tantalus with Greece and with Pelops	466
As to the seat of his power	470
Homeric notices of Pelops	471
The Achæans rose with him	472
They came from Thessaly	474
The Dorians appropriate the Pelopid succession	477
Protest against the popular tradition of the Hellenidæ	480
Which, however, bears witness to the connection with Thessaly	481
Case of Agamemnon summed up	482
The cases of Anchises and Æneas	484
Presumptive evidence as to Anchises	486
Presumptive evidence as to Æneas	864
Evidence from the Dardanid genealogy	489
From the horses of Tros	490
Evidence summed up	491
Signs of kin between Trojans and Greeks	492
Signs connected with the Hellic name	496
The Hellespont of Homer	497
The gift of Echepolus Anchisiades	499
Twofold bond, Hellic as well as Pelasgic	499
Case of Augeias stated	500

CONTENTS.

Notes of connection between Elis and the North 502
Relation of Augeias to the name Ephyre 504
Cluster of apparently cognate names 505
The race of Φῆρες 509
Common root of all these names 510
Probable signification of 'Εφύρη 513
Places bearing the name 'Εφύρη 515
Summary of the evidence for Augeias 519
Case of Euphetes 520
The site of his Ephyre 521
Case of Eumelus 526
The ἄναξ ἀνδρῶν is descended from Jupiter 529
The four notes of the ἄναξ ἀνδρῶν 531
Negative proofs 532
Persons with the four notes but without the title 536
Its disappearance with Homer 538
Signs in the Iliad of political disorganization 539
More extensively in the Odyssey 542
General significancy of the title ἄναξ ἀνδρῶν 543

SECT. X.

On the connection of the Hellenes and Achæans with the East.

The Achæan name has no mark of a Greek origin 545
Means for pursuing the inquiry 546
The two groups of Indo-European languages 547
Corresponding distinction of races 548
Province of Fars or Persia proper 549
Ascendancy of the Persians 550
Relation of the Germani to the Celts 551
And to the Hellenes 552
The Persian tribe of Γερμάνιοι 554
The Homeric traces of the Persian name 555
The Achæan name in Persia 556
Its probable etymology 557
The Persians according to Herodotus 558
The comparison as to religious belief 561
As to ritual, and other resemblances 563
Evidence of the Behistun inscription 565

CONTENTS.

The organization established by Darius 566
Presumptions from the term Βασιλεύς 567
Hellenic traits in modern Persia 568
The Eelliats... 571
Media a probable source of the Pelasgi 571

ADDENDA 573

STUDIES ON HOMER

AND

THE HOMERIC AGE.

I. PROLEGOMENA.*

SECT. 1.—*On the State of the Homeric question.*

WE are told that, in an ancient city, he who had a new law to propose made his appearance, when about to discharge that duty, with a halter round his neck. It might be somewhat rigid to re-introduce this practice in the case of those who write new books on subjects, with which the ears at least of the world are familiar. But it is not unreasonable to demand of them some such reason for their boldness as shall be at any rate presumably related to public utility. Complying with this demand by anticipation, I will place in the foreground an explicit statement of the objects which I have in view.

These objects are twofold: firstly, to promote and extend the fruitful study of the immortal poems of Homer; and secondly, to vindicate for them, in an age of discussion, their just degree both of absolute and, more especially, of relative critical value. My desire is to indicate at least, if I cannot hope to establish, their proper

* Revised and enlarged from the 'Essay on the place of Homer in Classical education and in Historical inquiry,' which was contained in the 'Oxford Essays' for 1857, published by Mr. J. W. Parker.

place, both in the discipline of classical education, and among the materials of historical inquiry. When the world has been hearing and reading Homer, and talking and writing about him, for nearly three thousand years, it may seem strange thus to imply that he is still an 'inheritor of unfulfilled renown,'[a] and not yet in full possession of his lawful throne. He who seems to impeach the knowledge and judgment of all former ages, himself runs but an evil chance, and is likely to be found guilty of ignorance and folly. Such, however, is not my design. There is no reason to doubt that Greece

Dum fortuna fuit

knew right well her own noble child, and paid him all the homage that even he could justly claim. But in later times, and in most of the lands where he is a foreigner, I know not if he has ever yet enjoyed his full honour from the educated world. He is, I trust, coming to it; and my desire is to accelerate, if ever so little, the movement in that direction.

As respects the first portion of the design which has been described, I would offer the following considerations. The controversy *de vitá et sanguine*, concerning the personality of the poet, and the unity and antiquity of the works, has been carried on with vigour for near a century. In default of extraneous testimony, the materials of warfare have been sedulously sought in the rich mine which was offered by the poems themselves. There has resulted from this cause a closer study of the text, and a fuller development of much that it contains, than could have been expected in times when the student of Homer had only to enjoy his banquet, and not to fight for it before he could sit down. It is not merely, however, in warmth of feeling that he may

[a] Shelley's Adonais.

have profited; the Iliad and the Odyssey have been, from the absolute necessity of the case, put into the witness-box themselves, examined and cross-examined in every variety of temper, and thus, in some degree at least, made to tell their own story. The result has been upon the whole greatly in their favour. The more they are searched and tested, the more does it appear they have to say, and the better does their testimony hang together. The more plain does it become, that the arguments used on the side of scepticism and annihilation are generally of a technical and external character, and the greater is the mass of moral and internal evidence continually accumulated against them. In consequence, there has set in a strong reaction among scholars, even in Germany (in England the destructive theories never greatly throve), on behalf of the affirmative side of all, or nearly all, the main questions which had been raised. Mure,[b] the last and perhaps most distinguished of British writers on this subject, has left the debate in such a state that those who follow him may be excused, and may excuse their readers, from

[b] While speaking of this eminent labourer in the field of Homeric inquiry, I must not pass by the sympathising spirit and imagination of Mr. H. Nelson Coleridge, the admirably turned Homeric tone of the ballads of Dr. Maginn, or the valuable analysis contained in the uncompleted 'Homerus' of Archdeacon Williams. But of all the criticisms on Homer which I have ever had the good fortune to read, in our own or any language, the most vivid and entirely genial are those found in the 'Essays Critical and Imaginative' of the late Professor Wilson. In that most useful, and I presume I may add standard, work, Smith's 'Dictionary of Classical Biography and Mythology,' I am sorry to find that the important article Homerus, by Dr. Ihne, though it has the merit of presenting the question in a clear light, yet is neither uniformly accurate in its references to the text of Homer, nor at all in conformity with the prevailing state at least of English opinion upon the controversy.

systematic preliminary discussion; and may proceed upon the assumption that the Iliad and Odyssey are in their substance the true offspring of the heroic age itself, and are genuine gifts not only of a remote antiquity but of a designing mind; as well as that he, to whom that mind belonged, has been justly declared by the verdict of all ages to be the patriarch of poets. These controversies have been 'bolted to the bran;' for us at least they are all but dead, and to me it seems little better than lost time to revive them.

Having then at the present day the title to the estate in some degree secured from litigation, we may enter upon the fruition of it, and with all the truer zest on account of the conflict, which has been long and keenly fought, and in the general opinion fairly won. It now becomes all those, who love Homer, to prosecute the sure method of inquiry and appreciation by close, continued, comprehensive study of the text; a study of which it would be easy to prove the need, by showing how inaccurately the poems are often cited in quarters, to which the general reader justifiably looks for trustworthy information. To this we have been exhorted by the writer already named:[c] and we have only to make his practice our model. That something has already been attained, we may judge by comparison. Let us take a single instance. In the year 1735 was published 'Blackwell's Inquiry into the Life and Writings of Homer.' Bentley, as it would appear from Bishop Monk's Life[d] of that extraordinary scholar, was not to be taken in by a book of this kind: but such men as Bentley are not samples of their time, they are living symbols and predictions of what it will require years or

[c] Mure's History of Grecian Literature, vol. i. p. 10.
[d] 4to ed. p. 622, n.

generations to accomplish. We may rather judge of the common impression made by this book, from the Notes to Pope's Preface to the Iliad, where Warton[e] extols it as 'a work that abounds in curious researches and observations, and places Homer in a new light.' But no reader of Homer, in our own time, would really, I apprehend, be the poorer, if every copy of it could be burned.

Since the time of Blackwell's work, important aids have been gained towards the study of Homer, by the researches of travellers, fruitful in circumstantial evidence, and by the discovery of the Venetian Scholia, as well as by the persevering labours of modern critics. We have been gradually coming to understand that these precious works, which may have formed the delight of our boyhood, have also been designed to instruct our maturer years. I do not here refer to their poetic power and splendour only. It is now time that we should recognise the truth, that they constitute a vast depository of knowledge upon subjects of deep interest, and of boundless variety; and that this is a knowledge, too, which can be had from them alone. It was the Greek mind transferred, without doubt, in some part through Italy, but yet only transferred, and still Greek both in origin and in much of its essence, in which was shaped and tempered the original mould of the modern European civilization. I speak now of civilization as a thing distinct from religion, but destined to combine and coalesce with it. The power derived from this source was to stand in subordinate conjunction with the Gospel, and to contribute its own share towards the training of mankind. From hence were to be derived the forms and materials of thought, of imaginative

[e] Warton's Pope, vol. iv. p. 371, n.

culture, of the whole education of the intellectual soul, which, when pervaded with an higher life from the Divine fountain, was thus to be secured from corruption, and both placed and kept in harmony with the world of spirits.

This Greek mind, which thus became one of the main factors of the civilized life of Christendom, cannot be fully comprehended without the study of Homer, and is nowhere so vividly or so sincerely exhibited as in his works. He has a world of his own, into which, upon his strong wing, he carries us. There we find ourselves amidst a system of ideas, feelings, and actions, different from what are to be found anywhere else; and forming a new and distinct standard of humanity. Many among them seem as if they were then shortly about to be buried under a mass of ruins, in order that they might subsequently reappear, bright and fresh for application, among later generations of men. Others of them almost carry us back to the early morning of our race, the hours of its greater simplicity and purity, and more free intercourse with God. In much that this Homeric world exhibits, we see the taint of sin at work, but far, as yet, from its perfect work and its ripeness; it stands between Paradise and the vices of later heathenism, far from both, from the latter as well as from the former; and if among all earthly knowledge, the knowledge of man be that which we should chiefly court, and if to be genuine it should be founded upon experience, how is it possible to over-value this primitive representation of the human race in a form complete, distinct, and separate, with its own religion, ethics, policy, history, arts, manners, fresh and true to the standard of its nature, like the form of an infant from the hand of the Creator, yet mature, full, and finished, in its own sense, after its own laws, like some masterpiece of the sculptor's art.

The poems of Homer never can be put in competition with the Sacred Writings of the Old Testament, as regards the one invaluable code of Truth and Hope that was contained in them. But while the Jewish records exhibit to us the link between man and the other world in the earliest times, the poems of Homer show us the being, of whom God was pleased to be thus mindful, in the free unsuspecting play of his actual nature. The patriarchal and Jewish dispensations created, and sustained through Divine interposition, a state of things essentially special and exceptional: but here first we see our kind set to work out for itself, under the lights which common life and experience supplied, the deep problem of his destiny. Nor is there, perhaps, any more solemn and melancholy lesson, than that which is to be learned from its continual downward course. If these words amount to a begging of the question, at least, it is most important for us to know whether the course was continually downwards; whether, as man enlarged his powers and his resources, he came nearer to, or went farther from his happiness and his perfection. Now, this inquiry cannot, for Europe and Christendom at least, be satisfactorily conducted, except in commencing from the basis which the Homeric poems supply. As regards the great Roman people, we know nothing of them, which is at once archaic and veracious. As regards the Greeks, it is Homer that furnishes the point of origin from which all distances are to be measured. When the historic period began, Greece was already near its intellectual middle-age. Little can be learned of the relative movements of our moral and our mental nature severally, from matching one portion of that period with another, in comparison with what we may gather from bringing into neighbourhood and contrast the pristine and youthful Greece of Homer on the one hand, and, on the other, the developed and finished Greece of the age of the tragedians or the orators.

The Mosaic books, and the other historical books of the Old Testament, are not intended to present, and do not present, a picture of human society, or of our nature drawn at large. Their aim is to exhibit it in one master-relation, and to do this with effect, they do it, to a great extent, exclusively. The Homeric materials for exhibiting that relation are different in kind as well as in degree: but as they paint, and paint to the very life, the whole range of our nature, and the entire circle of human action and experience, at an epoch much more nearly analogous to the patriarchal time than to any later age, the poems of Homer may be viewed, in the philosophy of human nature, as the complement of the earliest portion of the Sacred Records.

Although the close and systematic study of the Homeric text has begun at a date comparatively recent, yet the marked development of riches from within which it has produced, has already been a real, permanent, and vast addition to the mental wealth of mankind. We can now better understand than formerly much that relates to the fame and authority of this great poet in early times, and that we may formerly have contemplated as fanciful, exaggerated, or unreal. It was, we can now see, with no idle wonder that, while Greek philosophers took texts from him so largely in their schools, the Greek public listened to his strains in places of thronged resort, and in their solemn assemblages, and Greek warriors and statesmen kept him in their cabinets and under their pillows; and, for the first and last time in the history of the world, made the preservation of a poet's compositions an object of permanent public policy.

SECT. 2.—*The Place of Homer in Classical Education.*

Now, from these considerations may arise the important question, Does Homer hold in our English education the place which is his due, and which it would be for our advantage to give him? An immense price is paid by the youth of this country for classical acquirement. It is the main effort of the first spring-tide of their intellectual life. It is to be hoped that this price will continue to be paid by all those, who are qualified to profit by the acquisition; and that though of other knowledge much more will hereafter be gained than heretofore, yet of this there shall on no account be less. Still, viewing the greatness of the cost, which consists in the chief energies of so many precious years, it highly concerns us to see that what we get in return is good both in measure and in quality. What, then, are the facts with respect to the study of Homer in England at the present day?

I must here begin with the apology due from one who feels himself to be far from perfectly informed on the case of which it is necessary to give an outline. But even if I understate both the amount of Homeric study, and its efficiency, there will, I am confident, remain, after every due allowance shall have been made for error, ample room for the application of the general propositions that I seek to enforce. They are these: that the study of Homer in our Universities is as yet below the point to which it is desirable that it should be carried, and that the same study, carried on at our Public Schools, neither is, nor can be made, a fitting substitute for what is thus wanting at the Universities.

In my own day, at Oxford, now a full quarter of a century ago, the poems of Homer were read chiefly by way of exception, and in obedience to the impulse of individual tastes. They entered rather materially into those examinations by which scholarship was principally to be tested, but they scarcely formed a substantive or recognised part of the main studies of the place, which were directed to the final examination in the Schools for the Bachelor's degree. I do not recollect to have ever heard at that time of their being used as the subject matter of the ordinary tutorial lectures; and if they were so, the case was certainly a rare one. Although the late Dr. Gaisford, in the estimation of many the first scholar of his age, during his long tenure of the Deanery of Christ Church, gave the whole weight of his authority to the recommendation of Homeric study, it did not avail to bring about any material change. The basis of the Greek classical instruction lay chiefly in the philosophers, historians, and later poets; and when Homer was, in the academical phrase, ' taken up,' he was employed ornamentally, and therefore superficially, and was subjected to no such searching and laborious methods of study as, to the great honour and advantage of Oxford, were certainly applied to the authors who held the first rank in her practical system. I am led to believe that the case at Cambridge was not essentially different, although, from the greater relative space occupied there by examinations in pure scholarship, it is probable that Homer may, under that aspect at least, have attracted a greater share of attention.

When, however, the University of Oxford brought to maturity, in the year 1850, a new Statute of examinations, efforts were made to promote an extended study of Homer. Those efforts, it happily appears, have produced a considerable effect. Provision was made by that statute for dividing the study of the poets from the philosophical and historical studies, and for including the former in the intermediate, or, as it is termed, 'first public' examination, while both the latter were reserved for the final trial, with which the period of undergraduateship is usually wound up. All candidates for honours in this intermediate examination are now required to present not less than twelve Books of Homer on the list of works in which they are to be examined. And I understand that he has also taken his place among the regular subjects of the tutorial lectures. This is a great sign of progress; and it may confidently be hoped that, under these circumstances, Homer will henceforward hold a much more forward position in the studies of Oxford. There remains something to desire, and that something, I should hope, any further development of the Examination Statute of the University will supply.

It is clear, that the study of this great master should not be confined to preparation for examinations which deal principally with language, or which cannot enter upon either primitive history, or philosophy, or policy, or religion, except by way of secondary illustration. Better far that he should be studied simply among the poets, than that he should not be studied at all. But as long as he is read only among the poets, he cannot, I believe, be read effectively for the higher and more varied purposes of which Homeric study is so largely susceptible.

The grammar, metre, and diction, the tastes, the

whole poetic handling and qualities of Homer, do, indeed, offer an assemblage of objects for our consideration at once and alike singular, attractive, extended, and profitable. The extraneous controversies with which his name has so long been associated as to his personality and date, and as to the unity and transmission of his works, although they are for us, I trust, in substance nearly decided, yet are not likely to lose their literary interest, were it only on account of the peculiarly convenient and seductive manner in which they open up many questions of primitive research; presenting these questions to us, as they do, not in the dull garb pieced out of antiquarian scraps, but alive, and in the full movement of vigorous debate. All this is fit for delightful exercise; but much more lies behind.

There is an inner Homeric world, of which his verse is the tabernacle and his poetic genius the exponent, but which offers in itself a spectacle of the most profound interest, quite apart from him who introduces us to it, and from the means by which we are so introduced. This world of religion and ethics, of civil policy, of history and ethnology, of manners and arts, so widely severed from all following experience, that we may properly call them palæozoic, can hardly be examined and understood by those, who are taught to approach Homer as a poet only.

Indeed, the transcendency of his poetical distinctions has tended to overshadow his other claims and uses. As settlers in the very richest soils, saturated with the fruits which they almost spontaneously yield, rarely turn their whole powers to account, so they, that are taught simply to repair to Homer for his poetry, find in him, so considered, such ample resources for enjoyment, that, unless summoned onwards by a distinct and separate call, they are little likely to travel further. It was thus that Lord Bacon's brilliant fame as a philosopher diverted public attention from his merits as a political historian.[f] It was thus, to take a nearer instance, that most readers of Dante, while submitting their imaginations to his powerful sway, have been almost wholly unconscious that they were in the hands of one of the most acute and exact of metaphysicians, one of the most tender, earnest, and profound among spiritual writers. Here, indeed, the process has been simpler in form; for the majority, at least, of readers, have stopped with the striking, and, so to speak, incorporated imagery of the 'Inferno,' and have not so much as read the following, which are also the loftier and more ethereal, portions of the 'Divina Commedia.' It may be enough for Homer's fame, that the consent of mankind has irrevocably assigned to him a supremacy among poets, without real competitors or partners, except Dante and Shakspeare; and that, perhaps, if we take into view his date, the unpreparedness of the world for works so extraordinary as his, the comparative paucity of the traditional resources and training he could have inherited, he then becomes the most extraordinary, as he is also the most ancient, phenomenon in the whole history of purely human culture. In particular points he appears to me, if it be not presumptuous to say so much, to remain to this day unquestionably without an equal in the management of the poetic art. If Shakspeare be supreme in the intuitive knowledge of human nature and in the rapid and fertile vigour of his imagination, if Dante have the largest grasp of the 'height and depth' of all things created, if he stand first in the power of exhibiting and producing ecstasy,

[f] The remark is, I think, Mr. Hallam's.

and in the compressed and concentrated energy[g] of thought and feeling, Homer, too, has his own peculiar prerogatives. Among them might perhaps be placed the faculty of high oratory; the art of turning to account epithets and distinctive phrases; the production of indirect or negative effects; and the power of creating and sustaining dramatic interest without the large use of wicked agents, in whom later poets·have found their most indispensable auxiliaries. But all this is not enough for us who read him. If the works of Homer are, to letters and to human learning, what the early books of Scripture are to the entire Bible and to the spiritual life of man; if in them lie the beginnings of the intellectual life of the world, then we must still recollect that that life, to be rightly understood, should be studied in its beginnings. There we may see in simple forms what afterwards grew complex, and in clear light what afterwards became obscure; and there we obtain starting-points, from which to measure progress and decay along all the lines upon which our nature moves.

Over and above the general plea here offered for the study of Homer under other aspects than such as are merely poetical, there is something to be said upon his claims in competition with other, and especially with other Greek poets. The case of the Latin poets, nearer to us historically, more accessible in tongue, more easily retained in the mind under the pressure of after-life, more readily available for literary and social purposes, must stand upon its own grounds.

In considering what is the place due to Homer in education, we cannot altogether exclude from view the

[g] This is the σφοδρότης, which Longinus (c. ix.) commends in the Iliad, but which was perhaps excelled in the Divina Commedia.

question of comparative value, as between him and his now successful and overbearing rivals, the Greek tragedians. For we are not to expect that of the total studies, at least of Oxford and Cambridge, any larger share, speaking generally, can hereafter be given to Greek poetry, as a whole, than has heretofore been so bestowed. It is rather a question whether there should be some shifting, or less uniformity, in the present distribution of time and labour, as among the different claimants within that attractive field.

I do not dispute the merits of the tragedians as masters in their noble art. As long as letters are cultivated among mankind, for so long their honours are secure. I do not question the advantage of studying the Greek language in its most fixed and most exact forms, which they present in perfection; nor their equal, at least, if not greater value than Homer, as practical helps and models in Greek composition. But, after all allowances on these, or on any other score, they cannot, even in respect of purely poetic titles, make good a claim to that preference over Homer, which they have, nevertheless, extensively enjoyed. I refer far less to Æschylus than to the others, because he seems more to resemble Homer not only in majesty, but in nature, reality, and historical veracity: and far less again to Sophocles, than to Euripides. But it may be said of them, generally, though in greatly differing degrees, that while with Homer everything is pre-eminently fresh and genuine, with them, on the contrary, this freshness and genuineness, this life-likeness, are for the most part wanting. We are reminded, by the matter itself, of the masks in which the actors appeared, of the mechanical appliances with the aid of which they spoke. The very existence of the word, ἐκτραγῳδεῖν,[h] and other[i] like compounds, shows us that, in the Greek tragedy, human nature and human life were not represented at large; they were got up; they were placed in the light of certain peculiar ideas, with a view to peculiar effects. The dramas were magnificent and also instructive pictures, but they taught, as it were, certain set lessons only: they were pictures *sui generis*, pictures marked with a certain mannerism, pictures in which the artist follows a standard which is neither original, nor general, nor truly normal. Let us try the test of an expression somewhat kindred in etymology: such a word as ἐξομηροῦν would carry upon its face a damning solecism. Again, let us mark the difference which was observed by the sagacity of Aristotle.[k] With the speeches in the Iliad, he compares the speeches in the tragedians; those most remarkable and telling compositions, which we have occasion so often to admire in Euripides. But, as he says, the Characters of the ancients, doubtless meaning Homer, speak πολιτικῶς, those of the moderns, ῥητορικῶς. I know no reason why the speeches of Achilles should not be compared with the finest passages of Demosthenes: but no one could make such a comparison between Demosthenes and the speeches, though they are most powerful and effective harangues, which we find in the Troades, or the Iphigenia in Aulide. This contrast of the earnest and practical with the artificial, runs, more or less, along the whole line which divides Homer from the tragedians, particularly from Euripides.

When we consider the case in another point of view, and estimate these poets with reference to what they

[h] Used by Longinus xv. Polyb. vi. 56, 8.
[i] Steph. Lex. iii., 1353.
[k] Aristot. Poet. c. 15.

tell, and not to the mere manner of their telling it, the argument for assigning to Homer a greater share of the attention of our youth, becomes yet stronger. For it must be admitted that the tragedians, especially the two later of the three, teach us but very little of the Greek religion, history, manners, arts, or institutions. At the period when they wrote, the religion of the country had become political or else histrionic in its spirit, and the figures it presented were not only multiplied, but were also hopelessly confused: while morals had sunk into very gross corruption, of which, as we have it upon explicit evidence, two at least of them largely partook. The characters and incidents of their own time, and of the generations which immediately preceded it, were found to be growing less suitable for the stage. They were led, from this and other causes, to fetch their themes, in general, from the remote period of the heroic or pre-historic ages. But of the traditions of those ages they were no adequate expositors; hence the representations of them are, for the most part, couched in altered and degenerate forms. This will be most clearly seen upon examining the Homeric personages, as they appear in the plays of Euripides. Here they seem often to retain no sign of identity except the name. The 'form and pressure,' and also the machinery or physical circumstances of the Greek drama, were such as to keep the tragedians, so to speak, upon stilts, while its limited scope of necessity excluded much that was comprised in the wide circle of the epic action; so that they open to us little, in comparison with Homer, of the Greek mind and life: of that cradle wherein lie, we are to remember, the original form and elements, in so far as they are secular, of European civilization.

If I may judge in any degree of the minds of others by my own experience, nothing is more astonishing in Homer, than the mass of his matter. Especially is this true of the Iliad, which most men suppose to be little more than a gigantic battle-piece. But that poem, battle-piece as it is, where we might expect to find only the glitter and the clash of arms, is rich in every kind of knowledge, perhaps richest of all in the political and historical departments. It is hardly too much to say, in general, that besides his claims as a poet, Homer has, for himself, all the claims that all the other classes of ancient writers can advance for themselves, each in his separate department. And, excepting the works of Aristotle and Plato, on either of which may be grafted the investigation of the whole philosophy of the world, I know of no author, among those who are commonly studied at Oxford, offering a field of labour and inquiry either so wide or so diversified, as that which Homer offers.

But, if Homer is not fully studied in our universities, there is no adequate consolation to be found in the fact, that he is so much read in our public schools.

I am very far indeed from lamenting that he is thus read. His free and genial temperament gives him a hold on the sympathies of the young. The simple and direct construction of almost all his sentences allows them easy access to his meaning; the examination of the sense of single words, so often requisite, is within their reach; while it may readily be believed that the large and varied inflexions of the Greek tongue, in his hands at once so accurate and so elastic, make him peculiarly fit for the indispensable and invaluable work of parsing. It may be, that for boyhood Homer finds ample employment in his exterior and more obvious aspects.

But neither boyhood nor manhood can read Homer effectively for all purposes at once, if my estimate of those purposes be correct. The question therefore is, how best to divide the work between the periods of life severally best suited to the different parts of it.

It is, indeed, somewhat difficult, as a general rule, beneficially and effectively to use the same book at the same time as an instrument for teaching both the language in which it is written, and the subject of which it treats. What is given honestly to the one purpose, will ordinarily be so much taken or withheld from the other. For the one object, the mind must be directed upon the thought of the author; for the other, upon the material organ through which it is conveyed; or, in other words, for the former of these two aims his language must be regarded on its material, for the latter on its intellectual, side. The difficulty of combining these views, taken of necessity from opposite quarters, increases in proportion as the student is young, the language subtle, copious, and elaborate, the subject diversified and extended. In some cases it may be slight, or, at least, easily surmountable; but it is raised nearly to its maximum in the instance of Homer. There are few among us who can say that we learned much of the inward parts of Homer in our boyhood; while perhaps we do not feel that our labours upon him were below the average, such as it may have been, of our general exertions; and though other generations may greatly improve upon us, they cannot, I fear, master the higher properties of their author at that early period of life. Homer, if read at our public schools, is, and probably must be, read only, or in the main, for his diction and poetry (as commonly understood), even by the most advanced;

while to those less forward he is little more than a mechanical instrument for acquiring the beginnings of real familiarity with the Greek tongue and its inflexions. If, therefore, he is to be read for his theology, history, ethics, politics, for his skill in the higher and more delicate parts of the poetic calling, for his neverending lessons upon manners, arts, and society, if we are to study in him the great map of that humanity which he so wonderfully unfolds to our gaze,—he must be read at the universities, and read with reference to his deeper treasures. He is second to none of the poets of Greece as the poet of boys; but he is far advanced before them all, even before Æschylus and Aristophanes, as the poet of men.

But no discussion upon the general as well as poetical elevation of Homer, can be complete or satisfactory without a more definite consideration of the question—What is the historical value of his testimony? This is not settled by our showing either his existence, or his excellence in his art. No man doubts Aristo's, or Boiardo's, or Virgil's personality, or their high rank as poets; but neither would any man quote them as authorities on a point of history. To arrive at a right view of this further question, we must be reasonably assured alike of the nature of Homer's original intention, of his opportunities of information, and of the soundness of his text. To these subjects I shall now proceed; in the meantime, enough may have been said to explain the aim of these pages so far as regards the more fruitful study of the works of Homer, the contemplation of them on the positive side in all their bearings, and the clearing of a due space for them in the most fitting stages of the education of the youth of England.

SECT. 3.—*On the Historic Aims of Homer.*

For the purposes of anatomy every skeleton may be useful, and may sufficiently tell the tale of the race to which it belongs. But when we come to seek for high beauty and for approaches to perfection, of how infinite a diversity, of what countless degrees, does form appear to be susceptible! How difficult it is to find these, except in mere fragments; and how dangerous does it prove, in dealing with objects, to treat the whole as a normal specimen, simply because parts are fine, or even superlative. When, again, we pass onward, and with the body regard also the mind of man, still greater is the range of differences, and still more rare is either the development of parts in a degree so high as to bring their single excellence near the ideal standard, or the accurate adjustment of their relations to one another, or the completeness of the aggregate which they form.

Now, it appears to me, that in the case of Homer, together with the breadth and elevation of the highest genius, we have before us, and in a yet more remarkable degree, an even more rare fulness and consistency of the various instruments and organs which make up the apparatus of the human being—constituted as he is, in mind and body, and holding, as he does, on the one side of the Deity, and on the other, of the dust. Among all the qualities of the poems, there is none more extraordinary than the general accuracy and perfection of their minute detail, when considered with reference to the standards at which from time to time they aim. Where other poets sketch, Homer draws; and where they draw, he carves. He alone, of all the now famous epic writers, moves (in the Iliad especially) subject to the stricter laws of time and place;

he alone, while producing an unsurpassed work of the imagination, is also the greatest chronicler that ever lived, and presents to us, from his own single hand, a representation of life, manners, history, of morals, theology, and politics, so vivid and comprehensive, that it may be hard to say whether any of the more refined ages of Greece or Rome, with their clouds of authors and their multiplied forms of historical record, are either more faithfully or more completely conveyed to us. He alone presents to us a mind and an organization working with such precision that, setting aside for the moment any question as to the genuineness of his text, we may reason in general from his minutest indications with the confidence that they belong to some consistent and intelligible whole.

It may be right, however, to consider more circumstantially the question of the historical authority of Homer. It has been justly observed by Wachsmuth[1], that even the dissolution of his individuality does not get rid of his authority. For if the works reputed to be his had proceeded from many minds, yet still, according to their unity of colour, and their correspondence in ethical and intellectual tone with the events of the age they purport to describe, there would arise an argument, founded on internal evidence, for the admissibility of the whole band into the class of trustworthy historical witnesses.

But, first of all, may we not ask, from whence comes the presumption against Homer as an historical authority? Not from the fact that he mixes marvels with common events; for this, to quote no other instance, would destroy along with him Herodotus. Does it not arise from this—that his compositions are poeti-

[1] Historical Antiquities of the Greeks, vol. i. Appendix C.

cal—that history has long ceased to adopt the poetical form—that an old association has thus been dissolved—that a new and adverse association has taken its place, which connects poetry with fiction—and that we illogically reflect this modern association upon early times, to which it is utterly inapplicable?

If so, there is no burden of proof incumbent upon those, who regard Homer as an historical authority. The presumptions are all in favour of their so regarding him. The question will, of course, remain—In what proportions has he mixed history with imaginative embellishment? And he has furnished us with some aids towards the consideration of this question.

The immense mass of matter contained in the Iliad, which is beyond what the action of the poem requires, and yet is in its nature properly historical, of itself supplies the strongest proof of the historic aims of the poet. Whether, in the introduction of all this matter, he followed a set and conscious purpose of his own mind, or whether he only fed the appetite of his hearers with what he found to be agreeable to them, is little material to the question. The great fact stands, that there was either a design to fulfil, or, at least, an appetite to feed—an intense desire to create bonds and relations with the past—to grasp its events, and fasten them in forms which might become, and might make them become, the property of the present and the future. Without this great sign of nobleness in their nature, Greeks never could have been Greeks.

I have particularly in view the great multitude of genealogies; their extraordinary consistency one with another, and with the other historical indications of the poems; their extension to a very large number, especially in the Catalogue, of secondary persons;

I take again the Catalogue itself, that most remarkable production, as a whole; the accuracy with which the names of the various races are handled and bestowed throughout the poems; the particularity of the demands regularly made upon strangers for information concerning themselves, and especially the constant inquiry who were their parents, what was, for each person as he appears, *his* relation to the past? and further, the numerous legends or narratives of prior occurrences with which the poems, and particularly the more historic Iliad, is so thickly studded. Even the national use of patronymics as titles of honour is in itself highly significant of the historic turn. Nay, much that touches the general structure of the poem may be traced in part to this source; for all the intermediate Books between the Wrath and the Return of Achilles, while they are so contrived as to heighten the military grandeur of the hero, are so many tributes to the special and local desires in each state or district for commemoration of their particular chiefs, which Homer would, of course, have to meet, as he itinerated through the various parts of Greece.

Now, this appetite for commemoration does not fix itself upon what is imaginary; it may tolerate fiction by way of accessory and embellishment, but in the main it must, from its nature, rely upon what it takes to be solid food. The actions of great men in all times, but especially in early times, afford it suitable material; and there is nothing irrational in believing that the race which in its infancy produced so marvellous a poet as Homer, should also in its infancy have produced great warriors and great statesmen. Composing, with such powers as his, about his own country, and for his own countrymen, he could scarcely fail, even independently of conscious purpose, to convey to us a great mass of such matter as is in reality of the very highest historic truth and value. If, indeed, we advance so far as to the conviction that his hearers believed him to be reciting historically, the main question may speedily be decided. For each generation of men, possessed of the mental culture necessary in order to appreciate Homer, knows too much of the generations immediately preceding to admit of utter and wholesale imposition. But it is a fair inference from the Odyssey, that the Trojan War was thus sung to the men and the children of the men who waged it. Four lays of bards[m] are mentioned in that poem; one of Phemius, three of Demodocus; and out of the four, three relate to the War, which appears to show clearly that its celebrity must have been both instantaneous and overpowering; the more so, as the only remaining one has reference not to any human transaction, but to a scene in Olympus. And I shall shortly advert to the question, whether the Homeric poems themselves were in all probability composed not later than within two generations of the War itself.

It may be true that, with respect to some parts of his historical notices, the poet, adapting himself to the wishes and tastes of his hearers, might take liberties without fear of detection, most of all where he has filled in accessories, in order to complete a picture; but I think we should be wrong in supposing that in the interest of his art he would have occasion to make this a general practice, or to carry it in historical subjects beyond matters of detail. Nor can I wholly disregard the analogy between his history and his equally copious and everywhere intermixed geographical notices: such

[m] Od. i. 326, viii. 72-82, 266-366, 499-520.

of them, I mean, as lay within the sphere of Greek experience. These indeed, he could not, under the eyes of the men who heard him, cast into the mould of fiction; yet there could be no call of popular necessity for his unequalled and most minute precision, and it can only be accounted for by the belief that accurate record was a great purpose of his poems. If he was thus careful to record both classes of particulars alike, and if, as to the one, we absolutely know that he has recorded them with exemplary fidelity, that fact raises a corresponding presumption of some weight as to the other.

But there is, I think, another argument to the same effect, of the highest degree of strength which the nature of the case admits. It is to be found in the fact that Homer has not scrupled to make some sacrifices of poetical beauty and propriety to these historic aims. For if any judicious critic were called upon to specify the chief poetical blemish of the Iliad, would he not reply by pointing to the multitude of stories from the past, having no connexion, or at best a very feeble one, with the War, which are found in it? Such brief and minor legends as occur in the course of the Catalogue, may have a poetical purpose; it appears not improbable that they may be introduced by way of relief to the dryness of topographical and local enumeration. But in general the narratives of prior occurrences are (so to speak) rather foisted in, and we must therefore suppose for them a purpose over and above that, which as a mere poet Homer would have in view. It is hard to conceive that he would have indulged in them, if he had not been able to minister to this especial aim by its means. Thus, again, the curious and important genealogy of the Dardanian House[n] is given by Æneas, in answer to Achilles,

[n] Il. xx. 213-41.

who had just shown by his taunt that he, at least, did not want the information, but knew very well º the claims and pretensions of his antagonist. Again, the long story told by Agamemnon, in the assembly held for the Reconciliation, when despatch was of all things requisite, may best be accounted for by the desire to relate the circumstances attending the birth of the great national hero, Hercules. It certainly impedes the action of the poem, which seems to be confessed in the rebuke insinuated by the reply of Achilles:—

νῦν δὲ μνησώμεθα χάρμης
αἶψα μάλ'· οὐ γὰρ χρὴ κλοτοπεύειν ἐνθάδ' ἐόντας
οὐδὲ διατρίβειν· ἔτι γὰρ μέγα ἔργον ἄρεκτον. Ρ

Still more is this the case when Patroclus, sent in a hurry for news by a man of the most fiery impatience, is (to use the modern phrase) button-held by Nestor, in the eleventh Book, and, though he has 'no time to sit down,' yet is obliged to endure a speech of a hundred and fifty-two lines, ninety-three of which, containing the account of the Epean contest with Pylos, are absolutely and entirely irrelevant. It may be said, that these effusions are naturally referable to the garrulous age of Nestor, and to false shame and want of ingenuousness in Agamemnon. In part, too, we may compare them with the modern fashion among Orientals of introducing parables in common discourse. But many of these have no parabolic force whatever: and from all of them poetical beauty suffers. On the other hand, the historic matter introduced is highly curious and interesting for the Greek races: why, then, should we force upon Homer the charge of neglect, folly, or drowsiness,[q] when an important purpose for these interpolations appears to lie upon the very face of them?

º Il. xx. 179-83.   ᵖ Il. xix. 148–50.   ᵠ Hor. A.P. v. 359.

It will be observed, that if this reasoning in reference to the interlocutory legends be sound, it supplies an historical character to the poem just in the places where the general argument for it would have been weakest; inasmuch as these legends generally relate to times one or two generations earlier than the Troica, and are farther removed, by so much of additional interval, from the knowledge and experience of his hearers.

But, over and above the episodes, which seem to owe their place in the poem to the historic aim, there are a multitude of minor shadings which run through it, and which, as Homer could have derived no advantage from feigning them, we are compelled to suppose real. They are part of the graceful finish of a true story, but they have not the showy character of what has been invented for effect. Why, for instance, should Homer say of Clytæmnestra, that till corrupted by Ægisthus she was good?[r] Why should it be worth his while to pretend that the iron ball offered by Achilles for a prize was the one formerly pitched by Eetion?[s] Why should he spend eight lines in describing the dry trunk round which the chariots were to drive?[t] Why should he tell us that Tydeus was of small stature?[u] Why does Menelaus drive a mare?[x] Why has Penelope a sister Iphthime, 'who was wedded to Eumelus,' wanted for no other purpose than as a *persona* for Minerva in a dream?[y] These questions, every one will admit, might be indefinitely multiplied.

But, after all, there can be no point more important for the decision of this question, than the general tone of Homer himself. Is he, for ethical and intellectual

[r] Od. iii. 266.
[s] Il. xxiii. 826.
[t] Ibid. 326-33.
[u] Il. v. 801.
[x] Il. xxiii. 409.
[y] Od. iv. 797.

purposes, the child of that heroic age which he describes? Does he exhibit its form and pressure? Does he chant in its key? Are there a set of ideas of the writer which are evidently not those of his heroes, or of his heroes which are not those of the writer, or does he sing, in the main, as Phemius and Demodocus might themselves have sung? Wachsmuth says well, that Homer must be regarded as still within the larger boundaries of the heroic age. There are, perhaps, signs, particularly in the Odyssey, of a first stage of transition from it; but the poet is throughout identified with it in heart, soul, speech, and understanding. I would presume to argue thus; that Homer never would have ventured to dispense with mere description, and to adopt action as his sole resource—to dramatise his poem as he has dramatised it—unless he had been strong in the consciousness of this identity. It is no answer to say that later writers—namely, the tragedians—dramatised the subject still more, and presented their characters on the stage without even those slender aids from interjected narrative towards the comprehension of them, which Homer has here and there, at any rate, permitted himself to use. For the consequence has been in their case, that they entirely fail to represent the semblance of a picture of the heroic age, or indeed of any age at all. They produce remote occurrences or fables in a dress of feelings, language, and manners suited to their own time, as far as it is suited to any. Besides, as dramatists, they had immense aids and advantages of other kinds; not to mention their grand narrative auxiliary, the Chorus. But Homer enjoyed little aid from accessories, and has notwithstanding painted the very life. And yet, seeking to paint from the life, he commits it to his characters to paint themselves and one another.

Surely he never could have confined himself to this indirect process, unless he had been emboldened by the consciousness of his own essential unity with them all. He would have done as most other epic poets have done, whose personages we feel that we know, not from themselves, but from what the poet in the character of intelligencer has been kind enough to tell us; whereas we learn Achilles by means of Achilles, Ulysses by means of Ulysses, and so with the rest. Next to their own light, is the light they reflect on one another; but we never see the poet, so to speak, holding the candle. Still, in urging all this, I feel that more remains and must remain unspoken. The question, whether Homer speaks and paints essentially in the spirit of his own age, or whether he fetches from a distance both his facts and a manner so remarkably harmonizing with them, must after all our discussions continue one to be settled in the last resort not by arguments, which can only play a subsidiary part, but first by the most thorough searching and sifting of the text; then by the application of that inward sense and feeling, to which the critics of the destructive schools, with their ἀναποδεικταὶ φάσεις, make such copious appeals.

But the assumption by an effort of mind of the manners and tone of a remote age, joined with the consistent support of this character throughout prolonged works, is of very rare occurrence. In Greek literature there is nothing, to my knowledge, which at all approaches it; and this I think may fairly be urged as of itself almost conclusive against ascribing it to Homer. The later tragedians, in whose compositions we should look for it, do not apparently so much as think of it; and it is most difficult to suppose a poet so national as Homer to be in this cardinal respect entirely different from all others of his race. Indeed the supposition is radically at variance with the idea of his poetical character; of which the very groundwork lies in a childlike unconsciousness, and in the unity of Art with Nature[y].

May we not, however, go a good deal further, and say boldly that the faculty of assuming in literary compositions an archaic costume, voice, and manner, does not belong at all either to an age like that of Homer, or to any age of which the literary conditions at all resemble it?

In the first place, an inventor, working like Homer for the general public, must, by departing altogether from the modes of thought, expression, and action current in his own day, *pro tanto* lose his hold upon those on whose approval he depends. It seems to follow that this will not be seriously attempted, except in an age which has ceased to afford a liberal supply of the materials of romance. Is not this presumption made good by experience? The Greek tragedians, it is indisputable, did not find it necessary to aim, and did not aim, at reproducing the whole contemporary apparatus, which was in strictness appropriate and due to their characters. Virgil made no such attempt in the Æneid, of which, notwithstanding the manners abound in anachronisms of detail. The romance poets of Italy idealize their subject, not, however, by the revival of antique manners with their proper apparatus of incidents, but by means of an abundant preternatural machinery. Even in Shakespeare's King John, Henry IV, or Henry VIII, how little difference can be detected from the Elizabethan age, or (in this point) from one another[z]. Again,

---

[y] Nägelsbach, Homerische Theologie, Einleitung, pp. 1–3.

[z] Scott has paid, however, a tribute to Shakespeare on this ground in 'The Fortunes of Nigel.' Novels and Romances, vol. iii. p. 68, 8vo edition.

in Macbeth or Lear, enough is done to prevent our utterly confounding their ages with the common life of the hearers; but there is nothing that approaches to a complete characteristic representation of the respective times to which the personages are supposed to belong. So, again, in Coriolanus, Julius Cæsar, or Antony and Cleopatra, there is a sort of Roman *toga* thrown loosely over the figures; but we do not feel ourselves amidst Roman life when we read them. And, in truth, what is done at all in these cases is not done so much by reproducing as by generalizing, in the same sense as a painter generalizes his draperies. A great instance of the genuine process of reproduction is to be found in Sir Walter Scott. He, however, besides being a man of powerful genius, cast not in the mould of his own age, but in one essentially belonging to the past, was a master of antiquarian knowledge. And this leads me to name what seems to be the second condition of serious and successful attempts (I need not here speak of burlesques, of which all the touches must be broad ones) at disinterring and reviving bygone ages in the whole circle and scheme of their life. The first, as has been already said, is to live in an age itself socially old, so as not to abound in proper materials for high invention. The second is, to live in an age possessed of such abundant documents and records of a former time as to make it practicable to explore it in all points by historical *data*. This condition was wanting to Virgil, even supposing him to have had the necessary tastes and qualifications. It was not wanting to Scott, with reference especially to the period of the Stuarts, who, besides a vast abundance of oral and written traditions, had laws, usages, architecture, arms, coins, utensils, every imaginable form of relic and of testimony at his command, so that he could himself first live in the age of his works, and then, when himself acclimatised, invent according to it.

In all this it is not forgotten that a certain amount of archaism is indispensable in all works purporting to draw their subject from a long-past age. But this *minimum* need only be slight and general, as in the Æneid; and it consists rather in the exclusion of modern accessories, than in the revival of the original tone. And again, the very choice of subject, as it is grave and severe or light and gay, will to some extent influence the manners: the former will spontaneously lean towards the past, the latter, depending on the zest of novelty, will be more disposed to clothe itself in the forms of the present. Thus we have a more antique tone in Henry the Fifth, than in the Merry Wives of Windsor. But archaic colouring within limits such as these is broadly different from such systematic representation of the antique as Homer must have practised, if he had practised it at all.

As in romance and poetry, so in the progress of the drama, this method appears to be the business of a late age. The strength of dramatic imagination is always when the drama itself is young. It then confidently relies upon its essential elements for the necessary illusion; it knows little, and cares less, about sustaining it by elaborate attention to minor emblems and incidents. But when it has lived into the old age of civilized society, when the critical faculty has become strong and the imagination weak, then it strengthens itself by minute accuracy in scenery and costume,—in fact, by exact reproduction. This is indeed the novel gift of our own time: and by means of it theatrical revivals are now understood and practised among ourselves in a manner which former generations could not emulate, but did not require.

Nor must we forget the importance, with reference to this discussion, of Homer's minuteness, precision, and multitude of details. Every one of these, be it remembered, if we suppose him not to be painting from the life, affords an additional chance of detection, by the discrepancy between the life habitually present to the poet's experience, and that which he is representing by effort. But the voice of the Homeric poems is in this respect, after all, unisonous, like that of the Greeks, and not multiform, like that of the Trojan army[a]. We are driven, therefore, to suppose that Homer practised this art of reproduction on a scale, as well as with a success, since unheard of, and this at a period when, according to all likelihood and all other experience, it could only in a very limited sense be possible to practice it at all. The extravagance of these suppositions tells powerfully against them, and once more throws us back on the belief that the objects which he painted were, in the main, those which his own age placed beneath his view.

This view of the historical character of Homer, I believe, substantially agrees with that taken by the Greeks in general. If I refer to Strabo, in his remarkable Prolegomena[b], it is because he had occasion to consider the point particularly. Eratosthenes had treated the great sire of poets as a fabulist. Strabo confutes him. Eratosthenes had himself noticed the precision of the geographical details: Thisbe, with its doves; Haliartus and its meadows; Anthedon, the boundary; Lilæa by the sources of Cephissus; and Strabo retorts upon him with force—$\pi \acute{o} \tau \epsilon \rho o \nu$ $o \mathring{\vartheta} \nu$ $\acute{o}$ $\pi o i \hat{\omega} \nu$ $\tau a \hat{\upsilon} \tau a$ $\psi \upsilon \chi a \gamma \omega \gamma o \hat{\upsilon} \nu \tau \iota$

[a] Il. iv. 438.   [b] Strabo i. 2, p. 16.

ἔοικεν ἢ διδάσκοντι; his general conclusion is, that Homer used fiction, as his smith in the Odyssey used gold for plating silver:—

ὡς δ' ὅτε τις χρυσὸν περιχεύεται ἀργύρῳ ἀνήρ,

that so Homer adjoined mythical ornaments to true events. But history was the basis:—ἔλαβεν οὖν παρὰ τῆς ἱστορίας τὰς ἀρχάς[c]. And, in adopting the belief that Homer is to be taken generally for a most trustworthy witness to facts, I am far from saying that there are no cases of exception, where he may reasonably be suspected of showing less than his usual fidelity. The doctrine must be accepted with latitude: the question is not whether it is absolutely safe, but whether it is the least unsafe. We may most reasonably, perhaps, view his statements and representations with a special jealousy, when they are such as appear systematically contrived to enhance the distinctive excellencies of his nation. Thus, for instance, both in the causes and incidents of the war, and in the relative qualities and merits of Greeks and Trojans, we may do well to check the too rapid action of our judgments, and to allow some scope to the supposition, that the historical duties of the bard might here naturally become subordinate to his patriotic purpose in glorifying the sires of his hearers, that immortal group who became through him the fountain head to Greece, both of national unity and of national fame.

Indeed, while I contend keenly for the historic aim and character of Homer, I understand the terms in a sense much higher than that of mere precision in the leading narration. We may, as I am disposed to think, even if we should disbelieve the existence of Helen, of Agamemnon, or of Troy, yet hold, in all that is most

[c] Strabo i. 2, p. 20.

essential, by the historical character of Homer. For myself, I ask to be permitted to believe in these, and in much besides these; yet I also plead that the main question is not whether he has correctly recorded a certain series of transactions, but whether he has truly and faithfully represented manners and characters, feelings and tastes, races and countries, principles and institutions. Here lies the pith of history; these it has for its soul, and fact for its body. It does not appear to me reasonable to presume that Homer idealized his narration with anything like the license which was permitted to the Carlovingian romance; yet even that romance did not fail to retain in many of the most essential particulars a true historic character; and it conveys to us, partly by fact and partly through a vast parable, the inward life of a period pregnant with forces that were to operate powerfully upon our own characters and condition. Even those who would regard the cases as parallel should, therefore, remember that they too must read Homer otherwise than as a poet in the vulgar and more prevailing sense, which divests poetry of its relation to reality. The more they read him in that spirit the higher, I believe, they will raise their estimate of his still unknown and unappreciated treasures.

Sect. 4.—*The probable Date of Homer.*

In employing such a phrase as the date of Homer, I mean no reference to any given number of years before the Olympiads, but simply his relation in the order of history to the heroic age; to the events, and, above all, to the living type of that age.

When asserting generally the historic aims and authority of the poet, I do not presume to pronounce confidently upon the difficult question of the period at which he lived. I prefer to dwell upon the proposition that he is an original witness to manners, characters, and ideas such as those of his poems. It is not necessary, to make good this proposition, that we should determine a given number of years as the maximum that could have passed between the Trojan war and the composition of the Iliad or Odyssey. But the internal evidence seems to me very strongly to support the belief, that he lived before the Dorian conquest of the Peloponnesus. That he was not an eye-witness of the war, we absolutely know from the Invocation before the Catalogue[d]. It also appears[e] that he must have seen the grandchildren of Æneas reigning over the land of Priam. It is no extravagant supposition that forty or fifty years after the siege, perhaps even less, might have brought this to pass.

The single idea or form of expression in the poems, which at first sight tends to suggest a very long interval, is that quoted by Velleius Paterculus[f], the οἷοι νῦν βροτοί εἰσι[g]. But the question arises, whether this is an historical land-mark, or a poetical embellishment? In the former sense, as implying a great physical degeneracy of mankind, it would require us to suppose nothing less than a lapse of centuries between the Troica and the epoch of the poet. This hypothesis, though Heyne speaks of the eighth or ninth generation[h], general opinion has rejected. If it be dismissed, and if we adopt the view of this formula as an ornament, it loses all definite chronological significance. Thus it is lost in the phrase, common in our own time with respect to

[d] Il. ii. 486.
[e] Il. xx. 308.
[f] Hist. i. 5.

[g] Il.v.304;xii.383,449;xx.287.
[h] Exc. iii. ad Il. xxiv., vol. viii. p. 828.

38 I. *Prolegomena.*

the intellectual characters of men now no more, but yet not removed from us, perhaps, by more than from a quarter to half a century—'there were giants in those days.' Nay, the observation of Paterculus, especially as he was an enthusiastic admirer, itself exemplifies the little care with which these questions have been treated. For the Iliad itself supplies a complete answer in the speech of Nestor, who draws the very same contrast between the heroes of the Troica and those of his own earlier days:

κείνοισι δ' ἂν οὔτις
τῶν οἱ νῦν βροτοί εἰσιν ἐπιχθονίων μαχέοιτο[i].

And it is curious that we have in these words a measure, supplied by Homer himself, of the real force of the phrase, which seems to fix it at something under half a century, and thus makes it harmonise with the indication afforded by the passage relating to the descendants of Æneas. The argument of Mitford[j] on the age of Homer appears to me to be of great value: and, while it is rejected, it is not answered by Heyne[k]. Nor is it easy to conceive the answer to those who urge that, so far as the poet's testimony goes, the years from Pirithous to the siege are as many as from the siege to his own day[l]. But Pirithous was the father of Polypætes, who led a Thessalian division in the war.[m]

If this view of Homer's meaning in the particular case be correct, we can the better understand why it is that the poet, who uses this form of enhancement four times in the Iliad, does not employ it in the Odyssey, though it is the later poem, and though he had oppor-

[i] Il. i. 262–272.
[j] Hist. Greece, chap. iii. App.; vol. i. 169–74, 4to.
[k] Heyne, Exc. iii. ad Il. xxiv.; vol. viii. p. 226.
[l] Granville Penn on the Primary Arguments of the Iliad, p. 314. [m] Il. ii. 740.

tunities enough; such as the athletic exploits of Ulysses in Phæacia, and especially the handling of the Bow in Ithaca. For in the Iliad a more antique tone of colouring prevails, as it is demanded by the loftier strain of the action.

There is one passage, and one only, which is just capable of being construed as an allusion to the great Dorian conquest: it is that in the Fourth Book of the Iliad, where Juno tells Jupiter that she well knows he can destroy in spite of her, whensoever he may choose, her three dearest cities, Argos, Sparta, and Mycenæ[n]. It is probable that the passage refers to sacking such as had been practised by Hercules[o], and such as is pathetically described by Phœnix[p]. But, in the first place, we do not know that these cities were in any sense destroyed by the Dorian conquest, more than they had been by previous dynastic and territorial changes. If, on the other hand, it be contended, that we need not construe the passage as implying more than revolution independent of material destruction, then we need not introduce the idea of the Dorian conquest at all to sustain the propriety of the passage, for Homer already knew by tradition how those cities, and the territory to which they belonged, had changed hands from Danaïds to Perseids, and from Perseids to Pelopids.

But indications even far less equivocal from an isolated passage would be many times outweighed, in a case like that of Homer, by any conclusion justly drawn from features, whether positive or negative, that are rooted in the general body of the poems. Now such a conclusion arises from the admitted and total absence of any allusion in Homer to the general incidents of the great Dorian conquest, and to the consequent reconstruction of the old or European Greece,

[n] Il. iv. 51. [o] Il. ii. 660. [p] Il. ix. 593.

or to the migrations eastward, or to the very existence of the new Asiatic Greece which it is supposed to have called into being. Respecting the conquest itself, he might by a sustained effort of deliberate intention have kept silence: but is it possible that he could have avoided betraying by reference to results, on a thousand occasions, his knowledge of a change which had drawn anew the whole surface of society in Greece? It would be more rational, were we driven to it (which is not the case), even to suppose that the passage in question had been tampered with, than to imagine that the poet could have forborne through twenty-eight thousand lines, to make any other reference to, or further betray his knowledge of, events which must on this supposition have occupied for him so large a part of the whole horizon of life and experience.

Again, the allusions to the trumpet and the riding-horse found in illustrative passages, but not as used in the war, are by far too slight and doubtful, to sustain the theory that Homer saw around him a system of warfare different from that which he recorded; and require us to adopt no supposition for the explanation of them, beyond the very natural one that the heroic poet, without essentially changing manners, yet, within certain limits, insensibly projects himself and his subject from the foreground of every-day life into the mellowness of distance; and, therefore, that he may advisedly have excluded from his poem certain objects or practices, which notwithstanding he knew to have been more or less in use. Again, what are we to say to the minute knowledge of Greece proper and the Peloponnesus, which Homer has displayed? Why does he (apparently) know it so much better than he knew Asia Minor? How among the rude Dorians, just emerged from comparative barbarism, could he learn it at all? How strange, that Lycurgus should have acquired the fame of having first introduced the poems to the Peloponnesus, unless a great revolution and a substitution of one dominant race for another had come between, to obliterate or greatly weaken the recollection of them in the very country, which beyond all others they covered with a blaze of glory.

Of the very small number of passages in the poems which contain a reference to events later than the action, there are two, both relating to the same subject, for which at first sight it appears difficult to account. Why does Neptune obtrude upon the Olympian Court his insignificant and rather absurd jealousy, lest the work of defence, hastily thrown up by the Achæan army, should eclipse the wall built around Troy by Apollo and himself? Evidently in order to obtain from Jupiter the suggestion, that he should subsequently himself efface all traces of it. But why does Homer show this anxiety to account for its non-appearance? Why does he return subsequently to the subject, and most carefully relate how Jupiter by raining, and Apollo by turning the mouths of eight rivers, and Neptune with his trident, all cooperated to destroy the work, and make the shore smooth and even again? Had Homer lived many generations after the Trojan war, these passages would have been entirely without purpose, for he need not then have given reasons to show, why ages had left no trace still visible of the labour of a day. But if he lived near the period of the war, the case is very different. He might then be challenged by his maritime hearers, who, if they frequented the passage into the Sea of Marmora, would have had clear views of the camp of Agamemnon, and who would naturally require him to assign a cause for the disappearance even of such a work as a day's labour of the army could produce, and as the Trojan soldiery could make practicable for their chariots to drive over [q].

These particular indications appear to be worth considering: but the great reasons for placing the date of Homer very near to that of the War are, his visible identity with the age, the altering but not yet vanished age, of which he sings, and the broad interval in tone and feeling between himself, and the very nearest of all that follows him.

SECT. 4.—*The Probable Trustworthiness of the Text of Homer.*

Let us now proceed to consider the question, what assumption is it, on the whole, safest to make, or what rule can we most judiciously follow, as our guide in Homeric studies, with reference to the text of the Poems?

Shall we adopt a given form of completely reconstructed text, like that of Mr. Payne Knight?

Shall we, without such adherence to a particular pattern, assume it to be either indisputable or, at least, most probable that an extensive corruption of the text can hardly have been avoided[r]; and shall we, in consequence, hold the received text provisionally, and subject to excision or to amendment according to any particular theory concerning Homer, his age, its manners and institutions, which we may ourselves have thought fit to follow or construct?

Shall we admit as authoritative, the excisions of Aristarchus or the Alexandrian critics, and the *obeli*

[q] Il. vi. 445-64; xii. 10-33; xv. 384.
ii., vol. viii. p. 789; Lord Aberdeen's Inquiry, p. 65.

[r] Heyne, Exc. ii. ad Il. Ω. sect.

which he has placed against verses which he suspected?

Or shall we proceed, as a general rule, upon the belief, that the received text of Homer is in general sound and trustworthy, so far, at least, as to be very greatly preferable to any reconstructed or altered form whatever, in which it has hitherto been produced or proposed for our acceptance?

My decided preference is for the fourth and last of these alternatives: with the observation, however, in passing, that the third does not essentially differ from it with respect to the great body of the Poems, so far as we know what the Alexandrian text really was.

I prefer this course as by far the safest: as the only one which can be entered upon with such an amount of preliminary assent, as to secure a free and unbiassed consideration of Homeric questions upon a ground held in common: and as, therefore, the only one, by means of which it can be hoped to attain to solid and material results as the reward of inquiry. In order fairly to raise the issue, the two following propositions may be stated as fitting canons of Homeric study:—

1. That we should adopt the text itself as the basis of all Homeric inquiry, and not any preconceived theory, nor any arbitrary standard of criticism, referable to particular periods, schools, or persons.

2. That as we proceed in any work of construction by evidence drawn from the text, we should avoid the temptation to solve difficulties found to lie in our way, by denouncing particular portions of it as corrupt or interpolated: should never set it aside except upon the closest examination of the particular passage questioned; should use sparingly the liberty even of arraying presumptions against it; and should always let

the reader understand both when and why it is questioned.

Now, let us consider these rules, and the method which it is proposed by means of them to apply,

a. With reference to the failure of other methods.

b. With reference to the antecedent probabilities for or against the general soundness of the text.

c. With reference to the internal evidence of soundness or unsoundness afforded by the text itself.

The first of the two rules has been brought more and more into operation by the believers in Homer as the Poet of the Iliad and the Odyssey, in self-defence against the sceptical theories: and it has been both announced and acted upon by Mure with such breadth and completeness, as to leave to those, who adopt it, simply the duty of treading in his footsteps.

Again, as to the second, it may now be hoped that by the force of circumstances it is gradually coming into vogue, though perhaps less, as yet, by a distinct conviction of its reasonableness, than through the utter failure and abortiveness of all other methods. First to theorise rashly (with or without consciousness), and then rudely to excise from the Homeric text whatever clashes with our crude conceptions, is, after all, an essentially superficial and vulgar method of proceeding: and if it was excusable before the evidence touching the Poet and the text had been so greatly confirmed, as it has recently been, by closer scrutiny, it can hardly be forgiven now. The text of Homer cannot be faultless: but, in the first place, it is plain, as far as general consent can make it so, that the poems, as they stand, afford a far better and surer foundation than any other form of them which has been proposed, whether curtailed in their principal members, as by the destructive school, or only amended by free handling in detail. All the recasting processes which have yet been tried, have begotten ten solecisms, or another solecism of tenfold magnitude, for every one that they did away. In fact, the end of schemes, such as that of Lachmann[s], has been not to achieve any thing like real progress in a continuous work, but simply to launch so many distinct speculations, isolated, conflicting, each resting on its author's own hearty approval, and each drawing from the rest of the world no other sign than the shrug or the smile, which seems to be the proper reward of perverted ingenuity.

It would be presumptuous and unjust to treat the remarkable performance of Mr. Payne Knight as one of what may be called—to borrow a phrase from the commercial world—the Homeric bubble-schemes. It was anticipated with eagerness by Heyne. It was hailed by the calm judgment and refined taste of Lord Aberdeen. Yet this was not enough.

ἀμέραι δ' ἐπίλοιποι
μάρτυρες σοφώτατοι[t].

The ordeal of time has not destroyed the value of Mr. Payne Knight's Prolegomena, but it has been decidedly unfavourable to his text as a practical attempt at reconstruction. With the old text in the right hand, and Mr. Knight's in the left, who would doubt in which to look for the nearest likeness to Homer? Or who will ever again venture to publish an abridged or remodelled Iliad?

Apart, however, from the unsatisfactoriness of the results of attempts at reconstruction, have we reason to believe that the text of Homer has, as a whole, been

[s] In the Berlin Philosophical Transactions, 1839, and Fernere Betrachtungen, 1843.   [t] Pindar.

seriously vitiated by interpolation or corruption? The difficulties attending its transmission from the time of the poet are not to be denied. But I think we have scarcely enough considered the amount of means which were available, and which were actually employed, in order to neutralize those difficulties, and achieve the task. Although writing of some description appears to have existed at the epoch of the Poems, it can be probably proved, and may at any rate be fully admitted, that Homer did not write, but recited only. This is the first step: now for the second. I pass by the argument with those, who deny that poems of this length could be transmitted orally at all, as one already disposed of by the general verdict of the world. So, likewise, I leave behind me, at the point where Mure has placed them, all the reasonings of the *piecers*, who say that there were originally a number of Iliadic and Odyssean songs, afterwards made up into the poems such as we now have them: of the *amplifiers*, who look upon them as expanded respectively by gradual interpolations and additions from an original of small dimensions; of the *separators*, who will have just two Homers and no more, one for the Iliad, and one for the Odyssey. I assume for the present purpose the contrary of all these three propositions: and simply invite those who disbelieve them, but who also conceive that the text is generally unsafe and untrustworthy in its detail, to some consideration of that subject.

In attempting to weigh retrospectively the probable fortunes of the Homeric text, I presume that we may establish as our point of departure the judgment delivered by Heyne[u], that the manuscripts of Homer are satisfactory: that we possess all, or nearly all, that the

[u] Exc. ii. ad Il. Ω, sect. ii. vol. viii. pp. 790, 1.

Alexandrian critics possessed; and that by the advance of the critical art, we have now probably, on the whole, a better and truer Homer than that of Aristarchus, which is the basis of the modern text. The imperfect state of notation when writing first began to be used, and the changes in pronunciation, have not, we may also suppose with Heyne[x], done more than trifling or secondary damage to the copies.

The first serious question is this; how far was Homer mutilated, first, by the rhapsodists, or reciters, before he was put into writing, and secondly, by those who, in order to bring the lays of the Iliad into one body, must, it is assumed, have added and altered much, even if they had no whims of their own, and only sought to do what was needful *nexûs et juncturæ causâ*. It is, of course, admitted that these lays, even though ideally one as they came from their framer, were in many cases actually separated. And Heyne quotes the Scholiast of Pindar[y], complaining by report that Cinæthus and his school had interpolated largely, as well as the passage in which Josephus[z] (so he states) gives it as his opinion that the Iliad, from having been pieced together long after it was composed, presented many discrepancies. Now, even if this were the opinion of Josephus, it would have no more pretension to historical authority, than if it had been delivered yesterday. But the fact is, that Josephus mentions it simply as a current notion; φασὶν οὐδὲ τοῦτον ... ἀλλὰ διαμνημονευομένην ... καὶ διὰ τοῦτο πολλὰς ἐν αὐτῇ σχεῖν τὰς διαφωνίας. Indeed, it cannot be too carefully borne in mind, that if the positive notices of Homer in early times are slight, so as to throw us back very much upon the poems for their own vindication, yet, on the other hand, all

[x] Exc. ii. ad Il. Ω, sect. ii. vol. viii. pp. 790, 1.
[y] Pind. Nem. ii. 1.
[z] Joseph. contr. Ap. i. 2.

the authorities cited on the sceptical side, are chronologically so remote from the question in debate, that they are but opinions and not proofs, and that we may canvass and question them without the smallest scruple, or fear that we are pitting mere theory against legitimate evidence.

It is not to be denied that the condition of the Homeric poems, before they were committed to writing, was one of great danger. But the question may well be asked, how came poems of such length to be preserved at all by mere oral transmission through a period of undefined, and possibly of very great, length? It is plain that nothing but an extraordinary celebrity, and a passionate attachment on the part of the people, could have kept them alive. Now, if we suppose this celebrity and this attachment, let us inquire further, whether they may not have supplied the means of neutralizing and counteracting, in the main, the dangers to which the poems were exposed; and whether it is unreasonable to say, That which *could* have preserved them in their unity at all, *must*, in all likelihood, have preserved them in a tolerably genuine state. Fully admitting that the evidence in the case is imperfect, and can only lead to disputable conclusions, I nevertheless ask, What is the most probable supposition respecting the condition of the Homeric poems in the pre-historic times of Greece? Is it not this—that, with due allowance for a different state of circumstances, they were then, what they were in later times; the broad basis of mental culture; the great monument of the glory of the nation, and of each particular State or race; the prime entertainment of those prolonged festive gatherings which were so characteristic of early Greece; that they were not only the special charge and pride of particular poetical schools, but distinct objects of the care of legislators and statesmen; that in this manner they were recognised as among the institutions of the country, and that they had thus to depend for their transmission, not only on the fire of national and poetic feeling, but upon a jealous custody much resembling that which even a comparatively rude people gives to its laws?

I shall attempt a summary of the arguments and testimonies which appear to me to recommend, if they do not compel, the adoption of these conclusions.

1. Heraclides Ponticus, a pupil of Plato, in a fragment περὶ πολιτειῶν, declares that Lycurgus was the first to bring the poetry of Homer into Peloponnesus: τὴν Ὁμήρου ποίησιν, παρὰ τῶν ἀπογόνων Κρεοφύλου λαβὼν, πρῶτος διεκόμισεν εἰς Πελοπόννησον. This testimony is late with reference to the fact it reports, but not late in the history of Greek literature. Of the source from which it was derived by the author who gives it us, we know nothing. No light is thrown upon it by Ælian,[a] who adds the epithet ἀθρόαν to ποίησιν. Plutarch enlarges the expression of the tradition, but seems to add little to its matter, except that some portions of Homer were known before Lycurgus brought the whole from Crete.[b] It is stated in the Republic of Plato,[c] that Creophylus was a companion of Homer. Strabo[d] informs us that he was a Samian; and Hermodamas, the master of Pythagoras, is said by Diogenes Laertius[e] to have been his descendant. Now, we cannot call any part of these statements history; but they exhibit a body of tradition, of which the members, drawn from scattered quarters, agree with one another, and agree also with the general probability that arises out of a fact so astonishing as is in itself the actual preservation

[a] Var. Hist. xiii. 14.
[b] Plut. Lyc. p. 41.
[c] Plat. Rep. x. p. 600, B.
[d] Strabo xiv. p. 946.
[e] viii. 2.

of the poems of Homer. It is in truth this fact that lays the best ground for traditions such as the one in question. If they came before us artificially complete and embellished, that might be made a ground of suspicion. But appearing, as this one does, with an evident absence of design, there is every presumption of its truth. Before considering the full force which attaches to it if it be true, we will draw out the kindred traditions.

2. Of these, the next, and a most important one, is the statement of Herodotus respecting Clisthenes, the ruler of Sicyon, who, when he had been at war with Argos, ῥαψῳδοὺς ἔπαυσε ἐν Σικυῶνι ἀγωνίζεσθαι, τῶν Ὁμηρείων ἐπέων εἵνεκα, ὅτι Ἀργεῖοί τε καὶ Ἄργος τὰ πολλὰ πάντα ὑμνέαται[f]. He proceeds to say, that Clisthenes sought to banish the memory of Adrastus, as being an Argive hero, from Sicyon. It is not necessary to inquire what these Homeric poems may have included; but the conclusion of Grote, that they were 'the Thebais and the Epigoni, not the Iliad[g],' seems to me incredible. Nor is it correct that the Iliad fails to supply matter to which the statement may refer. In the Iliad, the name of Argos, though meaning it is true the country rather than a city, is nearly associated with the chief seat of power, and becomes representative of the whole Hellenic race in its heroic infancy. This is surely honour infinitely higher, than any local fame it could derive from the civil feud with Thebes. The Iliad, too, marks most clearly the connexion of Adrastus with Argos—for it names Diomed as the husband of his daughter or granddaughter, Ægialea[h]; it also marks the subordinate position of Sicyon,

ὅθ' ἄρ' Ἄδρηστος πρῶτ' ἐμβασίλευεν[i].

[f] Herod. v. 67. [g] Hist. Greece, ii. 174 n. [h] Il. v. 412-15.
[i] Il. ii. 572.

by making it a mere town in the dominions of Agamemnon, while Argos figures as a sovereign and powerful city. There may therefore perhaps be room to doubt whether Herodotus meant even to include the Thebais or Epigoni in the phrase 'Homeric poems.'

But the importance of the passage is not wholly dependent on these considerations. It shows,

a. That there were, at Sicyon, State-recitations of Homer six centuries before the Christian era, attended with rewards for the successful performers.

b. That these recitations were in conformity with common use; for they are named as something ordinary and established, which was then set aside, not as a custom peculiar to Sicyon.

c. That the recitations depended upon the Homeric poems, since they were entirely stopped on account of exceptionable matter which the Homeric poems were deemed to contain.

d. That these recitations were in the nature of competitive contests among the rhapsodists, when the best and most approved, of course, would obtain prizes. This implies that the recitations were not single, as if by poet laureates, but that many shared in them.

3. Next to this tradition, and nearly coeval with it, but reported by later authority, is that respecting Solon and Athens. Dieuchidas of Megara, an author of uncertain age, placed by Heyne[j] later than Alexander, is quoted in Diogenes Laertius[k] as testifying to the following effect concerning Solon: τά τε Ὁμήρου ἐξ ὑποβολῆς γέγραφε ῥαψῳδεῖσθαι. οἷον ὅπου ὁ πρῶτος ἔληξεν, ἐκεῖθεν ἄρχεσθαι τὸν ἐχόμενον. μᾶλλον οὖν Σόλων Ὅμηρον ἐφώτισεν, ἢ Πεισίστρατος. But we have also a better

[j] Heyne, Hom. viii., seq.   [k] I. 57.

witness, I think, in Lycurgus the orator, contemporary with Demosthenes,[1] who gives a most striking account of the political and martial use of the Homeric songs. He says, οὕτω γὰρ ὑπέλαβον ὑμῶν οἱ πατέρες σπουδαῖον εἶναι ποιητήν, ὥστε νόμον ἔθεντο καθ' ἑκάστην πενταετηρίδα τῶν Παναθηναίων μόνου τῶν ἄλλων ποιητῶν ῥαψῳδεῖσθαι τὰ ἔπη. 'It was with these songs in their ears,' he proceeds, 'that your fathers fought at Marathon; and so valiant were they *then*, that from among them their brave rivals, the Lacedæmonians, sought a general, Tyrtæus.'

a. Now, these words appear to carry the traditional origin of this law, as far as the authority of Lycurgus will avail, back to the early part of the seventh century, when Tyrtæus lived.[m]

b. Thus, at the period when Athens is just beginning to rise towards eminence, she enacts a law that the poems of Homer shall be recited at her greatest festival.

c. This honour she accords to Homer (whatever that name may have imported) alone among poets.

d. This appears, from the connexion with Tyrtæus, to be a tradition of a matter older still than the one mentioned by Dieuchidas. But the two are in thorough accordance. For Dieuchidas does not say that Solon introduced the recitations of Homer, nor does he refer simply to the Panathenaica. He pretty clearly implies, that Solon did not begin the recitations, but that he reformed—(by bringing them into regular succession, which implies a fixed order of the songs)—what had been introduced already; while Lycurgus seems to supply the notice of the original introduction as having occurred before the time even of Tyrtæus.

[1] In Leocritum, 104-8. [m] Smith's Dict. 'Tyrtæus.'

4. The argument from the sculptures on the chest of Cypselus, representing subjects taken out of the Iliad, refers to a period nearly corresponding with that of Tyrtæus, as Cypselus was probably born about B. C. 700: and tends to show that the Iliad was famous in Corinth at that date.[n]

5. The next of the specific traditions is that relating to Pisistratus. To his agency it has been the fashion of late years to assign an exaggerated, or even an exclusive, importance. But whereas the testimonies respecting Lycurgus, Clisthenes, and Solon, (as well as the Athenian legislators before him,) are derived from authors probably, or certainly, of the fourth and fifth centuries B. C., we have none at all respecting Pisistratus earlier than the Augustan age.[o] Cicero says he first disposed the Homeric books in their present order; Pausanias,[p] that he collected them, διεσπασμένα τε καὶ ἀλλαχοῦ μνημονευόμενα; Josephus,[q] who, as we have seen, merely refers to the report that the Iliad was not committed to writing until after Homer's time, is wrongly quoted[r] as a witness to the labours of Pisistratus. An ancient Scholion, recently discovered,[s] names four poets who worked under that prince. And it may be admitted, that the traditions respecting Pisistratus have this distinctive mark—that they seem to indicate the first accomplishment of a critical and literary task upon Homer's text under the direct care and responsibility of the sovereign of the country.

Thus, the testimony concerning Pisistratus is of an

---

[n] See the Homerus of Archdeacon Williams, pp. 9—11.
[o] Cic. de Or. iii. 34.
[p] Paus. vii. 26. p. 594. add Suidas in voc. Ὅμηρος. Eustath.
Il. i. 1.
[q] Contra Ap. i. 2.
[r] Smith's Dict., Art. 'Homerus :' and elsewhere.
[s] Ibid. from Ritschl.

order decidedly inferior to that which supports the earlier traditions, and cannot with propriety be put into the scale against them where they are in conflict with it; but there is no reason to reject the report that he fixed the particular order of the poems, which the law of Solon may have left open in some degree to the judgment of the reciters, although they were required by it to recite in order.

6. The dialogue, doubtfully ascribed to Plato under the name of Hipparchus, states that that sovereign—

τὰ Ὁμήρου πρῶτος ἐκόμισεν ἐς τὴν γῆν ταυτηνὶ, καὶ ἠνάγκασε τοὺς ῥαψῳδοὺς Παναθηναίοις ἐξ ὑπολήψεως ἐφεξῆς αὐτὰ διιέναι, ὥσπερ νῦν ἔτι οἵδε ποιοῦσι [t].

As regards the matter of original introduction, this passage contradicts all the foregoing ones. From the uncertainty who is its author, it must yield to them as of less authority. But this is not all. It is on the very face of it incredible: for it asserts, not that his poetry was first arranged or adjusted, but first brought into the country by Hipparchus. This is in itself absurd: and it is also directly in the teeth of the statement, which can hardly be a pure fiction, that Solon by law required the poems of Homer to be recited at the Panathenæa. As regards the succession in reciting, it is quite possible that he may have put the last hand to the work of his father.

However, the passage may deserve notice as a sign of the general belief that the care of the poems of Homer, and provision for their orderly publication in the only mode then possible, was a fit and usual part of the care of States and their rulers.

The whole mass of the passages which have been cited may be thought to bear primarily on the contro-

[t] Hipparchus, § 4. (ii. 228.)

versies which I have waived. But they have a most important, even if secondary, bearing upon the question, whether the received text is generally sound in its structure. The dangers which menaced that text of course were referable to two sources: the one, want of due care; and the other, falsification for a purpose: and it is necessary to bring into one view the whole positive evidence with respect to the preservation and publication of the Homeric poems, in order to estimate the amount both of these dangers and of the safeguards against them. I resume the prosecution of this task.

From the word ἀγωνίζεσθαι, applied by Herodotus to the recitations at Sicyon, it is plain that they were matches among the rhapsodists. And as the match did not in the main depend upon the original compositions of the candidates, but on the repetition of what Homer was reputed to have composed, the question arises, on what grounds could the prize be adjudged? Partly, perhaps, for the voice and manner of the rhapsodist; but partly also, nay, we must assume principally, for his comparative fidelity to the supposed standard of his original. And, when we consider the length of the poems, we may the more easily understand how the retentiveness of memory required to give an adequate command of them, might well deserve and receive reward. True, the vanity of a particular rhapsodist might readily induce him to suppose that he could improve upon Homer. But surely such an one would be subject to no inconsiderable check from the vigilance, and the impartial, or more probably the jealous, judgment of his contemporaries and rivals. The aberrations, too, or interpolations, of each one inventor, would be immediately crossed by those of every other; and the intrinsic superiority of the great poet himself, and the extraordinary reverence paid to his name, would thus derive powerful aid from the natural play of human passions. I look upon the circumstance that these recitations were competitive, and probably open to all comers, as one of the utmost importance. Freedom, in such a case, would be far more conservative than restriction.

The force of such considerations is abated indeed, but it is not destroyed, by the fact that poems not composed by Homer were esteemed to be Homeric. We have no means of knowing whether this false estimation reached in general beyond the character of mere vulgar rumour. We find, indeed, that Callinus ascribed the Thebais to Homer, Thucydides the Pythian Hymn, and Aristotle the Margites. But, of these three, the last judgment, for all we know, may have been a true one. The Thebais was judged by Pausanias to be the best of the epics, after the Iliad and Odyssey. It does not therefore follow, that because a poet might assign this to him, he would also have assigned others. Few authors show more slender marks of critical acumen than Herodotus; but even he treats the notions that the Cyprian epic or the Epigoni belonged to Homer in terms such as to show, that they were at most mere speculations, and not established public judgments.[u]

Now, even in a critical age, it seems to be inevitable, that authors of conspicuous popularity shall be followed on their path, not only by imitators, but, where there is the least hope of even temporary success, by forgers. We see, in the present day, attempts to vent new novels under the name of Walter Scott. I have myself a volume, purchased in Italy, of spurious verses,

[u] Herod. ii. 117. iv. 32.

printed under the name of her great, though not yet famous, modern poet, Giacomo Leopardi. In periods far less critical, impostors would be bolder, and dupes more numerous. But it cannot be shown that a number of other epics, or even that any single one, had been generally ascribed to Homer with the same confidence as the Iliad and Odyssey; nor that the same care, public or private, was taken in any other case for the keeping and restoration of the text.

Again, though the Spartan and Athenian traditions take no specific notice of competition, yet we are justified in supposing that it existed, because the practice can be traced to an antiquity more remote than any of them. It is true that in Homer we have no example of competition among bards actually exhibited; but neither do the poems furnish us with an occasion when it might have been looked for. The ordinary place of the bard was as a member of a king's or chieftain's household. At the great assemblages of tribes, or of the Greek race, to which the chiefs repaired in numbers, more bards than one would also probably appear. Some light is thrown upon this subject by the passage relating to Thamyris in the second Book of the Iliad.[v] He met his calamity at Dorion, when on a journey; and it caught him Οἰχαλίηθεν ἰόντα παρ' Εὐρύτου Οἰχαλιῆος. Homer's usual precision justifies our arguing that, when he says he came, not simply from a place, but also from, or from beside, the lord of a place, the meaning is, that he was attached to that lord as the bard of his court or household. Again, he was on a journey. Whither bound, except evidently to one of these contests? This is fully shown by the lines that follow, for they contemplate a match as then about to take place forth-

[v] Il. ii. 594-600.

with. For the form of his boast was not simply that he could beat the Muses, but (to speak in our phraseology) he vauntingly vowed that he would win, even though the Muses themselves should be his rivals.

στεῦτο γὰρ εὐχόμενος νικήσεμεν, εἴπερ ἂν αὐταὶ
Μοῦσαι ἀείδοιεν.

Institutions which embrace competition have, from the character of man's nature, a great self-sustaining power; and there is no reason to suppose that between the time of Thamyris and that of the Sicyonian rhapsodists this method of recitation had at any time fallen into abeyance. In a fragment of Hesiod[x], quoted by the Scholiast on Pindar, we find the phrase ῥάπτειν ἀοιδήν; but on account of its mention of Homer as a contemporary, this fragment is untrustworthy. In other places, however, he distinctly witnesses to the matches and prizes of the bards, and says that at the match held by Amphidamas in Aulis, he himself won a tripod[y]. Again, Thucydides finds an unequivocal proof of the competition of bards in the beautiful passage which he quotes from the very ancient *Hymn* to Apollo[z].

I do not think it needful to dwell in detail upon the means privately taken for the transmission of the Homeric songs. Cinæthus of Chios (according to the Scholiast on Pindar[a], quoting Hippostratus, a Sicilian author of uncertain date), ἐρραψῴδησε τὰ Ὁμήρου ἔπη (about 500 B.C.), for the first time at Syracuse. It may be observed that this passage may probably imply the foundation of public recitations there. Eustathius[b],

[x] Fragm. xxxiv.
[y] Op. ii. 268–75.
[z] Hymn. Apoll. 166—73; 146–50.
[a] Schol. Pyth. vi. 4; Nem. ii. 1.
[b] Il. A. p. 6.

quoting, as Heyne[c] observes, inaccurately, charges Cinæthus with having corrupted the Homeric poems; but the words of the Scholiast need not mean more than that he composed certain poems and threw them into the mass of those which were more or less taken to be Homeric. We need not enlarge upon Creophylus[d], or upon the Homeridæ mentioned by Pindar, and, according to Strabo, claimed as her own by Chios[e]. That name appears to be used freely by Plato[f], without explanation, as if in his own time they formed a well-known school. According to Athenæus[g], quoting Aristocles, a writer of uncertain date, the name Ὁμηρισταὶ was given to the rhapsodists generally.

The Iliad and the Odyssey were known to Herodotus under their present titles, as we find from his references to them. But it is justly argued by Heyne, that there must have been known poems of their scope and subject at the time when the other Cyclic poems were written, which fill up the interval between them, and complete the Troic story[h]; that is to say, not long after the commencement of the Olympiads.

Again, it is needless to do more than simply touch upon the relation of Homer to Greek letters and culture in general. He was the source of tragedy, the first text-book of philosophers, and the basis of liberal education; so much so, that Alcibiades is said to have struck his schoolmaster for having no MS. rhapsody of the Iliad[i], while Xenophon quotes Niceratus as saying that his father made him learn the Iliad and Odyssey, and that he could repeat the whole of them by heart[k].

[c] Heyne, viii. p. 811.
[d] Sup.
[e] Pind. Nem. ii. 1, and Strabo, xiv. i. p. 645.
[f] Plat. Phædrus, iii. 252, and Republ. B. i.; ii. 599.
[g] Athen. iv. p. 174.
[h] Heyne, viii. 814.
[i] Plut. Apoph., p. 186 D.
[k] Xenoph. Sympos. iii. 5.

I. *Prolegomena.*

Cassander, king of Macedon, according to Athenæus, could do nearly as much. He had by heart τῶν ἐπῶν τὰ πολλά.[1]

Passing on from this evidence of general estimation, I come to what is more important with respect to the question of the text—that is, the state of the poems at the time of the Alexandrian recensions, as it is exhibited by Villoison, from the Venetian Scholia on the Iliad which he discovered. From this source appears to me to proceed our best warrant for believing in the general soundness of the text.

The first tendencies of the Alexandrian school, as they are represented by Zenodotus, appear to have been towards very free excision and emendation. Aristarchus, its highest authority, is considered to represent a reaction towards more sober handling. The plan of expressing suspicion by *obeli* was a good one—it raised the question of genuineness without foreclosing it. The passages which he excluded stand in the text, and many among them are not much damaged by the condemnation. One particularly, in the speech of Phœnix,[m] appears to me alike beautiful and characteristic. After all, the *obelos* is generally attached to lines of amplification and poetic ornament; which could be dispensed with, and yet leave the sense not vitally mutilated. But we may quote Aristarchus as a witness, on the whole, to the substantial soundness of the text. For it is plain that the affirmation of all his doubts would still leave us with the substance of the Iliad as it is; while it seems that the judgment of mankind, or rather its feeling, which in such a matter is worth more than its judgment, has refused to go as far as he did, for his doubts or adverse verdicts are recorded, but the

[1] Athen. xiv. p. 620.   [m] Il. ix. 458–61.

lines and passages remain, are still read and taught as Homer, and are not pretended to be distinguishable by any broad mark of intrinsic inferiority. It is not meant that the soundness of each line has been considered and affirmed to be free from doubt, but that it has been felt that, while clear discrimination in detail was impracticable, retention was, on the whole, safer than exclusion. Nor is this because a principle of blind credulity has prevailed. On the contrary, the same judgment, feeling, or instinct, be it what it may, of civilised man, which has found it safest to adhere to the traditional text of Homer, has likewise thought it safest to rule the case of authorship adversely as to the Hymns. Under all the circumstances, I find no difficulty in understanding such accounts as that which tells us that the inquiry, which is the best edition of Homer? was met with the answer, 'the oldest;'—or such a passage as that of Lucian,[n] who introduces Homer in the Shades, declaring that the ἀθετούμεναι στίχες, the suspected and rejected verses, were all his; whereupon, says Lucian, I recognised the abundant frigidity of the school of Zenodotus and Aristarchus. This is in an ironical work; but ironical works are often used as the vehicles of real opinions.

The Venetian Scholiast is full of familiar references to the different editions of the text of the Iliad, as being standards perfectly well known; and he thus exhibits to us, in a considerable degree, the materials which the Alexandrian critics found existing, and with which they went to work upon that poem.

The multitude of editions (ἐκδόσεις) which they had before them, were partly state editions (αἱ πολιτικαὶ, αἱ κατὰ πόλεις, αἱ διὰ τῶν πόλεων, αἱ ἀπὸ τῶν πόλεων), and

[n] Lucian, Ver. Hist. ii. 117.

partly those due to private care (οἱ κατ' ἄνδρα). These latter seem to have obtained the name in two ways. The first was, when it was taken from particular editors who had revised the text, such as Antimachus (contemporary with Plato), Callimachus, and, above all, Aristotle, who prepared for Alexander the Great the copy ἐκ νάρθηκος, and, again, the edition of Zenodotus, that of Aristophanes, and the two separate editions of Aristarchus, all of the Alexandrian school; or else they were named from the persons who possessed them, and for whom they had been prepared by the care of learned men. Among such possessors was Cassander, king of Macedonia.

The existence of these State editions is a fact full of meaning. It appears to show nothing less than this, that the text was under the charge of the public authorities in the several States. We have particular names for six of these editions through the Venetian Scholiast—those of Marseilles, Chios, Cyprus, Crete, Sinope, Argos. On beholding this list, we are immediately struck by the fact that while it contains names from the far East, like Sinope, and far West, like Marseilles, it does not contain one name of a city in Greece Proper, except Argos, and that a city having perhaps less communion than almost any other considerable place with Greek literature in general. We ask why do not Athens, Sparta, Thebes, Corinth, why do not Syracuse and the great Greek towns of Sicily and Italy, appear with their several Homeric texts? The most likely answer appears to be, not that these six enumerated cities were more distinguished than others by the carefulness of their provisions for the safety of the Homeric text, but that for some reason, possibly from their lying less within the circle of Greek letters at large, they still retained each their particular text, whereas an approximation had been made to a common text,—of which the cities most properly Greek in general availed themselves. For sometimes there are certain signs supplied in the Scholia of a common text prevailing in the State or national, and another in the private editions, and this without reference to the six cities above mentioned. In the supposition of such a tendency to divaricate, there is nothing beyond likelihood; for private editors would be more free to follow their own judgments or conjectures, whereas the public curators would almost, as a matter of course, be more rigidly conservative. At any rate, there are traceable indications before us to this effect; for the Scholiast cites for particular readings—

αἱ ἐκ τῶν πόλεων, xxi. 351.
αἱ ἀπὸ πόλεων, xxii. 51.
αἱ ἀπὸ τῶν πόλεων, xix. 386.

and on the other hand—

αἱ κατ' ἄνδρα, xxii. 103.

as well as in other places, τινὲς τῶν πολιτικῶν (e. g. xxiv. 30), and αἱ πλείους τῶν κατ' ἄνδρα (xxiii. 88). It is therefore likely that there was a national text, approximating to uniformity, and used in common by those cities, the principal ones of Greece, which are not quoted as having had texts of their own; for there is no reason, that I am aware of, to suppose that the phrases αἱ πολιτικαί, and the rest of those equivalent to it, are confined to the six editions. Now, while the six State editions indicate a care probably dating from very early times for the soundness of the text, the common State recension, if, as appears probable, there was one, indicates a gradual convergence of critical labours and of the public judgment in the generality of those States, of which the people had the oldest, strongest, and most direct interest in the Homeric poems.

There is a third form of common text, less perfect than either of the others, of which abundant traces are found. We find mention of the editions or copies called αἱ κοιναὶ, αἱ δημοτικαὶ, αἱ δημώδεις, and they are sometimes described collectively, as on Iliad ii. 53, ἐν δὲ ταῖς κοιναῖς ἐγέγραπτο καὶ τῇ Ζηνοδοτείῳ, βουλήν. Sometimes the greater part of these κοιναὶ or δημώδεις have a particular reading. They all, of all classes, varied more or less, and are distinguished according to their merits, as φαυλαὶ, εἰκαιότεραι, μέτριαι, χαριέστάται. These ordinary or public (not national) editions, prepared for sale in the open book-market, were probably founded, in the main, on the national text, but being intended for general sale, and not prepared by responsible editors, they were ordinarily inferior. This Venetian Scholiast was himself a critic, and wrote when the Æolic and Ionic dialects were still in use, as appears from his references to them.[p]

The Scholia to the Odyssey supply the names of some editions besides those which have been mentioned. One of these is the Αἰολὶς, or Αἰολική;[q] another is ἡ ἐκ Μουσείου,[r] which is explained to refer to the depositary near the School at Alexandria; and a third ἡ Κυκλική,[s] which is interpreted to mean an edition in which the poems of Homer were placed in a series with those of the Cyclical authors.

On the one hand, then, it may be readily admitted that the Homeric poems were exposed, before they were reduced to writing, to the powerful and various action

---

[p] Villoison, Proleg. p. xxvii. *in loc.*
[q] Od. xiv. 280.
[r] Od. xiv. 204, and Buttmann *loc.*
[s] xvi. 195, and Buttmann *in*

of disintegrating causes. Among these we may name neglect, inability to cope with the real difficulties of their transmission, the personal vanity of the rhapsodists, and the local vanity of communities. But I think we have also disclosed to us, both by the fragmentary notices of the history of the poems if taken in their collective effect, and by the state of things in and upon which the Alexandrian critics laboured, the operation of an immense amount of restorative counter-agency. All chance of our arriving at a sober judgment must depend upon our duly weighing these two sets of forces in their relation to one another. There were indeed tendencies, which may well be called irresistible, to aberrations from the traditional standard; but there were barriers also insurmountable, which seem to have confined those aberrations within certain limits. They could not proceed beyond a given point without awakening the consciousness, that Homer, the priceless treasure of Greece, and perhaps the first source of its keener consciousness of nationality, was in danger of being disfigured, and deformed, and so lost; and that sense, when once awakened, without doubt generated such reactions as we find exemplified in the proceedings of Pisistratus.

We may indeed derive directly, from the force of the destroying element, when viewed in detail, the strongest proof that there must have been an original standard, by recurrence to which its ravages could from time to time be repaired. For if that element had worked without such means of correction, I do not see how we could now have been in possession of an Iliad and an Odyssey. As with regard to religions after they are parted from their source, the tendency would have been to continually-increasing divergence. The dissimilarities arising from omission, alteration, and interpolation, would have grown, so as to embrace larger and larger portions of the poems, and at this day, instead of merely questioning this or that line in a few places, and comparing this with that reading, we should have been deliberating among a dozen Iliads and a dozen Odysseys, to discover which were the true.

If, then, it be said that the proceedings of Pisistratus or of Solon, bear testimony not to the soundness but to the incessant corruption of the text, my answer is, they bear witness to its corruption, just as the records of the repairs of Westminster Abbey might be said, and truly said, to bear testimony to its disrepair. That partial and local faults, and dislocations, would creep in, is as certain as that wind and weather act upon the stoutest fabric: but when we read of the repairs of a building, we infer that pains were taken to make it habitable; and when we read of the restorations of Homer, we perceive that it was an object of public solicitude to keep the poems in a state of soundness. As, indeed, the building most used will *cæteris paribus* require the most frequent repairs, so the elementary causes of corruption, by carelessness, might operate most powerfully in a case where the poet might be recited by every strolling minstrel at a local festivity: but it is also clear that in these very cases there would be the greatest anxiety to detect and to eliminate the destructive elements, when once they were seen to be making head. But, in truth, the analogy of a building does not represent the case. Edifices are sometimes disfigured by the parsimony of aftertimes: but there was no time, so far as we know, when Greece did not rate the value of Homer more highly than the cost of taking care of him. Again, the architects of degenerate ages think, as Bernini did of Michael Angelo, that they can improve upon their designs: but the name of no Greek has been recorded who thought he could improve upon Homer, and the vanity of the nameless was likely to be checked by their companions and competitors.

We have principally had in view the question, whether Homer was, in a peculiar degree, guarded against any profound and radical corruption which might grow out of unchecked carelessness; but the result will be not more unfavourable, if we ask how did he stand in regard to the other great fountain-head of evil, namely, falsification with a purpose? Now, the fact, that in any given case provision is made for jealous custody against any attack from without, affords no proof, or even presumption, against the subsistence of destroying causes within. But the Greeks, as a nation, had no motive to corrupt, and had every motive to preserve the text of Homer. His national office and position have been admirably expressed by Statius, in verses on the Trojan expedition:—

> Tum primùm Græcia vires
> Contemplata suas: tum sparsa ac dissona moles,
> In corpus vultumque coït[t].

His works were the very cradle of the nation; there it first visibly lived and breathed. They were the most perfect expression of every Greek feeling and desire: in the rivalry between the Hellenic race and the (afterwards so called) βάρβαροι of Asia, they gave, in forms the most effective and the most artful, everything worth having to the former, and left the later Greek nothing to add. What void to be filled could even

[t] Achilleis, i. 456.

vanity discover, when so many Greek chieftains, inferior, in a degree never measured, to Achilles, were, nevertheless, each of them, too strong for the prince of Trojan warriors?

But it may perhaps be replied that, even supposing that collective Greece could gain nothing by corrupting Homer, yet the relative distribution of honour among the principal States might be affected to the profit of one and the prejudice of another. Now it is plain that, in this delicate and vital point, the sectional jealousies of the Greeks would afford the best possible security to the general contents of the text: something of the same security that the hatred of the Jews and the Samaritans supplied, when they became rival guardians of the books of the Old Testament. Argos, deeply interested for Diomed, and Lacedæmon for Menelaus, and both for Agamemnon, were watchmen alike powerful and keen against Athens, if she had attempted to obtain for herself in the Iliad a place at all proportioned to her after-fame. There were numerous parts of Homer's Greece, both great and small, that fell into subsequent insignificance, such as Pylos, Ithaca, Salamis, Locris: the relative positions of Thessaly and Southern Greece were fundamentally changed in the historic times. But all, whether they exulted in the longlived honours of their States, or whether they fondly brooded on the recollections of former fame, were alike interested in resisting interlopers who might seek to trespass for their own advantage, as well as in the general object of preserving the priceless national monument from decay. Nor is there any room to suppose, that these questions of primeval honour were indifferent to the later Greeks. The citation from the Catalogue by the Athenian envoys before Gelon in Herodotus (to take a single instance), affords conclusive proof to the contrary: and, even so late as in the day of Pausanias, he tells us that Argolis and Arcadia were the States, which even then were still keenly disputing with Athens the palm of autochthonism.

It, therefore, appears to me that the presumptions of the case are on the whole favourable, and not adverse, to the general soundness of the Homeric text.

I confess myself to be very greatly confirmed in this view of the presumptions, by the scarcely measurable amount of internal evidence which the text supplies to substantiate its own integrity. Almost the whole of the copious materials which recent writers have accumulated to prove the unity and personality of the author, is available to show the soundness of the text. The appeal need not be only to the undisturbed state of the main *strata* of the poems, the consistent structure and relations of the facts; the general *corpus* of the poems might have been sound, and yet a bad text would, when subjected to a very searching ordeal on the minutest points, have revealed a multitude of solecisms and errors: but, instead of this, the rigid application of the microscope has only shown more clearly a great perfection in the workmanship. The innumerable forms of refined and delicate coincidence in names and facts, in the use of epithets, the notes of character, the turn of speeches and phrases, and the like, are so many rills of evidence, which combine into a stream of resistless force, in favour of that text which has been found so admirably, as a mirror, to reflect the image and the mind of Homer, and which, like a mirror, could not have reflected it truly unless it had itself been true.

Indeed, I must proceed a step further; and admit

that the arguments *ab extra*, which I have here put forward respecting the historic aims of the poet, his proximity in time to his subject, and the probable soundness of the text, are rather answers to objections, than the adequate materials of affirmative conviction.

After having myself tested the text as to its self-consistency and otherwise, in several thousand places, I find scarcely one or two places in each thousand, where it seems to invite expurgation in order to establish the consistency of its contents. The evidence on which I really place reliance is experimental evidence: and that I find in the poems, accumulated to a degree which no other human work within my knowledge approaches. I do not presume to hope more than that the more remote and general arguments, which have now been used, may assist in removing preliminary barriers to the consideration of the one cardinal and paramount argument, the text itself and its contents.

And here a brief reference must be made to the scepticism in miniature which has replaced the more sweeping incredulity of Wolf and his school. Editors of great weight, refusing to accompany even the Chorizontes in separating the authorship of the poems, nevertheless freely condemn particular passages. I do not deny that there are various passages, of which the genuineness is fair matter for discussion. But I confess that I find such grounds of excision, as those commonly alleged by critics recommending it, very indeterminate, and of a nature to leave it doubtful where their operation is to stop. They generally involve arbitrary assumptions either of construction or of history, or the application of a more rigid and literal rule of consistency than poetry either requires or can endure, or else the capital error, as I cannot but consider it, of bringing Homer to be tried at the bar of later and inferior traditions. And there is a want of common principles, a general insecurity of standing ground, and an appearance of reforming Homer not according to any acknowledged laws of criticism, but according to the humour of each accomplished and ingenious man: which, in a matter of this weight, is no sufficient guarantee. I therefore follow in the line of those, whose recommendation is to draw every thing we can out of the present text; and to see how far its contents may constitute a substantive and consistent whole, in the various branches of information to which they refer. When we have carried this process as far as it will bear, we may find, first that many or some of the seeming discordancies are really embraced within a comprehensive general harmony, and secondly that with a fuller knowledge of the laws of that harmony we may ourselves be in a condition at least of less incapacity to pronounce what is Homeric and what is not. I will only say that were I to venture into this field of criticism, I should be governed less than is usual by discrepancies of fact often very hastily assumed; and much more than is usual by any violence done to the finer analogies of which Homer is so full, and by departures from his regular modes of thought, feeling, and representation.

SECT. 6.—*The Place and Authority of Homer in Historical Inquiry.*

The principal and final purpose, which I wish to present in the most distinct manner to the mind of the reader, is that of securing for the Homeric traditions, estimated according to the effect of the foregoing considerations, a just measure of relative as well as absolute appreciation.

It appears to me that there has prevailed in this respect a wide-spread and long-continued error, assuming various forms, and affecting in very different degrees, without doubt, the practice of different writers, but so extended and so rooted, as at this stage in the progress of criticism to require formal challenge. I mean, that it is an error to regard and accept all ancient traditions, relating to the periods that precede regular historic annals, as of equal value, or not to discriminate their several values with adequate care. Above all, I strongly contend that we should assign to the Homeric evidence a primary rank upon all the subjects which it touches, and that we should make it a rule to reduce all other literary testimony, because of later origin, to a subordinate and subsidiary position.

Mere rumours or stories of the pre-historic times are not, as such, entitled to be called traditions. A story of this kind, say in Apollodorus, may indeed by bare possibility be older than any thing in Homer; but if it comes to us without the proper and visible criteria of age, it has no claim upon our assent as a truthful record of the time to which it purports to refer. Traditions of this class only grow to be such, as a general rule, for us, at the time when they take a positive form in the work of some author, who thus becomes, as far as his time and circumstances permit, a witness to them. It is only from thenceforward, that their faithful derivation and transmission can be relied on as in any degree probable.

Again, I cast aside statements with respect to which the poet, being carried beyond the sphere of his ordinary experience, must, on that account, not be presumed to speak historically; yet even here, if he is speaking of matters which were in general belief, he is a witness of the first class with respect to that belief, which is itself in another sense a matter of history; and here also those, who have followed him at a remote date, are witnesses of a lower order.

Or there may be cases, as, for instance, in the stubborn facts of geography, where the laws of evidence compel us rudely to thrust aside the declaration of the bard; or cases where his mode of handling his materials affords in itself a proof that he did not mean to speak historically, but, in the phrase of Aristotle, ἐκπληκτικῶς, or for poetic effect.

Or again, it is conceivable, though I do not know whether it has happened, that Homeric testimony might come into conflict, not with mere counter-assertion, but with those forms of circumstantial evidence which are sometimes conclusively elicited by reasoning from positive *data* of architecture, language, and ethnology. I claim for Homer no exemption from the more cogent authority which may attach to reasoning of this kind.

Clearing the question of these incumbrances, I wish to submit to the suffrages of those, who may be more competent than myself to estimate both the proposition and the proof, the following thesis: that, in regard to the religion, history, ethnology, polity, and life at large of the Greeks of the heroic times, the authority of the Homeric poems, standing far above that of the whole mass of the later literary traditions in any of their forms, ought never to be treated as homogeneous with them, but should usually, in the first instance, be handled by itself, and the testimony of later writers should, in general, be handled in subordination to it, and should be tried by it, as by a touchstone, on all the subjects which it embraces.

It is generally admitted that Homer is older by some

generations than Hesiod, by many than the authors of the Cyclical Poems; and older by many centuries than the general mass of our authorities on Greek antiquity, beginning with Æschylus and Herodotus, and coming down to Dionysius of Halicarnassus, Diodorus Siculus, Strabo, Ælian, Pausanias, Diogenes Laertius. Nor is it by time alone, that his superior proximity and weight are to be measured. Of all the ages that have passed since Homer, it may be truly said that not one has produced a more acute, accurate, and comprehensive observer. But, above all, writing of the heroic time, he, and he alone, writes like one who, as from internal evidence we may confidently assert, stood within its precinct, and was imbued from head to foot with its spirit and its associations.

It is, of course, quite possible, that in one particular or another, Homer may be in error, and the later tradition, it is also just possible, may be correct. But so, also, the evidence of an eye-witness in a court of justice may be erroneous, while by chance the merest hearsay may be true. This does not divert men from a careful classification of evidence according to its presumptive value, where they have purposes of utility, according to the common and limited sense of the term, in their view. In regard to the early Greek history, the practice has often been otherwise; partly in the works of scholars, and yet more, as we might expect, in the more popular forms of tuition. It has been to lump together the heterogeneous mass of traditions embodied in the literature of a thousand years. All that the sport of fancy and imagination had conceived—all that national, or local, or personal vanity had suggested—all that motives of policy had forged in history or religion—or so much of this aggregate as time has spared to us, has been treated without any systematic recognition of the different value of different orders of tradition. I admit that it is towards the close of the Greek literature that we find the principal professed inquirers into antiquity; and their aim and method may have redressed, in great part, any inequality between themselves and writers of the time of Thucydides or Plato. But nothing can cancel, nothing, it might almost be said, can narrow, the enormous interval, in point of authority, between Homer, who sang in the heroic age, and those who not only collected their materials, but formed their thoughts, after it was closed, and after its floating reminiscences had become subject to the incessant action of falsifying processes.

For a length of time the temper of our ancient histories was one of unquestioning reception. But where much was self-contradictory, all could not be believed. Under these circumstances, it was not unnatural that those writers who were full and systematic, should be preferred, rather than that the labour should be undergone of gathering gold in grains from the pages of Homer, of carefully collecting facts and presumptions singly from the text, and then again estimating the amount and effect of their bearings upon one another. Hence the Catalogues of Apollodorus, or the downright assertions of Scholiasts, have been allowed to give form to our early histories of Greece; and the authentic, but usually slighter notices of Homer, have received little attention, except where, in some detail or other, they might suit the argument which each particular writer happened to have in hand. Again, because Herodotus was by profession an historian and nothing else (at least, I can discern no better reason), more importance seems to be attached to his notices of prior ages than to the less formally presented notices of Homer, who, according to the statement of Herodotus himself, preceded him by four hundred years. I do not mean by this remark to imply that Herodotus and Homer are particularly at variance with one another, but only to illustrate what seems to me a prevailing source of error.

In general, where the traditions reported by the later writers are preferred to those of Homer, it is perhaps because, although they may conflict with probability as well as with one another in an infinity of points, yet they are in themselves more systematic and complete. They represent to us for the most part *pasticcios* arbitrarily made up of materials of unequal value, but yet made up into wholes; whereas, the evidence which he supplies is original though it is fragmentary. Had he been followed by a continuous succession of authors, we should, no doubt, do wisely in consenting to view the subjects of fact, with which he dealt, mainly as they were viewed by those who trod in his steps. But, on the contrary, they were separated from him by a gulf both wide and deep; over which his compositions floated, in despite of difficulties so great that many have deemed them positively insurmountable, only by their extraordinary buoyancy.

It is in the Cyclic poems that we should naturally seek for materials to enlarge, expound, or correct Homer. But there is not a line or a notice remaining of any one of them, which would justify our assigning to them any historical authority sufficient to qualify them for such a purpose. Their reputed authors, from Arctinus downwards, all belong to periods within the dates of the Olympiads[u]. They all bear marks of hav-

[u] Mure, ii. 282.

Place and Authority of Homer in Historical Inquiry. 77

ing been written to fill the gaps which Homer had left unoccupied, and so to enter into a partnership, if not with his fame, yet with his popularity; with the popularity, of which his works, as we can well judge from more recent experience, would be sure to shed some portion upon all compositions ostensibly allied with them, and which then, as now, presented the most cogent inducements to imitators who had their livelihood to seek by means of their Muse.

Homer, without doubt, gave an immense addition of celebrity and vogue to the subject of the Trojan war, much as Boiardo and Ariosto did to the whole circle of the romances of which Orlando is the centre. One of these poems, the Ἰλίου Πέρσις, is a simple expansion, as Mure has observed[x], of the third lay of Demodocus in the Eighth Odyssey[y]. They seem to bear the mark of being, not composed first-hand from actions of men, but from a stock of compositions in which heroic actions had already been enshrined; so little do they appear to have been stamped with the individuality which denotes original design. And accordingly the usual manner of quoting them is not as the certain works of a given person, but the form of citation is (ὁ γράψας τὴν μικρὰν Ἰλιάδα, ὁ ποιήσας τὰ Κύπρια ἔπη), the writer of the little Iliad, the composer of the Cyprian Songs, and the like. Heyne[z] holds even the commencement of the Cyclic poems to have been at least a century after the date of the Iliad and Odyssey.

Mr. Fynes Clinton, whose name can never be mentioned without a grateful recognition of his merits and services, supplies, in the early part of his Fasti Hellenici, many valuable suggestions for the sifting of early

[x] Mure, ii. 286.   [y] Od. viii. 499.   [z] Exc. i. ad Æn. ii.

Greek history. But he nowhere acknowledges, or approaches (I believe) to the acknowledgment of the rule, that for the heroic age the authority of Homer stands alone in kind. In the Fasti Hellenici many statements, dating long after Homer, are delivered as if of equal authority with his in regard to the history of that age; and Mr. Clinton seems to have been led into a snare, to which his duty as a chronologer probably exposed him, in assuming that history and chronology may be expected to begin together; an assumption, I apprehend, not supported by probability. Mr. Mitford has admirably pointed out the importance of veracity to Homer's function, and to his fame as a poet, at a time when a poet could be the only historian[a], the probability and singular consistency of his scattered anecdotes, and the remarkable contrast between the clearness of his history, and the darkness and uncertainty which follow after him, and continue until the historic age begins; nor does he scruple to declare that 'for these early ages Homer is our best guide[b].' But even this is still short of my desire, which is not merely to recognise him as *primus inter pares*, but to treat his testimony as paramount, and as constituting a class by itself, with which no other literary testimony can compete. And so once more Bishop Marsh, in his able work on the Pelasgi, assigns no special office, I might perhaps say no peculiar weight, to the Homeric testimony.

But I am glad to shelter myself under the authority afforded me by the practice of Buttmann, who, in the Preface to his admirable Lexilogus, declares his rule of philological investigation in Homer to be this: to take,

---

[a] Hist. of Greece, chap. i. sect. iv. p. 62. 4to.
[b] Ibid. sect. iii. p. 47.

first, the evidence of the text itself in its several parts; secondly, that of the succeeding epic poetry, and along with this the testimony of the prime after-ages of Greek literature ; thirdly, grammatical tradition.

And yet the extensive contrariety between the old and the new is admitted. 'The Iliad and the Odyssey,' says Mr. Grote[c], 'and the remaining Hesiodic fragments, exhibit but too frequently a hopeless diversity, when confronted with the narratives of the logographers.' And the author of the Minos[d] cleared away the fabulous and defaming accounts of that sovereign, to return to the representations of Homer and of Hesiod ; καίτοι γε πιθανώτεροί εἰσιν ἢ σύμπαντες οἱ τραγῳδοποιοὶ, ὧν σὺ ἀκούων ταῦτα λέγεις. The great ancient writers, indeed, seem never to have questioned the authority of Homer as a witness ; nor could any one wish to see him enthroned at a greater elevation than that assigned to him as late as in the pages of Strabo. Virgil systematically made light of him, but he was in a manner compelled by his subject to make light of historical veracity altogether.

Historical scepticism, which has come of late years into possession of the ground, has not redressed, as affecting Homer, the wrong that had been done by historical credulity. We once exalted into history the general mass of traditions relating to the ages which next preceded those of continuous historic records ; we now again decline the labour of discrimination, and reduce them all alike into legend. The name of Mr. Grote must carry great weight in any question of Greek research: but it may be doubted whether the force and aptitude of his powerful mind have been as successfully applied to the Homeric as to the later

[c] History of Greece, vol. i. p. 146 ; chap. vi. Introd.
[d] Minos, 12, in Plato's Works.

80   I. *Prolegomena.*

periods. He presents us, indeed, with even more goodly and copious catalogues than historians are wont of Æolids, of Pelopids, of ruling families in every corner of Greece, and from the earliest times; but he, too, fixes a chronological point for the commencement of history, namely, the first recorded Olympiad [e]. He seems to think that the trustworthy chronology of Greece begins before its real history. He declines to take his start from disinterred Pelasgi [f]; he conceives that we have no other authority for the existence of Troy than we have for the theogonic revolutions [g]; the immense array of early names that he presents are offered as names purely legendary. He will not attempt to determine how much or how little of history these legends may contain; he will not exhibit a picture from behind the curtain, because, as he forcibly says, the curtain is the picture, and cannot by any ingenuity be withdrawn [h]. He deals in the main alike with Homer, Hesiod, the tragedians and minor Greek poets, the scattered notices of the historians, of the antiquarian writers near the Christian era, and of the Scholiasts. Of course, therefore, he cannot be expected to rectify the fault, if such there has been, in regard to the appreciation of the poems of Homer.

I may, however, observe that in this, as in other cases, extremes appear to meet. Attempts to winnow the legendary lore, and to separate the historic or primitive kernel from the husk, were clearing the stage of a multitude of mythical personages unknown to the earliest tradition; all of whom now are ushered in once

[e] Preface, p. xi.
[f] Ibid. p. xii.
[g] Vol. i. p. 2.
[h] An accomplished critic in the Quarterly Review July, (1856) treats this renunciation as one of Mr. Grote's main titles to praise.

more; they are, indeed, labelled as unhistorical; but they are again mixed up wholesale with those, from whose company critical observation had expelled them. In thus reimparting a promiscuous character to the first scenes of Grecian history, we seem to effect a retrogressive and not a progressive operation. At any rate it should be understood that the issue raised embraces the question, whether the personality of Achilles and Agamemnon has no better root in history than that of Pelasgus, of Prometheus, or of Hellen. And again, whether all these, being equal to one another, are likewise equal, and no more than equal, in credit to Ceres, Bacchus, or Apollo. As to all alike, what proportion of truth there may be in the legend, or whether any, ' it is impossible to ascertain, and useless to inquire [i];' all alike belong to a region, essentially mythical, neither approachable by the critic, nor measurable by the chronologer.

If the opinions which have been here expressed are in any degree correct, we must endeavour to recover as substantial personages, and to bring within the grasp of flesh and blood some of those pictures, and even of those persons, whom Mr. Grote has dismissed to the land of Shadow and of Dream.

In this view, the earliest Greek history should be founded on the text of Homer, and not merely on its surface, but on its depths. Not only its more broad and obvious statements should be registered, but we should search and ransack all those slighter indications, suggestions, and sources of inference, in which it is so extraordinarily rich; and compel it, as it were, to yield up its treasures. We cannot, indeed, like the zoologist, say the very words, Give me the bone, and I will dis-

[i] Grote's Hist., vol. i. pp. 58, 9, 72.

inter the animal; yet so accurately was the mind of Homer constructed, that we may come nearer to this certainty in dealing with him, than with any other child of man. The later and inferior evidence should be differently handled, and should not be viewed as intrinsically authoritative. But that portion of it, which fills up the gaps or confirms the suggestions of Homer, becomes thereby entitled to something of historic rank. Again, widely extended and uniformly continued traditions may amount to proof of notoriety, and may, not by their individual credit, but by their concurrence, supply us with standing ground of tolerable firmness. Beyond all this we may proceed, and may present to view, where for any cause it seems desirable, even ill-supported legends, but always as such, with fair notice of any circumstances which may tend to fix their credit or discredit, and with a line sufficiently marked between these and the recitals which rest upon Homeric authority. Thus, the general rule would be to begin with Homer: *a Jove principium*. We should plant his statements each in their place, as so many foundation stones. While he leads us by the hand, we should tread with comparative confidence; when we quit his guidance, we should proceed with caution, with mistrust, with a tone no higher than that of speculation and avowed conjecture.

In many instances, the application of these principles will require the rudiments of early Greek history to be recast. In illustration of this statement, I will refer to a legend, which has heretofore been popularly assumed as in a great degree the ethnological starting point of Greek history.

The current ideas respecting the distribution of the Greek races are founded upon the supposition that there was a certain Hellen, and that he had three sons, Dorus, Æolus, and Xuthus, the last of whom died and left behind him two sons, Ion and Achæus. This Hellen was (so runs the story) the son of Deucalion, and Deucalion was the son of Prometheus, and the husband of Pyrrha, who again was the daughter of Epimetheus and of Pandora, the first-made woman. From the agency of Deucalion and Pyrrha, the human race took a new commencement after the Deluge. The nation at large were called Hellenes, after Hellen; and from his two surviving sons, and his grandsons Ion and Achæus, were named the four great branches of the common stem. Such is the legend as it stands in Apollodorus [k]; and that part of it which describes Hellen and his three sons, but no more, is found in a fragment of Hesiod, quoted by Tzetzes on Lycophron [l].

It is obvious that any one, setting about the invention of a story with the compound purpose, first, of uniting the Greeks in a common bond of race; secondly, of referring them to a common country as their cradle; and, thirdly, of carrying up their origin to an extreme antiquity, could hardly have done better than invent this tale. And that, which might have been done at a stroke by an individual mind, was done no less effectually by the common thought and wish of the Greek people moulding itself by degrees into tradition. The tale has a symmetry about it, most suggestive of design and invention. How clearly it connects all the celebrated families or groups of the Greek nation; with what accuracy it fixes their relation to the common stem; and with how much impartial consideration for the self-love of every one among them, and for their several shares of fame.

Not only in general, but even in detail, we may

[k] I. vii. 2 and 3.   [l] Hes. Fragm. xxviii from Tzetzes ad Lyc. 284.

watch the gradual formation of this tradition adapting itself to the state of Greece. In Homer we find no Hellenes greatly distinguished, except Æolids and Achæans. This is the first stage. But when the Dorians attain to power[m], they claim a share in the past answerable to their predominance in the present: and they receive accordingly the first place in the genealogy as it stands in Hesiod, where Dorus is the first-named among the three sons of Hellen. The Achæans, now in depression, do not appear as Hellenes at all. But with the lapse of time the Ionians of Athens, becoming powerful, desire to be also famous: therefore room must be made for them: and the Achæans too by their local intermixture with the same race, and their political sympathy with Athens, once more come to be entitled to notice: Xuthus accordingly, in the final form of the tradition is provided with two sons, Ion and Achæus, and now all the four branches have each their respective place.

This tradition, however, is neither in whole nor in part sustained by Homer, and can by no effort be made to fit into Homer; to say nothing of its containing within itself much incongruity. If we exclude Xuthus, as a mere mute, it gives us five persons as the eponymists of five races, the four last included in the first. But of the five persons thus placed upon the stage, Homer gives us but one; that one, Æolus, has no race or tribe, but only two or three lines of descendants named after him. Again, the two or three children of Æolus in Homer become five in Hesiod, twelve in Apollodorus, and by additions from other writers reach a respectable total of seventeen[n]. Thus as to persons,

[m] Hermann, Griech. Staats-Altherthum, Sect. 8.
[n] See the list in Clinton, F. H. Vol. I., p. 46, note.

Homer has indeed an Æolus, but he has no Hellen, no Dorus, no Ion, no Achæus. Now as to races. He mentions, without doubt, Hellenes, Achæans, Dorians, Ionians; but affords hardly any means of identifying Dorians with Hellenes, and as to Ionians, supplies pretty strong presumptions that they were not Hellenic[o]. Nor does he establish any relation whatever between any of the four races and any common ancestor or eponymist. Again, the Deucalion of this legend is two generations before its Æolus; but the Deucalion of Homer, who may be reckoned as three generations before the fall of Troy, is also three generations later than his Æolus. In fact, this legend of Hellen and his family is like an ugly and flimsy, but formal, modern house, built by the sacrilegious collection of the fragments of a noble ruin.

It may be thought dangerous, however, in setting up the authority of Homer, to pull down that of Hesiod, who comes nearest to him. But, firstly, Hesiod is only responsible for so much of the legend as connects two persons named Æolus and Dorus with Hellen as their source; which is at any rate no more than a poetical dress given to an hypothesis substantially not in conflict with the Homeric traditions. Secondly, as respects literal truth, the name Hellen at once bears the strongest evidence against its own pretensions to an historical character such as that assigned to it, because its etymology refers it to the territorial name Ἑλλάς, and through this to the national name Ἕλλοι[p]. Lastly, the essential difference in point of authority lies between Homer and Hesiod, not between Homer together with Hesiod on the one side, and those who came after Hesiod on the other. Homer was fully within the sphere and spirit of the

[o] See inf. II. Sect. 2.   [p] Mure, Lit. Greece, vol. i., p. 39, n.

heroic age; Hesiod was as plainly outside it. He is apparently separated from the mighty master by a considerable term, even as measured in years. That term it would be difficult to define by any given number; but it is easy to see that even when defined it would convey an utterly inadequate idea of the interval of poetic and personal difference, and of moral and social change, between Hesiod and Homer. It is not to be found in this or that variation, for it belongs to the whole order of ideas; all the elements of thought, the whole tone of the picture, the atmosphere in which persons and objects are seen, are essentially modified.

I venture one remark, however, upon Hesiod's very beautiful account of the Ages. None can fail to be struck by the order in which he places them. Beginning with the Golden, he comes next to the Silver age, and then to Brass. But, instead of descending forthwith the fourth and last step to the Iron age, he very singularly retraces his steps, and breaks the downward chain by an age of heroes, of whom he says that it was

δικαιότερον καὶ ἄρειον,
ἀνδρῶν ἡρώων θεῖον γένος, οἱ καλέονται
ἡμίθεοι προτέρῃ γενεᾷ κατ' ἀπείρονα γαῖαν[q].

These, he goes on to explain, were the men, partly slain in the Theban and Trojan wars, partly translated by Jupiter to the ends of the earth, the islands of the blest. After this, the scale drops, at once, to the lowest point, the Iron age, the age without either Νέμεσις or Αἰδώς, the age of sheer wickedness and corruption.

This very curious turn in the arrangement of the Hesiodic Ages, and especially the insertion, in a regular figurative series taken from the metals, of a completely heterogeneous passage, calls for explanation;

[q] Hes. Op. 157.

and I venture to suggest that this passage should be construed as disclosing to us that brilliant halo, which the Homeric poems had cast over an age still recent, so as not only to hold it above the one that followed, but also to raise it even above that which had preceded it; above the age of Bellerophon, of Tantalus, of Sisyphus, of Minos, and even of Hercules. The splendour of the fame of heroes really depended on the Bard. The great Bard of Greece had lifted Achilles and Ulysses to a height surpassing that of the older Heroes, who remained unsung by him; and he had promised Menelaus, in the Fourth Odyssey[r], that very seat in the regions of the blest, to which allusion is here made by Hesiod. While the apparent poetic solecism of this passage is thus accounted for, it becomes, at once, both an emphatic testimony to the immense power exercised by the verse of Homer, and a distinct declaration by Hesiod of the wide social interval, by which he was himself separated from the heroic period; a declaration entirely accordant with the internal evidence of the poems of Hesiod generally, and amounting by implication to the double statement from this poet, that Homer belonged to the heroic age, and that he himself did not belong to it.

The tradition of Hellen and his sons, then, exhibits one of the cases in which we must take our choice between the testimony of Homer, and what are apparently the inventions of the later Greeks.

Another of these cases, which will be my second and last illustration, relates to Helen of Troy.

It has been much disputed whether this celebrated character is to be regarded as historical or fictitious. A writer of no less judgment and authority than the

[r] Od. iv. 561-9.

Bishop of St. David's, adopts the latter alternative, upon various grounds. The strongest among them all, in his view, is, that 'in the abduction of Helen, Paris only repeats an exploit, also attributed to Theseus[s].' This exploit, the Bishop thinks, was known to Homer, as he introduces Æthra, the mother of Theseus, in the company of Helen at Troy. And other writers have further developed these ideas, by finding absurdity in the Homeric tale of Helen, on the ground that she must have been eighty years old when the supposed abduction by Paris took place.

Now, the basis of these statements entirely depends upon the assumption that the later traditions are entitled to be treated either as upon a par, or, at any rate, as homogeneous with those of Homer. The tradition which assigns a rape of Helen to Theseus, is only available to discredit the tale of Homer, on the supposition that it rests upon authority like that of Homer. But if it was a late invention, then it is more probably to be regarded as a witness to the fame of the Homeric personages, and the anxiety of Attica to give her hero the advantage of similar embellishments, than as an original tradition which Homer copied, or as a twin report with that which he has handed down.

The tradition of the rape of Helen by Theseus is mentioned by Herodotus[t] as a tale current among the Athenians. He testifies apparently to the fact, that the Deceleans of Attica enjoyed certain immunities in Sparta, and were spared by the Lacedæmonian forces when they invaded Attica; which was ascribed by the Athenians to their having assisted in the recovery of Helen from Theseus, by pointing out to the Tyndaridæ

[s] Bp. Thirlwall's Hist. of Greece, chap. v.   [t] Herod. ix. 73.

the place of her concealment. Herodotus, however, does not affirm the cause stated by the Athenians, nor the abduction by Theseus, which afterwards became, or had even then become, an established tradition. Isocrates[u] handles it without misgiving, and it is methodized in Plutarch, with a multitude of other particulars, our acceptance of which absolutely requires the rejection of Homer's historical authority.

And so again with regard to Æthra, the daughter of Pittheus, whom the later ages have connected with Theseus. We have no right to treat her introduction in the company of Helen[x], as a proof that Homer knew of a story connecting Helen with Theseus, unless we knew, which we do not, from Homer, or from authority entitled to compete with Homer, that there was a relation between Æthra and Theseus.

Now, the story of Homer respecting Helen, is perfectly self-consistent: and so is his story respecting Theseus: but the two are separated by an interval of little less than two generations, or say fifty years. For Theseus[y] fought in the wars against the Φῆρες, in which Nestor took part: and he wooed and wedded Ariadne, the aunt of Idomeneus, who was himself nearly or quite one generation older than the Greek kings in general. On the other hand, Homer shows the age of Helen to have been in just proportion to that of Menelaus: for she had a daughter, Hermione, before the abduction, and might, so far as age was concerned, have borne children after their conjugal union was resumed[z]. Why, then, if Homer be the paramount authority, should we, upon testimony inferior to his, introduce conflict and absurdity into two traditions, which he

[u] Encom. Hel. 21 et seq.   [x] Il. iii. 144.
[y] Il. i. 262.   [z] See Od. iv. 12.

gives us wide apart from one another and each self-consistent, by forging a connexion between them?

I have stated these two cases, not by way of begging the question as to the superiority in kind of Homer's testimony, but to show how important that question is; and in how many instances the history of the heroic age must be rewritten, if we adopt the principle, that Homer ought to be received as an original witness, contemporary with the manners, nay, perhaps, even with some of the persons he describes, and subject only to such deductions as other original witnesses are liable to suffer: whereas the later traditions rest only upon hearsay; so much so, that they can hardly be called evidence, and should never be opposed, on their own credit, to the testimony of Homer.

In bringing this discussion to a close, I will quote a passage respecting Homer, from the Earl of Aberdeen's *Inquiry into the Principles of Beauty in Grecian Architecture*, which, I think, expresses with great truth and simplicity the ground of Homer's general claim to authority, subject, of course, to any question respecting the genuineness of the received text:

In treating of an age far removed from the approach of regular history, it is fortunate that we are furnished with a guide so unerring as Homer, whose general accuracy of observation, and minuteness of description, are such as to afford a copious source of information respecting almost everything connected with the times in which he composed his work: and who, being nearly contemporary with the events which he relates, and, indeed, with the earliest matter for record in Greece, cannot fall into mistakes and anachronisms in arts, or manners, or government, as he might have done had he lived at a more advanced and refined period [a].

It was said of a certain Dorotheus, that he spent his

---

[a] Lord Aberdeen's Inquiry, p. 62. (1822)

whole life in endeavours to elucidate the meaning of the Homeric word κλισίη. Such a disproportion between labour and its aim is somewhat startling; yet it is hardly too much to say, that no exertion spent upon any of the great classics of the world, and attended with any amount of real result, is really thrown away. It is better to write one word upon the rock, than a thousand on the water or the sand: better to remove a single stray stone out of the path that mounts the hill of true culture, than to hew out miles of devious tracks, which mislead and bewilder us when we travel them, and make us more than content if we are fortunate enough to find, when we emerge out of their windings, that we have simply returned to the point in our age, from which, in sanguine youth, we set out.

As rules of the kind above propounded can' only be fully understood when applied, the application of them has accordingly been attempted, in the work to which these pages form an Introduction. In this view, it may be regarded as their necessary sequel. I commit it to the press with no inconsiderable apprehension, and with due deference to the judgments of the learned: for I do not feel myself to have possessed either the fresh recollection and ready command of the treasures of ancient Greece, or the extended and systematic knowledge of the modern Homeric literature, which are among the essential requisites of qualification to deal in a satisfactory manner with the subject. I should further say, that the poems of Homer, to be rightly and thoroughly sounded, demand undoubtedly a disengaged mind, perhaps would repay even the study of a life. One plea only I can advance with confidence. The work, whatever else it be, is one which has been founded in good faith on the text of Homer. Whether in statement or in speculation, I have desired and endeavoured that it should lead me by the hand: and even my anticipations of what we might in any case expect it to contain have been formed by a reflex process from the suggestions it had itself supplied:

> Oh degli altri poeti onore e lume!
> Vagliami il lungo studio, e il grande amore
> Che m' án fatto cercar lo tuo volume;
> Tu sei lo mio maestro, e il mio autore [b].

Finally, though sharing the dissatisfaction of others at the established preference given among us to the Latin names of deities originally Greek, and at some part of our orthography for Greek names, I have thought it best to adhere in general to the common custom, and only to deviate from it where a special object was in view. I fear that diversity, and even confusion, are more likely to arise than any benefit, from efforts at reform, made by individuals, and without the advantage either of authority or of a clear principle, as a groundwork for general consent. I am here disposed to say, '$οὐκ\ ἀγαθὸν\ πολυκοιρανίη$;' and again with Wordsworth,

> 'Me this unchartered freedom tires.'

Yet I should gladly see the day when, under the authority of Scholars, and especially of those who bear rule in places of education, improvement might be effected, not only in the points above mentioned, but in our solitary and barbarous method of pronouncing both the Greek and the Latin language. In this one respect the European world may still with justice describe the English at least as the *penitus toto divisos orbe Britannos*.

[b] Inferno, I. 32.

II. ETHNOLOGY.

SECT. I.

Scope of the Inquiry.

I NOW proceed to attempt, in a series of inquiries, the practical application of the principles which have been stated in the preliminary Essay. The first of these inquiries might on some grounds be deemed the most hazardous. It is an inquiry into the Early Ethnology and Ethnography of Greece: or the Composition of the Greek nation, and the succession and Distribution of its races, according to the text of Homer. The religion, the politics, the manners, the contemporary history, of the Iliad and Odyssey, may justly be considered to form essential parts of the plan of the Poet, and to have been distinctly contemplated by his intention. But into anterior legends he only dips at times: and of the subject of the succession and distribution of races it probably formed no part of his purpose to treat at all; so that in the endeavour to investigate it we are entirely dependent, so far as he is concerned, upon scattered and incidental notices.

But here it is, that the extraordinary sureness and precision of the mind of Homer stands us in such admirable stead. Wherever, amidst the cloud and chaos of pre-Homeric antiquity, he enables us to discern a luminous point, that point is a beacon, and indicates ground on which we may tread with confidence. The materials, which at a first glance appear upon the face of the poems to be available for our purpose, may indeed be but slender. But the careful gathering together of many dispersed indications, and the strict observation of their relative bearings has this effect, that each fragment added to the stock may both receive illustration from what is already known, and may give it in return, by helping to explain and establish relations hitherto doubtful or obscure. And as the total or gross accumulation grows, the nett result increases in a more rapid ratio: as a single known point upon a plane tells us of nothing besides itself, but two enable us to draw a line, and three a triangle, and each further one as it is added to construct a multitude of figures: or as in the map-puzzles, constructed to provoke the ingenuity of children, when once a very few countries have been laid in their right places, they serve as keys to the rest, and we can lay out with confidence the general order. Even so I am not without hope that, as to some parts at least of this ethnical examination, the Homeric indications may, when brought together, warrant our applying to them words used by Cicero for another purpose: *est enim admirabilis continuatio seriesque rerum, ut aliæ ex aliis nexæ, et omnes inter se aptæ conligatæque videantur*[a].

I must not, however, step over the threshold of the investigation without giving warning, that we have to meet at the outset an opinion broadly pronounced, and proceeding from a person of such high authority as Mr. Grote, our most recent historian of Greece, to the effect that these inquiries are futile. This intimation is so important that it shall stand in his own words. "In going through historical Greece," says Mr. Grote, "we are compelled to accept the Hellenic aggregate with

[a] Cic. de Nat. Deor. i. 4.

its constituent elements as a primary fact to start from, because the state of our information does not enable us to ascend any higher. By what circumstances, or out of what pre-existing elements, this aggregate was brought together and modified, we find no evidence entitled to credit[b]." And then, in condemnation particularly of Pelasgic inquiries, he resumes: "if any man is inclined to call the unknown ante-Hellenic period of Greece by the name of Pelasgic, it is open to him to do so: but this is a name carrying with it no assured predicates, no way enlarging our insight into real history, nor enabling us to explain—what would be the real historical problem—how or from whom the Hellens acquired that stock of dispositions, aptitudes, arts, &c. with which they began their career..... No attested facts are now present to us—none were present to Herodotus and Thucydides even in their age, on which to build trustworthy affirmations respecting the ante-Hellenic Pelasgians."

In answer to these passages, which raise the question no less broadly than fairly, it may first be observed, that at least Herodotus and Thucydides did not think what we are thus invited to think for them, and that of the judgment of the latter, as an inquirer into matters of fact, Mr. Grote has himself justly expressed the highest opinion[c]. Mr. Grote, placing in one category all that relates to the legendary age, finds it as a whole intractable and unhistorical, with a predominance of sentimental attributes quite unlike the practical turn and powers of the Greek mind in later times[d]. But has not this disturbance of equilibrium happened chiefly because the genuine though slender historic materials

[b] Grote's Hist. vol. ii. pp. 349–51. part ii. ch. 2.   [c] Preface p. ix.
[d] Preface p. xvii.

of the heroic age, supplied by the poems of Homer, have been overborne and flooded by the accumulations made by imagination, vanity, resentment, or patriotism, during a thousand years? Even of the unsifted mass of legend, to which the distinguished historian refers, it may be doubted, whether it is not, when viewed as a whole, bewildering, formless, and inconsistent, rather than sentimental. It has been everywhere darkened by cross purposes, and by the unauthorized meddling of generations, which had ceased to sympathize with the heroic age. At any rate, I crave permission to try what we can make of that age in the matter of history, by dealing first and foremost with him who handled it for the purposes of history, apart from those, I mean the after poets, tragedians, and logographers, to whom it was little more than a romance.

I trust that the recent examples of men so learned and able as Bishop Thirlwall and K. O. Müller, neither of whom have thought subjects of this kind too uninviting to reward inquiry, may avail both to prevent the interposition of a preliminary bar to the discussion, and to protect it against an adverse prejudgment. By anticipation I can reasonably make no other answer to a condemnatory sentence, than that which is conveyed in the words 'let us try.' But at any rate, *est. operæ pretium*: the stake is worth the venture. He would be indeed a worthless biographer who did not, so far as his materials carried him, pursue the life of a hero back to the nursery or even the cradle: and the same faithful and well-grounded instincts invest with a surpassing interest all real elucidation of the facts and ideas, that make up the image of the Greek nation either in its infancy or even in its embryo.

There are three and only three names of ordinary

use in the Iliad, by which the poet designates the people that had been banded together against Troy. This same people afterwards became famous in history, perhaps beyond all others, first by the name of Hellenes, which was self-applied; and secondly by the name of Greeks, which they acquired from their Italian conquerors and captives. Greece is now again become Hellas.

These names, prominent far beyond all others, are,
1. Δαναοὶ, Danaans.
2. Ἀργεῖοι, Argeians or Argives.
3. Ἀχαιοὶ, Achæans.

They are commonly treated as synonymous. It appears at least to have been assumed that they are incapable of yielding any practical results to an attempt at historic analysis and distribution. To try this question fully, is a main part of my present purpose. Thus much at least is clear: that they seem to be the equivalents, for the Troic period, of the Hellenic name in later times.

But there are other names, of various classes, which on account of their relations to the foregoing ones it is material to bring into view.

First, there are found in Homer two other designations, which purport to have the same effect as the three already quoted. They are
1. Παναχαιοὶ, Panachæans.
2. Πανέλληνες, Panhellenes.

Next come three names of races, whose relations to the foregoing appellations will demand scrutiny. These are
1. Πελασγοὶ, Pelasgians.
2. Ἕλληνες, Hellenes.
3. Θρῆκες, Thracians, or rather Thraces.

Lastly, there are a more numerous class of names,

H

which are local in this sense, that Homer only mentions them in connection with particular parts of Greece, but which being clearly tribal and not territorial, stand clearly distinguished from the names which owed, or may have owed, their origin to the different cities or districts of the country, such as Phocian (Il. ii. 517), Rhodian (654), Elian (Il. xi. 670), or Ithacan (Odyssey *passim*): and likewise from the names which already were, or afterwards came to be, in established connection with those of districts, though they have no appearance of having been originally territorial: such as Arcadian (Il. ii. 603, 11), Bœotian (Il. ii. 494), Athenian (Il. ii. 546, 551).

Of the class now before us there are some which are of importance in various degrees with regard to the views of primitive history to be gathered from the Homeric poems. As such I rank

1. Καδμεῖοι, Cadmeans, in Thebes, Il. iv. 388 and elsewhere: and with this, as an equivalent, Καδμείωνες, Il. iv. 385 and elsewhere.

2. Ἰάονες, Ionians, in Athens, Il. xiii. 685.

3. Δωριέες, Dorians, in Crete, Od. xix. 177. A town Dorion is also mentioned in the Catalogue as within the territories of Nestor, Il. ii. 594.

4. Κεφάλληνες, Cephallenes, in the islands under Ulysses, Il. ii. 631.

5. Ἐφυροὶ, Ephyri, in Thessaly, Il. xiii. 301.

6. Σελλοὶ or Ἑλλοὶ, Helli, in northern Thessaly, Il. xvi. 234.

7. Καύκωνες, Caucones, in southern Greece, Od. iii. 366: (and among the Trojan allies, Il. x. 429, xx. 329.)

8. Ἐπειοὶ, Epeans, in Elis, Il. ii. 619, and on the opposite or northern coast and islands of the Corinthian Gulf: compare Il. ii. 627, and xiii. 691.

9. Ἄβαντες, Abantes, in Euboea, Il. ii. 536.
10. Μυρμίδονες, Myrmidones, in Phthia, Il. ii. 684.
11. Κουρῆτες, Curetes, in Ætolia, Il. ix. 529.
12. Φλεγύαι, Phlegyæ, in Thessaly, Il. xiii. 301.
13. Φῆρες, in Thessaly, Il. i. 267, 8. ii. 733, 4.

And lastly it may be mentioned that in the single word Γραῖα, used (Il. ii. 498) to designate one of the numerous Bœotian towns, we have an isolated indication of the existence in the heroic times of the germ of the names *Greece* and *Greek*, which afterwards ascended to, and still retain, such extraordinary fame.

The Homeric text will afford us means of investigation, more or less, for the greater part of these names, but the main thread of the inquiry runs with these five; Pelasgians, Hellenes, Danaans, Argeians, Achæans.

In conjunction with the present subject, I shall consider what light is thrown by Homer on the relations of the Greeks with other races not properly Greek: the Lycians, the Phœnicians, the Sicels, the Egyptians, the people of Cyprus, and finally the Persians. The name of the Leleges will be considered in conjunction with that of the Caucones.

SECT. II.

The Pelasgians; and with these,

a. Arcadians.   *b.* Γραικοὶ or Græci.   *c.* Ionians.
d. Athenians.   *e.* Egyptians.   *f.* Thraces.
g. Caucones.   *h.* Leleges.

It will be most convenient to begin with the case of the Pelasgians: and the questions we shall have to investigate will be substantially reducible to the following heads:

1. Are the Pelasgians essentially Greek?
2. If so, what is their relation to the Hellenes, and to the integral Greek nation?
3. What elements did they contribute to the formation of the composite body thus called?
4. What was their language?
5. What was the derivation of their name?
6. By what route did they come into Greece?

The direct evidence of the Homeric poems with respect to the Pelasgians is scattered and faint. It derives however material aid from various branches of tradition, partly conveyed in the Homeric poems, and partly extraneous to them, particularly religion, language, and pursuits. Evidence legitimately drawn from these latter sources, wherever it is in the nature of circumstantial proof, is far superior in authority to such literary traditions as are surrounded, at their visible source, with circumstances of uncertainty.

I. The first passage, with which we have to deal, is that portion of the Catalogue of the Greek armament, where Homer introduces us to the contingent of Achilles in the following lines:

The Pelasgians: Pelasgic Argos.

Νῦν αὖ τοὺς ὅσσοι τὸ Πελασγικὸν Ἄργος ἔναιον,
Οἵ τ' Ἄλον οἵ τ' Ἀλόπην οἵ τε Τρηχῖν' ἐνέμοντο,
Οἵ τ' εἶχον Φθίην ἠδ' Ἑλλάδα καλλιγύναικα,
Μυρμιδόνες δὲ καλεῦντο καὶ Ἕλληνες καὶ Ἀχαιοί,
Τῶν αὖ πεντήκοντα νεῶν ἦν ἀρχὸς Ἀχιλλεύς[d].

All evidence goes to show, that Thessaly stood in a most important relation to the infant life of the Greek races; whether we consider it as the seat of many most ancient legends; as dignified by the presence of Dodona, the highest seat of religious tradition and authority to the Greeks; as connected with the two ancient names of Helli and Pelasgi: or lastly in regard to the prominence it retained even down to and during the historic age in the constitution of the Amphictyonic Council[e]. All these indications are in harmony with the course of Greek ethnological tradition.

Now the Catalogue of the Greek armament is divided into three great sections.

The first comprises Continental Greece, with the islands immediately adjacent to the coast, and lying south of Thessaly. The second consists of the Greek islands of the Ægean. The third is wholly Thessalian: and it begins with the lines which have been quoted.

What then does Homer mean us to understand by the phrase τὸ Πελασγικὸν Ἄργος in this passage? Is it

1. A mere town, or town and district, like Alos, Alope, and others which follow; or is it

2. A country comprising several or many such? And if the latter, does it describe

  1. That country only over which Peleus reigned, and which supplied the Myrmidon division; or

  2. A more extended country?

[d] Il. ii. 681-5.   [e] Hermann Gr. Staats-alt. sect. 12.

First let us remark the use of the article. It is not the manner of Homer to employ the article with the proper names of places. We may be sure that it carries with it a distinctive force: as in the Trojan Catalogue he employs it to indicate a particular race or body of Pelasgians[f] apart from others. Now the distinctive force of the article here may have either or both of two bearings.

1. It may mark off the Argos of the Pelasgians from one or more other countries or places bearing the name of Argos.

2. Even independently of the epithet, the article may be rightly employed, if Argos itself be not strictly a proper name, but rather a descriptive word indicating the physical character of a given region. Thus 'Scotland' is strictly a proper name, 'Lowlands' a descriptive word of this nature: and the latter takes the article where the former does not require or even admit it. And now let us proceed to make our selection between the various alternatives before us.

Whichever of the two bearings we give to the article, it seems of itself to preclude the supposition that a mere town or single settlement can be here intended: for nowhere does Homer give the article to a name of that class.

Secondly, in almost every place where Homer speaks of an Argos, he makes it plain that he does not mean a mere town or single settlement, but a country including towns or settlements within it. The exceptions to this rule are rare. In Il. iv. 52 we have one of them, where he combines Argos with Sparta and Mycenæ, and calls all three by the name of cities.

[f] Il. ii. 841.

The line Il. ii. 559 probably supplies another. But in a later Section[g] the general rule will be fully illustrated.

It will also clearly appear, that the name Argos is in fact a descriptive word, not a proper name, and is nearly equivalent to our 'Lowlands' or to the Italian 'campagna.'

Thirdly: in many other places of the Catalogue, Homer begins by placing in the front, as it were, the comprehensive name which overrides and includes the particular names that are to follow; and then, without any other distinctive mark than the use of the faint enclitic copulative τε, proceeds to enumerate parts included within the whole which he has previously named. Thus for instance

οἱ δ' Εὔβοιαν ἔχον...
Χαλκίδα τ' Εἰρετρίαν τε κ.τ.λ.   v. 535, 6.

'Those who held Euboea, both Chalcis and Eretria'... Or in the English idiom we may perhaps write more correctly, 'Those who held Euboea, that is to say Chalcis, and Eretria'.... and the rest.

Again,

οἱ δ' εἶχον κοίλην Λακεδαίμονα κητώεσσαν
Φαρίν τε Σπάρτην τε...   v. 581, 2.

'Those who held channelled Laconia, abounding in wild beasts, namely, the several settlements of Pharis and Sparta,' and the rest.

So with Arcadia, v. 603, and Ithaca, v. 631.

We may therefore consider the verse 681,

Νῦν αὖ τοὺς, ὅσσοι τὸ Πελασγικὸν Ἄργος ἔναιον·

as prefatory, and I print it, accordingly, so as to mark a pause.

But, again, is it prefatory only to the division of Achilles, and is it simply the integer expressing the

[g] Inf. sect. viii.

whole territory from which his contingent was drawn, or is it prefatory to the whole remainder of the Catalogue, ending at v. 759, and does it include all the nine territorial divisions described therein? There is no grammatical or other reason for the former alternative, while various considerations recommend the latter.

There is no sign in the poems of any connection between Achilles with his Myrmidons, or between the kingdom of his father Peleus, and any particular part of Thessaly under the name of Argos, or Pelasgic Argos. Although the division of Achilles did not embrace the whole of the Phthians[g], yet Phthia appears to be the proper description of his territory, so far as it has a collective name: and there are signs, which will be hereafter considered, that the name of Phthia itself was embraced and included within the wider range of another name.

Again, the Pelasgic name, as will be further observed, is not in Homer specially connected with the South of Thessaly, where the realm of Peleus lay, but rather with the North, the towns and settlements of which are enumerated, not in the first, but in the later paragraphs of this portion of the Catalogue.

In the invocation of the Sixteenth Book, to which reference will shortly be made, Achilles at once addresses Jupiter as Pelasgic, and as dwelling afar ($\tau\eta\lambda\acute{o}\theta\iota$ $\nu\alpha\acute{\iota}\omega\nu$): therefore, the special Thessalian seat of the god could not be in the dominions of Peleus.

We have observed, again, in the earlier parts of the catalogue various collective names, afterwards explained distributively, for the various contingents: but there is not one of this class of names employed for any of the Eight Divisions which follow that of Achilles. They

[g] Il. xiii. 686, et seqq.

all seem to bear the form of particular distributive enumerations, belonging to the comprehensive head of Pelasgic Argos or Thessaly.

There is also something in the obvious break in the Catalogue, signified by the words

νῦν αὖ τοὺς, ὅσσοι...

which indicate, as it were, a completely new starting point. There is nothing else resembling them. They form the introduction to a new chapter of the lists, after a geographical transition from the islands: and there is no reason for these marked words, if Pelasgic Argos was either a mere town district, or a local sovereignty, but a very good reason, if Pelasgic Argos meant that great integral portion of the Greek territory, the vale of Thessaly, the particular parts of which the Poet was about to set forth in so much detail.

It may therefore be inferred, that the epithet Πελασγικὸν is applied by Homer to the Thessalian vale collectively, as it is contained between the mountains of Pindus to the west, Œta and Olympus to the north, Othrys to the south, and Ossa or the sea to the east. We might, without geographical error, translate the phrase τὸ Πελασγικὸν Ἄργος of the second Iliad by that name of Thessaly[h], which the country afterwards acquired: but the idea which it properly indicates to us, is, *that Argos which had been settled by the Pelasgians.*

It is the only geographical epithet which, applied to the name Argos, belongs to the north of Greece: and it is so applied by way of distinction and opposition to other uses of the name Argos in other parts of the poems, which we shall hereafter have to examine, namely, the Achaic and the Iasian Argos.

[h] So Strabo, p. 221.

II. Perhaps the most solemn invocation of Jupiter as the great deity of the Greeks in the whole of the Poems is where Achilles, sending forth Patroclus to battle, prays that glory may be given him. It runs thus (Il. xvi. 233–5):

Ζεῦ ἄνα, Δωδωναῖε, Πελασγικὲ, τηλόθι ναίων,
Δωδώνης μεδέων δυσχειμέρου· ἀμφὶ δέ σ' Ἑλλοὶ
σοὶ ναίουσ' ὑποφῆται ἀνιπτόποδες χαμαιεῦναι.

It seems not too much to say upon this remarkable passage, that it shows us, as it were, the nation pitching its first altar upon its first arrival in the country. It bears witness that those who brought the worship of Dodonæan Jupiter were Pelasgians, as well as that the spot, which they chose for the principal seat of their worship, was Dodona. For the appeal of Achilles on this occasion is evidently the most forcible that he has it in his power to make, and is addressed to the highest source of Divine power that he knew.

It has been debated, but apparently without any conclusive result, what was the site of the Dodona so famous in the after-times of Greece[h]. It seems clear, however, that it was a Dodona to the westward of Pindus, and belonging to Thesprotia or Molossia. But this plainly was not the position of the Dodona we have now before us. For in a passage of the Catalogue Homer distinctly places this Dodona in Thessaly, giving it the same epithet, δυσχείμερος, as Achilles applies to it in Il. xvi. Gouneus, he says, was followed by the Enienes and Perrhæbi,

οἳ περὶ Δωδώνην δυσχείμερον οἰκί' ἔθεντο,
οἵ τ' ἀμφ' ἱμερτὸν Τιταρήσιον ἔργ' ἐνέμοντο[i].

[h] The discussion is reviewed in Cramer's Greece, vol. i. 115.
[i] Il. ii. 750.

Both the name of the Perrhæbi and that of the river Titaresius fix the Dodona of Homer in the north of Thessaly. And the character assigned to this Titaresius, so near Dodona, as a branch of Styx, 'the mighty adjuration of the gods,' well illustrates the close connection between that river, by which the other deities were to swear, and Jupiter, who was their chief, and was in a certain sense the administrator of justice among them. In the Odyssey, indeed, Ulysses, in his fictitious narrations to Eumæus and Penelope, represents himself as having travelled from Thesprotia to consult the oracle of Jupiter, that was delivered from a lofty oak[j]. But no presumption of nearness can be founded on this passage such as to justify our assuming the existence of a separate Dodona westward of the mountains in the Homeric age: and there was no reason why Ulysses should not represent himself as travelling through the passes of Mount Pindus[k] from the Ambracian gulf into Thessaly to learn his fate. Nor upon the other hand is there any vast difficulty in adopting the supposition which the evidence in the case suggests, that the oracle of Dodonæan Jupiter may have changed its seat before the historic age. The evidence of Homer places it in Thessaly, and Homer is, as we shall see, corroborated by Hesiod. After them, we hear nothing of a Dodona having its seat in Thessaly, but much of one on the western side of the peninsula. As in later times we find Perrhæbi and Dolopes to the westward of Pindus, whom Homer shows us only on the east, even so in the course of time the oracle may have travelled in the same direction[l]. It is highly improbable, from the manner in

[j] Od. xiv. 327; xix. 296.   [k] Cramer's Ancient Greeee, i. 353.
[l] Cramer's Greece, i. 370.

which the name is used, that there should have been two Greek Dodonas in the Homeric age.

However, the very passage before us indicates, that revolution had already laid its hand on this ancient seat of Greek religion. For though the Dodona of Homer was Pelasgic by its origin, its neighbourhood was now inhabited by a different race, the Selli or Helli, and these Helli were also the ὑποφῆται or ministers of the deity. While their rude and filthy habits of life mark them as probably a people of recent arrival, who had not themselves yet emerged from their highland home, and from the struggle with want and difficulty, into civilized life, still they had begun to encroach upon the Pelasgians with their inviting possessions and more settled habits, and had acquired by force or otherwise the control of the temple, though without obliterating the tradition of its Pelasgic origin. The very fact, that the Helli were at the time the ministers of Jupiter, tends to confirm the belief that the Pelasgians were those who originally established it; for how otherwise could the name of the Pelasgian race have found its way into an Hellenic invocation?

Thus, as before we found that what we term Thessaly is to Homer 'the Argos of the Pelasgians,' so we now find that people associated with the original and central worship of the Greek Jupiter, as having probably been the race to whom it owed its establishment.

And thus, though the Pelasgians were not politically predominant in Thessaly at the epoch of the *Troica*, yet Thessaly is Pelasgian Argos: though they were not possessed of the Dodonæan oracle, yet Jupiter of Dodona is Pelasgian Jupiter: two branches of testimony, the first of which exhibits them as the earliest known colonisers of the country, and the second as the reputed founders of the prime article of its religion.

We must not quit this subject without referring to the evidence of Hesiod, which, though second in importance to that of Homer, is before any other literary testimony. He refers twice to Dodona. Neither time does he appear to carry it to the westward. In one passage he connects it immediately with the Pelasgians;

Δωδώνην, φηγόν τε, Πελασγῶν ἕδρανον, ἦκεν[m].

In the other passage, he associates it with the Hellic name through the medium of the territorial designation Hellopia:

ἐστί τις Ἑλλοπίη πολυλήϊος ἠδ' εὐλείμων,
ἔνθα τε Δωδώνη τις ἐπ' ἐσχατίῃ πεπόλισται[n].

Thus, in exact accordance with Homer, he associates Dodona with two and only two names of race, the same two as those with which it is associated in the invocation of Achilles.

III. Next, we find in Homer a widely spread connection between Thessaly and the islands which form as it were the base of the Ægean sea.

From these islands he enumerates four contingents furnished to the Greek army:

1. From Crete, under Idomeneus (Il. ii. 645).
2. From Rhodes, under Tlepolemus (653).
3. From Syme, under Nireus (671).
4. From Nisyrus, the Calydnæ, and other minor islands, under Pheidippus and Antiphus (676).

1. As to Crete. Universal tradition connects the name of Deucalion with Thessaly. But he was the son, according to Homer, of Minos, who was the ruler or warden of Crete (Κρήτῃ ἐπίουρος, Il. xiii. 450): and he

[m] Hesiod ap. Strab. vii. 327.   [n] Schol. ad Trach. v. 1169.

was also the father of Idomeneus, leader of the Cretans before Troy (Il. xiii. 452), and ruler over many of them (ibid.), but not, so far as appears, over the whole island.

Now Minos was not only king of all Crete, but son of Jupiter (ibid., and Od. xi. 568) by a Phœnician damsel of great note (Il. xiv. 321); we must therefore regard him, or his mother, as having come from Phœnicia into Crete. The inference would be, that Deucalion came from Crete to Thessaly, and that he, or Idomeneus his son, re-migrated to Crete. Homer does not indeed state that Deucalion was ever in Thessaly: but he indirectly supports the tradition both by placing Idomeneus in a different position in Crete from that of his grandfather Minos, and otherwise[o]. This supposition would at once reconcile the later tradition with Homer, and explain to us why the grandson of Minos only filled an inferior position.

Again, as we see that Thessaly is Pelasgic, and that the Thessalian Myrmidons are called Achæans, so likewise we find among the five nations of Crete both Pelasgians and Achæans[p]. Here, according to Strabo, Staphylus described these two races as inhabiting the plains, and Andron reported them, as also the Dorians, to have come from Thessaly: erroneously, says Strabo (x. 4., p. 476), making the mother city of the Dorians a mere colony from the Thessalians. And the ancient tradition which places the infant Jupiter in Crete ('Jovis incunabula Creten'), concurs with the idea which the above-named facts would suggest, that the Pelasgians may have come, at least in part, from the southern islands of the Ægean.

2. As to Rhodes. Tlepolemus, its chieftain, is the son of Hercules, and of Astyochea, whom, in the course

[o] Vid. inf. sect. iii.   [p] Od. xix. 175.

of his raids, he took from Ephyra by the river Selleeis. It is questioned which Ephyra, and which Selleeis, for of both there were several, these may have been. If they were in Thessaly[q], we have thus a line of connection established between Thessaly and Rhodes.

3. As to the contingent from Nisyrus, the Calydnæ, and Cos. Firstly, it was commanded by Pheidippus and Antiphus (678), sons of Thessalus, the son of Hercules. The connection between Hercules and Thessaly, which is agreeable to the general course of tradition, also harmonises with the most natural construction which can be put upon this passage of Homer: namely, that this Thessalus was the person who afterwards became the eponymist of Thessaly, that he was a native or inhabitant of the country, and that either he, or more probably his sons, were emigrants from it to the islands.

His name, latent for a time, may afterwards have attained to its elevation, as a means of connecting Thessaly with Hercules, when the descendants of that hero had become predominant in the South. Perhaps the appearance of the post-Homeric name 'Doris' may be explained in the same manner.

Secondly, Cos is described as the city of Eurypylus. This may mean a city which he had founded; or a city which was then actually under his dominion. Beyond all doubt, it indicates a very special connection of some kind between Cos and Eurypylus. Now, his name is mentioned without adjunct. Had he been a deceased founder of the city, he would probably have been called $\theta\epsilon\hat{\iota}o\varsigma$ like Thoas (Il. xiv. 230). If he was living, who was he? We have in the Iliad one very famous Eurypylus, who appears among the nine foremost of the

[q] This question is discussed, inf. sect. ix.

Greek heroes (Il. vii. 167), and whose rank entitled him (xi. 818) to be called Διοτρεφής; an epithet confined, as is probable, to Kings[r]. Now although Homer allows himself, when he is dealing with secondary persons, to apply the same name to more than one individual, without always caring to discriminate between them, there is no instance in which he does this for a person of the class of Eurypylus. This probably, therefore, is the same Eurypylus, as meets us in other parts of the poem, the son of Euæmon. But from the Catalogue[s], it appears that he commanded the contingent from Ormenium in Thessaly. If then, the same person, who founded or had some special relation to Cos, was also the commander of a Thessalian force, here we have a new track of connection between Thessaly and the islands to the southward.

4. Nireus, named by Homer for his beauty alone, with his three ships from Syme, can scarcely be said to make an unit in the Greek catalogue.

With this one inconsiderable exception, we find in all the cases of island contingents a connection subsisting between them and Thessaly, and this connection not appearing to be mediate, along the line of mainland which reaches from Thessaly to within a short distance from Crete, but apparently maintained directly by the maritime route: a fact of importance in considering the probable extension and movement of the Pelasgic race, which we find existing in both regions. We know from Homer[t] that the southern islands were a common route connecting Greece with the East. There are also abundant traces of migration by the northern coast of the Ægean. Thus it is at both those gates of Greece,

[r] See inf. sect. ix.   [s] Il. ii. 735.
[t] Od. iv. 83. xiv. 199, 245. xvii. 448.

that we find the Pelasgian name subsisting in the time of Homer, when in the nearer vicinity of the centre of Achæan power it was already extinct.

IV. Again, I think we may trace the near connection between the Pelasgians and the Greek nation in the laudatory epithets with which the former are mentioned by Homer. We must here keep in mind on the one hand the extraordinary skill and care with which the Poet employed his epithets, and on the other hand, his never failing solicitude to exalt and adorn every thing Greek.

Homer names the Pelasgians only thrice, and each time with a laudatory epithet.

In Il. x. 429, where they form part of the Trojan camp, and again in Od. xix. 177, where they are stated to be found in Crete, they are $\delta\tilde{\iota}οι$. Homer never applies this word except to what is preeminent in its kind: in particular, he never attaches it to any national name besides the Pelasgi, except 'Αχαιοὶ, which of itself amounts to a presumption that he regarded his countrymen as in some way standing in the same class with the Pelasgians.

In the remaining passage where he names the Pelasgians, that in the Trojan Catalogue (Il. ii. 340), he calls them ἐγχεσίμωροι. He uses this epithet in only three other places. Of itself it is laudatory, because it is connected with the proper work of heroes, the σταδίη ὑσμίνη. In one of the three places he applies it individually to two royal warriors, one Munes the husband of Briseis, and the other Epistrophus (Il. ii. 693), a warrior associated with Munes. In the second (Il. vii. 134), he gives it to the Arcadians; whom in the Catalogue (ii. 611), he has already commended as ἐπιστάμενοι πολεμίζειν. In the third passage (Od. iii. 188), he applies the epithet to the Myrmidons themselves. From each of these uses, the last especially, we may draw fresh presumptions of his high estimate of the Pelasgian name.

V. Again. In the case of a race, unless when it can be traced to an Eponymus or name-giver, the plural name precedes the singular in common use. There must be Celts before there can be a Celt, and Pelasgians before there can be a Pelasgian. The use therefore of the singular, in the names of nations, is a proof of what is established and long familiar.

For example, Homer never calls a single Greek Δαναός, nor Ἄργειος (though in the particular cases of Juno and of Helen he uses the singular feminine, of which more hereafter), but only Ἀχαιός; and we shall find, that this fact is not without its meaning. It is therefore worthy of note, that he uses the term Πελασγὸς in the singular. The chiefs of the Pelasgian ἐπίκουροι at Troy were Hippothous and Pulæus, (Il. ii. 843,) who were

υἷε δύω Λήθοιο Πελασγοῦ Τευταμίδαο.

And again, (xvii. 288),

Λήθοιο Πελασγοῦ φαίδιμος υἱός.

'The illustrious son of Lethus the Pelasgian.' It seems uncertain, from their place in the Trojan Catalogue, whether these Pelasgians were European or Asiatic; nor is it material to which region they belonged.

VI. It is further observable, that Homer implies distinctly the existence of various tribes of Pelasgi under that same name in various and widely separated places. He says,

Ἱππόθοος δ' ἄγε φῦλα Πελασγῶν ἐγχεσιμώρων
τῶν, οἳ Λάρισσαν ἐριβώλακα ναιετάουσιν.

Strabo justly observes upon the use of the plural φῦλα in this passage as implying considerable numbers.

And the words τῶν οἱ in the following line, signifying "namely those Pelasgi, who," show that the poet found it necessary to use a distinctive mark in order that these Pelasgi might not be confounded with other Pelasgi. Again, as this is in the Trojan Catalogue, where as a matter of course no Greeks would be found, he could hardly need to distinguish them from any Pelasgi connected with the Greeks, and we may assume it as most probable that he meant thus to distinguish them from other Pelasgi out of Greece rather than in Greece. At the same time, he may have had regard to other Pelasgians of Pelasgic Argos. In that country, as we may conclude with confidence from the appellation itself, they were known to form the bulk of the population, and as we hear of no such Pelasgian mass elsewhere in Homer, he may possibly have had them particularly in his mind, when he described the Trojan Pelasgians as Pelasgians of Larissa.

Some light is also thrown upon the character and habits of nations by the epithets attached to their places of abode. Homer mentions Larissa but twice: once here, and once where he relates the death of Hippothous, τῆλ' ἀπὸ Λαρίσσης ἐριβώλακος (Il. xvii. 301). The fertility of Larissa tends, as far as it goes, to mark the Pelasgi as a people of cultivators, having settled habits of life.

There is some difficulty, however, connected with the particular sign which Homer has employed to distinguish these Pelasgians. 'Hippothous led the Pelasgi, those Pelasgi, I mean, who inhabit productive Larissa.' From this it would appear that in the days of Homer, though there were many Pelasgi in various places, there was but one Larissa. And, accordingly, the name never appears within the Greece of Homer, either in the Catalogue, or elsewhere. Yet tradition hands down to us many Larissas, both in Greece and beyond it: and critics hold it to be reasonably presumed, wherever we find a Larissa, that there Pelasgi had been settled. But this name of Larissa apparently was not, and probably could not have been, thus largely employed in Homer's time; for if it had been so, the poet's use of the term Larissa would not have been in this case what he meant it to be, namely, distinctive. Yet the Pelasgians were even at that time apparently falling, or even fallen, into decay. How then could they have built many new cities in the subsequent ages? And, except in that way, how could the name Larissa have revived, and acquired its peculiar significance?

In six places of the Iliad we hear of a particular part of the city of Troy which was built upon a height, and in which the temple of Apollo was situated (v.446). This affords us an example of a separate name, $Πέργαμος$, affixed to a separate part of a city, that part apparently being the citadel. In like manner the citadel of Argos (which stood upon an eminence) had, at a later date, a distinct name, which was Larissa[x], and was said to have been derived from a daughter of Pelasgus so called[y]. Now it may have been the general rule to call the citadels of the Pelasgian towns Larissa. If so, then we can readily understand that so long as the towns themselves, or rather, it might be, the scattered hamlets, remained, the name of the citadels would be rarely heard: but when the former fell into decay, the solid masonry which the Pelasgi used for walls and for public buildings, but which did not extend to private dwellings, would remain. Thus the citadels would naturally retain their own old name, which had been

[x] Strabo viii. 6. p. 370.   [y] Cramer's Greece, iii. 244.

originally attached to them with reference to their fortifications. This hypothesis will fully account for the absorption of the particular and separate names of towns in the original and common name of their citadels.

Where an agricultural settlement was made upon ground, some particular spot of which afforded easy means of fortification, convenience would probably dictate the erection of a citadel for occasional retreat in time of danger, without any attempt to gather closely into one place and surround with walls the residences of the settlers: a measure which, as entailing many disadvantages, was only likely to take place under the pressure of strong necessity. Such I have presumed to have been the ordinary history of the Pelasgian Larissas. That which, while it flourished as a Pelasgian settlement, might be an Argos[z], would, perhaps, after a conquest, and the changes consequent upon it, become at last a Larissa.

But cases might arise in which the most fertile lands, lying entirely open and level, would, on the one hand, offer peculiar temptations to the spoiler, and, on the other, offer no scarped or elevated spot suitable for a separate fortification. In such a case the name ἐριβώλαξ would be best deserved, and in such a case too the probable result would be, to build a walled town including all the habitations of the colonists. This walled town would, for the very same reason as the citadels elsewhere, be itself a Larissa: and thus this Pelasgian name might be a distinctive one in the time of Homer, and yet might become a common one afterwards.

All this corresponds with the general belief on the two points, (1) that the Pelasgians dwelt, as in Attica, κωμηδὸν, and (2) that the Larissas are Pelasgian.

[z] Inf. sect. viii.

II. *Ethnology.*

But moreover it is supported by particular instances. Troy, for example, had its Pergama on a lofty part of the site where it stood: and from the epithets αἰπείνη, ὀφρυόεσσα, ἠνεμόεσσα, applied to the name Ἴλιος but never to Τροίη (of course I mean when this latter word is used for the city, the only class of cases in point), it may justly be inferred that Ilus[a] built the Pergama when he migrated into the plain. But the wall surrounding the entire city was only built in the next generation, under King Laomedon, who employed Neptune and Apollo for the purpose.

Another, and perhaps more marked instance, is to be found in the case of Thebes. We know from Thucydides[b] that Bœotia was, from its openness and fertility, more liable to revolutions from successive occupancy than other parts of Greece. With this statement a passage of the Odyssey[c] is in remarkable accordance. Homer tells us that Amphion and Zethus, probably among the very earliest Hellic immigrants into Middle Greece, first settled on the site of Thebes; and, he adds specially, that they fortified it. But apparently it could not have been the usual practice of the time to surround entire cities, at least, with fortifications, because he goes on to assign the special reason for its being done in this case, namely, that, even powerful as they were, they could not hold that country, so open (εὐρύχορος, Od. xi. 265) and rich, except with the aid of walls. This would appear to be a case like the Λαρίσση ἐριβώλαξ of the seventeenth Iliad, and both alike were probably exceptions to the general rule.

I have now done with the direct notices of the Pelasgi in Homer. But we have still a considerable har-

[a] Il. xx. 215 and seqq.   [b] Thuc. i. cap. 2.
[c] Od. xii. 260–5.

vest of indirect notices to gather. Particularly, in discussing the meaning of the name Ionians, we shall hereafter find reason to suppose that Homer's Athenians were Pelasgic: and I propose here to refer to some similar indications with respect to the Arcadians.

The Arcadians in Homer.

Like the Pelasgians, the Arcadians are, as we have seen, happy in never being mentioned without Homer's commendation. In Il. ii. 611 they are ἐπιστάμενοι πολεμίζειν. In Il. vii. 134 they are ἐγχεσίμωροι.

In the Catalogue he also throws some light upon the habits of the Arcadians: first, by describing them as heavy armed, ἀγχιμάχηται: secondly, by stating that they had no care for maritime pursuits. In both respects their relation to the Trojans is remarkable. With the exception of the Arcadians, the epithet ἀγχιμάχηται is nowhere used except for the substantive Δάρδανοι, and the position of the Dardanians in Troas very much corresponded with that of the Arcadians in Greece. Again, the Trojans, as we know, were so entirely destitute of ships, that Paris had to build them by way of special undertaking. These resemblances tend to suggest a further likeness. As the Trojans appear to have been peculiarly given to the pursuits of peace, it is reasonable to suppose the poet had the same idea of the Arcadians. The ἀγχιμάχηται is connected with the habits of settled cultivators. A peasantry furnishes heavy infantry, while light troops are best formed from a population of less settled habits and ruder manners. And as the use of ships had much less to do with regular commerce than with piracy and war,[d] so the

[d] This state of ideas and habits is well illustrated by Odyss. xiv. 222-6: and see inf. sect. 7.

absence of maritime habits tends, for the heroic age, to imply a pacific character. In those days the principal purpose of easy locomotion was booty: and there was no easy locomotion for bodies of men, except by ships. Though inclosed by hills, Arcadia was a horse feeding[e], therefore relatively not a poor country. In later times it was, next to Laconia[f], the most populous province of the Peloponnesus; and even in Homer, although its political position was evidently secondary, it supplied no less than sixty ships with large crews to each[g]. All this is favourable to the tradition which gives it a Pelasgian character.

Again, the Arcadians were commanded by Agapenor the son of Ancæus[h]. He would appear not to have been an indigenous sovereign. For we learn from a speech of Nestor in the twenty-third Book[i], that games were celebrated at the burial of Amarynceus by the Epeans, in which he himself overcame in wrestling Ancæus the Pleuronian. Ancæus therefore was not an Arcadian but an Ætolian: and his son Agapenor was probably either the first Arcadian of his race, or else a stranger appointed by Agamemnon to command the Arcadians in the Trojan war. Their having ships from Agamemnon, and a chief either foreign or of non-Arcadian extraction, are facts which tend to mark the Arcadians as politically dependent, and therefore *pro tanto* as Pelasgian: for it cannot be doubted that whatever in Greece was Pelasgian at the epoch of the *Troica*, was also subordinate to some race of higher and more effective energies.

Again. It will hereafter (I think) be found that the

[e] Strabo viii. p. 383.
[f] Xenoph. Hell. vii. 1, 23, and Cramer iii. 299.
[g] Il. ii. 610.
[h] Il. ii. 609.
[i] 630–5

institution of all gymnastic and martial games was Hellenic and not Pelasgic[k]. In the passage last quoted there is a very remarkable statement, that there were present at the games Epeans, Pylians, and Ætolians: that is to say, all the neighbouring tribes, except the Arcadians. Thus we have a strong presumption established that these games were not congenial to Arcadian habits: and if the same can be shown from other sources with respect to the Pelasgians, there is a strong presumption that the Arcadians were themselves Pelasgian.

Once more. In the sixth book Nestor relates, that in his youth the Pylians and Arcadians fought near the town of Pheiæ and the river Iardanos. The Arcadians were commanded by Ereuthalion, who wore the armour of Areithous. Areithous had met his death by stratagem from Lycoorgos, who appropriated the armour, and bequeathed it to his θεραπών, or companion in arms, Ereuthalion. Nestor, on the part of the Pylians, encountered Ereuthalion, and by the aid of Minerva defeated him.

From this tale it would appear, first, that Lycoorgus was king of Arcadia. His name savours of Pelasgian origin, from its relation to Λυκαών of the later tradition respecting Arcadia, and to Lycaon son of Priam, descended by the mother's side from the Leleges; again, to Lycaon the father of Pandarus; possibly also to the inhabitants of Lycia. The allusion to his having succeeded by stratagem only, is very pointed (148),

τὸν Λυκόοργος ἔπεφνε δόλῳ, οὔτι κράτεί γε,

and the terms employed appear to indicate a military inferiority: which accords with the probable relation of the Arcadians, as Pelasgi, to their Hellenic neighbours.

[k] See inf. sect. vii.

And this again corresponds with the close of the story; in which Nestor, fighting on the part of the Pylians who were Achæan, and therefore Hellenic, conquers the Arcadian chieftain Ereuthalion (Il. vi. 132–56).

It may be remarked once for all, that this military inferiority is not to be understood as if the Pelasgi were cowards, but simply as implying that they gave way before tribes of more marked military genius or habits than themselves; as at Hastings the Saxons did before the Normans; or as the Russians did in the late war of 1854–6 before the Western armies.

Lastly, the δῖος applied to Ereuthalion (Il. v. 319), accords with the use of that epithet for the Pelasgi elsewhere.

Thus a number of indications from Homer, slight when taken separately, but more considerable when combined, and drawn from *all* the passages in which Homer refers to Arcadia, converge upon the supposition that the Arcadians were a Pelasgian people.

They are supported by the whole stream of later tradition; which placed Lycaon, son of Pelasgus, in Arcadia, which uniformly represented the Arcadians as autochthonic[1], and which made them competitors with the Argives for the honour of having given to the Pelasgians their original seat in the Peloponnesus.

Here too philology steps in, and lends us some small aid. The name of Προσέληνοι, which the Arcadians took to themselves, and which is assumed to mean older than the moon, appears, when so understood, to express a very forced idea: it is difficult indeed to conceive how such a name could even creep into use. But if we refer its origin to πρὸ and Σελλοὶ or Σέλληνες, it then becomes the simple indication of the historical

[1] Xenoph. Hell. vii. 1. 23.

fact we are looking for, namely, that they, a Pelasgic population, occupied Arcadia before any of the Hellic or Sellic races had come into the Peloponnesus.

From its rich pastures, Arcadia was originally well adapted for Pelasgian inhabitants. Defended by mountains, it offered, as Attica did through the poverty of its soil, an asylum to the refugees of that race, when dispossessed from other still more fertile, and perhaps also more accessible tracts of the Peloponnesus[m]. Hence it is easy to account both for its original Pelasgian character, and for the long retention of it.

We seem then to find the Arcadians of Homer (first) politically dependent, and (secondly) commanded by a foreigner, but yet (thirdly) valiant in war. It would thus appear that what they wanted was not animal or even moral courage, but the political and governing element, which is the main element in high martial talent. All this we shall find, as we already have in some degree found, to be a Pelasgian portraiture. And if it should seem to have been drawn with the aid of conjecture, let it at any rate be observed that it is supported by the Arcadian character in the historic ages. They appear from various indications to have been for many generations the Swiss of Greece: not producing great commanders, and obscure enough, until a very late date, in the political annals of the country, but abounding in the materials of a hardy soldiery, and taking service with this or that section of the Greeks as chance might dictate. For in Xenophon they boast that when any of the Greeks wanted auxiliaries (ἐπίκουροι) they came to Arcadia to obtain them: that the Lacedæmonians took them into company when they invaded Attica, and that the Thebans did the very same

[m] Thuc. i. 2.

when they invaded Lacedæmon[n]. And Thucydides tells us that, in the Sicilian war, the Mantineans, with a portion of their brother Arcadians, fought for hire with the Athenians on one side, while another contingent from the very same State assisted the Corinthians, who had come in force to aid in the defence of Syracuse against them[o].

Two other circumstances, slight in themselves, still remain for notice.

1. It was through the authority and practice of the Romans that the name of Greeks or Graians came ultimately to supplant that of Hellenes. Out of this fact, which is the most important piece of evidence in our possession, arises the presumption, that as it was the Pelasgians who may be said to have supplied the main link between Greece and Italy, and between the Hellenic and the Roman language, the Graians could not but have been a branch or portion of that people. Now we know that the Pelasgians were cultivators of the plains. Bœotia is, as we have seen, indicated by Thucydides[p] as the richest plain[q] of Greece, and on that account among the parts most liable to the displacement of their inhabitants. It was therefore probably a plain where the Pelasgi would have settled early and in numbers: and it deserves notice, that the Catalogue[r], placing the town of Graia in Bœotia, places it where we naturally assume a large, though now, as in Thessaly, subordinate Pelasgian population to have existed.

Nor is the passage in which Aristotle notices the Γραικοὶ adverse to the belief that they were a Pelasgian race. He states that the deluge of Deucalion was in the

[n] Xenoph. Hellen. vii. 1. 23.
[o] Thucyd. vii. 57.
[p] B. i. 2.
[q] See also Müller, Orchomenus p. 77, and his references.
[r] Il. ii. 498.

ancient Hellas: which is the country reaching from Dodona to the Achelous (αὕτη δ' ἐστὶν ἡ περὶ τὴν Δωδώνην καὶ τὸν Ἀχελῷον). This may include either great part, or the whole, of Thessaly: whether we understand it of the little and Thessalian Achelous, near Lamia, which was within thirty *stadia* of the Spercheus[s]: or of the great Achelous, which skirted the western border of that country, and whose line of tributaries was fed from the slopes of Pindus. If we understand the Dodona of Epirus, this will give a considerable range of country, all of it outside Thessaly. Aristotle proceeds to say, that there dwelt the Selli, and those then called Γραικοὶ but now Hellenes (καὶ οἱ καλούμενοι τότε μὲν Γραικοὶ νῦν δὲ Ἕλληνες). Thus he describes as Γραικοὶ those who, together with the Selli, were the inhabitants of the country that Homer calls Pelasgic Argos: so that according to him the Γραικοὶ were not Sellic: and the time, when they were thus neighbours of the Selli, was the pre-Hellenic time. This is nearly equivalent to an assertion by Aristotle that the Graians were Pelasgic, for we know of no other pre-Hellenic race in Thessaly[t].

2. In vv. 695, 6 we find that (Πύρασος) Pyrasus in Thessaly (probably deriving its name from πυρὸς wheat, grain), is described as Δήμητρος τέμενος: and it is the only ground consecrated to Ceres that Homer mentions. It is material that this should be in Thessaly, the especially Pelasgic country: for both slight notices in Homer, and much of later tradition, connect the Pelasgi in a peculiar manner with the worship of that deity. For example, Pausanias mentions a temple of Δημήτηρ Πελασγὶς[u] at Corinth even in his own time. This connection in its turn serves to confirm the character of the Pelasgi as a rural and agricultural people.

[s] Strabo ix. p. 433. [t] Aristot. Meteorol. i. 14.
[u] Paus. ii. 22. 2.

So far as this part of the evidence of Homer is concerned, it goes to this only, that with the aid of Hesiod it serves to exhibit Ceres in direct relations with two countries; both with Thessaly, and, as will now be shown, with Crete; in which also, as we know from Homer (brought down by Hesiod to a later date), the Pelasgian name still remained when it had apparently been submerged elsewhere in Greece; and in which therefore it may be inferred that the Pelasgian element was more than usually strong and durable.

In the fifth Odyssey[x] we are told that Ceres fell in love with a son of Iasus (Iasion, in Hesiod Iasios), whom she met νειῷ ἐνὶ τριπόλῳ; in what country Homer does not say, but Hesiod, repeating the story, adds it was in Crete, Κρήτης ἐν πίονι δήμῳ[y]. Thus the double connection is made good.

Over and above this, the name Iasus goes of itself to establish a Pelasgian origin.

1. Because Ἴασον Ἄργος is an old name for the Peloponnesus, or else a large portion of it; whereas the Hellenic name was, as we know, Ἀχαικὸν Ἄργος. And the Ἰασίδαι reigned in Orchomenus[z] two or three generations before the Neleids. This probably touches a period when no Hellic tribes had, as far as we know, found their way into the Peloponnesus[a], and when the dynasties even of the middle and north were, as is probable, chiefly Pelasgian.

2. Because Ἴασος[b] was the name of one of the Athenian leaders, and the Athenians were, as we shall find, manifestly Pelasgian. His father Sphelus is also the son of Boucolus, a name which will be shown to be of Pelasgic and not Hellenic character[c].

[x] Od. v. 125.
[y] Hesiod. Theog. 971.
[z] Od. xi. 281-4.
[a] See inf. sect. 8.
[b] Il. xv. 332, 7.
[c] Inf. sect. vi.

3. Because Dmetor the son of Iasus was the ruler of Cyprus at the epoch of the Troica, and that island seems to have stood in an anomalous relation of half-dependence to Agamemnon, which is best capable of explanation if we suppose it to have been inhabited by a population still retaining its Pelasgian character. To this question I shall shortly have occasion to return in a more full consideration of the case of Cyprus.

Of later tradition, there is abundance to connect Ceres with the Pelasgians: their character as tillers of the soil, and hers as the giver of grain: the worship of her at Eleusis, dating from time immemorial, and purporting to be founded upon rites different from those in vogue at a later epoch: this too taken in connection with the Pelasgian origin of Athens, and its long retention of that character. In the ancient hymn to Ceres, estranged from Jupiter and the other gods, she comes to Eleusis, and there herself founds the worship; and she announces in her tale that she was come from Crete:

νῦν αὖτε Κρήτηθεν, ἐπ' εὐρέα νῶτα θαλάσσης,
ἤλυθον, οὐκ ἐθέλουσα[d].

I even venture to suggest it as possible that the existence of a τέμενος (or land devoted to the service of any deity) at all, affords a presumption of a Pelasgic population and institutions. For we find only three other cases of such endowments: all in places strongly marked with a Pelasgic character. One is that of the river Sperchius in Thessaly: a second that of Venus in Cyprus; and the third that of Jupiter in Gargarus[e].

The Ionians.

The notices of the Ionians contained in Homer are

[d] Hymn, Cer. 123.   [e] Il. xxiii. 148. Od. viii. 362. Il. viii. 48.

II. *Ethnology.*

faint and few: but they are in entire contradiction with the prevailing tradition.

The word Ἰάονες occurs only once in the poems, where we find the five contingents of Bœotians, Ionians, Locrians, Phthians, and Epeans, united in resisting, but ineffectually, Hector's attack upon the ships. They are here termed ἑλκεχίτωνες[f], an epithet which is unfortunately nowhere else employed by the poet. The order in which they are named is,

    1. Bœotians,   2. Ionians,   3. Locrians,
             4. Phthians,   5. Epeans.

A description thus commences in three parts, of which the first is (689–91),

οἱ μὲν Ἀθηναίων προλελεγμένοι· ἐν δ' ἄρα τοῖσιν
ἦρχ' υἷος Πετεῶο, Μενεσθεύς· οἱ δ' ἄμ' ἕποντο
Φείδας τε Στιχίος τε, Βίας τ' ἐΰς·

The second describes the leaders of the Epeans: the third of the Phthians, and these, it says, meaning apparently the Phthian force, fought in conjunction with the Bœotians, μετὰ Βοιωτῶν ἐμάχοντο (700). No Bœotian leaders are named: the absence of Oilean Ajax, who officially led the Locrians, is immediately accounted for by saying that he was with his inseparable friend, the Telamonian chief.

These Ἰάονες ἑλκεχίτωνες then were the προλελεγμένοι, a chosen band of the Athenian force; or else they were the force composed of men picked among the Athenians. But no distinguished quality or act of war is recounted of the Athenians, either here or elsewhere in the Iliad. They are simply called μήστωρες ἀϋτῆς,[g] but this is a mere general epithet, has no reference to any particular conduct, and is not sustained by any relation of their feats in arms. The five divisions above named fight in order to be beaten by the Trojans: and we

[f] Il. xiii. 635.   [g] Il. iv. 328.

The Athenians in the Catalogue.

may be sure that Homer does not produce the flower of the Greeks for such a purpose. Nor has their chief Menestheus any distinction whatever accorded to him, even in the much questioned passage of the Catalogue, except that of being excellent at marshalling forces.

The passage Il. ii. 546–56, describing the Athenians in the Catalogue, is of so much historical interest through the various points it involves, as to deserve a particular consideration, which it may best receive in this place. Upon it depends some part of the Homeric evidence relating to the signs of a Pelasgian origin.

Three lines of it must in any case be allowed to remain, in order to describe the Athenian contingent and its commander.

οἱ δ' ἄρ' Ἀθήνας εἶχον, ἐϋκτίμενον πτολίεθρον... (v. 546.)
τῶν αὖθ' ἡγεμόνευ' υἱὸς Πετεῶο Μενεσθεύς. (552.)
τῷ δ' ἅμα πεντήκοντα μέλαιναι νῆες ἕποντο. (556.)

To the supposition that this jejune *minimum* represents the passage in its original form, it is certainly an objection, that in no other place of the whole Catalogue has Homer dispatched quite so drily and summarily any important division of the force.

The remainder of the passage falls into three portions, of which the first is separable from the two others, and the first with the second is also separable from the third. They are as follows:

(1)—vv. 546–9.

οἱ δ' ἄρ' Ἀθήνας εἶχον, ἐϋκτίμενον πτολίεθρον,
δῆμον Ἐρεχθῆος μεγαλήτορος, ὅν ποτ' Ἀθήνη
θρέψε Διὸς θυγάτηρ, τέκε δὲ ζείδωρος Ἄρουρα,
κὰδ δ' ἐν Ἀθήνῃσ' εἶσεν, ἑῷ ἐνὶ πίονι νηῷ.

There is a reading of Ἀθήνης for Ἀθηνησ': it is disputed whether τέκε applies to δῆμον or to Erechtheus; whether ἑῷ is to be understood of Erechtheus or of

K

Minerva; and again, what is the meaning of πίονι as applied to νηῷ? The variety of lection is not material: the application of τέκε is clearly to Erechtheus, as seems also that of ἑῷ to Minerva[h]. Again, the application of the epithet πίονι to the temple is perhaps sufficiently supported by Od. xii. 346, πίονα νηὸν, and Il. v. 512, μάλα πίονος ἐξ ἀδύτοιο.

It does not appear that these lines, or the two which follow, were rejected by the Alexandrian critics, but the Pseudo-Herodotus, in the Life of Homer, c. 28, states that they were interpolated.

The objections from internal evidence are stated by Payne Knight[i].

1. That the Greeks had no temples at the time of the *Troica*.

2. That as Ἄρουρα is *superficies non orbis Terræ*, so it was not a known personification at the time of Homer.

As to the first of these, we hear of Trojan temples in the Iliad; probably also of the Greek temple of Apollo in Il. ix. 404; and of Greek temples in the Odyssey, beyond all reasonable doubt. We hear of Ætolian priests in Il. ix. 575; while it is not likely that there should have been priests without temples.

Again, the circumstances of the Greeks in the Iliad were not such as to lead to the mention of temples usually or frequently. Therefore this is not a ground of suspicion against the passage.

As to the second objection, it should be borne in mind that the Earth, Γαῖα, as well as Ἄρουρα, was apparently to Homer, not less than to the other ancients, a surface, not a solid (κυκλοτερὴς ὡς ἀπὸ τόρνου, Herod. iv. 36.) The objection really is, that Ἄρουρα

[h] Heyne in loc.   [i] In loc.

means a particular class of ground, namely, arable or cultivable land; and that to personify this class of land by itself is artificial, far-fetched, and not in the manner of Homer.

To me it appears clear that it would be unnatural for us, but very doubtful whether it was so for Homer. We could not in poetry well treat Corn-field or Garden as a person: but the corn-bearing Earth ($\zeta\epsilon i\delta\omega\rho o\varsigma$ Ἄρουρα) had for the Greeks in their early days a vividness of meaning, which it has not for us. To us, to the modern European mind, the gifts of Ceres are but one item in an interminable list of things enjoyable and enjoyed: to man when yet youthful, while in his first ruder contact with his mother Earth and the elements, while possessed of few instruments and no resources, this idea was as determinate, as it was likewise suggestive and poetical. The Latins have no word by which to render the word Ἄρουρα in its full meaning, though *arvum* must have been taken from it, or from the same root with it. It nearly corresponds with the English 'glebe' in its proper use[j]. It signifies not only corn land, but all productive land, for instance, vine land, in Il. iii. 246. But to them, so pregnant was the idea, that besides a crop of epithets such as πολύφορβος and τραφέρη, it threw off its own inverted image in the epithet, habitual with Homer, of ἀτρύγετος for θάλασσα, the uncornbearing sea. Now when the idea of corn land had been thus vividly conceived, the next step, that of viewing Ἄρουρα as Γαῖα, was one not very hard to take. The objection seems to arise out of our unconsciously

[j] From the Greek βῶλος, according to Richardson, who quotes *The Fox* (v. 2.)
                  If Italy
   Have any glebe, more fruitful than these fallows,
   I am deceived.

132 II. Ethnology.

reading Homer in the false light of our own familiar associations.

His text affords evidence in support of these views. May it not be said that the phrase πάτρις Ἄρουρα[k] for *patria* shows us a great step towards personification? In the Νεκυία (Od. xi. 489), ἐπάρουρος is equivalent to 'alive;' compare Il. xvii. 447. Again, Ulysses, the moment he escapes from the river mouth to the shore, kisses the ζείδωρος Ἄρουρα[l] among the reeds: which seems to show an use of the term nearly synonymous with Γαῖα or earth. And again, praying for the glory of Alcinous[m], he says,

τοῦ μέν κεν ἐπὶ ζείδωρον ἄρουραν
ἄσβεστον κλέος εἴη.

The fame of Alcinous could not be confined to fields. So the setting sun casts shadows on the ἐρίβωλος Ἄρουρα[n]. In both cases the term so approximates to the meaning of Earth, doubtless by metonymy, as to be indistinguishable from it. Again Il. iv. 174, σέο δ᾽ ὄστεα πύσει Ἄρουρα. Surely the meaning here is Earth, for we are not to suppose Homer meant to say the bodies of his warriors would lie on the cultivable land only. But another passage brings us up to actual personification, that respecting Otus and Ephialtes

οὓς δὴ μηκίστους θρέψε ζείδωρος Ἄρουρα[o].

This objection to Ἄρουρα therefore will not hold good: and the passage cannot be condemned upon internal evidence. It is referred to by Plato, in the first Alcibiades[p].

(2)—Vss. 550, 1.

ἐνθάδε μιν ταύροισι καὶ ἀρνειοῖς ἱλάονται
κοῦροι Ἀθηναίων, περιτελλομένων ἐνιαυτῶν.

[k] Od. i. 407. [l] Od. v. 463. [m] Od. vii. 332.
[n] Il. xxi. 232. [o] Od. xi. 309. [p] (ii. 132 Serr. Steph.)

Some refer μιν to Minerva, and construe the passage with reference to the Panathenaic celebration. When so interpreted, as it is contended, the words betray a palpable anachronism.

Again it is alleged, (1) Homer does not in the Catalogue introduce general descriptions of the religious rites of Greece, and it is scarcely likely he should mention here a celebration, which he does not report to have had anything peculiar in its character. (2) From xi. 729 it appears that cows were sacrificed to Minerva, not bulls: (3) the tenour of the sentence directs us to Erechtheus, and it involves worship offered to a local hero.

With respect to the Panathenaica, a difficulty would undoubtedly arise, if we were obliged to suppose that it contained a reference to gymnastic games, which we have every reason to treat as having borne in the age of Homer a marked Hellenic character[q]. But the words imply no such reference. They speak, at the most, of no more than periodical sacrifices. This implies an established festival, and nothing beyond it. Now such a signification raises no presumption whatever against the genuineness of the passage: because we have one distinct and unquestionable case in Homer of an established festival of a deity, that namely of Apollo in the Odyssey. The day of the vengeance of Ulysses was the ἑορτὴ τοῖο Θεοῖο ἁγνή[r].

So considering the passage, let us next examine the objection taken to it, that it involves hero-worship[s], which was not known in the Homeric age.

Now we have in the Odyssey, as well as here in the Iliad, cases of mortals translated to heaven and to the company of immortals.

[q] Inf. sect. 7.   [r] Od. xxi. 255.   [s] Payne Knight in loc.

In the Odyssey we have, for example, the case of Castor and Pollux, who enjoyed a peculiar privilege of life after death, and revisited earth in some mysterious manner on alternate days[t]. And this, too, although they were buried[u].

Their τίμη πρὸς Ζηνὸς was such that, as the passage in Od. xi. proceeds to state, they vied with deities;

τίμην δὲ λελόγχασ' ἶσα θεοῖσιν.

This τίμη must have included honour paid on earth: to be in heaven, unless in connection with earth and its inhabitants, was not of itself a τίμη, much less was it the τίμη of the gods. The subject of hero-worship will be further examined in a later portion of this work: but for the present it appears sufficiently, that this comes near to hero-worship. The passage about Erechtheus is no more than a development of the expression relating to the Tyndarid brothers; and, though by some steps in advance of it, can hardly be rejected on this ground alone as spurious. All passages cannot be expected to express with precisely the same degree of fulness the essential ideas on which they are founded; and we are not entitled to cut off, on that ground alone, the one which happens to be most in advance.

But although the application to Erechtheus might not convict the passage, I very much question whether we ought so to apply it. It is quite against the general bearing of the passage, which would much more naturally refer it to Minerva. The reason for it is that cows or heifers were offered to her, and not rams or bulls. No doubt, in the particular cases mentioned to us, (Il. vi. 94, x. 292, xi. 729, and Od. iii. 382,) cows or heifers only are spoken of. But in Od. iii. 145 we are

[t] Od. xi. 302–4. [u] Il. iii. 243.

told that ἑκατομβαὶ were to be offered to her, which we can hardly limit so rigidly: and considering that the cases of cows mentioned by Homer are all special, while this passage speaks of what was ordinary and periodical, I think we should pause before admitting that the application of the lines to Minerva is on this ground indefensible.

The word περιτελλομένων[v] is taken to mean not annual revolutions, but the revolutions of periods of years. I question the grounds of this interpretation: but, if it could be established, it would certainly rather weaken the passage; for Homer nowhere else mentions periodical celebrations of any kind divided by any number of years, and I doubt whether such an idea does not involve greater familiarity with numerical combinations than the Poet seems to have possessed.

Leaving these two lines subject to some doubt, but by no means fully convicted, let us proceed to the third and last of the contested portions of the passage.

(3)—Vss. 553-5.
τῷ δ' οὔπω τις ὁμοῖος ἐπιχθόνιος γένετ' ἀνὴρ
κοσμῆσαι ἵππους τε καὶ ἀνέρας ἀσπιδιώτας·
Νέστωρ οἶος ἔριζεν· ὁ γὰρ προγενέστερος ἦεν.

These lines were condemned by Zenodotus[w], upon the ground that we have no other mention of these gifts of Menestheus, and no example of his putting them in exercise. Mr. Payne Knight[x] also urges that Menestheus, here so commended with respect to chariots as well as infantry, does not even appear as a competitor in the chariot-race at the funeral games of Patroclus, although, in order to enlarge the competition, even the slow horses of Nestor are put in requisition.

[v] Eustath. in loc. et alii.   [w] Schol. A. in loc.   [x] In loc.

II. Ethnology.

The Scholiast answers, with regard to the first objection, and Heyne[y] accepts the defence as sufficient, that other persons are praised in the gross, of whom no details are given anywhere: as Machaon is called ἀριστεύων in Il. xi. 506. But a mere general epithet is very different from a set passage of three lines expressing extraordinary preeminence in particular accomplishments.

Again, the word applied to Machaon is by no means one of abstract panegyric, but is itself a description of the activity in the field by which he was at the moment baffling the energies of Hector, and would, says the Poet, have continued to baffle them, had not Paris wounded him. Thus the word is not a vague epithet: the words παῦσεν ἀριστεύοντα Μαχάονα simply mean, that the manful exertions of Machaon were arrested.

There is another objection to the passage in the rather inflated character of its compliment to an undistinguished man. Even Nestor[z], it says, did not beat him, but only (ἔριζεν) vied with him: and this not as an abler, but only as an older, man.

On the other hand, some of the Scholiasts ingeniously suggest that these verses are given to Menestheus by way of compensation; τοῦτο χαρίζεται αὐτῷ, ἐπεὶ μὴ εὐδοκιμήσει ἐν ταῖς μάχαις[a]. But Homer does not usually deal out compensation, among the Greeks, by abstract praises, for the want of the honour earned by deeds: and all the other martial eulogies on chiefs in the Catalogue are well borne out in the poem.

On the whole, Mr. Payne Knight's objection, and the judgment of the Alexandrine Critics, seem to leave this part of the passage in a state so questionable, that nothing ought to be rested on it. The best point in

[y] Obss. in loc.   [z] Eustath. in loc.   [a] Schol. BL. in loc.

its favour is, that the Athenian Legates before Gelon are represented by Herodotus as confidently relying on it, when there would have been an interest on his part in demurring to its authority, for it was a question of military precedence that was at issue: τῶν καὶ ῞Ομηρος ὁ ἐποποιὸς ἄνδρα ἄριστον ἔφησε εἰς ῎Ιλιον ἀπικέσθαι, τάξαι τε καὶ διακοσμῆσαι στράτον[b].

On the other hand, it may be observed with justice that the compliment here paid to Menestheus is the very best of which the case admitted; perhaps the only one that an interpolator would have been safe in selecting. For he would have known that any panegyric relating to strength or prowess in action would be conclusively belied by the rest of the poem in its entire tenour.

But while we cannot confidently rely upon these three lines, there appears to be no reason why we should not use the evidence supplied by the rest of the passage as most probably good historic matter. It undoubtedly represents a strong course of old local tradition[c]: for there was in Athens a most ancient temple dedicated to Minerva and Erechtheus in conjunction.

The Homeric evidence then up to this point stands as follows with reference to Athens and the Athenian contingent, or the principal and picked men of it, whichever be the best term for the passage. They were

1. Ionians, Il. xiii. 685.
2. ἑλκεχίτωνες, ibid.
3. Autochthonous, Il. ii. 547.
4. Undistinguished in the war.
5. Under the special patronage of Pallas or Minerva, Il. ii. 546, and Od. xi. 323, where the epithet ἱεράων, given to Athens, indicates a special relation to a deity.

[b] Herod. vii. 161.   [c] Lord Aberdeen's Inquiry, p. 100.

II. *Ethnology.*

The epithet ἑλκεχίτωνες suggests unwarlike habits, and, though more faintly, it also betokens textile industry. It stands in marked contrast with the ἀμιτροχίτωνες[d] of the valiant Lycians, whose short and spare tunic required no cincture to confine it. It corroborates the negative evidence afforded by the Iliad of some want of martial genius in the primitive Athens. It coincides with the tutelage of Pallas, for the Minerva of Homer has no more indisputable function than as the goddess of skilled industry[e]. All this tends to betoken that the inhabitants of the Homeric Attica were Pelasgian.

Again, the autochthonic origin, ascribed to the Athenians in the person of Erechtheus, amounts to an assertion that they were the first known inhabitants of the country: in other words, that they were Pelasgian.

The negative evidence is also important. There is nothing in Homer that tends to associate Athens with the Hellenic stem. The want of military distinction deserves a fuller notice.

It can hardly be without meaning, that of all the chiefs, considerable in the Iliad by their positions and commands, there are but two who are never named as in actual fight, or with any other mark of distinction, and these two are the heads of the two (as we suppose) emphatically Pelasgian contingents, from Athens and Arcadia respectively. Agapenor, who (being however of Ætolian extraction) leads the Arcadians, is named nowhere but in the Catalogue: Menestheus is repeatedly named, but never with reference to fighting. In the only part of the action of the poem where he is put forward, he shudders[f], and shows an anxiety for his personal safety, much more like a Trojan leader than a

[d] Il. xvi. 419.   [e] See Od. xx. 72.   [f] Il. xii. 331.

Greek one. Yet they were sole commanders, the first of no less than sixty ships, the second of fifty. There are no similar cases. The nearest to them are those (1) of Prothous[g], who commands 40 ships of the Magnesians, and Gourieus[h], who leads 22 of the Enienes and Perrhæbi: both of these are remote, Thessalian, and very probably Pelasgian tribes: (2) of Podarkes, who commands 40 ships, but only as deputy for his deceased brother Protesilaus, who is said to have been not only the elder, but the more valiant[i].

Agapenor, indeed, was evidently dependent in a peculiar sense on Agamemnon, in whose ships he sailed: but this could not affect his position as to personal prowess. The case of Menestheus is the more remarkable from this circumstance, that he is the only independent and single commander in charge of so many as fifty ships, who is not invested with the supreme rank of Βασιλεὺς or King. His father Peteos is however called Διοτρεφὴς βασιλεὺς (Il. iv. 338), which marks him as having probably been a person of greater importance.

And what is true of the commanders is true also of the troops. Athens, and with her Arcadia, may justly be regarded as the only two undistinguished in Homer among those states of Greece which afterwards attained to distinction. For among the States which acquired fame in the historic ages, Argolis, Achaia, and Laconia hold through their chiefs very high places in the poem: Elis and Bœotia are conspicuous in the anterior traditions which it enshrines. Only Attica and Arcadia fail in exhibiting to us signs of early pre-eminence in the arts of war: which in a marked manner confirms the suppositions we have already obtained, as to the Pelasgian character of their inhabitants.

[g] Il. ii. 756.   [h] Il. ii. 748.   [i] Ibid. 703–7.

A sign, though a more uncertain one, that points in the same direction, is afforded by the choice of Athens, on the part of Orestes[j], as his place of habitation during the tyranny of Ægisthus in Mycenæ. The displaced, if they do not fly to the strong for protection, go among those who are weaker, and where they may most easily hold their ground, or even acquire power afresh. In other words, in the case before us, an Hellenic exile would very naturally betake himself among a Pelasgian people.

While however the indications of a predominating Pelasgian character among the Athenians at the epoch of the *Troica* appear to be varied and powerful, I must admit that they are crossed by one indication, which is at first sight of an opposite character, I mean that which is afforded by their name. Even though we were to surrender the entire passages in the Catalogue respecting them, it would still be difficult to contend that the name of Athens and of Athenians is forged in six other places of the poems where one or the other of them is found, besides that there is a second allusion to Erechtheus in the Odyssey. Here we have then, attached to a people whom we suppose Pelasgian, a name connecting them immediately with a deity commonly reputed to be of strong Hellic propensities: connecting them, indeed, in a manner so special as to be exclusive, because no other city or population in Homer takes its name from a deity at all. This indicates a relation of the closest description: and it is quite independent of the suspected passage, which represents Minerva as the nurse or foster-mother of Erechtheus.

Now it will be found, upon close examination, that

[j] Od. iii. 307.

Minerva plays a very different part in the Iliad from Juno, the great protectress of the Greeks, and from Neptune, their actual comrade in fight. The difference even at first sight is this, that theirs appears to be a national, hers more a personal and moral sentiment. In Juno, it is sympathy with the Greeks as Greeks; in Neptune, antipathy to the Trojans as Trojans: but both cases are plainly distinguishable from the temper and attitude of Minerva.

Her protection of Ulysses, whose character is the human counterpart of her own, is the basis of the whole theurgy of the Odyssey, and is also strongly marked in the Δολώνεια. Again, she comes, in the first book[k], at the instance of Juno, to restrain and guide Achilles: for Juno, it is stated, loved both Agamemnon and Achilles alike; which may imply, that this was not the exact case with Minerva. So again, she inspires Diomed[l] for the work of his ἀριστεῖα, with a view to his personal distinction[m]. On each of the two occasions when the two goddesses come down together from heaven, it is Juno that makes the proposal. When Minerva prompts Pandarus to treachery, it is by the injunction of Jupiter, issued on the suggestion of Juno[n]. In the seventh book, however, she descends of herself on seeing that the Greeks lose ground, tells Apollo that she was come, as he was, with the intention to stay the battle[o], and the result of their counsel is one of the single fights (that between Hector and Ajax), which were sure to issue in glory to the Greek heroes. Still she has not the rabid virulence against Troy which distinguishes Juno, which makes her exact the decision for its destruction in the Olympian assembly, and which leads Jupiter to say to

[k] Il. i. 194. [l] Il. v. 1–8. [m] V. 2, 3.
[n] Il. iv. 64–74. [o] Il. vii. 34.

her sarcastically, that if she could but eat Priam and his children and subjects raw, then her anger would be satiated.

In fact, Juno has all the marks of a deity entirely Hellic: both in the passionate character of her attachment, and in the absence of all signs whatever of any practical relation between her and the Trojan people.

It is not so with Pallas. Pitilessly opposed to the Trojans in the war, she is nowhere so identified with the Greeks as to exhibit her in the light of one of those deities, whose influence or sympathies were confined to any one place or nation. Her enmity to Troy is mythologically founded on the Judgment of Paris [p]: but it has a more substantive ethical ground in the nature of the quarrel between the two countries.

Unlike Juno and Neptune, she was regularly worshipped at Troy, where she had a priestess of high rank, and a temple placed, like that of Apollo, on the height of Pergamus.

Distinct proof, however, that Minerva was neither originally at war with the Trojans, nor unknown to them by her beneficial influences, is afforded by the case of Phereclus son of Harmonides, the carpenter; this Phereclus was the builder of the ships of Paris, and was a highly skilled workman [q] by her favour,

ἐξόχα γάρ μιν ἐφίλατο Πάλλας Ἀθήνη.

The name of Harmonides may be fictitious; but the relation to Pallas deserves remark, if we assume Troy to have been fundamentally Pelasgian; and it affords a strong presumption, that there was nothing in the character of Minerva to prevent her being propitious to a Pelasgian country. Her attributes as the goddess of industry, or more strictly, in our phrase, of manu-

[p] Il. xxiv. 25-30.   [q] Il. v. 59.

facture, were indeed in no special harmony with the character of the Pelasgians, as she had nothing to do with works of agriculture: but neither was there any antagonism between them.

There is also something that deserves notice in the speech in which Minerva expresses to Juno her resentment at the restraint put upon her by Jupiter. She accuses him of forgetting the services she had so often rendered to Hercules when he was oppressed by the labours that Eurystheus had laid upon him, and declares that it was she who effected his escape from Hades[r]. Now this has all the appearance of being the fabulous dress of the old tradition, which reports that the children of Hercules had taken refuge in Attica, and had been harboured there; that Eurystheus invaded the country in consequence of the protection thus given, and that he was slain while upon the expedition. It seems therefore possible, that this reception of the Heraclids may have had something to do with the special relation, at the epoch of the *Troica*, between Athens and Minerva as its tutelary goddess? In connection with Hercules personally, the Iliad affords us another mark that friendly relations might subsist between Troy and Pallas. She, in conjunction with them,

Τρῶες καὶ Πάλλας Ἀθήνη[s],

erected the rampart in which Hercules took refuge from the pursuing monster.

But the full answer to the objection is of a wider scope, and is to be found in the general character of this deity, which did not, like inferior conceptions, admit of being circumscribed by the limits of a particular district or people.

[r] Il. viii. 362-9: cf. Od. xi. 626.   [s] Il. xx. 146.

II. *Ethnology.*

It will hereafter be shewn, that, like Latona and Apollo in particular, Minerva in Pagan fiction represents a disguised and solitary fragment of the true primeval tradition[t]. All such deities we may expect to find, and we do find, transmitted from the old Pelasgians into the mythologies both of Greece and Rome, or those common to Pelasgian and Hellene. We expect to find, and we do find, them worshipped both among the Greeks and among the Trojans as gods, not of this or that nation, but of the great human family. In theory, exclusive regard to the one side or the other comports far better with the idea of such deities as represent unruly passions or propensities of our nature like Mars and Venus, or Mercury; or chief physical forces like Neptune; or such as, like Juno, are the sheer product of human imagination reflected upon the world above, and have no relation to any element or part of a true theology. But the Homeric Jupiter, in so far as he is a representative of supreme power and unity, and the Pallas and Apollo of the poems by a certain moral elevation, and by various incidents of their birth or attributes, show a nobler parentage[u].

In the capacity of a traditive deity, Minerva is with perfect consistency worshipped alike among Trojans and Greeks, Hellenic and Pelasgian tribes. There is nothing strange, then, in our finding her the patroness of a Pelasgian people. The only strangeness is her being (if so she was) more specially their patroness than of any other people. The very fact that, for the purposes of the war, Homer gives her to the Greeks, might perhaps have prepared us to expect that we should find her special domicile among the Hellic portions of that nation: but it supplies no absolute and conclusive reason

[t] See inf. Religion and Morals, Sect. II.   [u] Vid. inf. as before.

for such a domicile. But I close the discussion with these observations. In the first place, the Pelasgian character of the Athenians in early times is established by evidence too strong to be countervailed by any such inference as we should be warranted in drawing to a contrary effect from the special connection with Minerva. Again, it may be that the connection of both with Hercules may contain a solution of the difficulty. But lastly, if, as we shall find reason to believe, the traditive deities were the principal gods of ancient Greece, and if the entrance of the Hellic tribes brought in many new claimants upon the divine honours, it may after all seem not unreasonable that we should find, in one of the most purely Pelasgian States, the worship of this great traditive deity less obscured than elsewhere by competition with that of the invaders, and consequently in more peculiar and conspicuous honour.

An examination of the etymology of certain names in Homer will hereafter, I trust, confirm these reasonings on the Athens of the heroic age: with this exception, we may now bid adieu to the investigation of the Homeric evidence of Pelasgianism in.Attica.

That evidence certainly receives much confirmation, positive and negative, from without. In the first place, though Hesiod supplies us with an Hellen, and with a Dorus and Æolus among his sons, he says not a word of an Ion; and the tradition connecting Ion with Hellen through Xuthus is of later date: probably later than Euripides, who makes Ion only the adopted son of Xuthus an Achæan[x], and the real son of Creusa, an Erectheid; with Apollo, a Hellic, but also a Pelasgian deity, for his father. Again, in the legendary times we do not hear of the Athenians as invaders and con-

[x] Eurip. Ion 64. 1590. Grote i. 144.

querors, which was the character of the Hellic tribes, but usually as themselves invaded; for example, by Eurystheus from the Peloponnesus.

In ancient tradition generally, the Athenians appear on the defensive against Bœotians[y], Cretans, or others. And the reputed Pylian and Neleid descent of the Pisistratid family is a curious illustration of the manner in which Attica was reported to have imported from abroad the most energetic elements of her own population[z], and also of the (so to speak) natural predominance of Hellic over Pelasgic blood.

Thucydides[a] informs us, that the Athenians were first among the Greeks to lay aside the custom of bearing arms, and to cultivate ease and luxury. Of this we have perhaps already had an indication in the words ἑλκεχίτωνες.

He also states that, on account of the indifferent soil[b], which offered no temptation comparable to those supplied by the more fertile portions of Greece, there was no ejection of the inhabitants from Attica by stronger claimants. Τὴν γοῦν 'Αττικὴν, ἐκ τοῦ ἐπὶ πλεῖστον διὰ τὸ λεπτογέων ἀστασίαστον οὖσαν, ἄνθρωποι ᾤκουν οἱ αὐτοὶ ἀεί. This is simply stating in another form what was usually expressed by declaring them autochthons. It is part of their Pelasgian title.

A remarkable passage in Herodotus covers the whole breadth of the ground that has here been taken; and it is important, because no doubt it expresses what that author considered to be the best of the current traditions, founded in notoriety, and what Crœsus likewise learned upon a formal inquiry, undertaken with a view to alliances in Greece, respecting the origin of

[y] Thirlwall, vol. ii. p. 2. [z] Herod. v. 65.
[a] Thuc. i. 6. [b] i. 2.

the Athenians. Herodotus, like Homer, makes the Athenians Ionian; and in conformity with the construction here put upon Homer, he declares the Ionians not to be Hellenic, but to be Pelasgian[c]. The Attic people, he goes on to say, having once been Pelasgian became Hellenic[d]. According to some opinions[e], this change occurred when the Ionians came into Attica: but the evidence of Homer, I think, makes Athens Ionian at the same epoch when it is Pelasgian. I therefore construe the statement of Herodotus as signifying that the Athenians, in the course of time, received among themselves Hellenic immigrants from the more disturbed and changeful parts of Greece, and these immigrants impressed on Attica, as they had done on other states[f], the Hellenic character and name; only with the difference that, instead of a conflict, and the subjugation of the original inhabitants, there came a process of more harmonious and genial absorption, and in consequence, a development of Greek character even more remarkable for its fulness than in any other Grecian race. Even in the case of Attica, however, the Hellenic character was not finally assumed without a collision, though perhaps a local and partial one only, which ended in the ejectment of the Pelasgians. This conflict is reported to us by Herodotus from Hecatæus[g], and if we find that in it, according to the Athenian version of the story, the Pelasgians were the wrong-doers, it is probably upon the ground that the winner is always in the right: and the Athenians had the more need of a case, because their policy demanded a justification, when, under Miltiades, they followed the Pelasgians to Lemnos, and again subdued them there. Each version

[c] Herod. i. 56.   [d] i. 57.   [e] Höck's Creta ii. 109.
[f] Thuc. i. 3.   [g] Herod. vi. 137, 8.

of the Attican quarrel contains indications of being related to the truth of the case: for the Pelasgians are made to declare, that the Athenians drove them out from the soil of which they were the prior occupants, and which they cultivated so carefully as to arouse their envy, while the Athenians alleged that when, before the days of slavery, their children went to draw water at the Nine-Springs ('Εννεάκρουνοι), the Pelasgians of the district insulted them. What more likely than that, when the Hellenic part of the population was coercing the other portion of it into servitude, their resentment should occasionally find vent in rustic insolence to boys and maidens?

The doctrine thus propagated by Herodotus concerning Attica is even more strongly represented in Strabo as respects its Ionian character. Τὴν μὲν Ἰάδα τῇ παλαιᾷ Ἀτθίδι τὴν αὐτὴν φαμέν· καὶ γὰρ Ἴωνες ἐκαλοῦντο οἱ τότε Ἀττικοὶ, καὶ ἐκεῖθεν εἰσιν οἱ τὴν Ἀσίαν ἐποικήσαντες Ἴωνες, καὶ χρησάμενοι τῇ νῦν λεγομένῃ γλώττῃ Ἰάδι [g]. The poverty of their soil kept them, he adds, apart as of a different race (ἔθνος), and of a different speech (γλώττη).

And thus again Herodotus reports that the same letter which the Dorians called San, the Ionians called Sigma. Is not this more than a dialectic difference, and does it not indicate a deeper distinction of race?[h]

The connection of the Pelasgians with ancient Attica will receive further illustration from our inquiry hereafter into the general evidence of the later tradition respecting that race.

Egypt.

If we are to venture yet one step further back, and ask to what extraneous race and country do the Pelasgic

[g] B. viii. p. 333.   [h] Herod. i. 139.

ages of Greece appear particularly to refer us as their type, the answer, as it would seem, though it can only be given with reserve, must be, that Egypt and its people appear most nearly to supply the pattern. A variety of notes, indicative of affinity, are traceable at a variety of points where we find reason to suspect a Pelasgian character: particularly in Troy, and in the early Roman history, more or less in Hesiod and his school, and in certain parts of Greece. Many of these notes, and likewise the general character that they indicate, appear to belong to Egypt also.

The direct signs of connection between Egypt and Greece are far less palpable in Homer, than between Greece and Phœnicia. We have no account from him of Egyptians settled among the Greeks, or of Greeks among the Egyptians. The evidence of a trading intercourse between the two countries is confined to the case of the pseudo-Ulysses, who ventures thither from Crete under circumstances[i] which seem to show that it was hardly within the ordinary circle of Greek communications. He arrives indeed in five days, by the aid of a steady north-west wind: but a voyage of five days[k] across the open sea, which might be indefinitely prolonged by variation or want of wind, was highly formidable to a people whose only safety during their maritime enterprises lay in the power of hauling up their vessels whenever needful upon a beach. It was near twice the length of the voyage to Troy[l]. Hence we find that Menelaus was carried to Egypt not voluntarily, but by stress of weather: and Nestor speaks with horror of his crossing such an expanse, a passage that even the birds make but once a year[m]. If this be

[i] Od. xiv. 243.   [k] Ibid. 257.   [l] Il. ix. 363.
[m] Od. iii. 318.

II. *Ethnology.*

deemed inconsistent with the five days' passage, yet even inconsistency on this point in Homer would be a proof that the voyage to Egypt was in his time rare, strange, and mysterious to his countrymen, and so was dealt with freely by him as lying beyond experience and measurement.

There is nothing in Homer absolutely to contradict the opinion that Danaus was Egyptian; but neither is there anything which suffices conclusively to establish it. And if he considered the Egyptians to approach to the Pelasgian type, this may cast some slight doubt on the Egyptian origin of Danaus. The Poet certainly would not choose a Pelasgian name, unless fully naturalized, for one of the characteristic national designations of the Achæans. But he is too good a Greek to give us particular information about any foreign eminence within his fatherland. It seems, however, possible that in the name ἀπίη, given to Peloponnesus, there may lie a relation to the Egyptian Apis. Apis was the first of the four divine bulls of Egypt[n]; and the ox was the symbol of agriculture which, according to the tradition conveyed by Æschylus[o], Danaus introduced into the Peloponnesus.

The paucity of intercourse however between Greece and Egypt in the time of Homer does not put a negative on the supposition that there may have been early migration from the latter country to the former.

It has been questioned how far the ancient Egyptians were conversant with the art of navigation. The affirmative is fully argued by Mr. M'Culloch[p] in his commentaries on Adam Smith's Wealth of Nations. But it is plain that the Egyptians were not known to Homer as a nautical people. Not only do we never

[n] Döllinger Heidenthum und Judenthum vi. 136. p. 427.
[o] Inf. p. 176.   [p] Note xvii.

Egypt and the Pelasgians. 151

on any occasion hear of them in connection with the use of ships, but we hear of the plunder of their coast by pirates, when they confined themselves to resistance by land. This want of nautical genius agrees with all that we learn of them in Holy Scripture. And it places them in marked resemblance to the Pelasgian races generally: to the Arcadians[p]; to the Trojans; to the early Romans, who paid no serious attention to the creation of a fleet until the second Samnite War B. C. 311, or, as Niebuhr thinks, then only first had a fleet at all[q]: and again, to the landsmanlike spirit of Hesiod, who calls himself

οὔτε τι ναυτιλίης σεσοφισμένος, οὔτε τι νηῶν,

limits it entirely to a certain season, never was at sea except crossing from Aulis to Euboea, and considers the whole business of going to sea one that had better be avoided[r].

That with Homer the fabulous element enters into his view of the Egyptians seems plain, from his calling them the race of Paieon, in the same way as he calls the Phæacians the race of Neptune: and in some degree also from the place which he gives them in the wanderings of Menelaus, since they lay, like those of Ulysses, in the exterior and unascertained sphere of geography.

Proteus is called Αἰγύπτιος, but in all probability the meaning is Proteus of the Nile, which is the proper Αἴγυπτος in the masculine gender; while the country, derivatively called from it as the γῆ Αἴγυπτος, takes the feminine. We shall hereafter see how Proteus belongs to the circle of nautical and therefore Phœnician tradition[s]. That deity has upon him all the marks of the

[p] Il. ii. 614.
[q] Smith, Antiq. p. 331. Niebuhr, Hist. iii. 282.
[r] Works and Days 616 et seqq.

[s] Vid. inf. sect. 4. Nägelsbach (Hom. Theol. ii. 9.) may be consulted in an opposite sense.

outer and non-Grecian world. He is no less an admirable type of the τρωκτής, than a regular servant of Neptune, Ποσειδάωνος ὑποδμώς (Od. iv. 386). This connection with Neptune by no means makes him Greek: Neptune was the god of the θάλασσα, which extended beyond the circle of Greek experience, even to the borders of Ocean. We see set upon the whole of this adventure the same singular religious token as upon the remote adventures of Ulysses, namely this, that Menelaus passes beyond the ordinary charge of the Hellenic deities. The means of deliverance are pointed out to him, not by Minerva, but by Eidothea, daughter of Proteus himself, whose name, function, and relationship alike remind us that it was Ino Leucothea, daughter of the Phœnician Cadmus, who appeared to Ulysses for his deliverance, in a nearly similar border-zone of the marine territory lying between the world of fable and the world of experience; for the position of Egypt was in this respect like that of Phæacia. It would seem, then, as if Homer himself knew Egypt mainly through a Phœnician medium.

Of the Phœnician intercourse with that country we may safely rest assured, from their proximity, from their resort thither mentioned in Homer[t], and from the traces they left in Egypt itself.

It seems a probable conjecture that they had from a very early date a colony or factory in Egypt, by which they carried on their commerce with it. In the time of Herodotus, there was at Memphis a large and well-cared-for τέμενος or demesne of Proteus, whom the priests reported to be the successor of Sesostris on the Egyptian throne. This demesne was surrounded by the habitations of the 'Tyrian Phœnices,' and the whole

[t] Od. xiii. 272. xiv. 228.

plain in which it stood was called the Τυρίων στρατόπεδον. There is another tradition in Herodotus, according to which the Phœnicians furnished Egypt with the fleet, which in the time of Necho circumnavigated Africa[u].

Homer affords us little or no direct evidence of a connection between the religion of Greece and an Egyptian origin, to which Herodotus conceived it to be referable; but yet it may very well be the case, that Egypt was the fountain-head of many traditions which were carried by the Phœnicians into Greece. In Homer, for example, we find marks that seem to connect Dionysus with Phœnicia: but the Phœnicians may have become acquainted with him in Egypt, where Diodorus[x] reports that Osiris was held to be his original. There are two marks, however, of Egyptian influence, which seem to be more deeply traced. One is the extraordinary sacredness attached to the oxen of the Sun. The other, the apparent relation between the Egyptian Neith and the Athene of Attica, taken in conjunction with the Pelasgian character of the district[y]. But certainly our positive information from Homer respecting the Egyptians may be summed up in very brief compass. They would appear to have been peaceful, rich, and prosperous: highly skilled in agriculture, and also in medicine, if we are not rather to understand by this that they knew the use of opium, which might readily draw fervid eulogiums from a race not instructed in its properties. But the testimony to their agricultural excellence cannot be mistaken. Twice their fields are. mentioned, and both times as περικάλλεες ἀγροί: in exact correspondence with the tradition which we find subsisting in Attica respecting those fields which were tilled by the

[u] Herod. iv. 42.   [x] i. 13.   [y] Inf. Religion and Morals, sect. iii.

Pelasgians[y]. And this case of the Egyptians is the only one throughout the Poems in which Homer bestows commendation upon tillage. Again, they fought bravely when attacked[z]. We find also the name Ægyptius naturalized in Ithaca. Lastly, they appear to have been hospitable to strangers, and placable to enemies[a]. This is a faint outline: but all its features appear to be in harmony with those of the Pelasgian race.

It is worthy of remark, that the Lotophagi visited by Ulysses correspond very much with the Egyptians, such as Homer conceived them. Locally, they belonged to the Egyptian quarter of the globe: they received the companions of Ulysses with kindness[b]; and they gave them to eat of the lotus, which appears in its essential and remarkable properties exactly to correspond with the $νήπενθες$[c] that Helen had obtained from Egypt. As every figure of the Phœnician traditions, except perhaps Æolus, is essentially either hard, or cruel, or deceitful, even so, whether on account of neighbourhood or otherwise, it seems to have been the poet's intention to impress the less energetic but more kindly character of the Egyptians on this particular people, which perhaps he conceived to be allied to them.

There is indeed one suggestive passage of the Odyssey from which it is open to us to conjecture that there was more of substantive relation between Greece and Egypt than Homer's purpose as a national poet led him fully to disclose. Menelaus, when he returns to Egypt after hearing from Proteus of the death of Agamemnon, raises in Egypt a mound in honour of his brother[d], $ἵν'$ $ἄσβεστον$ $κλέος$ $εἴη$. But this mound could not contribute to the glory of the slain king, unless Greece and its inhabitants were tolerably well known in Egypt.

[y] Sup. p. 148. [z] Od. xiv. 271. [a] Od. v. 278–86.
[b] Ibid. ix. 84, 94. [c] Ibid. iv. 220. [d] Ibid. 584.

Upon the whole, the evidence of the Homeric poems does not correspond with those later traditions which refer principally to Egypt as the origin of what is Greek. In considering this subject, we ought indeed to bear in mind Homer's systematic silence as to the channels by which foreign influences found their way into Greece. For it throws us entirely upon such indirect evidence as he may (so to speak) involuntarily afford. And we must also recollect firstly that the Egyptian influence, whatever it may have been, may perhaps have operated more in the Pelasgian period, than in that Achæan age to which the representations of Homer belong. Secondly, that much may have reached Greece, as to religion or otherwise, in a Phœnician dress, which the Phœnicians themselves may have derived from Egypt.

There are other features, well known from all history to be Egyptian, though not traced for them by the hand of Homer, which tend strongly to confirm their relationship to the Pelasgian race, partly as it is delineated in the Homeric outlines, and partly as it is known from later tradition. One of these points is the comparatively hard and unimaginative character of its mythology, conforming to that of the race. It is interesting to notice how the Greeks, with their fine sense of beauty, got rid at once, in whatever they derived from Egypt, of the mythological deformities of gods incarnate in beasts, and threw them into the shapes of more graceful fable.

A second point of Pelasgian resemblance is the strong ritual and sacerdotal development of religion. A third is the want of the political energies which build and maintain extensive Empire. With all its wealth, and its early civilization, this opulent state could never make acquisitions beyond its own border, and has usually been in subordination to some more masculine Power. A fourth is, the early use of solid masonry in public edifices. The remains in Greece and Italy which are referred to the Pelasgians are indeed of much smaller dimensions than those of Egypt: but the Pelasgians of these countries, so far as we know, had not time to attain any higher political organization than that of small communities, with comparatively contracted means of commanding labour. A fifth is their wealth itself, which causes Egyptian Thebes to be celebrated both in the Iliad and in the Odyssey, perhaps the only case in which the poet has thus repeated himself, Il. ix. 381, and Od. iv. 126.

Lastly, the reputed derivation of the oracle at Dodona from Egypt harmonises with the Pelasgian character assigned to that seat of worship by Homer. The tradition to this effect reported by Herodotus[e] was Greek, and not Egyptian: it was obtained by him on the spot: and if Homer's countrymen partook of the poet's reserve, and his dislike of assigning a foreign source to anything established in Greece, a presumption arises that this particular statement would not have been made, had it not rested on a respectable course of traditionary authority.

It may however be asked, if the Pelasgians are to be regarded as Greeks, and as the base of the Greek nation, and if Homer was familiar with their name and position in that character, how happens it that he never calls the Greeks Pelasgians, as he calls them Danaans, Argeians, and Achæans, and never even gives us in the

[e] Herod. ii. 54. According to the Egyptian tradition there reported, the Phœnicians carried into Greece the priestess who founded the Dodonæan oracle. This again leads us to view the Phœnicians as the chief medium of intercourse between Egypt and Greece.

Iliad a Pelasgian race or tribe by name as numbered among the Greeks?

Now it is not a sufficient answer to say, that the Pelasgian race and name were falling under eclipse in the age of Homer; for we shall see reason hereafter to suppose that the appellations of Danaan and Argeian were likewise (so to speak) preterite, though not yet obsolete, appellations; still Homer employs them freely.

Their case is essentially different, however, as we shall find, from that of the Pelasgians, since those two names do not imply either any blood different from that of the Achæan or properly Greek body, or any particular race which had supplied an element in its composition: one of these the Pelasgian name certainly does imply. Those names too, without doubt, would not be used, unless they shed glory on the Greeks: the Pelasgian name could have no such treasure to dispense.

It should, however, here be observed, that an examination presently to be made of the force of the Argeian name will help us to account for the disappearance from Greece of the Pelasgian name, which it may perhaps have supplanted.

Let me observe, that if the Pelasgians did, in point of fact, supply an element to the Greek nationality, which had, while still remaining perceptibly distinct, become politically subordinate in Homer's time, that is precisely the case in which he would be sure not to apply the name to the Greeks at large, nor to any Greek state, as its application could not under such circumstances be popular. His non-employment of it, therefore, for Greeks is *pro tanto* a confirmation to the general argument of these pages.

If, again, there were a distinct people of Pelasgians

among the Trojan auxiliaries, and on the Greek side a large but subordinate Pelasgic element, this would be ample reason both for his naming the Pelasgic allies of the Trojans, with a view to the truth of his recital, and for his not using the Pelasgic name in connection with the Greeks; for in no instance has he placed branches of the same race or tribe on both sides in the struggle. Glaucus and Sarpedon, the transplanted Æolids, cannot be considered as exceptions, first, from the old date of their Greek extraction: and secondly, because they are individuals, whereas we now speak of tribes and races. The name, too, was more suited to the unmixed Pelasgians of the Trojan alliance, than to a people, among whom it had grown pale beneath the greater splendour of famous dynasties and of more energetic tribes.

The application of this reasoning to the Pelasgi is fortified by its being applicable to other Homeric names.

It can hardly be doubted that the name Θρῆξ is akin to Τραχὶν and τρῆχυς[f], that it means a highlander, or inhabitant of a rough and mountainous country, and that it included the inhabitants of territories clearly Greek. This extended signification of the term explains the assertion of Herodotus[g], that the Thracians were the most numerous of all nations, after the Indians.

Now Homer makes Thamyris the Bard a Thracian; yet it is clear from his having to do with the Muses, and from the geographical points with which Homer connects his name, that he must be a Greek[h]. They are, Δώριον in the dominions of Pylos, where he met his calamity, and the Œchalia of Eurytus in Thessaly, from whence he was making his journey[i]. Strabo tells us

[f] Mure, Lit. Greece, vol. i. p. 153 n.   [g] Herod. v. 2.   [h] Il. ii. 594–600.   [i] Il. ii. 730.

that Pieria and Olympus were anciently Thracian[k], and moreover, that the Thracians of Bœotia consecrated Helicon to the Muses. Orpheus, Musæus, Eumolpus, were held to be Thracians by tradition, yet it also made them write in Greek. I think we may trace this descriptive character of the name Θρῆκες, and its not yet having acquired fully the force of a proper name with Homer, in his employment of it as an adjective, and not a substantive. It is very frequently joined in the poems with the affix ἄνδρες, which he does not employ with such proper names as are in familiar and established use, such as Danaan, Argive, or Achæan. He says Achæan or Danaan heroes, but never joins the names to the simple predicate 'men.' When he says Ἀχαιὸς ἄνηρ, it is with a different force; it is in pointing out an individual among a multitude. Indeed in Homer it is not Θρῇξ but Θρηίκιος which means Thracian, of or belonging to the country called Thrace, Θρῄκη. There is then sufficient evidence that Greeks of the highlands might be Thraces; and there may very probably have been whole tribes so called among the Greeks. Yet we never have Thracians named by Homer on the Greek side, while on the Trojan side they appear as supplying no less than two contingents of allies: one in the Catalogue, and another which had just arrived at the period of the Δολώνεια [l].

These two appear to be entirely distinct tribes: because no connection is mentioned between them; because the first contingent is described as being composed not of all the Thracians, but of all the Thracians within the Hellespont: and lastly, because the new comers have their own βασιλεὺς with them, as the first contin-

---

[k] Strabo x. p. 471. [l] Il. ii. 844, and x. 434.

gent had its leaders, Acamas and Peirous. The Hellespont meant here seems to be the strait, because it is ἀγάρροος. And it is therefore possible, that while the first contingent was supplied by the nearer tribes, the second may have been composed of those Thracians who lay nearer the Greek border.

Notwithstanding that Mars, who is so inseparably associated with Thrace, fights on the Trojan side, we have no evidence from Homer which would warrant the assumption that he intended to connect the Thracians more intimately with the Pelasgians than with the Hellenes. It may be that the poet's ethnical knowledge failed him. The wavering of Mars seems to indicate a corresponding uncertainty in his own mind. Perhaps with both the Thracian and Pelasgian names it was the breadth of their range that constituted the difficulty. Some part of Thrace is with him ἐριβώλαξ[1]; it is the part from which the first contingent came, as the son of Peirous belonged to it. And that part is less mountainous than the quarter which I have presumed may have supplied the contingent of Rhesus. The epithet is the very same as is applied to the Pelasgian Larissa[m]: and the Larissan Pelasgians are placed next to the first Thracian contingent in the Trojan Catalogue.

The most probable supposition for Thracians as well as Pelasgians is, that they had affinities in both directions; that they existed among the Greeks diffusively, and were absorbed in names of greater splendour: but that on the Trojan side they still had distinct national existence, and therefore they are named on that side, while to avoid confusion silence is studiously maintained about them on the other. The whole race, says Grote, present a character more Asiatic than European[n].

[1] Il. xx. 485.   [m] Il. ii. 841.   [n] Hist. Greece, iv. 28.

Many other races have been recorded in the later traditions as having in pre-historic times inhabited various parts of Greece. Such are Temnices, Aones, Hyantes, Teleboi. Of these Homer makes no mention. But there are two other races whom he names, the Leleges and Caucones, and with respect to whom Strabo[o] has affirmed, that they were extensively diffused over Greece as well as over Asia Minor.

Homer has proceeded, with respect to the Caucones, exactly in the same way as with respect to the Pelasgi In the Iliad he names them[p] among the Trojan allies, and is wholly silent about them in dealing with the Greek races. But in the Odyssey, where he had no national distinctions to keep in view, he names them as a people apparently Greek, and dwelling on the western side of Greece. The pseudo-Mentor is going among them on business, to obtain payment of a debt[q]: and the manner in which they are mentioned, without explanation, shows that the name must have been familiar to Nestor and the other persons addressed. Probably therefore they were a neighbouring tribe: certainly a Greek tribe, for we do not find proof that the Homeric Greeks carried on commerce except with their own race.

The poet names them with a laudatory epithet: they are the Καύκωνες μεγάθυμοι. This may remind us of his bounty in the same kind to the Pelasgians: and it seems as though he had had a reverence for the remains of the ancient possessors of the country.

We have abundant signs of the Leleges on the Trojan side in the war. In the Tenth Book they appear as a contingent: but besides this, Priam had

[o] Strabo viii. 7. p. 321, 2.   [p] Il. x. 429; xx. 329.
[q] Od. iii. 366.

M

II. Ethnology.

for one of his wives Laothee, daughter of Altes, king of the Lelegians, who are here called Φιλοπτόλεμοι[r]. What is more important, we find the expressions Λέλεγες καὶ Τρῶες[s] used together in such a way, as implies the wide extension of the former as a race. In the Twentieth Iliad, Æneas in speaking of Achilles refers to his former escape from the great warrior. He fought, says Æneas, under the auspices of Minerva: who shed light before him, and bid him slay Lelegians and Trojans,

ἠδ' ἐκέλευεν
ἔγχεϊ χαλκείῳ Λέλεγας καὶ Τρῶας ἐναίρειν.

The Trojan force was in two main portions, each with many subdivisions: first, the army of Priam, with those of his kindred or subordinate princes: and, secondly, the allies, with their numerous and widely dispersed races. In the passage just quoted, the word *Leleges* must either mean the great body of allies, or else it must, conjointly with *Troes*, signify the whole mass of what we may call the indigenous troops. Now the former is highly improbable. Such differences as are implied in the combination of Thracians, Lycians, and Pelasgians, could not well be, and nowhere else are comprehended by Homer under a single name as one race or nation, though the Lycians, on account of their excellence, are sometimes[t] taken to represent the whole body of the allies. And again, if the Leleges meant the whole body of allies, the Pelasgians would appear as a branch of them, which is contrary to all evidence and likelihood. If then the two words together represent those indigenous troops, as contradistinguished from the allies, who were arrayed in the five divisions that are enumerated in vv. 816–39 of the

[r] Il. xxi. 85.   [s] Il. xx. 96.   [t] Inf. p. 182.

Second book, the question is, how is the sense to be distributed between them. And here there is not much room for doubt. The name Τρῶες had been assumed four generations before the war from King Tros, and was therefore a political or dynastic name, not a name of race. It most probably therefore indicates either the inhabitants of Priam's own city and immediate dominions, or else the ruling race, who held power here, as elsewhere, among a subject population. In either case we must conclude that the word Leleges is meant to indicate the blood, and also the blood-name (so to speak) of the bulk of the population through a considerable tract of country: and it will be observed that in the fourth and fifth of the divisions[u] in the Trojan Catalogue Homer specifies no blood-name or name of race whatever.

This being so, we find an important light cast upon the meaning of the word Leleges. As we proceed with these inquiries, we shall find accumulating evidence of the Pelasgianism of the mass of the population on the Trojan side: and thus when it appears that that mass or a very great part of it was Lelegian, it also appears probable that the Leleges were at least akin to the Pelasgians, though some have taken them to be distinct[v].

In answer therefore to the question, who were these Caucones and these Leleges, while we are deficient in the means of detailed and particular reply, we may, I think, fall back with tolerable security upon the words used by Bishop Thirlwall in closing an ethnological survey:

" The review we have just taken of the Pelasgian settlements in Greece appears inevitably to lead to the

[u] Il. ii. 828–39. [v] Höck's Creta, ii. p. 7.

conclusion that the name Pelasgians was a general one, like that of Saxons, Franks, or Alemanni : but that each of the Pelasgian tribes had also one peculiar to itself[x].'

Upon our finding, as we find, the Pelasgian name in certain apparent relations with others, such as Leleges and Caucones, it appears more reasonable to presume a relationship between them, than the reverse: for nothing can be more improbable than the simultaneous presence at that early period of a multitude of races, radically distinct from each other, and yet diffused intermixedly over the same country upon equal terms, and if there was a relationship, it would most probably be that of subdivision, under which Leleges and Caucones might be branches of the widely spread Pelasgian family.

This opinion is supported, not only by presumptions, but by much indirect evidence. It is indisputable that various names were applied, by the custom of the Homeric age, to the same people, and at the same period. The poet calls the inhabitants of Elis both Elians and Epeans. The people of Ithaca are Ithacesians ('Ιθακήσιοι), but they are also 'Αχαιοί[y], and in the Catalogue they are included under the Cephallenians[z]. The Dolopians in the speech of Phœnix[a] are included under the Phthians; and are also within the scope of the other names applied by the Catalogue to the followers of Achilles, who were called by the name of Myrmidons, or of Hellens, or of Achæans. Of these the first seems to be the denomination, which the ruling race of that particular district had brought with it into the country. The third probably belongs to the Myrmidons, as members of that tribe, of Hellic origin, which

[x] Thirlwall's Hist. of Greece, Ch. ii. Vol. i. p. 41. 12mo.   [y] Od. passim.   [z] Il. ii. 631.
[a] Il. ix. 184, and xvi. 196.

at the time predominated in Greece generally. The second, as we shall find, was the common name for all Greek tribes of that origin, and was the name which ultimately gained a complete ascendancy in the country. Of the five nations of Crete in the Seventeenth Odyssey[b], either all or several are probably included in the Κρῆτες of the Second Iliad[c]. Nay, we may now declare it to be at least highly probable[d], that the Ionian name was a sub-designation of the Pelasgians. Thus we have abundant instances of plurality in the designations of tribes. On the whole, we shall do best to assume that the names in question of Leleges and Caucones indicated Pelasgian subdivision. The inquiry is, however, one of ethnical antiquarianism only; these names are historically insignificant, for, apart from the Pelasgian, they carry no distinctive character or special function in reference to Greece.

[b] Od. xix. 175.   [c] Il. ii. 645.
[d] See supr. p. 126.

Erratum.—I have inadvertently, in p. 103, rendered κητώεσσαν 'full of wild beasts.' It ought to have been translated 'deep-sunken.' See Buttmann's Lexilogus, *in voc.*

SECT. III.

Pelasgians continued: and certain States naturalised or akin to Greece.

    a. Crete.   *b.* Lycia.   *c.* Cyprus.

This appears to be the place for a more full consideration of the testimony of Homer with respect to, probably, the greatest character of early Greek history, and one who cannot be omitted in any inquiry concerning the early Pelasgians of Greece: in as much as they stand in a direct Homeric relation to Crete, of which he was the king.

In the poems of Homer, Minos appears to stand forth as the first great and fixed point of Greek nationality and civilization. He is not indeed so remote from the period of Homer himself as others, even as other Europeans, whom the poet mentions, and whom he connects by genealogy with the Trojan period, particularly the Æolids. But the peculiarities meeting in his case, as compared with most of them, are these:

1. That he is expressly traced upwards as well as downwards.

2. That he is connected with a fixed place as its sovereign.

3. That so much is either recounted or suggested of his character and acts.

4. That the Homeric traditions as to Minos are so remarkably supported from without.

Minos is mentioned, and somewhat largely, in no less than six different passages of the Iliad and Odyssey. Homer has given us a much fuller idea of him, than of the more popular hero Hercules, although he is not named in nearly so many passages; and it is singular, that the more ancient of the two personages is also by much the more historical. Again, the poet has told us more about Minos, although he is of foreign extraction, than he has said about all the rest of the older Greek heroes put together. Of Theseus, Pirithous, Castor, Pollux, Meleager, Perseus, Jason, and the rest, his notices are very few and meagre. In dealing with Homer, I should quote even this fact of the greater amount of his references, which in the case of most other poets would be immaterial, as a strong presumption of the superior historical importance of the person concerned.

Minos, according to Homer, had Jupiter for his father, a Phœnician damsel for his mother, and Rhadamanthus for his younger brother. The name[e] of his mother is not recorded, but Jupiter calls her far-famed. This fame, if due to her beauty, would probably have kept her name alive; but as it has not been preserved, it is more probably a reflection from the subsequent greatness of her son.

The story thus far appears probably to indicate that Minos was a Phœnician by birth, but without a known ancestry, and raised into celebrity by his own energies and achievements.

The mode, by which he rose to fame, was by the government of men and the foundation of civil institutions. At nine years old he received, such is the legend, revelations from Jupiter,[f] and reigned, in the great or mighty city ($\mu\epsilon\gamma\acute{a}\lambda\eta$ $\pi\acute{o}\lambda\iota\varsigma$) of Cnossus, over

[e] Il. xiv. 321. [f] Od. xix. 178.

Crete: such was the form, copied by the politic legislator of Rome, in which a title to veneration was secured for his laws. No other city, besides this capital, is described in Homer by the epithet μεγάλη, or by any equivalent word.

A further vivid mark of his political greatness is afforded us by that passage in the Odyssey, which exhibits him not simply as exercising in the world beneath[g] the mere office of a judge, but rather as discharging there a judicial function in virtue of his sovereignty. Such is the force of the word θεμιστεύειν,[h] which signifies rather to give law than to administer it: or, at least, to exercise the function of a king rather than of a judge[i] (ἴστωρ). He is described as still the illustrious son of Jupiter, Διὸς ἀγλαὸς υἱός. Even there he appears not as one of the suffering or bewildered inhabitants of that lower world, but in the exercise of power as an actual ruler among the spirits of the departed;

οἱ δέ μιν ἀμφὶ δίκας εἴροντο ἄνακτα.

He only is invested with any character of this kind. Every other apparition below is either in actual suffering, or gloomy and depressed.

The epithet ὀλοόφρων, applied to Minos in an earlier passage of the Νεκυία, might perhaps convey the same idea as Virgil has rendered by his *durissima* regna,[k] in the description of Rhadamanthus: and we may also compare the address of Menelaus in the Third Iliad to Jupiter,

Ζεῦ πάτερ οὔτις σεῖο θεῶν ὀλοώτερος ἄλλος.[l]

A reasonable construction would refer the word to the

---

[g] Od. xi. 568–71.
[h] Cf. Il. i. 238. ii. 205.
[i] Il. xviii. 501. xxiii. 436.
[k] Æn. vi. 566.
[l] Il. iii. 365.

commercial character of the Phœnician people, at once cunning and daring[m]; and there is much probability in the opinion of Höck, who interprets the word as meaning 'exactor of tribute,' or as alluding to the exaction by Minos of a tribute from Attica[n]. On this we shall shortly have to enlarge.

As to the family and kingdom of Minos, we should gather in the first place from Homer, that Crete had under him been preeminent in power. He was king of the island (Κρήτη ἐπίουρος)[o], and he reigned, at the age of nine years only (ἐννέωρος βασίλευε), in Cnossus over the five nations. The island had ninety, or in the rounder numbers, an hundred cities. Two generations had passed since Minos; Idomeneus his grandson did not apparently reign, like Minos himself, over the whole of it: for if this had been the case, it is very improbable, presuming that we may judge by the analogies which the order of the army in general supplies, that Meriones would have been made his associate, which in some manner he is, in the command; and again, the feigned story of Ulysses in the Odyssey, though it introduces Idomeneus, does not represent him as king of the whole island, but rather implies that his pretended brother, Æthon, also exercised a sovereignty there[p]. But even then the Cretan contingent, although the towns named as supplying it do not extend over the whole island[q], amounted to eighty ships, and thus exceeded any other, except those of Agamemnon and of Nestor. And then, when Minos had so long been dead, it was still the marked and special distinction of

[m] Nägelsbach, Homerische Théologie, p. 83.; and Vid. inf. sect. iv. pp. 120, 124.
[n] Höck's Creta, ii. 142, n.
[o] Il. xiii. 450. Od. xix. 179.
[p] Od. xix. 181-98.
[q] Höck's Creta, ii. 182.

the country, that it was the seat of his race. So Eumæus, describing the disguised stranger to Penelope, says[r],

φησὶ δ' Ὀδυσσῆος ξεῖνος πατρώϊος εἶναι,
Κρήτῃ ναιετάων, ὅθι Μίνωος γένος ἐστίν.

A passage which perhaps testifies that the family of Minos had been ξεῖνοι to the predecessors of Ulysses.

But perhaps there is no country in Greece which Homer so rarely mentions without a laudatory epithet. Though (περίρρυτος) sea-girt, it is not with him an island: it is Κρήτη γαῖα, Κρήτη εὐρεῖα, Κρήτη ἑκατόμπολις[s], and in the principal description, Homer exalts it more highly, I think, than any other territory,

Κρήτη τις γαῖ' ἐστὶ, μέσῳ ἐνὶ οἴνοπι πόντῳ
καλὴ καὶ πίειρα, περίρρυτος· ἐν δ' ἄνθρωποι
πολλοὶ, ἀπειρέσιοι, καὶ ἐννήκοντα πόληες[t].

If it should be thought that the evidence to the character of Minos as a lawgiver is slight, we must call to mind that even the word *law* is not found in Homer. The term afterwards used by the Greeks to express what we mean by a law, νόμος, only occurs with Homer in a sense quite different. He tells us of nothing more determinate than δίκαι and θέμιστες. But relatively to his pictures of other governors, the legislatorial character of Minos is as strongly marked as that of Numa is in Livy, relatively to other kings of Rome.

In conclusion, as to the region of Crete, it was inhabited by five races: namely,

1. Ἀχαιοί.   2. Ἐτεοκρῆτες.   3. Κυδῶνες.
4. Δωριέες.   5. Πελασγοί.

Of these the Achæans and Dorians are evidently Greek.

[r] Od. xvii. 523.   [s] Od. xiv. 199. Il. xiii. 453. Il. ii. 649.
[t] Od. xix. 172.

We are now examining at large the title of the Pelasgi to the same character. With respect to the Cydones, we may draw an inference from the facts, that they lived (Od. iii. 292), on a Cretan river Iardanus, and that this was also the name of a river of Peloponnesus (Il. vii. 133). I should even hold that this stream, which is not identified, was most probably in Arcadia: first, because in the contest with the Hellic tribes of Pylos, the Arcadians as Pelasgians would be on the defensive, and would therefore fight on their own ground: secondly, because the battle was on the ὠκύροος Κελάδων. These words are most suitable to some mountain feeder of the Iardanus, with its precipitate descent, rather than to the usually more peaceful course of a river near the sea, especially near the sea coast of sandy Pylus, which reached to the Alpheus[u]. This supposition respecting the Celadon will also best account for what otherwise seems singular; namely, that the battle was at once on the Celadon, and also about the Iardanus (Ἰαρδάνου ἀμφὶ ῥέεθρα[v]). Again, the battle was between Arcadians and Pylians, and therefore, from the relative situation of the territories, was probably on some Arcadian feeder of the Alpheus, lying far inland. Now if Iardanus was an Arcadian river, and if the Arcadians were Pelasgi, it leads to a presumption that the Cydonians of Crete, who dwelt upon an Iardanus, were Pelasgian also.

There remain the Ἐτεοκρῆτες, apparently so called, to distinguish them as indigenous from all the other four nations, who were ἐπήλυδες, or immigrant. This is curious, because it refers us elsewhere for the origin of the Pelasgi. It is the only case in which we hear of any thing anterior to them, upon the soils which they occupied. Lastly, Crete lay between Greece and Cy-

[u] Il. xi. 712. [v] Il. vii. 133, 5.

prus, and Cyprus is clearly indicated in the Odyssey as on the route to Egypt[w].

But we hear also of Rhadamanthus as the brother of Minos, of Deucalion as his son, and of Ariadne as his daughter[x]. And the notices of these personages in Homer all tend to magnify our conception of his power and his connections.

Theseus, who is glorified by Nestor as a first rate hero[y], and described as a most famous child of the gods[z], whom both Homer, and also the later legends connect with Attica, marries Ariadne, who dies on her way to Athens[a]. The marriages of Homer were generally contracted among much nearer neighbours. This more distant connection cannot, I think, but be taken as indicating the extended relations connected with the sovereignty of Minos and his exalted position.

The genealogy of Idomeneus runs thus[b]; 'Jupiter begot Minos, ruler of Crete. Minos begot a distinguished son, Deucalion. Deucalion begot me, a ruler over numerous subjects in broad Crete.'

Here it is to be remarked,

1. That while Minos and Idomeneus, the first and third generations, are described as ruling in Crete, Deucalion of the second is not so described.

2. That Idomeneus is nowhere described as having succeeded to the throne of his grandfather Minos, but only as being a ruler in Crete: and that, as we have seen, from the qualified conjunction of Meriones with him in the command, perhaps also from the limited range of the Cretan towns in the Catalogue, there arises a positive presumption that he had succeeded

[w] Od. xvii. 442.
[x] Od. xi. 321.
[y] Il. i. 260–5.
[z] Od. xi. 631.
[a] Ibid. 322–5.
[b] Il. xiii. 450–3.

only to a portion of the ancient preeminence and power of his ancestor.

Now there is no direct evidence in Homer connecting Deucalion with Thessaly. The later tradition, however, places him there: and this tradition may probably claim an authority as old as that of Hesiod. A fragment of that poet [c], with the text partially corrupt, speaks of Locrus, leader of the Leleges, as among those whom Jupiter raised from the earth for Deucalion. This reference to Locrus immediately suggests the name of the Locrian race, and so carries us into the immediate neighbourhood of Thessaly; and the general purport of the words is to express something a little like the later tradition about Deucalion, which had that country for its scene. Combining this with the negative evidence afforded by the Homeric text, we thus find established a communication seemingly direct between Crete under Minos, and Thessaly, to which country we have already found it probable that Deucalion immigrated, and where he may have reigned.

The usual statement is, that the name Deucalion was common to two different persons, one the son of Minos, and the other the king of Thessaly. But we must be upon our guard against the device of the later Greek writers, who at once unravelled the accumulated intricacies that had gradually gathered about their traditions, and enlarged the stock of material for pampering vanity, and exciting the imagination, by multiplying the personages of the early legends. As regards the case now before us; the tradition, which makes Hellen son of the latter of these Deucalions, would certainly make him considerably older than he could be if a

[c] Fragm. xi. Strabo vii. p. 332.

son of Minos. It must be admitted, that Homer repeats the name of Deucalion, for a Trojan so called is slain by Achilles in Il. xx. 478. It has pleased the fancy of the poet there to use the names of a number of dead heroes to distinguish the warriors who fell like sheep under the sword of the terrible Achilles: we find among them a Dardanus, a Tros, and a Moulius; and it is so little Homer's practice to use names without a peculiar meaning, that we may conjecture he has done it, in preference to letting Achilles slaughter a crowd of ignoble persons, in order that in every thing his Protagonist might be distinguished from other men. But the poet seems to take particular care to prevent any confusion as to his great Greek, and indeed as to all his great living, personages. I am not aware of more than one single passage in the Iliad [d], among the multitude in which one or other of the Ajaxes is named, where there can be a doubt which of the two is meant. It is exceedingly unlikely that if a separate Deucalion of Thessaly had been known to Homer, he should not have distinguished him from the Deucalion of Crete. This unlikelihood mounts to incredibility, when we remember (1) that this other Deucalion of Thessaly is nothing less than the asserted root of the whole Hellenic stock, and (2) that the poet repeatedly uses the patronymic Deucalides as an individual appellation for Idomeneus, whereas the adverse supposition would make all the Achæans alike Δευκαλίδαι. We may therefore safely conclude at least, that Homer knew of no Deucalion other than the son of Minos.

We come now to Rhadamanthus, who is thrice mentioned by Homer. Once[e], as born of the same parents with Minos[f]. Once, as enjoying like him honours from

[d] Il. xiii. 681.   [e] Il. xiv. 322.   [f] Od. iv. 564.

Jupiter beyond the term of our ordinary human life: for he is placed amidst the calm and comforts of the Elysian plain. The third passage is remarkable. It is where Alcinous[g] promises Ulysses conveyance to his home, even should it be farther than Euboea, which the Phæacian mariners consider to be their farthest known point of distance, and whither they had conveyed Rhadamanthus,

ἐποψόμενον Τίτυον, Γαιήιον υἱόν·

on his way to visit, or inspect, or look after, Tityus. This Tityus we find in the νεκυία suffering torture for having attempted violence upon Latona[h], as she was proceeding towards Pytho, through Panopeus. Panopeus was a place in Phocis, on the borders of Boeotia, and on the line of any one journeying between Delos and Delphi.

There is in this legend the geographical indistinctness, and even confusion, which we commonly find where Homer dealt with places lying in the least beyond the range of his own experience or that of his hearers, as was the case with Phæacia. If Tityus was in Panopeus, the proper way to carry Rhadamanthus was by the Corinthian gulf. But from various points in the geography of the Odyssey, it may, in my opinion, be gathered, that Homer had an idea, quite vague and indeterminate as to distance, of a connection by sea between the north of the Adriatic, and the north of the Ægean, either directly, or from the sea of Marmora: and it suited his representation of the Phæacians, and best maintained their as it were aerial character, to give them an unknown rather than a known route. However that might be, if we look into the legend in order to conjecture its historic

[g] Od. vii. 317–26.   [h] Od. xi. 580.

II. *Ethnology.*

basis, it appears to suggest the inferences which follow:

1. That according to tradition, the empire or supremacy of Minos, which may in some points have resembled that afterwards held by Agamemnon, embraced both Corcyra and likewise middle Greece, where Panopeus and Pytho or Delphi lay.

We must, however, presume the empire of Minos to have been in great part insular. There were contemporary kingdoms on the mainland, which give no sign of dependence upon it.

2. That the Phæacians acted as subjects of Minos in carrying Rhadamanthus by sea from one part of the dominions of that king to another.

3. That Rhadamanthus went to punish Tityus as an offender within the realm of Minos, and did this on the part and in lieu of Minos himself.

4. That though he was not Greek by birth, his person, and family, and empire were all Greek in the view of Homer.

This conjectural interpretation of the legend derives support from many quarters.

It is in thorough harmony, as to the extended rule of Minos, with the Eleventh Odyssey, which represents Minos as acting in the capacity of a sovereign in the shades below; which also exhibits, as suffering judicially the punishments that he awarded, offenders connected with various portions of Greek territory, and among them this very Tityus.

It is now time to look to the post-Homeric traditions.

The extent of the sway of Minos is supported by the tradition of Pelasgus, in the Supplices of Æschylus[i], which represents the whole country from (probably)

[i] Æsch. Suppl. 262.

Macedonia to the extreme south of the peninsula, as having been formerly under one and the same sway. The empire of Minos may have been magnified into this tradition.

The authority of Thucydides is available for the following points[i]:—

1. That Minos was the earliest known possessor of maritime power: thus harmonising with the hypothesis that the Phæacians, whose great distinction was in their nautical character, were acting as his subjects when they carried Rhadamanthus.

2. That his power extended over the Grecian sea, or Ægean ('Ελληνικὴ θάλασσα) generally (ἐπὶ πλεῖστον); thus indicating a great extent of sway.

3. That he appointed his children to govern his dominions on his behalf (τοὺς ἑαυτοῦ παῖδας ἡγεμόνας ἐγκαταστήσας): which supports the idea that his brother Rhadamanthus may have acted for him at a distance.

4. That he drove the Carians out of the islands of the Ægean. This statement receives remarkable confirmation from Homer, who makes the islands up to the very coast of Caria contributors to the force of the Greek army: while Lesbos and others, situated farther north, and more distant from Crete, appear to have been, like Caria itself, in the Trojan interest.

In the Minos ascribed to Plato[k] we find the tradition of his direct relations with Attica, which were well known to the theatre. This supports the notice in Homer of the marriage contracted between Theseus and his daughter Ariadne.

Aristotle[l], like Thucydides, asserts the maritime power of Minos and his sovereignty over the islands,

---

[i] Thucyd. i. 4.   [k] Minos, 16, 17.   [l] Pol. ii. 10. 4.

and adds, that he lost or ended his life in the course of an expedition to conquer Sicily[m].

Herodotus[n], like Thucydides, treats Minos as the first known sovereign who had been powerful by sea, He states, that Minos expelled his brother Sarpedon from Crete, and that Sarpedon with his adherents colonised Lycia, which was governed, down to the time of the historian himself, by laws partly Cretan[o]: and he also delivers the tradition that Minos was slain in an expedition against Sicily at Camicus, afterwards Agrigentum. A town bearing his name remained long after in the island.

Euripides laid the scene of his Rhadamanthus in Bœotia: and a Cretan colony is said to have established the Tilphosian temple there[p]. Höck finds traces of a marked connection between Crete and that district[q].

More important, however, than any isolated facts are the resemblances of the Lacedemonian and Cretan politics, noticed by Aristotle[r], in combination with the admission always made by the Lacedæmonians, that their lawgiver Lycurgus initiated the Cretan institutions[s], and with the universal Greek tradition that in Crete, first of all parts of Greece, laws and a regular polity had been established by Minos. Again, in the Dialogue printed among the works of Plato, the author of it seeks to establish the fundamental idea of law: puts aside the injurious statements of the tragedians who represented Minos as a tyrant, declares his laws to have been the oldest and the best in Greece, and the

[m] For a lucid sketch of the position of Minos as defined by tradition, see Thirlwall's Greece, vol. i. ch. 5.
[n] Herod. iii. 122.
[o] Herod. i. 173.
[p] Müller's Dorians, ii. 11. 8; Eurip. Fragm. i.
[q] Creta ii. 87.
[r] Pol. ii. 10.
[s] Ibid. ii. 10. 2.

models from which the prime parts of the Laconian legislation had been borrowed[t].

Among the resemblances known to us appear to be

1. The division between the military and the agricultural part of the community.

2. The περίοικοι of Crete, holding the same relation to the Cretans, as the Helots to the Spartans, and like them cultivating the land.

3. The institution of συσσίτια in both countries.

4. The organism of the government: the five ephors corresponding with the ten κοσμοὶ of Crete, and the βουλὴ being alike in both.

There also still remain etymological indications that Minos was the person who raised some tribe or class to preeminence in Crete, and depressed some other tribes or classes below the level of the free community. In Hesychius we read,

μνοῖα, οἰκετεία.
μνῆτοι, δοῦλοι.
μνῶα, δουλεία.

And Athenæus quotes from the Cretica of Sosicrates, τὴν μὲν κοινὴν δουλείαν οἱ Κρῆτες καλοῦσι μνοίαν· τὴν δὲ ἰδίαν ἀφαμιώτας· τοὺς δὲ περιοίκους, ὑπηκόους[u]. He also says, that, according to Ephorus, the general name for slave in Crete was κλαρώτης, and that it was derived from the custom of apportioning the slaves by lot. This remarkably fixes the character of Cretan slavery as owing its rise to some institutions public in the highest sense, for merely private slavery could not, it would appear, have had an origin such as to account for the name. It thus indirectly supports the idea implied in μνοία and μνῆτοι, that it was derived from Minos. Athenæus[v] again, quoting the *Cretica glossæ*

[t] Minos 11–17. [u] Athen. vi. p. 263. [v] Ibid. p. 267.

of Hermon, gives us the words μνώτας, τοὺς εὐγενεῖς (otherwise read ἐγγενεῖς) οἰκέτας, and thus pointing to the reduction to servitude of some of the previously free population of the country.

There can be little doubt that it was the Pelasgic part of the population which thus succumbed before the more active elements of Cretan society, and which continued in the manual occupation of husbandry, while war, policy, and maritime pursuits became the lot of their more fortunate competitors. For is it difficult to divine which were those more active elements, since Homer points out for us among the inhabitants of Crete at least two tribes, the Achæans and the Dorians, of Hellic origin. Bishop Thirlwall points also to a Phœnician element in Crete, and to Homer as indicating the Phœnician origin of Minos. This is suggested not only by his birth, and by his maritime pre-eminence, but by Homer's placing Dædalus in Crete[w]. For that name directly establishes a connection with the arts that made Sidon and Phœnicia so famous. The later tradition, indeed, places Dædalus personally in relations with Minos, as having been pursued by him after he had fled to Sicily[x].

Elsewhere I have shown reason for supposing that a second of the five Cretan nations, namely, the Κύδωνες, was Pelasgian: and there is a curious tradition, which supports this hypothesis. According to Ephorus[y], there were solemn festivals of the slave population, during which freemen were not permitted to enter within the walls, while the slaves were supreme, and had the right of flogging the free; and these festivals were held in Cydonia, the city of these Κύδωνες.

Our belief in a Cretan empire of Minos, founded on

[w] Il. xviii. 592.   [x] Paus. x. 17. 4.   [y] Ath. vi. p. 263.

the evidence of the Poems, and sustained by the statement of Thucydides, need not be impaired by the fact that we find little post-Homeric evidence directly available for its support. In early times the recollection of dynasties very much depended on the interest which their successors had in keeping it alive. Now the Minoan empire was already reduced to fragments at the time of the *Troica*. The supremacy over Greece was then in the hands of a family that held the throne of the Perseids and the Danaids, a throne older than that of Minos himself, though in his time probably less distinguished: a throne whose lustre would have been diminished by a lively tradition of his power and greatness. And it was from the Pelopids that the Dorian sovereigns of Sparta claimed to inherit. Therefore the great Greek sovereignty, from the *Troica* onwards, had no interest in cherishing the recollection of this ancient part of history; on the contrary, their interest lay in depressing it; and under these circumstances we need not wonder that, until the inquiring age of Greek literature and philosophy, when Athens gained the predominance, the traces of it should have remained but faint. But the traces of Cretans have been found extensively dispersed both over the islands, and on the coasts of the Ægean[z].

To complete the statement of this part of the case, it is necessary to turn to another country, holding, with its inhabitants, a very peculiar position in the Iliad. The attentive reader of the poem must often inquire, with curiosity and wonder, why it is that Homer everywhere follows the Lycian name with favour so marked, that it may almost be called favouritism. At every turn, which brings that people into view, we are met by the clearest indications of it: and few of Homer's

[z] Höck's Creta, b. ii. sect. 4. (ii. 222 and seqq.)

II. Ethnology.

indications, none of his marked indications, are without a cause and an aim.

Sarpedon, the Lycian commander in chief, performs the greatest military exploit on the Trojan side that is to be found throughout the poems[a]. That he does not obscure the eminence of Hector is only owing to the fact, that his share in the action of the poem is smaller, not to its being less distinguished. Everywhere he plays his part with a faultless valour, a valour set off by his modesty, and by his keen sense of public duty according to the strictest meaning of the term[b]; Jupiter, his father, sheds tears of blood for his coming death; and he is in truth the most perfect as well as the bravest man on the Trojan side. Glaucus, his second in command, is inferior to no Trojan warrior save Hector, though in the exchange of the arms with Diomed Homer has, as usual, reserved the superiority to the Grecian intellect.

The distinctions awarded to the Lycian people are in full proportion to those of their king Sarpedon. They formed one only among the eleven divisions of the auxiliary force, but the Lycian[c] name, and theirs only[d], evidently on account of their eminence, is often used to signify the entire body. In the great assault on the Greek trench and rampart, Sarpedon their leader commands all the allies, and chooses as his lieutenants Glaucus, and Asteropæus a Pæonian, but not the Pæonian general[e]. They are never mentioned with any epithet except of honour: and to them is applied the

[a] Il. xii. 397.
[b] See particularly his speech Il. xii. 310-28.
[c] There were also Lycians of Troas, with whom Pandarus was connected: and it is possible that these may be the persons meant.
(Schol. on Il. v. 105.)
[d] For the question whether the Leleges on one single occasion form an exception, see sup. p. 162.
[e] Il. xvii. 350, 1. ii. 848.

term ἀντίθεοι[f], which is given to no other tribe or nation in the Iliad, and in the Odyssey only to the Phæacians[g]; to these last it appertains doubtless on account of their relationship to the immortals. The Lycian attack in the Twelfth Book is the one really formidable to the Greeks[h], and in the rout of the Sixteenth Book we are told, that 'not even the stalwart (ἴφθιμοι) Lycians' held their ground after the death of Sarpedon[i]. They alone are appealed to in the name of that peculiar and sacred sentiment of military honour called αἰδώς, which, with this single exception, seems to be the exclusive property of the Greeks[j].

It is difficult to account for this glowing representation, so consistently carried through the poem, except upon the supposition, that Homer regarded the Lycians as having some peculiar affinity or other relation with the Greeks; and that he on this account raised them out of what would otherwise more naturally have been a secondary position.

There are many signs of a specific kind, that this was actually his view of them.

1. To make Sarpedon the son of Jupiter was at once to establish some relationship with the Greek races.

2. The legend of Bellerophon, delivered on the field of battle, was not required, nor is it introduced, merely to fill up the time during which Hector goes from the camp to the city. It required no filling up: but Homer turns the interval to account by using it to give us this interesting chapter of archaic history, doubtless in order to illustrate, as all his other legends do, the beginnings and early relations of the Hellenic races. Accordingly we find that Antea, wife of Prœtus the Argive king, was

---

[f] Il. xii. 408. xvi. 421. [g] Od. vi. 241. [h] Il. xii. 397.
[i] Il. xvi. 659. [j] Il. xvi. 422. xvii. 426.

II. *Ethnology.*

a Lycian: that a familiar intercourse subsisted between the two courts, such as probably and strongly implies that the nations had other ties: and lastly that an Æolid line of sovereigns, descended through Sisyphus, were the actual governors of Lycia at the period of the *Troica.*

3. The very same ideas of kingship and its offices, which prevailed in Greece, are expressed by Sarpedon in his speech to Glaucus[k], and there is an indication of free institutions which enlarges the resemblance. The force of this circumstance will be more fully appreciated, when we shall have examined the Asiatic tinge which is perceptible in the institutions of Troy itself.

4. Besides the Æolid sovereignty, the etymology of the names of Lycian warriors connects itself not only with the Greek race, but with the Hellic element in that race[l].

5. On the other hand Apollo, whom we shall hereafter find to be the great Pelasgian, though also universal, god, is even, according to Homer, in close and peculiar connection with Lycia, although he is not localized there by Homer as he is in the later tradition. First as being λυκηγενής. Secondly as the great bowman: while Lycia was so eminent in this art, that Æneas, addressing Pandarus with a compliment on his skill, says no man before Troy can match him, and perhaps even in Lycia there may not be a better archer[m]. Thirdly, this Pandarus the archer, and son of Lycaon, received the gift of his bow from Apollo himself[n]: and says, that Apollo prompted or instructed him, as he came from Lycia[o]. It may, however, be reasonably questioned, whether we are here to understand the Lycia of the South, or the district of kindred name in

---

[k] Il. xii. 310.   [l] Vid. inf. sect. vii.   [m] Il. v. 172.
[n] Il. ii. 827.   [o] Il. v. 105.

Troas. In any case, Apollo in Lycia would be no more than the counterpart of Minerva in Pelasgian Athens.

6. The prevalence of that Lycian name in other quarters, such as Arcadia, of a marked Pelasgian character, further supports the supposition that Lycia had probably a Pelasgian race for the bulk of its population, holding the same subordinate relation to another race as we find in corresponding cases. In Arcadia[p] Pausanias reports a Lycaon son of Pelasgus; a Lycosura, the city he founded; Lyceon, the hill where it stood; and Lycea, the games he established.

All this evidence combines to show some correspondence between Lycia and Greece, as to the constituent elements of the population. The agreement could not have been perfect: for the records of the Lycian language, I believe, show a prevalence of other elements than the Greek. But we have thus a reason to suppose, that the community of architecture and other arts which has been found to subsist between the two countries, was not merely dependent on later colonisation, but was owing to an affinity of races and similarity of manners which dates from the heroic age.

Lastly, the fragments of Homeric evidence respecting the Lycians are combined by a later tradition, which links them to Crete, the main subject of our recent inquiry. According to this tradition, there was a Sarpedon earlier than the Sarpedon of the *Troica*, who, besides being son of Jupiter, was brother to Minos. He is said to have been expelled, with his adherents, by that sovereign from Crete; to have repaired to Lycia, and to have colonised that country, or a part of it. In the time of Herodotus, as we have seen, it retained laws of Cretan. that is to say of Greek, origin. And at two later periods of its history, far remote from

[p] Paus. viii. 2. 1.

Homer and from one another, its inhabitants signalised themselves by the most desperate valour in defence of Xanthus, its capital[q].

For the origin of the group of names, having Λύκος or some similar word for their root, it seems most natural to infer its identity with the Latin *lucus*, essentially the same with *lupus*, and to presume that it had a Pelasgic source, but that the word corresponding with it, probably Λύκος, meaning a wood or grove, had become obsolete in the later Hellenic tongue. There is every reason for a supposition of this kind, as these words, etymologically connected, evidently hang round some common centre, which centre has reference to primitive and to Pelasgic life, as well as to the somewhat specially Pelasgic deity Apollo. Nor is it strange that the root of a name associated with the Pelasgi should have been lost to the Greek tongue, while the name itself remains: we have another example in Larissa.

But if there was such a word, with such a meaning, the link, which may perhaps connect it with Pelasgic life, is evident. For the first agricultural settlers must often be, as such, in a greater or less degree, dwellers in woods. It may be said that in the United States, at the present day, the proper name for an agricultural settler is 'backwoodsman.' In British colonies of Australia, they, who pass beyond the limits of existing settlement, in order to extend it, are said to go into the bush. Thus the idea at the root of the Lycian name is in all probability twin, or rather elder brother, to that which properly would indicate the agricultural settler.

It is however plain, that we cannot look to any thing simply Pelasgian in the Lycian population, as supplying the motive which has induced Homer to give the Lycians a marked preference over other populations, them-

[q] Grote, Hist. Greece, iv. 280.

selves of a Pelasgian character. This preference must be due to the other element, which associates them especially with the Hellenic race. And we may not irrationally suppose it to be founded on any one of such causes as these: the special connection in the royal line between the two countries: a larger infusion of the more lordly blood into a subordinate Lelegian or Pelasgian body in Lycia, just as in Greece, than in Troas and Asia Minor generally: or lastly, a more palpable and near connection between the dominant caste in Lycia and those Persian highlanders, from among whom may have proceeded[r] the forefathers of the Hellenic tribes. Everywhere we see this race branching forth, and, by an intrinsic superiority, acquiring a predominance over the races in prior occupation. Whether the stock came to Lycia by land, or from the eastern coast of the Mediterranean, it may be hard even to conjecture: but there is one particular note of relationship to Persia, which Lycia retains more clearly than Greece, and that is the high estimation in which, to judge from the connection with Apollo and from Il. v. 172, the use of the bow was held in that country. The case was the same in Persia. According to Herodotus, one of the three essential articles of education in Persia was the use of the bow[s]; and he is not contradicted by Ctesias, who calls him in most things a liar and a fabulist[t]. We must not, indeed, rely too strongly upon a circumstance like this. Cyaxares the Median had the art taught to his sons by Nomad Scythians[u]. We may however observe that alike on the Trojan and the Grecian side we never hear of the bow except in the hands of highborn persons, such as Paris, Pandarus, Teucer: and, in the games, Meriones[v].

[r] Vid. inf. sect. x.
[s] Herod. i. 136.
[t] Photii Bibliotheca 72. p. 107.
[u] Herod. i. 73.
[v] Il. xxiii. 860.

II. *Ethnology.*

In passing, it may deserve remark, that the Lycians alone, of all tribes or nations on either side, appear not under two leaders merely, but two kings, in the strict sense. I do not however believe that this indicates a political peculiarity. The origin of it may probably be found in the legend of Bellerophon, to whom, after his high exploits and great services, the reigning sovereign gave half his kingdom[w]. Now that king is nowhere stated to have had a son: and if we suppose a failure of issue in his own direct line, and the succession of one of the two descendants of his daughter to each moiety of the realm, it at once accounts for the exceptional position of Sarpedon and Glaucus.

The suppositions then towards which we are led are, that Minos was of Phœnician origin, that he came to Crete and acquired the sovereignty, that he ruled over a mixed population of Cretans, Pelasgians, and Hellic tribes, that he organised the country and established an extended supremacy, especially maritime and insular, beyond its limits; which however we must not consider as involving the consistent maintenance of sovereignty according to modern ideas, and which is in no degree inconsistent with the rule of Danaids or Perseids in Peloponnesus. Lastly, that in giving form to his social institutions, he depressed the Pelasgian element of Cretan society, and laid, in political depression, the foundations of their subsequent servitude.

If this be so, it is worth while further to observe, that there are traces of a somewhat analogous history in Cyprus, another acknowledged stepping-stone, according to Homer[x], between Greece and the East.

In the Seventeenth Book of the Odyssey[y], Ulysses, in one of his fictitious narrations, states to the Suitors, that the Egyptians, who had taken him prisoner and

[w] Il. vi. 193.   [x] Od. xvii. 442, 8.   [y] Ibid. 440–4.

reduced him to slavery, then made a present of him to their ξεῖνος Dmetor, a descendant of Iasus, who ruled 'with might,' that is, with considerable power over Cyprus (ὃς Κύπρου ἶφι ἄνασσεν); the same expression as he uses in the Eleventh Book with respect to Amphion, the Iasid, in Orchomenus. From all we know of the Iasian name[z], it may be inferred that this was a Pelasgian dynasty, and if so, then without doubt that it ruled over a Pelasgian people.

Ulysses does not mention the time of this transaction; and it must be remembered, that he spoke in the character of an aged person, so that the scene might be laid (so to speak) thirty or forty years back, and therefore long before the expedition to Troy.

But in the Eleventh Book of the Iliad[a], we find Agamemnon putting on a breastplate, which was evidently a marvel of workmanship, with its plates on plates of different metals, and its six dragons flashing forth the colours of the rainbow. Now we must observe, first, that this was evidently meant to be understood as a Sidonian or Phœnician work: secondly, that it was presented to Agamemnon by Cinyres of Cyprus, to conciliate his favour (—χαριζόμενος βασιλῆϊ, perhaps we might render it, to win the favour of *his* king—) upon the occasion of his hearing that the king was collecting an armament against Troy. That is to say, it was to compound with him for not appearing in person to join the Greek forces. Here then we must infer that there was some vague allegiance, which was due, or which at least might be claimed, from Cyprus to Agamemnon, under the πολλῇσιν νήσοισι[b].

Now we know nothing of the Pelopids before the *Troica* as conquerors: and especially, it would be diffi-

[z] Vid. sup. p. 125.   [a] Il. xi. 19–28.   [b] Il. ii. 108.

cult to apply the supposition that they were such in relation to a place so distant. Therefore the political connection, whatever it may have been, could probably rest upon an ethnical affinity alone; and, as we know nothing of any Hellic element in this quarter, that affinity seems to presume the Pelasgian character of the population. The inference, which may thus be drawn, coincides with that already suggested by the name of Iasus.

We may however justly be curious to learn what conditions they were which gave to Cinyres, and so far as we know to Cinyres alone, among princes, this very peculiar attitude at a critical juncture. It is obvious, that in proportion as his situation was remote from the Greek rendezvous, and from the scene of action, the service became more burdensome: but on the other hand, in proportion as he was distant from the centre of Achæan power, he was little likely to be coerced. How comes it then that Agamemnon had over Cinyres an influence which he does not seem to have possessed over the tribes of Macedonia and Thrace, though these lay nearer both to him, and to the way between him and the Troad, which he had to traverse by sea?

The hypothesis, that the population of Cyprus was purely or generally Pelasgian, appears to square remarkably with the facts. For then, upon the one hand, they would naturally be disinclined to interfere on behalf of the Greeks in a war where all purely Pelasgian sympathies would (as we must for the present take for granted) incline them towards Troy.

But further, we find among other notes of the Pelasgians this, that they were characterised by a want of nautical genius, while the more enterprising character of the Hellenes at once made them, and has kept them down to this very day, an eminently maritime people; and Homer himself, with his whole soul, evidently gloried and delighted in the sea. If then the population of Cyprus was Pelasgian, we can readily understand how, notwithstanding its sympathies and its remoteness, it might be worth the while of its ruler to propitiate Agamemnon by a valuable gift in order to avert a visit which his ships might otherwise be expected to pay; and how the Pelopid power over Cyprus, as an island, might be greater than over nearer tribes, which were continental.

It may aid us to comprehend the relation between Cyprus and Agamemnon, if we call to recollection the insular empire which Athens afterwards acquired.

There is another sign, which strongly tends to connect Cyprus with the Pelasgian races, especially those which belong to Asia. It is the worship of Venus, who had in that island her especial sanctuary, and who, upon her detection in the Odyssey[c], takes refuge there. In the war, she is keenly interested on the Trojan side: and the Trojan history is too plainly marked with the influence of the idea, that exalted her to Olympian rank. That Venus was known mythologically among the Hellenic tribes, we see from the lay of Demodocus. That she was worshipped among them, seems to be rendered extremely improbable by the fact, that Diomed wounds her in his $ἀριστεῖα$[d]. We must consider her as a peculiarly, and perhaps in Homer's time almost exclusively Pelasgian deity; and her local abode at Paphos may be taken as a marked sign, accordingly, of the Pelasgianism of Cyprus.

We have already seen Agapenor, a stranger, placed by Agamemnon in command of the Pelasgian forces of

[c] Od. viii. 362.   [d] See inf. Religion and Morals, Sect. iii.

Arcadia; and Minos, a stranger, acquire dominion over the partially, and perhaps mainly, Pelasgian population of Crete. It seems probable, that Cyprus in this too affords us a parallel. We have the following considerations to guide us in the question. First, the Pelasgians, not being a maritime, were consequently not a mercantile people. Secondly, from the description of the gift sent by Cinyres, we must understand it, on account of the preciousness of its materials and its ornaments, to have been a first rate example of the skill of the workers in metal of the period. Such things were not produced by Pelasgians; and we must, to be consistent with all the other Homeric indications, suppose this breastplate to have been of Sidonian or Phœnician workmanship. This supposition connects Cinyres himself with Phœnicia, while his people were Pelasgian. Again, on examining his name we find in it no Pelasgian characteristics; but it appears to be Asiatic, and to signify a musical instrument with strings, which was used in Asia[e]. All this makes it likely, upon Homeric presumptions, that he was a Phœnician, or a person of Phœnician connections, and that into his hands the old Pelasgic sovereignty of Minos had passed over from the Iasid family, which had reigned there shortly before the *Troica*.

The Homeric tradition with respect to Cinyres is supported to some extent from without[f]. Apollodorus so far agrees with it as to report, that Cinyres migrated from the neighbouring Asiatic continent into Cyprus with a body of followers, founded Paphos, and married the daughter of the king of the island. Apollodorus, Pindar, and Ovid, all treat Cinyres in a way which

[e] Gr. κινύρα, Hebr. kinnûr. Liddell and Scott, in voc.
[f] Apollod. Bibl. iii. 14. 3. Pind. Pyth. ii. 26. Ov. Met. x. 310.

especially connects him with the worship of Venus, as though he had introduced it into the island; and it is observable, that the points at which we find this deity in contact with the race are all in Asia, or on the way from it, that is to say, Troas, Cyprus, and lastly, Cythera: as if it were not original to the Greeks, but engrafted, and gradually taking its hold. Sandacus was, according to Apollodorus, the father of Cinyres, and had come from Syria into Cilicia.

The process which we thus seem to see going forward in the Pelasgian countries, and which was probably further exemplified in the Greek migrations to the coast of Asia Minor, was grounded in the natural, if we mean by the natural the ordinary, course of things. In the last century, John Wesley said, that the religious and orderly habits of his followers would make them wealthy, and that then their wealth would destroy their religion. So in all likelihood it was the peaceful habits of the Pelasgians that made their settlements attractive to the spoiler. They thus invited aggression, which their political genius and organization were not strong enough to repel; and the power of their ancient but feeble sovereignties passed over into the hands of families or tribes more capable of permanently retaining it, and of wielding it with vigour and effect.

I must not, however, pass from the subject of Homeric testimony respecting the Pelasgi, without adverting to one important negative part of it.

It must be observed, that, as anterior to the three appellatives which he ordinarily applies to the Greeks of the Trojan war collectively, Homer uses no name whatever other than the Pelasgic, which is not of limited and local application. Neither Ἀχαιοὶ, Ἀργεῖοι, nor Δαναοὶ, bear any one sign of being the proper designation of the original settlers and inhabitants of all Greece: and if the name for them be not Πελασγοὶ, there certainly is no other name whatever which can compete for the honour, none which has the same marks at once of great antiquity, and of covering a wide range of the country. And if, as I trust, it shall hereafter be shown, that all these came from abroad as strangers into a country already occupied, there then will be a presumption of no mean force arising even out of this negative, to the effect that the Pelasgians were the original base of the Greek nation, while we are also entitled to affirm, upon the evidence of Homer, that their race extended beyond the limits of Greece.

Such is the supposition upon which we already begin to find that the testimony of the poems as a whole appears to converge. It is, I grant, indirect, and fragmentary, and much of it conjectural; we may greatly enlarge its quantity from sources not yet opened: but I wish to direct particular attention to its unity and harmony, to the multitude of indications which, though separate and individually slight, all coincide with the theory that the Pelasgi supplied the *substratum* of the Greek population subsisting under dominant Hellic influences; and to the fact, I would almost venture to add, that they can coincide with nothing else.

We must proceed, however, to consider that portion of the evidence in the case, which is external to the Homeric Poems.

Besides what has been up to this point incidentally touched, there is a great mass of extra-Homeric testimony, which tends, when read in the light of Homer, to corroborate the views which have here been taken of the Pelasgi, as one of the main coefficients of the Greek nation.

In the first chapter of the able work of Bishop Marsh, entitled, *Horæ Pelasgicæ*[g], will be found an ample collection of passages from Greek writers, which, though many of them are in themselves slight, and any one if taken singly could be of little weight for the purpose of proof, yet collectively indicate that the possession of the entire country at the remotest period by the Pelasgi was little less than an universal and invariable tradition. I will here collect some portion of the evidence which may be cited to this effect.

Coming next to Homer in time and in authority, Hesiod supports him, as we have seen above[h], in associating Dodona both with the Pelasgic and with the Hellic races; placing it, just as Homer does, in the midst of the latter, and more distinctly than Homer indicating its foundation by the former. It may be observed that, in a Fragment, he questionably personifies Pelasgus[i].

Next we find the very ancient poet Asius, according to the quotation of Pausanias[j], assigning the very highest antiquity to the Pelasgian race, by making Pelasgus the father of men;

ἀντίθεον δὲ Πελασγὸν ἐν ὑψικόμοισιν ὄρεσσι
γαῖα μέλαιν' ἀνέδωκεν, ἵνα θνητῶν γένος εἴη.

Among the Greek writers, not being historians themselves, of the historic period, there is none whose testimony bears, to my perception, so much of the true archaic stamp, as Æschylus. It seems as if we could trace in him a greater piety towards Homer, and we certainly find a more careful regard both to his characters

[g] Cambridge, 1815.
[h] Sup. p. 108.
[i] Hist. Fragm. x. 2.
[j] Paus. viii. 1, 2.

and his facts, than were afterwards commonly paid to them. Nay he excels in this respect the Cyclic poets. They were much nearer in date to the great master, but he, as it were, outran them, by a deeper and nobler sympathy. In him, too, the drama had not yet acquired the character, which effaces or impairs its claims to historical authority: which earned for it the ἐκτραγῳδεῖν of Aristotle[k] and Polybius[l], and on which was founded the declaration of Socrates in the Minos, Ἀττικὸν λέγεις μῦθον καὶ τραγικόν[m]. Even where he speaks allegorically, he seems to represent the first form of allegory, in which it is traceably moulded upon history, and serves for its key. It is not therefore unreasonable to attach importance to his rendering of the public tradition respecting the Pelasgi, which we find in a remarkable passage of the Supplices;

τοῦ γηγενοῦς γάρ εἰμ' ἐγὼ Παλαίχθονος
ἶνις Πελασγὸς, τῆσδε γῆς ἀρχηγέτης.
ἐμοῦ δ' ἄνακτος εὐλόγως ἐπώνυμον
γένος Πελασγῶν τήνδε καρποῦται χθόνα[n].

Pelasgus, himself the speaker, then describes his dominions as reaching from Peloponnesus (χώρη Ἀπίη) in the south to the river Strymon in the north (πρὸς δύνοντος ἡλίου), and declares how Apis, coming from Acarnania, had fitted the country for the abode of man by clearing it of wild beasts. Acarnania marks the line of country, which formed the ordinary route from Thessaly to Peloponnesus. Taken literally, Pelasgus is the son of the Earthborn, and the name-giver of the Pelasgian race. What the passage signifies evidently is, that by ancient tradition the Pelasgians were the first occupants of the country, and that they reached from

[k] Rhet.
[l] Hist. vi. 56, 8.
[m] Minos 10.
[n] Æsch. Suppl. 256.

the north to the south of Greece. It is in the reign of this mythical Pelasgus, that Danaus reaches the Peloponnesus.

Of such an *eponymus* Thessaly, Argos, and Arcadia had each their separate tradition in its appropriate dress. Pausanias reports the Arcadian one very fully: and according to its tenour Pelasgus taught the use of dwellings and clothes, and to eat chestnuts instead of roots, grass, and leaves[o]. The tomb of Pelasgus was pretended to be shown at Argos.

Herodotus states that the Hellas of his day was formerly called Πελασγία[p]: gives to the Peloponnesian women of the era of Danaus the name of Πελασγιωτίδες γυναῖκες[q]: he denominates the Arcadians Πελασγοὶ Ἀρκάδες[r], the people of what was afterwards Achaia Πελασγοὶ Αἰγιαλέες[s], the Athenians Πελασγοὶ Κραναοὶ[t], whom also he describes as autochthonic[u]: and he shows, that recollections of the Pelasgian worship were preserved in his day at Dodona[x]. He furthermore mentions the Πελασγικὸν τεῖχος[y] at Athens; and he places the Pelasgian race in Samothrace, and Lemnos, and mentions their settlements upon the Hellespont, named Placia and Scylace.

Thucydides describes the spot or building called Πελασγικὸν under the Acropolis at Athens, the very situation, in which the original town would in all likelihood be placed for safety. This historian also sustains, with the weight of his judgment, the opinion that in pre-Hellenic times the prevailing race and name in Greece were Pelasgic; κατὰ ἔθνη δὲ ἄλλα τε καὶ τὸ Πελασγικὸν ἐπὶ πλεῖστον[z].

[o] Paus. viii. 2, 2.   [p] Herod. ii. 56.   [q] ii. 171.
[r] i. 146.   [s] vii. 94.   [t] i. 56.
[u] viii. 44.   [x] ii. 52.   [y] v. 64.   [z] Thuc. i. 3.

It is true, that in another passage[a], among the races of the βάρβαροι, he enumerates the Pelasgi : but the epithet itself, which was wholly inapplicable to the heroic age, shows that he spoke with reference to the demarcation established in his own time, which made every thing barbarous that was not Greek, either geographically or by known derivation. Barbarian with him and his contemporaries meant simply foreign, with the addition of a strong dash of depreciation. The fullgrown Hellenic character no longer owned kindred with the particular races, which nevertheless might have contributed, each in its own time and place, to the formation of that remarkable product. The relationship is, however, established by Thucydides himself; for he says these Pelasgi were of the same Tyrseni, who occupied Athens at an earlier period.

Theocritus, who flourished early in the third century B. C., has a passage where he distinguishes chronologically between different persons and races. He begins with the heroes of the Troica, and then goes back to the ἔτι πρότεροι, in which capacity he names the Lapithæ, the Deucalidæ, the Pelopids, and lastly the Ἄργεος ἄκρα Πελασγοί[b]. The word ἄκρα might mean either (1) the flower of Greece, or (2) the very oldest and earliest inhabitants of Greece[c]. Now as the Pelasgians were by no means the flower of Greece, we can only choose the latter meaning for this particular passage. The word Ἄργος is perhaps taken here in its largest sense[d].

Apollonius Rhodius, nearly a century later, adheres to part at least of the same tradition, and calls Thessaly

---

[a] Thuc. v. 109.   [b] Theocr. Idyll. xv. 136–40.
[c] Pind. Pyth. xi. 18. Soph. Aj. 285.   [d] See inf. sect. viii.

the πολυλήϊος αἶα Πελασγῶν[e]. The Scholiast on this passage adds an older testimony, stating that Sophocles, in the Inachus, declared that the Πελασγοὶ and 'Αργεῖοι were the same. According to Strabo, the Pelasgi were the most ancient race which had held power in Greece: τῶν περὶ τὴν 'Ελλάδα δυναστευσάντων ἀρχαιότατοι[f]. In the same place he calls the oracle of Dodona Πελασγῶν ἵδρυμα, a Pelasgian foundation. He expressly supports the construction which has been given above to the Πελασγικὸν ῎Αργος of Homer[g], in the words τὸ Πελασγικὸν ῎Αργος ἡ Θετταλία λέγεται, and he defines the country by the Peneus, Pindus, and Thermopylæ. He traces the Pelasgi in a multitude of particular places, and, on the authority of Ephorus, mentions Πελασγία as a name of Peloponnesus. He also gives us that fragment of Euripides, which states, in harmony with the testimony of Æschylus, that Danaus came to Greece, founded the city of Inachus, and changed the name of the inhabitants from Pelasgiotes to Danaans.

Πελασγιώτας δ' ὠνομασμένους τὸ πρὶν
Δαναοὺς καλεῖσθαι νόμον ἔθηκ' ἀν' 'Ελλάδα.

And Strabo considers that both the Pelasgiote and the Danaan name, together with that of the Hellenes, were covered by the Argive or Argeian name on account of the fame, to which the city of Argos rose[h].

The writings of Dionysius of Halicarnassus probably represent all, that a sound judgment could gather from the records and traditions extant in his time[i]. He pronounces confidently, that the Pelasgian race was Hellenic; which I take to mean, that it was one of the

[e] Argonaut. i. 580, and Schol. Paris. [f] Strabo vii. p. 327.
[g] Ibid. v. p. 221.   [h] Ibid.   [i] i. 17.

component parts of the body afterwards called Hellenic, not that the early Pelasgi were included among the early Hellenes. He considers that the race came from Peloponnesus, where many believed it to be autochthonic, into Thessaly, under Achæus, Phthius, and Pelasgus. It was unfortunate, as in other respects, so in being driven to frequent migrations. This idea of the frequent displacement of the Pelasgians was probably the product in the main of the two facts, first, that traces of them were found at many widely separated points, and secondly, that, according to tradition, they had sunk into a position of inferiority.

K. O. Müller, proceeding chiefly on the post-Homeric tradition, has strongly summed up the evidence as to the Pelasgi, to the following effect.

They were the original inhabitants of the plains and flat bottoms of the valleys, any one of which the ancients called by the name Ἄργος, as we see by the plains of the Peneus, and of the Inachus. If, as Strabo holds, this use of the word was in his time modern, and Macedonian or Thessalian, it may still have been a revival of a primitive usage, even as the very old word Γραικὸς had come back into use with the Alexandrian poets, through the old common tongue of Macedonia.

Their oldest towns were the Larissæ[k], and the number of these points out the Pelasgians as a city-founding people, expert in raising considerable and durable structures. These Larissæ were upon alluvial soils by rivers, and the Pelasgians were early diggers of canals[l]. Their pursuits were agricultural; hence they occupy the richest soils: hence Pelasgus is the host of

[k] See however p. 114 above.
[l] So the ὀχετηγὸς ἀνήρ already exists, as apart from the common labourer, in the time of Homer; Il. xxi. 257.

Ceres, and the inventor of bread: hence Tyrrhenian Pelasgi convert the stony ground by Hymettus into fruitful fields. The shepherd life of the Pelasgians is an Arcadian tradition, but Arcadia was not their only original seat, and, when displaced by Achæans and Dorians, they may have been driven to the hills. Such seats we find in Argos, Achaia, Peloponnesus generally, Thessalia, Epirus, and Attica, where they may be traced in the division of the tribes.

Treating as an error the tradition of their vagrant character, he conceives them to be generally and above all autochthonic. He quotes from Asius in Pausanias the lines which have already been quoted.

There is no record, he says, of their coming into Greece by colonization. They are a people distinct, he thinks, from Lelegians and Carians, as well as from the northern immigrants, Achæans, and Thessalians: and they are the basis and groundwork of the Greek nation[m].

In Niebuhr[n] will be found a comprehensive outline of the wide range of Pelasgian occupancy in Italy: and Cramer supplies a similar sketch for Asia Minor and for Greece[o].

I forbear to quote Latin authorities as to the Pelasgi of Greece. The strong Pelasgian character of Magna Græcia will of itself naturally account for the free use of the name by Romans to designate the Greek nation, and cannot therefore greatly serve to show even the later tradition concerning the ancient position of the Pelasgians in Greece, and their relations to its other inhabitants.

Marsh appears to assert too much, when he says

[m] K. O. Müller, Orchomenos, 119-22.   [n] Chap. iii.
[o] Cramer's Geogr. Ancient Greece, vol. i. p. 15.

that we may set down as peculiarly Pelasgian those places which retained the Pelasgian name in the historic ages. It does not follow from this retention, that Placia and Scylace were more genuinely Pelasgian than Thessaly, any more than we are entitled to say from Homer, that Thessaly was originally more Pelasgian than Attica or Peloponnesus, though it retained the name longer. The reason may have been, that no such powerful pressure from a superior race was brought to bear in the one class of cases, as in the other[o].

In holding that the Pelasgians were the base, so to speak, of the Greek nation, I mean to indicate it as a probable opinion, that they continued to form the mass of the inhabitants throughout all the changes of name which succeeded the period of their rule. But it would appear, that a succession of other more vigorous influences from the Hellic stock must have contributed far more powerfully in all respects, excepting as to numbers, to compose and shape the nationality of the people. The chief part of the Pelasgians of Attica may perhaps have lain among the 400,000 slaves, who formed the unheeded herd of its population; much as in Italy the serfs of the Greek colonists bore the Pelasgian name[p]. So large a body could scarcely have been formed in that limited territory, except out of the original inhabitants of the country. In early stages of society the bulk of society takes its impress from one, or from a few, of superior force: and the ruling families and tribes of a smaller, but more energetic and warlike

[o] The tradition that the Pelasgians were the original inhabitants of the Greek Peninsula appears to have been adopted into the literature of modern Greece. See Πετρίδης—'Ιστορία τῆς παλαιᾶς 'Ελλάδος ἀπὸ τοὺς ἀρχαιοτάτους χρόνους, Κερκύρα, 1830, chap. i. p. 2. Also that Pelasgi and Hellenes were the two factors (μέρη) of the Greek nation. Ibid. p. 3.

[p] Niebuhr, ibid.

race, finding for themselves a natural place at the head of societies already constituted, assume the undisputed direction of their fortunes, and become, by a spontaneous law, their sole representatives in the face of the world, and in the annals of its history.

We may, however, find no inconsiderable proof of the presence of a strong Pelasgian element in the Greek nation, in that portion of the evidence upon the case which is supplied by language. Those numerous and important words in the Latin tongue, which correspond with the words belonging to the same ideas in Greek, could only have come from the Pelasgian ancestry common to both countries; and, if coming from them, must demonstrate in the one case, as in the other, the strong Pelasgian tincture of the nation.

And as the language of a country connot be extensively impregnated in this manner, except either by numbers, or by political and social ascendancy (as was the case of the French tongue with the English), or by literary influence (as is now the case with us in respect to the Greek and Latin tongues), we must ask to which of these causes it was owing, that the Pelasgians so deeply marked the Greek language with the traces of their own tongue. It was not literary influence, for we may be sure that there existed none. It was not political ascendancy, for they were either enslaved, or at the least subordinate. It could only be the influence of their numbers, through which their manner of speech could in any measure hold its ground; and thus we arrive again at the conclusion, that they must have supplied the substratum of the nation.

It is true that Herodotus, as well as Thucydides, spoke of the Pelasgians as using a foreign tongue. So a German writer would naturally describe the English, and yet the English language, by one of its main ingredients, bears conclusive testimony to the Saxon element of the English nation, and also illustrates the relative positions, which the Saxon and Norman races are known in history to have occupied. The tongue of the Pelasgians had been subject within Greece to influence and admixture from the language of the Hellic tribes: beyond Greece it had received impressions from different sources; and naturally, after the consequences of this severance had worked for centuries, the speech of the Pelasgians would be barbarous in the eyes of the Greeks. Again, Marsh[q] observes that, in the very chapter where he distinguishes Pelasgic from Hellenic, Herodotus (i. 56) declares the Ionians to belong to one of these stocks, the Dorians to the other: both of which populations were in his time undoubtedly Greek. And the historian gives another strong proof that the Pelasgians were Greek, where he assigns to this parentage (ii. 52) the Greek name of the gods: θεοὺς δὲ προσωνόμασάν σφεας ἀπὸ τοῦ τοιούτου, ὅτι κόσμῳ θέντες τὰ πάντα πρήγματα κ.τ.λ.

Even if we suppose, as may have been the case, that the Pelasgi mentioned by Herodotus, and by Thucydides, spoke a tongue as far from the Greek actually known to either of them, as is German from the English language at the present day, yet by its affinities that tongue might still remain a conclusive proof, that the ancestors of those who spoke it must have formed an essential ingredient in the composition of the nation. The evidence, which we know to be good in the one case, might be equally valid in the other.

There is abundance of testimony among authors, both Greek and Roman, to establish the relation of the Pelasgi to the old forms of the language of both coun-

[q] Horæ Pelasg. ch. ii. p. 28.

tries. It is enough for the present to refer to the Second Chapter of Bishop Marsh's Horæ Pelasgicæ for a very able and satisfactory discussion of the question. I shall presently have to consider the particular complexion of the words which the Greek nation appear to have derived from Pelasgic sources, and the inferences which that complexion suggests. But this will best be done, when we have examined into the Homeric import of the Hellenic and Pelasgian proper names.

We have next to examine the question,

By what route is it most probable that this Pelasgian nation came into Greece?

On this subject there can hardly be any other than one of two suppositions: the first, that by Thrace, or by the islands of the north, they reached Thessaly: the other, that they crossed from Asia, to the south of the Ægean, by the islands which divide the spaces of that sea.

It is observed by Cramer[r], that the prevailing opinion among those ancient writers, who have discussed the subject, places the Pelasgians first in the Peloponnesus: this being maintained by Pherecydes, Ephorus, Dionysius of Halicarnassus, and Pausanias, without any dissentients to oppose them. This tradition evidently favours the opinion of a passage by the south.

Dionysius, who may be regarded as summing up the general results of Greek tradition, says[s] it placed the Pelasgians first in the Peloponnesus as autochthons; and represented them as having migrated to Thessaly in the sixth generation. In six generations more, they were, he conceives, expelled by the Ætolians and Locrians, then called Curetes and Leleges, and were dispersed into various quarters: indeed, here the tradition seems to become wholly vague or mythical, and to have

[r] Cramer's Greece i. 17.   [s] Antiq. Rom. i. 17, 18.

gathered into one mass most of the places in which there appeared signs of Pelasgic occupancy: it includes the report of a great migration to Italy.

Marsh[t] considers Thrace as the original seat in Europe of the Pelasgi; but the *data* on which he proceeds are too narrow; they have reference only to the islands of Lemnus, Imbrus, and Samothrace. There is no evidence of Pelasgians on the Continent to the north of the Ægean except what places them at a distance from Troy (τῆλε Hom. Il. xvii. 301), and if so, at a point which they may have reached from those islands, more probably, than by the continental route. It is on the whole more likely, however, that Pelasgians may have found their way into Greece both by the north (and if so, probably through the islands), and also by the south.

Homer affords no materials for conclusively determining the question. He gives us the Pelasgic name established in Thessaly, which favours our supposing the one passage, and likewise in Crete, which favours the other. He gives us the Pelasgic Jove of Dodona (a very weighty piece of testimony), and the τέμενος of Ceres in Thessaly, telling rather for the first; and he likewise gives us a perceptible connection between Ceres and Crete, and between Jupiter and king Minos, verging to the latter. But it is to be observed that, with the exception of Attica, the chief Homeric tokens of Pelasgianism lie in Northern and in Southern, but not in Middle, Greece: which favours the opinion, that there may have been a double line of entry.

The extra-Homeric tradition is on the whole most favourable to the supposition of a southern route. Hesiod makes Dodona in Thessaly Pelasgian, but distinctly associates Ceres with Crete: and the Theogony (479, 80)

[t] Horæ Pelasg. pp. 12-15.

Pelasgian route into Greece. 207

sends Jupiter as an infant to be reared in Crete. The Hymn to Ceres, as we have seen, brings her from thence to Eleusis; and the popular mythology in general treats that island as the cradle of Jupiter, therefore manifestly as the place from which the Greeks derived his worship. More than this; the tradition makes Peloponnesus the seat and centre of Pelasgic power, as we see from Æschylus, who makes Pelasgus reside in Peloponnesus, but rule as far as Macedonia. So likewise the names both of 'Απίη γαῖα and of 'Ιασὸν Ἄργος connect themselves originally with this part of Greece: especially when we consider that Apis in Egypt is the sacred bull, and that agriculture, the characteristic pursuit of the Pelasgians, was also the business of oxen. Again, Herodotus[u] reports that the local tradition of Dodona assigned to that oracle an Egyptian origin; and as Dodona was Pelasgic, this tradition somewhat favours the hypothesis of entry by the south.

There are several allusions in Homer to Crete, to Cyprus, or to both, as marking the route between Greece and Asia. Menelaus, after quitting Troy, and nearing Crete (Od. iii. 285–92), sailed afar

Κύπρον Φοινίκην τε καὶ Αἰγυπτίους ἐπαληθείς[x].

The pseudo-Ulysses sails from Crete to Egypt[y], and returns thence to Phœnicia, in one tale, and afterwards starts for Libya by Crete; in another legend, he is given over from Egypt to Cyprus; and Antinous[z], in the Seventeenth Odyssey, replying to the supposed beggarman, says, Get out of the way,

μὴ τάχα πικρὴν Αἴγυπτον καὶ Κύπρον ἵκηαι.

We already know the connection of Crete with Greece from the Iliad: and thus it appears as on the high road

[u] Herod. ii. 54–7.   [x] Od. iv. 83.
[y] Ibid. xiv. 246–58, 290, 293–300.   [z] Ibid. v. 442, 7, 8.

from Greece to Phœnicia, and by Phœnicia to Egypt. The unexampled populousness of that island would, as a matter of course, beget migration; and, of all the tracts lying to the west of the Ægean, the Thessalian plain would, from its extent, offer perhaps the greatest encouragement to agricultural settlers. The traditions reported by Herodotus from Dodona connect that place closely with Egypt and the East, and the route now supposed by Crete establishes that connection in what is probably the simplest and most obvious line.

The continental country from Thessaly to the north and east was held as it would appear to a great extent by a martial and highland race Θρῆκες and Θρηίκιοι. It is not likely that the Pelasgians had much in common with that people, or could make their way to Greece either with or in despite of them. Perhaps the coast where we find Cicones and Pæones apart from the Thracians, may have afforded a route, and we must remember the traditional traces of them both on the coast of the Hellespont and in the islands[a].

This may be the place most convenient for observing, that there can be little hesitation in regarding the northern route as that by which the Hellic tribes came into Greece. They, a highland people, came along a mountain country. They left their name upon the Hellespont, the sea of Helle, which means not the mere strait so called in later times, but the whole northern Ægean[b]; and upon the river Selleeis, which discharges itself into the sea of Marmora. We first hear of them in Homer at the extreme north of Thessaly:

[a] Perhaps the use of the word ἤπειρος for mainland may suggest, that it is due to an insular people, who would appropriately describe a continent as the unlimited (land). It is derived from *a* and πέρας, an end or stop; consider also περάω, to pass over, ἀντιπέραια, Il. ii. 635, and πέρην ἱερῆς Εὐβοίης, ibid. 535.

[b] See inf. sect. vi.

then we find them giving their name, Hellas, to that country, or to some part of it. The people of Hellas, when their connection with their sires of the mountain had become faint in comparison with their relation to the territory they occupied, called themselves Hellenes, from the region they inhabited; and lost sight, as it were, of the ruder parent tribe. In the meantime, they had struck out offshoots through Greece, and the name Hellas had, as will be seen[c], probably come, even in the time of Homer, to be applied in a secondary and comprehensive sense to the whole northern and central parts of it.

It is remarkable and undeniable, with reference both to Pelasgic and to Hellenic times, that in whatever part of the country ruling tribes or families might first make their appearance, the permanent seat of power for Greece was uniformly in the Peloponnesus. Every movement of political importance appears to direct itself thither, and there to rest in equilibrium. The old tradition of Pelasgus, the dynasties of Danaids, Perseids, and Pelopids, the great Heraclid and Doric invasion, evidently aiming at laying hold on the centre of dominion, and yet more, that Spartan primacy ($\dot{\eta}\gamma\epsilon\mu o\nu\acute{\iota}a$), which endured for so many centuries, all tell the same tale; finally the train of evidence is crowned by the strong local sympathies of Juno. It was only in the fifth century before the Christian era that Athens acquired the lead: nor did she keep it long. Her sway, after an interval, was followed by another shortlived ascendancy, that of Thebes, in the fourth century. But Greece ended as she had begun: and the last splendours of her national sentiment and military courage were flung from its pristine seats in Peloponnesus: from La-

[c] Inf. sect. vi.

cedæmon, and Achaia. The old Amphictyonic Union alone remained, throughout the historic times of Greece, to bear witness to the fact that it was in the north of the Isthmus, and above all in Thessaly, that the Hellic tribes first organised themselves as distinct political integers, united in substance, if not in form, in respect of their common religious worship, and their common blood.

It was probably greater security, which gave this advantage, in early times, to Southern over Northern and Midland Greece. Only one narrow neck of land led into the Peloponnesus, and that passage was so circuitous, or dangerous, or both, that it was not the highway of immigrant tribes, who seem usually to have crossed the Corinthian gulf into Elis. This tract of land had not indeed the whole, but it had much, of the advantage enjoyed by England. It was not quite, but it was almost,

> A precious stone, set in the silver sea,
> Which serves it in the office of a wall,
> Or as a moat defensive to a house[c].

When reached, it was the highway to nothing. The fat lands of Bœotia were a road onwards for all who came from Thessaly: there was here a choice between barrenness and poverty, on the one hand, like those of Attica in early times, and insecurity of tenure in the rich soils, which were the object of desire to each tribe as it went upon its march. The Peloponnesus was richer than the one, far more secure than the other: it throve accordingly; and in the Trojan war this small territory supplied four hundred and thirty ships, probably including the greatest number of large vessels, while the other two divisions of continental Greece together gave no more than five hundred and thirty.

[c] Richard II., act ii., sc. 1.

And it seems to have had altogether a more vigorous and concentrated political organisation; for while the five hundred and thirty were in fifteen divisions, under twenty-six leaders, the Peloponnesian force was in six divisions, under nine leaders only, and of the six three at least, namely, those of Mycenæ, Lacedæmon, and Arcadia, were virtually under the direct command of Agamemnon.

Various derivations have been suggested for the name of the Pelasgi. Some will have it to come from Peleg, mentioned in the tenth chapter of Genesis, whose name, said to mean division, is taken to allude to the partition of the earth's surface among the various tribes of the human race. Marsh well observes, that this amounts to no more than possibility: that the meaning of the word will not serve to attach it to the Pelasgi in particular, as in the early ages of the world migration, with partition and repartition, was a continuous process: and that, even if true, it tells us nothing of them antecedent to their European settlement[d]: nothing, that is to say, of a material kind, except what we know independently of it, viz. their being, in common with all other races, of eastern origin. Clinton gives other reasons for rejecting this etymology[e], while he sees force in the reference of the names of Iapetus and Ion to Japheth and Javan respectively. It seems plain that we could not safely build upon even a complete similarity of name, in a case where the interval of time that separates Peleg and Pelasgi, the terms we are to compare, is so vast and so obscure.

So also the name πελαργοὶ, meaning storks, has been taken to be the foundation of Πελασγοί; and the explanation has been given, that the stork is a migratory

[d] Horæ Pelasg. ch. i. sub fin.   [e] Clinton, Fast. Hell. i. p. 97.

bird, and that the Pelasgi were called after it on account of their wanderings.

This explanation, which seems worse than the former, rests in part upon a statement of Herodotus misconstrued. He calls the Dorians ἔθνος πουλυπλάνητον κάρτα[f], and this has been erroneously applied to the Pelasgians, of whom, on the contrary, he says, οὐδαμῇ κω ἐξεχώρησε. This statement from a writer of the age of Herodotus, fully neutralises the statement of Dionysius, who describes them as itinerant, and never securely settled[g]. He may, indeed, mean no more than Thucydides means, when he says (i. 2), that the occupants of good soils were the most liable to dispossession. But does this idea of itinerancy correspond with the migrations of the stork, which seem to have reference to the steady periodical variations of climate, and to be as far as possible from the idea implied in 'much-roving?'

It appears to have been the understood characteristic of that bird, to draw to and dwell about the settled habitations of men. It seems highly improbable, and without precedent, that a widely spread nation should take its name from a bird: but may not the bird have taken its name from the nation? If it were a nation emphatically of settlers, as opposed to pirates, robbers, nomads, and rovers of all kinds, dwelling with comfort in fixed abodes, as opposed to the ἀνιπτόποδες χαμαιεῦναι[h], might not birds, which seemed to share these settlements, be reasonably named after the people?

It by no means appears as if Aristophanes, in the passage where he uses the term, intended a mere pun. It is in the comedy of the Birds[i], and is an allusion to that law of the Athenians, evidently here signified

---

[f] Herod. i. 56.
[g] Dion. Hal. i. 17.
[h] Il. xvi. 235.
[i] Ὄρνιθες, v. 1359.

under the name of storks, which required children to provide for their parents[j]. The passage is clearly a testimony to the Pelasgic origin of the Athenians: and it may be based upon the belief, that the storks took their name from the Pelasgi, and that the similarity lay in their habit of settling on the roofs of houses and the like, almost as if inhabitants, in the villages of which the Pelasgi were the first Greek founders. It also gives room for the conjecture that Πελαργοὶ may have been the old form of the name. The stork, it may be remembered, was one of the sacred birds of the Egyptians.

Again, the word πέλαγος has been suggested as supplying the true derivation of the Pelasgian name. Marsh[k] rejects it, because he conceives it is founded upon the hypothesis that the Pelasgi came across the Ægean, which he thinks improbable. But the evidence appears to be in favour of their having come principally by the islands, if not at once across the Ægean. It may also be questioned, whether the etymology must rest on this hypothesis exclusively. For, in the first place, the more natural construction would be, not that they came by sea, but that they came *from beyond sea*, an idea which might very well attach to any people of Asiatic origin. So it was that the too famous Pelagius, who is known to have been a Welshman, came by his classical name; a name bearing that very signification[1]. But is it not also possible, that πέλαγος may at one time have had the meaning of a plain? It properly signifies a wide open level surface, corresponding with the Latin *æquor*, and with our *main*. Hence Homer never attaches to the word πέλαγος any of his usual

[j] Potter's Antiq., b. i. ch. 26.
[k] Horæ Pelasg. ch. i. p. 17.
[1] See Hey's Norrisian Lectures, vol. iii. p. 142.

epithets for the sea, such as οἶνοψ, ἠχήεις, μεγακήτης, ἀτρύγετος, πολύφλοισβος; but only μέγα, great: and he uses the phrase ἅλος ἐν πελάγεσσι [m], which would be mere tautology, if πέλαγος properly and directly meant the sea. So Pindar has πόντιον πέλαγος, Æschylus ἅλς πελαγία, and Apollonius Rhodius πέλαγος θαλάσσης [n]. There were in Macedonia, as we learn from Strabo, a people called Pelagones [o], and in Homer we find the names Πελάγων and Πηλέγων. Again, we have in Hesychius, among the meanings of πελαγίζειν, ψεύδεσθαι μεγάλα, and for πέλαγος he gives μέγεθος, πλῆθος, βύθος; as well as πλάτος θαλάσσης. It seems not impossible that the Pelasgi may owe their name to the word πέλαγος, in its primary sense of plain and open surface: as the word Θρῇξ, in this view its exact counterpart, was derived from τρῆχυς, and at one time meant simply the inhabitant of a rough and rocky place, a mountaineer or highlander.

There is, however, another mode in which Πελασγοὶ may bear the sense of inhabitants of the plain, or rather (for it is in this that the word will most comprehensively apply to them, and most closely keep to its proper meaning), of the cultivable country, which would include valleys as well as plains properly so called: and indeed this derivation, suggested by K. O. Müller, is the simplest possible, if only we can clear the first step, which *assumes* the identity of Πελασγοὶ and Πελαργοί. He says it is compounded of πέλω and ἄργος. The first meaning of πέλω seems to imply motion with repetition or custom. Afterwards it is *to be*, and especially *to be*

[m] Od. v. 335.
[n] Ol. vii. 104; Persæ 427; Scott and Liddell in πέλαγος. I venture to suggest πελάζω as the root, and 'accessible,' 'easily travelled,' 'open'(compare εὐρυαγυῖα) as the meaning.
[o] Strabo, p. 327, 331.

wont to be. Thus it will, while yet very near its fountain, have the sense, *to frequent* or *inhabit.* To the same origin he refers πόλις, πολέω; and also the πελώρια, the harvest feast of Thessaly, taken as the feast of inhabitation[p] or settlement.

The subject of this name will again come into view, when the later name of Ἀργεῖοι is examined. In the mean time, let it be observed, that if the Pelasgi were thus called from being, or if only they in fact were, inhabitants of the plains, we find in this some further explanation of the tradition, which can hardly have been an unmixed error, of their vagrant character. For the plains contained the most fertile soils: and, especially as they were of limited extent, their inhabitants could not but rapidly increase, so as to require more space for the support of their population. Further, these rich tracts offered a prize to all the tribes who were in want of settlements; according to the just observation of Thucydides[q], already quoted, that the most fertile parts of Greece, namely, Bœotia, Thessaly, and much of Peloponnesus, most frequently changed hands. This would be more and more applicable to a given people, in proportion as it might be more addicted to peaceful pursuits. Manifestly, it is as inhabitants of the plains, or the cultivable country, that Homer especially marks the Pelasgi: both by calling the great plain of Thessaly Pelasgic, and by the epithet ἐριβώλαξ which he applies (Il. ii. 841. and xvii. 301), to their Larissa, on the only two occasions when he mentions it. And the etymological inquiry seems, upon the whole, to direct us, although the particular path be somewhat uncertain, towards a similar conclusion.

[p] Orchomenos, p. 119 and n.   [q] Thuc. i. 2.

SECT. IV.

On the Phœnicians, and the Outer Geography of the Odyssey.

The text of Homer appears to afford presumptions, if not of close affinity between the Phœnician and Hellenic races, yet of close congeniality, and of great capacity for amalgamation; although the former were of Semitic origin.

The Phœnician name, as may be seen from Strabo, was widely spread through Greece: even in Homer we find the word Φοῖνιξ already used, (1) for a Phœnician, (2) for a Greek proper name, (3) for purple, and (4) for the palm tree (Od. v. 163).

We find the ancient family of Cadmus established as a dynasty in Bœotia, about the same time, according to the common opinion, with the earliest appearances of the Hellenic race in the Greek peninsula. We have no reason to suppose that they were themselves of Hellic extraction: but we find them invested with the same marks of political superiority as the Hellenic families, and figuring among the Greek sovereigns in successive generations. They must have ejected previous occupants: for Amphion and Zethus first settled and fortified Thebes, and they were the sons of Jupiter and Antiope[a].

Ino Leucothee, the daughter of Cadmus, was already a deity in the time of Homer. She appears in that capacity to Ulysses, when he is tossed upon the waters between Ogygia and Phæacia; that is to say, when he was still beyond the limits of the Greek or Homeric world,

[a] Od. xi. 260.

and within the circle of those traditions, lying in the unknown distance, which the Greeks could only derive from the most experienced and daring navigators of the time; namely, the Phœnicians. This appears to mark Ino herself, and therefore her father Cadmus, as of Phœnician birth. And accordingly we may set down the position of this family in Greece, as the earliest token of relations between Phœnicia and Greece.

It is followed by one more significant still, and more clearly attested in Homer. Minos, a Phœnician, appears in Crete and founds an empire: he marries his daughter Ariadne to the Athenian hero Theseus; and so quickly does this empire assume the national character, that in the time of the *Troica*, Hellenic races are established in the island, the Cretan troops are numbered without distinction among the followers of Agamemnon; and Idomeneus, only the grandson of Minos, appears to be as Grecian as any of the other chiefs of the army. The grandfather himself is appointed to act as judge over the shades of Greeks in the nether world[b]: and his brother Rhadamanthus has a post of great dignity, if of inferior responsibility, in being intrusted with the police of Elysium[c].

Nowhere is Homer's precision more remarkable, than in the numerous passages where he appears before us as a real geographer or topographer. Indeed, by virtue of this accuracy, he enables us to define with considerable confidence the sphere of his knowledge and experience; by which I mean not only the countries and places he had visited, but those with respect to which he had habitual information from his countrymen, and unrestricted opportunities of correcting error.

[b] Od. xi. 568.   [c] Od. iv. 564.

218   II. *Ethnology.*

In the direction of the west, it seems plain that he knew nothing except the coast of Greece and the coastward islands. Phæacia hangs doubtfully upon his horizon, and it is probable that he had only a very general and vague idea of its position. Towards the north, there is nothing to imply, that his experimental knowledge reached beyond the Thracian coast and, at the farthest, the Sea of Marmora. He speaks of Ida, as if its roots and spurs comprised the whole district, of which in that quarter he could speak with confidence[d]. To the east, he probably knew no region beyond Lycia on the coast of Asia Minor, and to the south Crete was probably his boundary: though he was aware, by name at least, of the leading geographical points of a maritime passage, not wholly unfrequented, to the almost unknown regions of Cyprus, Phœnicia, and Egypt. The apparent inconsistency however of his statements[e] respecting the voyage to Egypt, affords proof that it lay beyond the geographical circle, within which we are to consider that his familiar knowledge and that of his nation lay.

While he is within that circle, he is studious alike of the distances between places, the forms of country, and the physical character of different districts: but, when he passes beyond it, he emancipates himself from the laws of space. The points touched in the voyage of Ulysses are wholly irreconcilable with actual geography, though national partialities have endeavoured to identify them with a view to particular appropriation. Some of them, indeed, we may conceive that he mentally associated with places that had been described to him: nay, he may have intended it in

---

[d] Il. ii. 824; and xii. 19.
[e] Od. iii. 320–2; and xiv. 257.

all: but the dislocated knowledge, which alone even the navigators of the age would possess, has suffered, by intent or accident, such further derangement in its transfer to the mind of Homer, that it is hopeless to adjust his geography otherwise than by a free and large infusion of fictitious drawing. This outer sphere is, however, peopled with imagery of deep interest. For the purposes of the poem, the whole wanderings both of Menelaus and Ulysses lie within it, and beyond the limits of ordinary Greek experience. And throughout these wanderings the language of Homer is that of a poet who, as to facts, was at the mercy of unsifted information; of information which he must either receive from a source not liable to check or scrutiny, or else not receive at all: and who wisely availed himself of that character of the marvellous with which the whole was overspread, to work it up into pictures of the imagination, which were to fill both his contemporaries and all succeeding generations with emotions of interest and wonder.

In Homer we find that Greek navigation already extends, yet it is very slightly, beyond the limits of Greek settlement. The Pseudo-Ulysses of the Fourteenth Odyssey made nine voyages[f], ἀνδρὰς ἐς ἀλλοδάπους; and at length, inspired as he says by a wild impulse from on high, he planned and executed a voyage to Egypt. But he is represented as a Cretan, and the early fame of Crete in navigation is probably due to its connection through Minos with Phœnicia. Here too the representation is, that he is a Cretan of the highest class, the colleague of Idomeneus in his command[g], and thus, according to the law of poetical likelihood, to be understood as probably of a family

[f] Od. xiv. 231, 243-8. [g] Od. xiv. 237; Il. xiv. 321.

belonging to the Phœnician train of Minos. The Thesprotian ship of the Fourteenth Odyssey trades for corn to Dulichium only. The Taphians, indeed, who from the xenial relation of their lord, Mentes[h], to Ulysses, must in all likelihood have lived in the neighbourhood of Ithaca, are represented as making voyages not only to an unknown Temese, which was in foreign parts (ἐπ' ἀλλοθρόους ἀνθρώπους[i]), but likewise to Phœnicia; the latter voyage, however, is only mentioned in connection with the purpose of piracy[j]. But these Taphians appear to have formed an insignificant exception to the general rule: we do not hear any thing of them in the great armament of the Iliad. Speaking generally, we may say that the Achæans had no foreign navigation: it was in the hands of the Phœnicians.

It is to that people that we must look as the established merchants, hardiest navigators, and furthest explorers, of those days. To them alone as a body, in the whole Homeric world of flesh and blood, does Homer give the distinctive epithet of ναυσικλυτοὶ ἄνδρες[k]. He accords it indeed to the airy Phæacians, but in all probability that element of their character is borrowed from the Phœnicians[l], and if so, the reason of the derivation can only be, that the Phœnicians were for that age the type of a nautical people. To them only does he assign the epithets, which belong to the knavery of trade, namely, πολυπαίπαλοι and τρῶκται. When we hear of their ships in Egypt or in Greece, the circumstance is mentioned as if their coming was in the usual course of their commercial operations. Some force also, in respect to national history, may be assigned to the general tradition, which almost makes the Me-

[h] Od. i. 105; ii. 180. [i] Od. i. 183. [j] Od. xv. 425.
[k] Od. xv. 415. [l] See Wood on Homer, p. 48.

diterranean of the heroic age 'a Phœnician lake;' to their settlements in Spain, and the strong hold they took upon that country; and to the indirect Homeric testimony, as well as the judgment of Thucydides, respecting the maritime character of the Minoan empire.

Again, Homer knew of a class of merchants whom he calls πρηκτῆρες in the Eighth Odyssey (v. 152). But where Eumæus enumerates the δημιόεργοι, or 'trades and professions' of a Greek community, there are no πρηκτῆρες among them[m]. Again, as the poet knew of the existence of this class on earth, so he introduced them into his Olympian heaven, where gain and increase had their representative in Mercury. From whence could the prototype have been derived, except from intercourse with the Phœnicians?

But the imaginative geography of the Odyssey goes far beyond the points, with which Homer has so much at least of substantive acquaintance, as to associate them historically with the commerce or politics of the age. The habitations of the Cyclops, the Læstrygones, the Lotophagi, of Æolus, the Sirens, Calypso, and Circe, may have had no 'whereabout,' no actual site, outside the fancy of Homer; still they must have been imagined as repositories in which to lodge traditions which had reached him, and which, however fabulously given, purported to be local. Again, with respect to the tradition of Atlas, it is scarcely possible to refuse to it a local character. He knows the depths of every sea, and he holds or keeps the pillars that hold heaven and earth apart. This must not be confounded with the later representations of Atlas carrying the globe, or with his more purely geographical character, as representing the mountain ranges of Northern Africa. Here

[m] Od. xvii. 383.

he appears[n] as the keeper of the great gate of the outer waters, namely, of the Straits of Gibraltar: that great gate being probably the point of connection with the ocean, and that outer sea being frequented exclusively by the Phœnicians, who in all likelihood obtained from Cornwall the tin used in making the Shield of Agamemnon, or in any of the metal manufactures of the period. Rocks rising on each side of a channel at the extreme point of the world, as it was known to Greek experience, or painted in maritime narrative, could not be represented more naturally than as the pillars which hold up the sky. This figure follows the analogy of the pillars and walls of a house, supporting the roof, and placed at the extremities of the interior of its great apartment[o]. With equal propriety, those who are believed alone to have reached this remote quarter, and to frequent it, would be said to hold those pillars[p].

Even in a less imaginative age than that of Homer, the love of the marvellous, both by the givers and by the receivers of information, would act powerfully in colouring all narratives, of which the scene was laid in tracts unknown except to the narrator. But a more powerful motive might be found in that spirit of monopoly, which is so highly characteristic of the earlier stages, in particular, of the development of commerce[q]. To clothe their relations in mystery and awe, by the aid both of natural and supernatural wonders, would be, for a people possessed of an exclusive navigation,

[n] Nägelsbach, Homerische Theologie 80-3.

[o] There were columns outside the doors, for example, of the palace of Ulysses in Ithaca. Od. xvii. 29. This construction of the metaphor would come nearly to the same point, by making it mean the doors of Ocean.

[p] Hermann Opusc. vii. 253. Nägelsbach, ii. 9, note.

[q] Blakesley's Introduction to Herodotus, p. xiv.

a powerful means of deterring competitors, and of maintaining secure hold upon profits either legitimate or piratical.

We have before us these facts in evidence: on the one hand, a people who in maritime enterprise had far surpassed all others, and had a virtual monopoly of the knowledge of the waters and countries lying beyond a certain narrow circle. Then, on the other hand, we have a multitude of adventures laid by Homer in this outer sphere, and associated wholly with the persons and places that belong to it. Upon these grounds it seems hardly possible to avoid the conclusion, that the Phœnicians must have been the people from whom Homer drew, whether directly or mediately, his information respecting the outer circle of the geography of the Odyssey. Such is the judgment of Strabo. He says τοὺς δὲ Φοίνικας λέγω μηνυτάς; he considers that even before the time of Homer they were masters of the choice parts of Spain and Africa: and it appears that the traces of their colonization remained until his day[r].

But further; the traditions themselves bear other unequivocal marks, besides their lying in parts known to Phœnicians only, of a Phœnician character; and whether these marks were attached by Homer, or came ready made into his hands, has no bearing upon the present argument.

I have spoken of the tradition of Atlas; and of the likelihood that the Phœnicians would cast a veil over the regions of which they knew the profitable secrets. In conformity with these ideas, the island of Ogygia is the island of Calypso, the Concealer: and this Calypso is the daughter of Atlas.

Phæacia is, in the Odyssey, the geographical middle

[r] Strabo iii. 2. 13, 14. pp. 149, 50.

term between the discovered and the undiscovered world; Ogygia is the stage beyond it, and the stage on this side of it is Ithaca. I do not understand the Phæacians to be a portrait of the Phœnicians[r]: but the very resemblance of name is enough to show that Homer had this people in his eye when he endowed his ethereal islanders with the double gift, first, of unrivalled nautical excellence, and, secondly, of forming the medium of communication between the interior space bounded by the Greek horizon, and the parts which lay beyond it.

But in many instances we find Homer's peculiar and characteristic use of epithets the surest guide to his meaning. Now in Minos we have, according to Homer, a firmly grounded point of contact with Phœnicia. Of Minos, as the friend of Jupiter, and the Judge of the defunct, we must from the poems form a favourable impression. Yet is Ariadne Μίνωος θυγάτηρ ὀλοόφρονος. What is the meaning of the word ὀλοόφρων? I think an examination of the use of kindred words will show, that in the mind of Homer it does not mean anything actually wicked or criminal, but hard, rigid, inexorable; or astute, formidable to cope with, one who takes merciless advantage, who holds those with whom he deals to the letter of the bond; and, in consequence, often entails on them heavy detriment.

In this view, it would be an epithet natural and appropriate for a people, who represented commerce at a time when it so frequently partook of the characters of unscrupulous adventure, war, and plunder; and an epithet which might pass to Minos as one of the great figures in their history, or as a conqueror. Again, it is worth while to review Homer's use of the adjective ὀλοός. This epithet is applied by him to the lion, the boar,

[r] Mure, Greek Literature, i. 510.

and the water-snake[r]. Achilles, when complaining of Apollo for having drawn him away from the Trojan wall, calls him θεῶν ὀλοώτατε πάντων[s]. Menelaus, combating with Paris, when his sword breaks in his hand, complains of Jupiter that no god is ὀλοώτερος[t]. Philætius, in the Twentieth Odyssey, astonished that Jupiter does not take better care of good men, uses the same words[u]. And Menelaus applies the same epithet to Antilochus, who has stolen an advantage over him in the chariot-race[v]. In the positive degree, it is applied to old age, fire, fate, night, battle, to Charybdis (Od. xii. 113), and even to the hostile intentions of a god, such as the ὀλοὰ φρονέων of Apollo (Il. xvi. 701), and in θεῶν ὀλοὰς διὰ βουλὰς (Od. xi. 275).

But the characteristic force of the epithet applied to Minos becomes most clear, and its effect in stamping a Phœnician character upon certain traditions undeniable, when we examine the remaining instances of its use; and likewise that of the cognate, indeed nearly synonymous, phrase ὀλοφώϊα εἰδώς.

Only two persons besides Minos receive in Homer the epithet ὀλοόφρων[x]. One of them is Atlas, the father of Calypso: the other is Æetes, the brother of Circe. Again, the phrase ὀλοφώϊα εἰδὼς is applied to Proteus[y]; and it is used nowhere else except by Melanthius, where he means to describe Eumæus as a person dangerous and to be suspected[z]. Again, the ὀλοφώϊα of Proteus are his tricks[a]: and moreover we have the ὀλοφώϊα δήνεα of Circe[b]. Thus it would appear that Homer virtually confines these epithets within one particular circle of traditions; for Proteus, Æetes, Circe,

[r] Il. xv. 630. xvii. 21. ii. 723.   [s] Il. xxii. 15.   [t] Il. iii. 365.
[u] Od. xx. 201.   [v] Il. xxiii. 439.   [x] Od. i. 52 and x. 137.
[y] Od. iv. 460.   [z] Od. xvii. 248.   [a] Od. iv. 410.   [b] Od. x. 289.

Atlas, all belong to the Outer Geography of the Odyssey[c]: and the use of one of them for Minos, with his already presumable Phœnician extraction[d], leads us, in concurrence with many other signs, to conclude that the epithet is strictly characteristic, and the circle of traditions Phœnician. One of the slightest, is also perhaps one of the most curious and satisfactory signs of the Phœnicianism of the whole scheme. Tiresias is employed in the Eleventh Odyssey to predict to Ulysses his coming fortunes: and in doing it he uses many of the very lines, which are afterwards prophetically spoken by Circe. Now why is Tiresias made the informant of Ulysses? He is nowhere else mentioned in the poems; yet he is introduced here, in possession of the only gift of prophecy permitted in the nether world. Why have we not rather Amphiaraus, or Polupheides, those Seers at the top of all mortal renown[e]? Surely there can be but one reason; namely, that Tiresias was a Theban, a native of the only Greek State, except Crete, where he could have been the subject of a Phœnician dynasty[f]. It was doubtless this Phœnician connection, which qualified him to speak of regions, of which a Greek Seer would, in right of his nation, have possessed no knowledge.

Nor is it only upon the epithets that we may rely; but upon the characters, too, of those to whom they are appropriated. They are full of the elements of cunning and deception. Proteus, Circe, Calypso, the Sirens, the Læstrygones, the Cyclopes, all partake of this element, while in some it is joined with violence, and in others

[c] As perhaps does Amphitrite, mentioned four times in the Odyssey, never in the Iliad.

[d] I shall consider further the construction of Il. xiv. 321, as it bears on the connection of Minos with Phœnicia, in treating the subject of the Outer Geography.

[e] Od. xv. 252, 3.

[f] Od. x. 492.

with refinement or sensuality. In all of these we recognise so many variations of the one Phœnician type.

It has been observed, that Virgil seems to recognise Proteus as an eastern counterpart of Atlas, in the lines

Atrides Protei Menelaus ad usque columnas, &c.

This is a recognition by Virgil of the Phœnician character of the tradition: but I see no evidence that Homer meant to place Proteus and Atlas in relations to one another as representing the East and West of the Mediterranean, though this theory is adopted by Nägelsbach[g] and others.

The office of the god Mercury, and his relationship to Calypso, will be found to confirm these conclusions[h].

The moral signs of the Greek character, though not identical with those of the Phœnician, yet establish a resemblance between them; in so far that both possessed vigour, hardihood, and daring, and that the intelligence, which directed and sustained these great qualities, was susceptible of alliance with craft. In the censure upon the πρηκτῆρες, which Homer has conveyed through the mouth of Euryalus, we may read a genuine effusion of his own nature: but the gifts of Mercury to Autolycus appear to show, that the Phœnician character easily amalgamated with the Greek by its cunning, as well as by its strength. And certainly we may well marvel at the tenacity of tissue, with which these characters were formed, when we find that still, after the lapse of three thousand years, one race is distinguished beyond all others for aptitude and energy in prosecuting the pursuits of honourable commerce; that in England, now the centre of the trade of the whole world, the Greeks of the present day alike excel all other foreigners who frequent her great emporia, and the children of

[g] Nägelsbach ii. 9.   [h] See Studies on Religion, sect. iii.

her own energetic and persevering people; themselves perhaps the offspring of the Thesprotians, who went for corn to Dulichium; of the Taphians, who carried swarthy iron to Temese; of the Cretans, who made much money in Egypt; and of the Lemnians, who obtained metals, hides, captives, and even oxen, in return for their wine, from the jovial Greeks of the army before Troy.

The more we attempt an examination of the geography of the Odyssey, the more we find that, impossible as it is to reconcile with the actual distribution of earth and sea, it has marks of being derived from the nation, who navigated in the remote waters where its scenes are laid. The fundamental article of the whole is the circumscription of the known seas by the great river Ocean, which, alike in the Iliad and the Odyssey, flows round and round the earth, returning upon itself, ἀψόρροος[h], like what is called an endless rope. And the two keys, as I believe, to the comprehension of it are to be found in the double hypothesis,

(1) That Homer placed to the northward of Thrace, Epirus, and the Italian peninsula, an expanse, not of land, but of sea, communicating with the Euxine. Or, to express myself in other words, that he greatly extended the Euxine westwards, perhaps also shortening it towards the east; and that he made it communicate, by the Gulfs of Genoa and Venice, with the southern Mediterranean.

(2) That he compounded into one two sets of Phœnician traditions respecting the Ocean-mouth, and fixed the site of them in the North East.

[h] I have given the accepted, and perhaps the more probable meaning; but the word is also well adapted to signify the *tidal* Ocean. In the Mediterranean, as is well known, the tidal action is not perceived.

It would carry us too far from the line of ethnological inquiry, were I now to examine the extensive question with which these propositions are connected. I will only observe in this place, that all the features of this outer geography, when viewed at large, are of such a nature as to favour, or perhaps rather to compel, the supposition, that it was founded on foreign, that is to say, on Phœnician information. Its extended range, its reach, by the routes of Menelaus on the one side, and of Ulysses on the other, over all the points of the compass, its vague, indeterminate, and ungeographical character as to distances and directions, and yet its frequent, though inconsistent and confused, resemblances at almost every point to some actual prototype, of which the poet may have had possibly or probably a vision in his eye;—all this agrees with the belief, that it represents a highly manufactured work, made up from Phœnician materials, and can scarcely agree with any thing else.

Reserving this much agitated subject for a fuller separate discussion, I will here only proceed to consider that limited portion of it which bears upon ethnology; I mean the evidence afforded us by Homer in the Odyssey, and particularly in connection with the Wanderings, as to the site and character (1) of the Siceli and of Sicania: (2) of the Thesprotians and Epirus: and (3) with respect to the family of Cadmus, which general tradition connects immediately with Phœnicia in the person of its founder, and which Homer, by indirect testimony, I think, justifies us in considering as derived from that source.

The Siceli and Sicania.

Notwithstanding his use of the name Thrinacie, the

poet appears to have had no geographical knowledge of Sicily, at least beyond its shape; for I think it may be shown that he places the site of the island in the immediate neighbourhood of the Bosphorus. But he might still have heard of the eastern coast of Italy immediately adjoining, afterwards the country of the Bruttii, which forms the sole of the foot rudely described by the configuration of southern Italy. For this coast is much nearer to Greece; it probably would be taken by mariners on their way from Greece to Sicily, and might be visited by them before they had pushed their explorations to the more distant point. The Athenian fleet in the Peloponnesian war touched first at the Iapygian promontory, and then coasted all the way[k]. This possibility grows nearly into a certainty, when we find that Homer speaks of a race, evidently as transmarine, which from history would appear probably to have inhabited that region at some early period.

I venture to argue that this Bruttian coast, the sole of the Italian foot, reaching from the gulf of Tarentum down to Rhegium, is the country which appears to us in the Odyssey under the name of Sicania.

In the fabulous account which Ulysses gives of himself to his father Laertes before the Recognition, he speaks as follows:

εἰμὶ μὲν ἐξ Ἀλύβαντος, ὅθι κλυτὰ δώματα ναίω,
υἱὸς Ἀφείδαντος Πολυπημονίδαο ἄνακτος·
αὐτὰρ ἐμοί γ' ὄνομ' ἐστὶν Ἐπήριτος· ἀλλά με δαίμων
πλάγξ' ἀπὸ Σικανίης δεῦρ' ἐλθέμεν οὐκ ἐθέλοντα·
νηῦς δέ μοι ἥδ' ἔστηκεν ἐπ' ἀγροῦ νόσφι πόληος[l].

In this passage Ulysses represents himself as a mariner, driven by some cross wind out of his course into Ithaca. Now this implies that his point of departure

[k] Thucyd. vi. 42, 44.   [l] Od. xxiv. 304-8.

should be one from which by a single change of wind he could easily be driven upon Ithaca. Again, Sicania must have been a region known to the Ithacans, or else, instead of merely naming it, he would have described it to Laertes, as he describes Crete to Penelope[m].

Now, to fulfil these conditions, no other country than the one I have named is available. It has only an open sea between it and Greece, and a passage of some two hundred or two hundred and fifty miles, so that a wind driving him from his course might readily carry him across. And there is no other tract on the western side of the Adriatic, which is so likely to have been intended by Homer. Iapygia, beyond the Tarentine gulf, lies northward even of Scheria; and, like Scheria, so Iapygia was, we may be assured, in the Outer or unknown sphere of geography for Homer.

On the other hand, the Bruttian coast might well be known in Greece, though by dim rumour, yet better than Sicily: first, because it was nearer; and secondly, inasmuch as it did not in the same manner present the appearance of an island, its bearings would be more easily determined, and therefore its site was less likely to be mistaken. Lastly, history assures us that the Sicanian name prevailed in Italy, before it passed over into Sicily. Therefore the country of the Bruttii is in all likelihood the Homeric Sicania.

But again, we hear in Homer of $\Sigma\iota\kappa\epsilon\lambda o\iota$, though not of a $\Sigma\iota\kappa\epsilon\lambda\iota a$. The Suitors advise Telemachus to send his guests to the $\Sigma\iota\kappa\epsilon\lambda o\iota$[n] for sale: adding that a good price, a renumerating price ($\mathring{a}\xi\iota o\nu$), would thus be obtained for them. On the other hand, a Sicelian female slave is the wife of Dolios, and looks after Laertes in his old age[o].

[m] Od. xix. 172.   [n] Od. xx. 383.   [o] Od. xxiv. 211, 366, 389.

II. *Ethnology*.

From these passages we may infer,

1. That the country of the Σικελοὶ was within the remoter knowledge of Ithacan seamen.

2. That they were a rich people; since they were able to pay a good price for slaves.

The first point, as we have seen, would make the Σικελοὶ suitable inhabitants of Sicania.

But likewise as to the second, Homer has given us some indications of their wealth: (*a*) in the name Ἀφείδας (the open-handed) ascribed by Ulysses to his father; (*b*) in that of Ἐπήριτος (object of contention) assumed for himself; (*c*) perhaps also in the name Ἀλύβας, akin to that of Ἀλύβη[p], where there was silver, and to that of Ἀρύβας a rich Sidonian[q]. This name probably indicates the possession of metallic mines, which for that period we may consider as a special sign of advancement and opulence.

Then if we turn for a moment to the historic period, it is in this very country that we find planted the great and luxurious cities of Sybaris and Crotona[r].

Now as the people called Siceli, and the country called Sicania, are thus placed in relations of proximity by Homer, so they continue throughout all antiquity. The reports collected by Thucydides represent the Sicanians as giving their name to Sicily, and displacing the former name Trinacria, which is identical with the Homeric Thrinacie. At a later time, the Sicilians passed from Italy into Sicily, and, as was said, upon rafts; that is to say, across the strait, and consequently from the country which, as I contend, is the Homeric Sicania. These Siceli were rumoured to have overcome the Sicani, and to have again changed the name of the

[p] Il. ii. 857. Schönemann Geog. Hom. p. 31.   [q] Od. xv. 426.   [r] Cramer's Italy, ii. pp. 354, 391.

island to Sicily. It is yet more material to note, that Thucydides says there were still Siceli in Italy when he himself lived: and he adds the tradition that Italus, a king of theirs, gave his name to the Peninsula[s].

To these reports, which form a part of the account given by Thucydides, we may add the statement of Dionysius, that the Σικελοὶ were the oldest inhabitants of Latium, and were displaced by the Pelasgi[t]. This implies their movement southward, and makes it probable that we should meet them in Bruttium, on their way to Sicily, perhaps pressing, in that region, upon the Sicani.

Such an hypothesis would be in entire agreement with Homer, who evidently represents the Sicanian as older than the Sicelian name: for the first had become territorial, when the latter was only tribal or national. And all this is in agreement with Thucydides in the essential point, that he makes the Sicanians precede the Siceli: while, though the tradition he reports brings the Sicani from Spain under pressure from the Ligures[u], he need not mean to exclude the supposition, that they may have come by land down the Italian peninsula. Though it is probably wrong to confound the Siceli with the Sicani[v], it would thus on all hands appear, that they were but successive waves of the tide of immigration advancing southward.

There is a further evidence that Homer meant to place Sicania within the Greek maritime world, and not beyond it. It is this. In his fabulous narrative to Laertes, Ulysses apprises the old man, that he had seen his son five years before in Sicania, hopeful of reaching his home[x]. Now this is a proof that the place was

[s] Thucyd. vi. 2.   [t] Dionys. i. 9.   [u] Thuc. ibid.
[v] Cramer's Italy, ii. p. 2.   [x] Od. xxiv. 309.

in the Inner or known sphere of geography: for in the outer circle, as for instance at Æolia, he never has any knowledge or reckoning of his own as to the power of reaching home: it was Æolus who gave him the Zephyr to take him home, not he who knew that if he got a Zephyr he would reach home. And in like manner he is supplied with express directions by Calypso: while Menelaus, not being absolutely beyond the known world, has no instructions for his voyage from Proteus, who plays for him the part of divine informant.

Thus then it appears, that Homer knew something of that part of the Italian continent, which we may term the sole of the foot. Again, if we look onward to the heel, Iapygia or Apulia, and observe its proximity to Corcyra or Scheria, we shall perceive that mariners in the time of Homer might take the route, which was afterwards pursued by the Athenian fleet under Nicias and his colleagues. But this is conjectural; and as Scheria was so faintly known, we must suppose Apulia to have been still more faintly conceived. Beyond Apulia Homer gives no sign of any acquaintance whatever with Italy. It therefore at once appears possible that he had no idea of the junction by land between the Greek and Italian peninsulas, and that he had imaged to the northward only an expanse of sea. I postpone, however, the further discussion of this subject.

Epirus and the Thesproti.

The Ithacan Suitors threaten to send Irus (Od. xviii. 84, 115), and again Ulysses (Od. xxi. 307), to a certain lawless and cruel king named Echetus; and in the two first passages we have the additional indication ἤπειρόνδε. This expression used in Ithaca can refer to no other mainland than that of the Greek Peninsula : of which even the nearer parts[y] pass by that name.

As on the one hand Echetus is savage, and evidently foreign (for we never find a Greek sold by Greeks as a slave to a Greek), he must be beyond the Greek limit : doubtless beyond the Thesproti, who were allies ($ἄρθμιοι$, Od. xvi. 427) of Ithaca. On the other hand, he could not be remote, or the Suitors would not have spoken so glibly of sending persons there. Hence we can hardly doubt, that this Echetus was a sovereign in the region of Epirus, between Scheria and the Thesproti: and the territorial name $Ἤπειρος$ may thus be at least as ancient as the Poet.

In like manner we find in the Sixth Odyssey a female slave named Eurymedusa, in the household of Alcinous, the old nurse of Nausicaa. She was brought by sea $Ἀπείρηθεν$, and is described as $γρηῦς\ Ἀπείραίη$[z]. This is probably meant to indicate some part of the same region.

Thus Epirus would appear to form, along with Scheria and Sicania, Homer's line of vanishing points, or extreme limits of actual geography, towards the northwest and west of Greece. To trace these vanishing points all round the circuit of his horizon, whenever it can be done, is most useful towards establishing the fundamental distinction between his Inner and Outer, his practical and poetical geography. In order to mark that distinction more forcibly, I would, if I might venture it, even call the former of these alone Geography, and the latter his territorial Skiagraphy.

More nearly within the circle of every day intercourse with Greece than the barbarous Echetus and his Epirus, and yet hovering near the verge of it, are the Thesprotians of the Odyssey.

[y] Od. xiv. 93. [z] Od. vi. 7–12.

Ulysses, in the Fourteenth Book, in the course of his fabulous narrative to Eumæus, relates that, when he was on his way from Crete to Libya, the ship in which he was sailing foundered, but that, by the favour of Jupiter, he floated on the mast for nine days, and, on the tenth, reached the land of the Thesprotians.

This statement suffices to fix that people to the north of the gulf of Ambracia (Arta). For had they lain to the south of that gulf, this would not have been the first land for him to make, as it would have been covered by the islands.

The narrative which follows is very curious. The Thesprotian king Pheidon, according to the tale of Ulysses, took good care of him without making him a slave (ἐκομίσσατο ἀπριάτην); which, as he was cast helpless on the shore, common usage would apparently have justified, and even suggested. The king's son, who found him in his destitute condition, had his share in this great kindness; for he took him home, like Nausicaa, and clothed him. Here, says the tale, he heard news of Ulysses, who had proceeded from thence to Dodona to inquire about his fate, and had left much valuable property in trust with these hospitable and worthy people. But he goes on to relate, still in the assumed character, that, instead of keeping him to wait for Ulysses, the Thesprotian king took advantage of the opportunity afforded by a Thesprotian ship about to sail to Dulichium for corn, and dispatched him by it as a passenger to his home. The crew, however, infected with the kidnapping propensities of navigators, maltreated and bound him, with the intention of selling him for a slave: but, when they landed on the Ithacan beach to make a meal, he took advantage of the opportunity, and made his escape[a].

[a] Od. xiv. 293-359.

This ingenious fable is referred to, and in part repeated in subsequent passages of the poem[b], with no material addition, except that the country is called (πίων δῆμος xix. 271) a rich one.

But another passage[c], quite independent of all the former, adds a highly characteristic incident. Antinous, the insolent leader of the Suitors, is sharply rebuked by Penelope, and is reminded that his father Eupeithes had come to the palace as a fugitive from the Ithacan people, dependent on Ulysses for deliverance from their wrath. The reason of their exasperation was, that Eupeithes had joined the buccaneering Taphians in a piratical expedition against the Thesprotians, who were allies of Ithaca.

We have here a very remarkable assemblage of characteristics, which all tend to prove, and I think very sufficiently prove, the Pelasgianism of the Thesprotians. The humane and genial reception of the stranded seafarer is in exact accordance with the behaviour of the Egyptian king[d], and his people to him on a previous occasion. The fact that he was not enslaved, suggests it as most probable, that there were no slaves in the Thesprotian country: which would entirely accord with the position of the Pelasgians, as themselves not the conquerors of a race that had preceded them, but the first inhabitants of the spots they occupied in the Greek peninsula. The richness of their country is further in harmony with the account of Egypt, and with their addiction to agricultural pursuits. The feigned deposit by Ulysses of his metallic stores with them proves, that they were not a predatory, and therefore proves, for that period, that they were not a poor people. The name Pheidon,

[b] Od. xvi. 65. xvii. 525, and xix. 269–99.
[c] Od. xvi. 424–30.   [d] Od. xiv. 278–86.

or thrifty, given to the king, agrees with the character which, as we shall elsewhere find, attaches in a marked manner to Pelasgian proper names. And lastly, they were the subject of attack by Taphian buccaneers; which tends to show their unoffending and unaggressive character.

On the other side, we find them trading by sea to Dulichium: and we find the crew of the trader attempting to kidnap Ulysses. But as the Pelasgians were not in general navigators, it may very well have happened that the trade of the country had fallen into the hands of some distinct, possibly some Lelegian, or even some Hellenic race, which may have settled there for the purpose of carrying on a congenial employment, and which, like other traders of the time, would be ready upon occasion to do a turn in the way of piracy. It is to be remembered that there was a Thesprotian[e] Ephyre; which proves, as I believe, an early infusion of some race connected with the Hellenic stem.

I conclude, therefore, from Homer, that the Thesprotians were Pelasgian. And this conclusion is strongly sustained by the extra-Homeric tradition. Herodotus states, that they were the parent stock from whence descended the Thessalians[f], a report which I only follow to the extent of its signifying an affinity between the early settlers on the two sides of Mount Pindus. And Dionysius[g] appears to imply the opinion, that they were Thesprotian Pelasgians who settled in Italy.

I have already stated, that I can hardly think Homer points out to us more than one Dodona in the Iliad and Odyssey respectively. At the same time, if the supposition of two Dodonas be admissible, the circum-

[e] Strabo vii. p. 324.   [f] Herod. vii. 176.   [g] Dion. Hal. i. 18.

stances suggested by him would help to account for it. For the Dodona of the Iliad is described as Pelasgic and also Hellic: that is, as we must I think suppose, having been Pelasgic, it had become Hellic. The Dodona of the Odyssey (on this supposition) is Thesprotian, that is to say Pelasgic, only. The solution would then be, that the Pelasgians of the original Dodona, when displaced, claimed to have carried their oracle along with them, while the Hellic intruders in like manner set up a counter-claim to have retained it in its original seat. The history of Christendom supplies us with cases bearing no remote analogy to this, in connection with the removal of a great seat of ecclesiastical power.

Cadmeans.

We have seen that the name of Ino Leucothee is sufficiently identified with a circle of Phœnician and outerworld traditions. And, as her name and position give us directly, or by suggestion, the principal testimony borne by Homer to Cadmus her father, this will be the most convenient place for considering his connection with Greece.

We are justified, I think, in at once assuming, first, from his relation to Ino, that he was Phœnician; secondly, from the deification of his daughter, that he was a ruler or prince. And thirdly, Ino appears to Ulysses in his distress as a protecting deity. Now as, when mortal, she had been Phœnician by extraction, and as she thus shows her sympathies with the Hellenic race, we must assume a link between these two facts. They would be associated in an appropriate manner, if the family of Cadmus her father had become naturalized in the possession of a Greek sovereignty.

Diodorus Siculus has handed down a tradition respecting Cadmus[h], which is important from its combination with circumstantial evidence; and which is in harmony with Homer, as it appears to represent the Phœnician immigrant at a well known and natural resting-place on his way towards Greece. It is to the effect, that Cadmus put into Rhodes, built there a temple of Neptune (and here we should remember the worship, and, as some think, the temple of Neptune[i] in Scheria), established a line of hereditary priests, and deposited offerings to Minerva of Lindos. Among these, there remained in after-times a finely wrought kettle or caldron, executed in an antique style of art, and bearing an inscription in the Phœnician character.

In connection with the name of Cadmus, we have the Homeric designations of Καδμεῖοι and Καδμείωνες. They appear to be synonymous: but the patronymical form of the latter corroborates the opinion that there was an individual Cadmus from whom the names proceeded, that they were properly dynastic, and not names taken from a nation or extended race.

We have next to inquire as to the period within which this race of Cadmeans held sway in Bœotia, the district where alone we hear of them. When did they begin, and when did they close?

The extra-Homeric tradition would throw Cadmus back to one of the very earliest periods, which would appear to be included within Homer's knowledge upwards. The generations are arranged as follows:

1. Cadmus.
2. Polydorus.
3. Labdacus.
4. Laius.
5. Œdipus.
6. Eteocles and Polynices.

[h] Diod. Sic. v. 58.   [i] Od. vi. 266.

The last-named brothers are contemporaries of Tydeus. It follows that Cadmus is placed seven generations before the Trojan war; he is made contemporary with Dardanus, and he appears in Greece about three and a half generations before Minos came to Crete.

Now this is not the presumption, to which the Homeric text would give rise. For it does not seem likely that, if a family of an active race like the Phœnicians made their way into Greece, and managed to establish a sovereignty within it seven generations before the *Troica*, upwards of a century should elapse before any other adventurer was found to repeat so advantageous a process.

Further, the Cadmeans were in Thebes. But Cadmus was not its founder. It was founded, as we are told in the Eleventh Odyssey[k], by Zethus and Amphion, sons of Jupiter and of Antiope, daughter of Asopus: two persons who have thus, on both sides of their parentage, the signs of being the first known of their own race in the country. From the appearance of Antiope in the Νεκυΐα, where none but Hellenic and naturalized Shades are admitted, we may infer that Amphion and Zethus were not Pelasgian but Hellene. Again, as they *first* founded and fortified Thebes, they must have preceded Cadmus there. What then was their probable date?

In the Νεκυΐα, so far as regards the women, Homer gives some appearance of meaning to introduce the persons and groups in chronological order.

The first of them all is Tyro[l], who seems to have been of the family of Æolus, and to have lived about four generations before the *Troica*.

[k] 260–5.   [l] See inf. sect. viii.

The next is Antiope, mother of Amphion and Zethus.

After her come (1) Alcmene, mother of Hercules,
(2) Epicaste, mother of Œdipus, and
(3) Chloris, mother of Nestor.

All of whom belong to a period three generations before the war.

After these follow Leda and Ariadne, with others whose epoch the text of Homer does not enable us to fix. But Ariadne, the bride of Theseus, and aunt of Idomeneus (the μεσαιπόλιος), stands at about one generation and a half before the war: and Leda, as the mother of Castor and Pollux who were dead, and of Helen whose marriageable age dated from so many years before the action of the Iliad, as well as of Clytemnestra, belongs to about the same date.

On the whole therefore it would appear, from the signs of chronological order, that Antiope can hardly have been older than Tyro, and therefore can only have been about four, and her sons about three generations before the War. We have no vestiges of their race in Homeric history, except that, in the Nineteenth Odyssey[m], there is recorded the death of Itylus, the son of Zethus, in his boyhood. The Amphion Iasides of Od. xi. 283, must be another person. But, if this reasoning be sound, Cadmus, who succeeds to them in Thebes, was probably much more recent than the later tradition makes him, and may have come into Greece only a short time before Minos.

His name appears to have been given as a dynastic name to his subjects, or the ruling class of them, and to have continued such under his descendants. For

[m] Od. xix. 522.

not only does it appear to have begun with him, but with the fall of the family it at once disappears.

In five different places of the poems, Homer has occasion to refer to occurrences, which took place at Thebes under the Cadmean dynasty, in the time of Œdipus and of his sons: and in these five passages he employs the names Καδμεῖοι and Καδμείωνες no less than eight times for the people, while he never calls them by any other name[n].

But when we come down to the time of the war, this dynasty has disappeared with Eteocles and Polynices: the country of Bœotia, which it had once governed, seems to have lost its cohesion, and its troops are led by a body of no less than five chiefs. And now, whenever Homer has occasion to refer to the inhabitants of the country, they are never Καδμεῖοι or Καδμείωνες, but they are Βοιωτοί. The words Βοιωτὸς and Βοιώτιος are found nine times in the Iliad.

Nations called by a name which is derived from a national source, are likely to retain it longer than those which are designated dynastically from the head of a ruling family: as they must change their dynasties more frequently than they can receive new infusions of race and blood, powerful enough to acquire a predominance over the old.

Strabo indeed says[o], that Homer calls the Cadmeans of the Troic war by the name of Minyæ. But no Minyæ are named in Homer at all, although he speaks of the Ὀρχόμενος Μινυήϊος, and of the ποταμὸς Μινυήϊος in Peloponnesus, and though there was perhaps there also a Minyan Orchomenos. Even if Minyæ were named in Homer as a race, it would be strange that

[n] Il. iv. 385, 388, 391. v. 804, 7. x. 208. xxiii. 680. Od. xi. 275.
[o] ix. p. 401.

Homer should without a reason alter, for the period of the war, that use of the Cadmean name, to which he adheres elsewhere so strictly, as to show that he is acting on a rule. Whereas the transition to Βοιωτοὶ is not only intelligible, but politically descriptive.

Upon the foregoing facts we may found several observations:

1. The Cadmean name would seem to be strictly dynastic: as it makes its first appearance on the spot where Cadmus has reigned, and disappears at the same point, along with the extinction of his family.

2. The use of the Cadmean name by Homer, compared with his departure from it, each having appropriate reference to the circumstances of different epochs, appears to be a marked example of a careful and historic manner of handling local names with reference to the exact circumstances of place, time, and persons, and not in the loose manner of later poetry.

3. Our whole view of Cadmus and the Cadmeans from Homer has been attained by circuitous inference: and, presuming it to be a just one, we have here a very singular example of the poet's reticence with respect to all infusion of foreign blood and influence into his country.

SECT. V.

On the Catalogue.

The Catalogue in the Second Book belongs more properly to the Geography, than to the Ethnology of the poems. But I advert to it here on account both of the historic matter it contains, and of the manner in which it illustrates the general historic designs of the Poet.

It is perhaps, in its own way, nearly as characteristic and remarkable a performance, as any among the loftier parts of the poem. Considered as a portion of the Iliad, it would be more justly termed the Array than the Catalogue; for it is a review, and not a mere enumeration. Considered with respect to history, its value can scarcely be overrated: it contains the highest title-deeds of whatever ancient honour the several States might claim, and is in truth the Doomsday Book of Greece.

We may consider the Greek Catalogue in three parts:

First, the Invocation or Preface.

Secondly, the Catalogue Proper.

Thirdly, the Postscript, so to call it, 761–779.

Before and after, he has graced the work with splendid similes. When all is concluded and, as it were, marked off, he proceeds to append to it the Trojan Catalogue; a work of less extent and difficulty, as also of less penetrating interest to his hearers, but yet constructed with much of care, and with various descriptive embellishments.

The Preface contains the most formal invocation of

the Muses among the few which are to be found in the poems. The others are,

Il. i. 1. Introduction to the Iliad: addressed to Θεά.
Il. ii. 761. In the Postscript to the Catalogue.
Il. xi. 218. Before the recital of the persons who were slain by Agamemnon.
Il. xiv. 508. Before the recital of the Greek chiefs, who, on the turn of the battle, slew various Trojans.
Il. xvi. 112. Before proceeding to relate, how the Trojans hurled the firebrands at the Grecian ships.
Od. i. 1. Introduction to the Odyssey: addressed to Μοῦσα.

In the cases of the Eleventh and Fourteenth Books, the invocation of the Muse stands in connection with a particular effort of memory; for the recitals prefaced by it consist of names not connected by any natural tie one with the other. But it is here that the Poet's appeal to the Muse most deserves attention.

If Homer was composing a written poem, the invocation is ill-timed and unmeaning. He has already, by a series of fine similes, elevated the subject to a proper level. Considered as a mere written Catalogue, it does not deserve or account for the prayer for aid: in this point of view, it was of necessity among the *sermoni propiora*, and was one of the easiest parts of the poem to compose. But if we consider the poem as a recitation, then the Catalogue was very difficult; because of the great multitude of details which are included in it, and which are not in themselves connected together by any natural or obvious link.

It is true that he begs the Muses to inform him, because they were omnipresent and omniscient, whereas he is dependent on report only (κλέος) for information.

Now this was equally true of the whole material of the poem: but the reason why he introduces the statement of this truth in so marked a manner, must be from the arduous nature of the task he was beginning; nor could it be arduous in any other way, than as an effort of memory.

The invocation contains another proof that the poems were composed for recitation in the words (vv. 489, 90)

οὐδ' εἴ μοι δέκα μὲν γλῶσσαι, δέκα δὲ στόματ' εἶεν
φωνὴ δ' ἄρρηκτος, χαλκέον δέ μοι ἦτορ ἐνείη.

Nothing can be more proper than to refer to the insufficient ability of the bodily organs of recitation, if he were about to recite: but nothing less proper, if he were engaged on a written poem. It has been a fashion however with poets to copy Homer in this passage, although the reason and circumstances on which it is founded had become wholly inapplicable: and their abusive imitation has blinded us to the significance of the passage as it stands in the Iliad.

Now as regards the list itself.

In this Catalogue, he had to go through the different States of Greece, furnishing twenty-nine contingents of various strengths, all indicated by the number of ships, to the army. These contingents are under forty-five leaders, many of them with genealogies, and coming from one hundred and seventy-one Greek towns. The proper names of the Greek Catalogue, strictly so called, are three hundred and ninety-six, and those of the Trojan one hundred and five, making in all five hundred and one. These must have been a selection from a larger number, for there were Greek towns (for example Φηραὶ of the Peloponnesus, Od. iii. 488, and the various towns named Ἐφύρη) not named in the Catalogue;

and this again increased the difficulty of keeping by memory to the list throughout. Again, it was difficult to adopt any arrangement that should not be wholly arbitrary, in displaying to us the parts of an army which comprised so many divisions, and which was drawn from sources so numerous, and dispersed over a territory of such extremely irregular formation.

Homer has however with great ingenuity adopted a geographical arrangement in the Greek Catalogue, which, so far as the various divisions were concerned, has enabled him to combine them into a kind of whole.

The territory, which supplied the army, consisted partly of continent, and partly of islands: and the islands again were partly such as, lying about the coast of the mainland, might be most conveniently remembered in conjunction with it, partly such as formed a group of themselves.

If we take the continent and islands together, we shall find that they form part of a curvilinear figure, not indeed circular, but elliptical, and more nearly approaching a circle than that group of islands in the Ægean, which afterwards obtained the name of Cyclades. This name, taken from the rude approximation to a geometrical figure, may possibly have been at first suggested to the Greeks by Homer's geometrical arrangement in the Catalogue. I speak of Homer's arrangement as geometrical, because the principle he has adopted is that of mental figure drawing: it is of course of the rudest kind, and he perhaps did not even know the correct mode of constructing a circle.

The proportion of the figure formed by the mainland and islands is about two-thirds of a complete circumference: the ends of the curve being Thessaly to the

The principle of arrangement. 249

north, and Calydnæ, with the other small islands, in the south-east.

Let us now proceed to notice, firstly, the primary division of the Catalogue into principal parts, and secondly, the subdivision in each of those parts.

It is worth while to remark, that the Poet has not adopted the mode of enumeration which might have been thought most obvious: namely, to begin at one of the extremities of this semicircle (so to call it), and then proceed towards the other. If the territorial subdivisions had been regular, this would have been convenient: but from their utter irregularity it would in this case have been wholly useless.

Again, he might have begun with Agamemnon, his immediate forces and dominion; and might then proceed through the States according to the political importance of their respective contingents. But to this course there were two objections. First, their order could not on this principle have been easily decided, especially after passing a few of the most considerable. But, secondly, he appears to have avoided, with a fixed purpose and with an extraordinary skill, both here and elsewhere, whatever could have excited feelings of jealousy as between the several States of Greece. Of course I do not refer to the admitted supremacy of Agamemnon: but if he had attempted to place the forces of Nestor, Diomed, Menelaus, of the Athenians, the Arcadians, the Phthians, in an order thus regulated, it would have been at variance with obvious prudence, and with his uniform rule of action. Perhaps, however, we may rightly consider, that if Homer had been writing his poems, he could not have failed to give Agamemnon the first place in this description. He has not then followed the general form of the territory, nor has he begun with the chief political member of the armament. Nor, lastly, has he even treated the Peloponnesus as a separate division of Greece: but he has introduced it, though it was the most important part of the country, between the eastern parts (Bœotia, with six other States) and the western parts (Ætolia, with two other States) of Middle Greece.

There are therefore various modes of arrangement, which either politically or geographically might be termed obvious, but which the Poet has passed by. Why has he passed them by? and why has he begun the Catalogue with the Bœotians? who were neither powerful, nor ancient, nor distinguished in a remarkable degree; nor did they lie at any one of the geographical extremities of the country.

Again, it might be asked, why has he not either divided all the islands from Continental Greece, or none? Instead of that, he reckons Eubœa, Cephallenia, Zacynthus, and Ithaca, in the same division with Continental Greece, but begins a new division with Crete.

Let us now carefully note what he has done, and see whether it does not suggest the reasons.

The three principal divisions of the Catalogue would appear to lie as follows:

I. Continental Greece south of mount Œta, including the Middle and the Southern division, with the islands immediately adjacent. This section furnishes sixteen contingents. (Il. ii. 494–644.)

II. Insular Greece, from Crete to Calydnæ: these islands furnish four contingents. (645–680.)

III. Thessalian Greece, from Œta and Othrys in the south, to Olympus in the north: which furnishes nine contingents. (681–759.)

These three divisions completely sever the line of

MAP I.

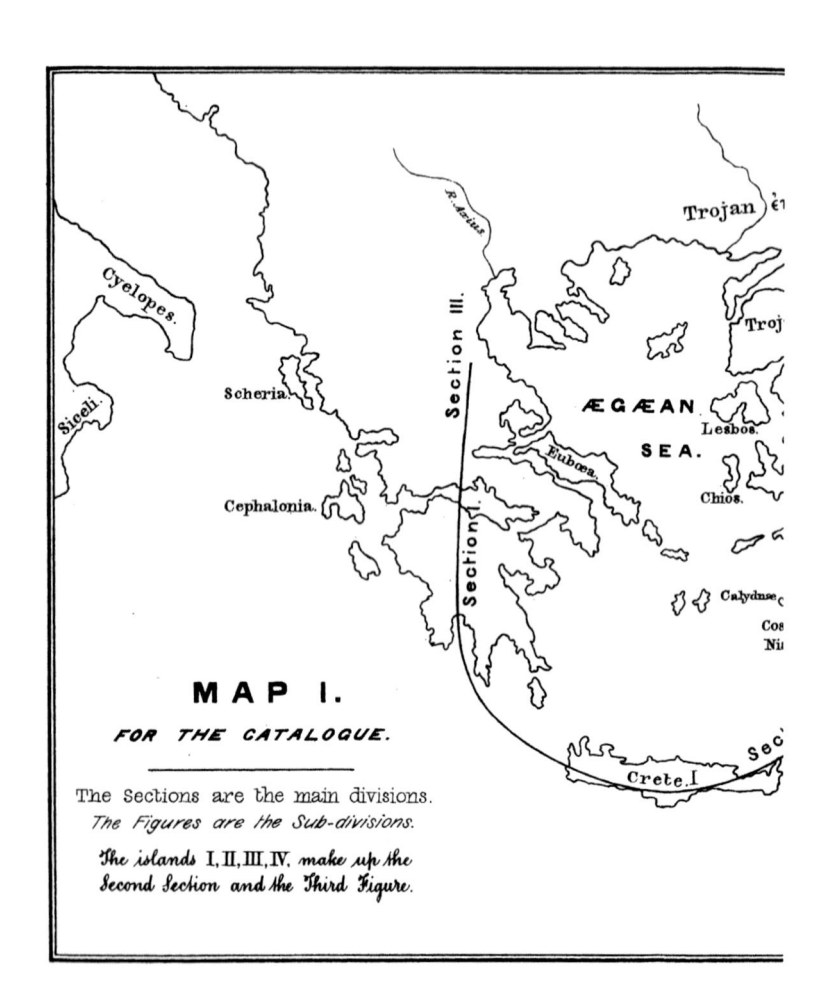

FOR THE CATALOGUE.

The Sections are the main divisions.
The Figures are the Sub-divisions.

*The islands I, II, III, IV, make up the
Second Section and the Third Figure.*

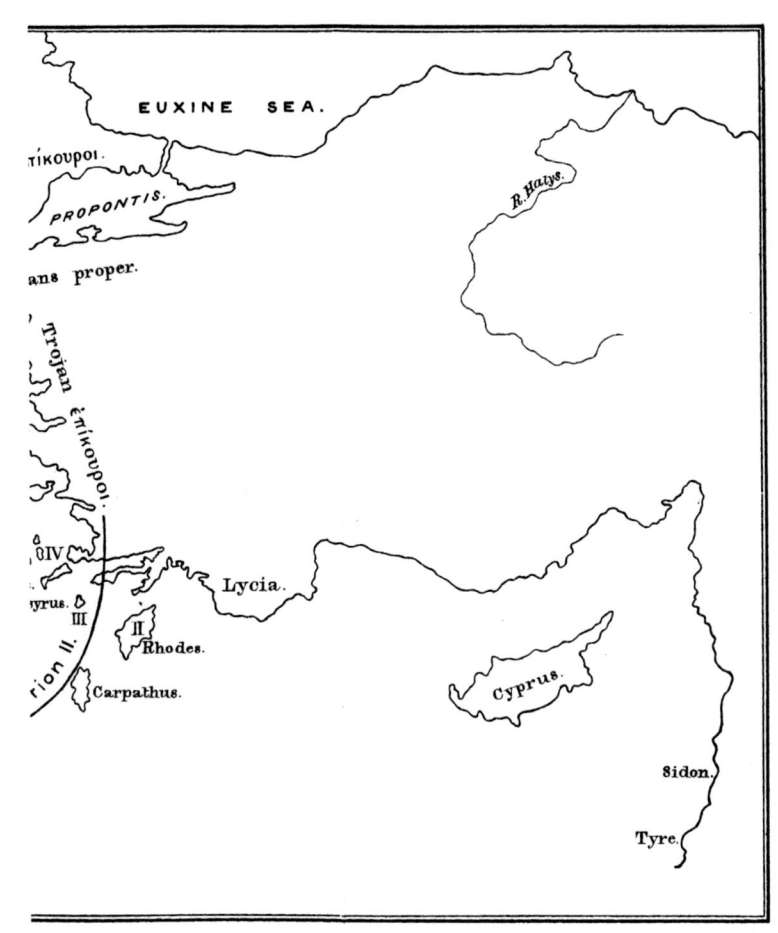

At p. 250.

the semicircular curve. It follows that in recitation he would be able to dispose of each part severally, as each forms a compact figure of itself: and this he could not have done, had he followed the seemingly more natural division into continent and islands. At the interval between the first and the second, he makes a spring from Ætolia to Crete: and another between the second and the third, from the Calydnæ to Thessaly.

The *desideratum* obviously was, to assist memory by such a geographical disposition, that the different parts might be made by association each to suggest that which was immediately to follow. So distributed, they would supply a kind of *memoria technica*.

We see how he prepares for this operation by his distribution in chief, which gives him the three sections of Greece, as they succeed one another on the line of the (completed) figure.

And, though we may not yet have in view a reason for his beginning with the Bœotians, we seem now at least to have a reason before us for his beginning with the middle section instead of one of the extremes; namely, that it was the principal one, as it not only supplied the largest number of ships and men, and nearly all the greater commanders, but also as it contains the seat of sovereignty, and supplied the forces of the Chief of the army.

Having the three sections before us, let us now observe the manner in which he manages the sub-distribution, so as to make each district of territory lead him on to the next.

And here he seems evidently to proceed upon these two rules: first, never to pass over an intervening territory, though he may cross a strait or gulf.

And secondly, to throw the several States into rude

II. *Ethnology.*

circles or other figures, round the arc or along the line of which his recollection moves from point to point.

His first figure may be called a circle, being elliptical[a]; and it includes nine contingents.

1. Bœotia.
2. Minyeian Orchomenus.
3. Phocis.
4. Locris.
5. Eubœa.
6. Attica.
7. Salamis.
8. Argolis.
9. Mycenæ.

His second is a zigzag, and includes seven contingents[b].

1. Lacedæmon.
2. Pylus.
3. Arcadia.
4. Elis.
5. The Dulichians.
6. The Cephallenians.
7. Ætolia.

We now part with the first section.

His third figure embraces the second section, or insular division of the Catalogue, and is again part of a rude circle or ellipse[c].

1. Crete.
2. Rhodes.
3. Syme.
4. Cos and other islands. Carpathus is included, which lay between Crete and Rhodes; being apparently in political union with Cos and the Calydnæ, and contributing to the same contingent, it could not but stand with them. Strabo observes that this principle of political division, according to what he terms δυνάστειαι[d], has been adopted by the Poet in his account of the Thessalian contingents.

By reference to the rude maps annexed, which mark

[a] Fig. i. in Map.　　[b] Fig. ii. in Map.　　[c] Fig. iii. in Map.
[d] ix. 5. p. 430.

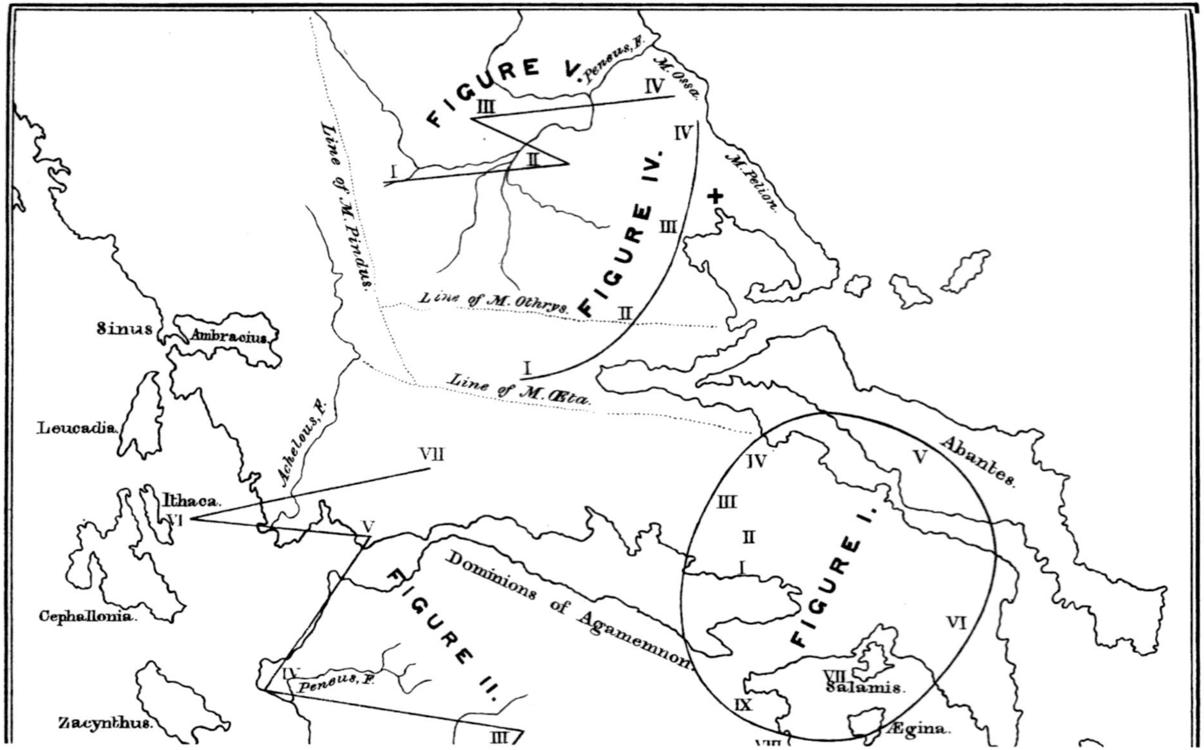
FIGURE V.
Peneus, F.
M. Ossa.
M. Pelion.
FIGURE IV.
Line of M. Pindus.
Line of M. Othrys.
Line of M. Œta.
Sinus
Ambracius.
Leucadia.
Achelous, F.
Ithaca.
Cephallonia.
Zacynthus.
Abantes.
FIGURE I.
Salamis.
Ægina.
Dominions of Agamemnon.
FIGURE II.
Peneus, F.

MAP II.
THE CATALOGUE.

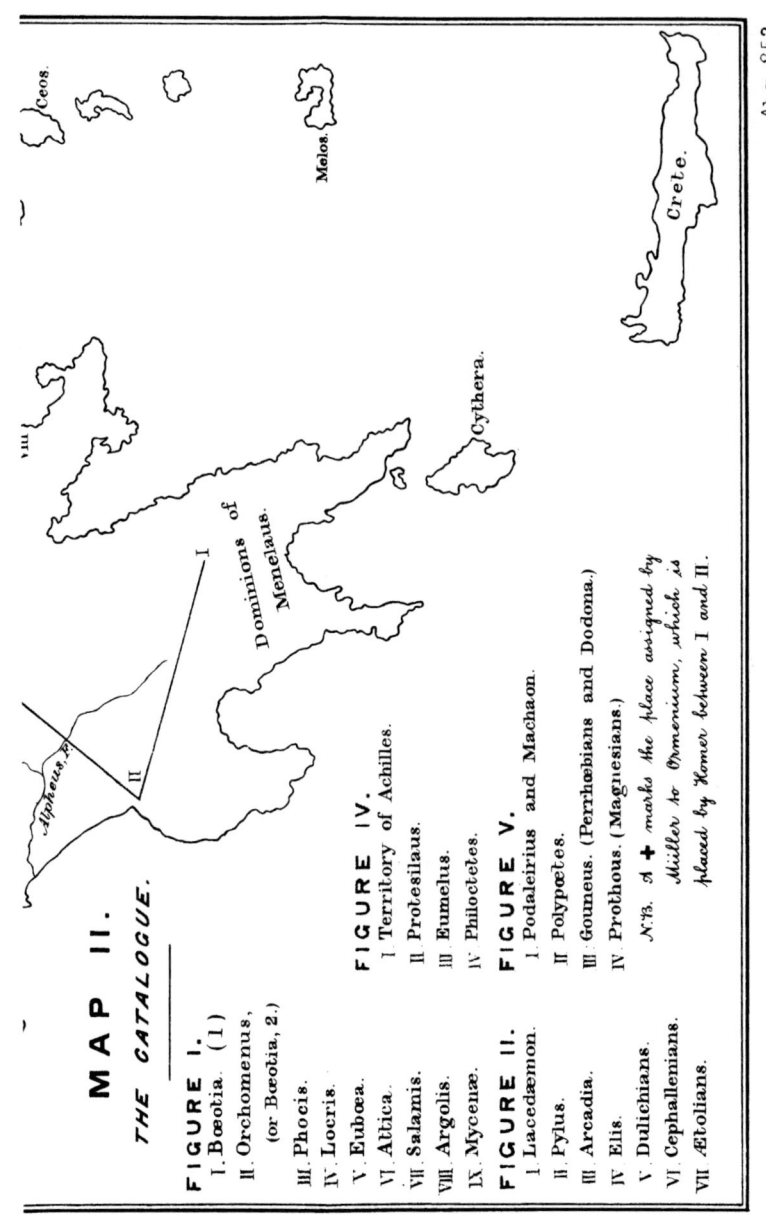

FIGURE I.
I. Boeotia. (1)
II. Orchomenus,
(or Boeotia, 2.)
III. Phocis.
IV. Locris.
V. Euboea.
VI. Attica.
VII. Salamis.
VIII. Argolis.
IX. Mycenae.

FIGURE II.
I Lacedaemon.
II Pylus.
III Arcadia.
IV Elis.
V Dulichians.
VI Cephallenians.
VII Aetolians.

FIGURE IV.
I Territory of Achilles.
II Protesilaus.
III Eumelus.
IV Philoctetes.

FIGURE V.
I Podaleirius and Machaon.
II Polypoetes.
III Gouneus. (Perrhoebians and Dodona.)
IV Prothous. (Magnesians.)

N.B. A + marks the place assigned by Müller to Ormenium, which is placed by Homer between I and II.

The order for Thessaly.

the several contingents by figures, the nature of this contrivance will be clearly seen.

It is more difficult to trace Homer's method of proceeding with respect to Thessaly.

This country furnishes nine contingents, which may best be described by the names of their leaders. There is no difficulty as to the first four, except that some of the boundaries are indeterminate. They form, like the last or insular group, an incomplete circle[e]. The leaders are;

I. Achilles (681–94).
II. Protesilaus (695–710).
III. Eumelus (711–15).
IV. Philoctetes (716–28).

There is more difficulty in describing the arrangement of the remainder. Strabo, who has followed the Catalogue in Thessaly with great minuteness, seems to have noticed the circular arrangement: at least he speaks of the κύκλος τῆς Θετταλίας, and the περιόδεια τῆς χώρας[f]. But when he comes to the sixth division, that of Eurypylus, he appears to find it impossible to fix with any confidence the site of Ormenium: and says, καὶ ἄλλα δ' ἐστὶν ἃ λέγοι τις ἄν, ἀλλ' οὖν ὀκνῶ διατρίβειν ἐπὶ πλέον[g]. And further on he observes, that the displacements and changes of cities, and mixtures of races, have confounded the names and tribes[h], so as to make them in part unintelligible to men of his day: where we are anew reminded of the passage of Thucydides, in which he tells us, that the most fertile tracts underwent the most frequent changes of population[i].

The δυναστεία of Eurypylus is in our maps commonly

[e] Fig. iv. in Map.   [f] Strabo ix. p. 435.
[g] Ibid. p. 439.   [h] Ibid. p. 442.   [i] Thuc. i. 2.

placed on the sea coast, but as it appears, with little authority of any kind: while, after all the proof we have seen of continuous arrangement, it seems incredible that, in this instance alone, Homer could have followed an order such that the δυναστεία should not march either with that which precedes, or that which follows, but should be severed from them by a line of territories intervening, which he has already disposed of.

To judge from analogy with the otherwise uniform rule of the Catalogue, the dominions of Eurypylus must have been somewhere conterminous both with those of the Asclepiads, and with those of Polypœtes. Waiving however any effort to fix positively their site, we find the other four remaining contingents connected by a zigzag line[k], like that which was used in southern Greece. The leaders are as follows:

I. Podaleirius and Machaon (729-33). (Eurypylus 734-7, omitted.)

II. Polypœtes (738-47).

III. Gouneus (Enienes, Perrhæbi, and Dodona, 748-55).

IV. Prothous (the Magnesians, 756-9).

In this view Homer appears to subdivide Thessaly into two figures, as he had done Southern Greece: and in both cases one of them is curvilinear, in which the eastern parts are arranged: the other a zigzag, which includes the western portions.

I have described this geometrical arrangement, as of great interest in connection with the question, whether the poems were written or recited; and also as it seems to be in itself highly ingenious.

It seems to distribute in rude but real symmetry before the eye of the mind, an assemblage of objects

[k] Fig. v. in Map.

between which it would at first sight appear almost impossible to frame any link of connection.

But in Homer, though there is much that is ingenious, there is nothing that is far-fetched: and the order he has followed might well, as to many parts at least of Greece, have been that of his own itinerancy as a minstrel. And, though complex in other respects, yet if it reduces a complex physical arrangement to the form, in which it becomes practically more manageable than in any other way for his purposes, it is evidently the one which may best be justified on the principles of common sense.

The Greek Catalogue is also full of proofs of the historical intention of Homer.

In the first place, such proof is afforded by the immense amount of its details, which are *prima facie* a load upon his verse, and which Homer seems to have so regarded, from the care he has taken to relieve the subject by the cluster of similes at the beginning. He must have had a purpose in facing this disadvantage. It is quite at variance with his own spirit, and the spirit of his age, to suppose that this purpose was merely to flatter the vanity of hearers by wholesale fiction.

The use of supernatural machinery is agreeable to the genius of the poet and his age, but not so the vulgar falsification of plain terrestrial facts. If the supposition of wholesale fiction cannot be maintained, there is no other alternative but that of an historical purpose.

Viewed at large, the Catalogue is an answer to that normal question, which expresses the anxiety of every Greek to make the acquaintance of a man first of all through what are colloquially termed his 'belongings.'

II. *Ethnology*.

Τίς; πόθεν εἰς ἀνδρῶν; πόθι τοι πόλις; ἠδὲ τοκῆες[1];

The chief indication of departure from this purpose is in the case of Nireus[m]. This paltry leader is almost the only person of legitimate birth, both of whose parents are named: and while he is evidently introduced for his beauty only, it is most suspicious that his father should be named Χάροψ, and likewise his mother Ἀγλαΐη. This savours of the names Δημόδοκος and Τερπιάδης, which Homer has given to his Bards in the Odyssey. And again of his Phronius, son of Noemon, whom he introduces to play the part of a considerate and serviceable Ithacan citizen[n]. With the insignificant island of Syme Homer might, for a special object, well take this liberty. And we may observe here, as elsewhere, that what is probably a departure from literal truth, may also be in a higher view historical: for doubtless his object is to commemorate impressively the wonderful beauty of Nireus, and this he does by inventing appropriate accessories.

Again, though an accurate geography would not of itself have proved the personal parts of the narrative to be historical, it is scarcely conceivable that he would have adopted one so minute and elaborate, as well as exact, if he had meant to combine with it a string of merely fictitious personalities.

Thirdly, besides many simple patronymics, there are found thirteen minor genealogies in the Catalogue, ten of them Greek, and three foreign. They are of three generations only in every case, with the single ex-

---

[1] Od. i. 170, *et alibi*.

[m] I am not prepared to contend that the numbers of the ships are to be taken as literally correct: but this subject will be discussed in conjunction with his general mode of using number, in the 'Studies on Poetry,' sect. iii.

[n] Od. ii. 386.

Genealogies of the Catalogue. 257

ception of the Orchomenian leaders, who have four: and in every case they attach to secondary heroes, who are thus treated in a mass, while provision is made in other parts of the poem for making known to us the descent (with the exception of Ajax) of all the greater heroes, as occasion serves to state it for each of them singly. Now it is inconceivable, even on general grounds, that the poet should have invented this mass of names; for they could surely have excited no sort of interest among his hearers, except upon one ground. They must have been true genealogical records of persons, who had played a part in the great national drama; one not perhaps of high importance, yet sufficient to be the basis of such traditions, as are justly deemed worthy of local record among a people eminently strong in their municipal, as well as their general patriotism. Over and above this, many points of these minor genealogies coincide with, and illustrate other historical notices in other parts of the poem.

Again, there are in all eight cases in the Catalogue, where the name of a mother is mentioned. These are,

1. Astyoche, mother of Ascalaphus and Ialmenus, Mars being the father, v. 513.

2. Aroura mother of Erechtheus, no father being mentioned, v. 548.

3. Astyochea mother of Tlepolemus, Hercules being the father, v. 658.

4. Aglaie mother of Nireus, Charops the father, v. 672.

5. Alcestis mother of Eumelus, Admetus the father, v. 715.

6. Rhene mother of Medon, Oileus the father, v. 728.

7. Hippodamia mother of Polypœtes, Pirithous the father, v. 742.

S

8. Venus is mentioned as the mother of Æneas, Anchises being the father, v. 820.

The second of these cases, if we are to regard the passage containing it as Homeric, must not be considered as an account of parentage, but simply as a mode of asserting autochthonism. Again, the parents of Nireus, whether true persons or not, are evidently named with reference to the consideration of beauty only, which is the key to the whole passage.

And the parentage of Æneas may also perhaps be named for the sole purpose of embellishment.

Described by the words θεὰ βροτῷ εὐνηθεῖσα, it does not appear to stand in the same class, or to be susceptible of the same explanations, as those Greek cases where Greek chieftains born out of wedlock have gods for their fathers; nor is there any case, among the Greeks, of illegitimate birth from a goddess. Of the five other cases three (1, 3, and 6), are obviously illegitimate births, one at least of them with a fabulous father. This raises the presumption that the name of the mother was mentioned as the only remaining means of recording the descent: inasmuch as the persons would otherwise have been οὐτίδανοι. It may reasonably be conjectured, that all these births were out of wedlock.

The epithets of the Catalogue are so accurately descriptive of the country, that they have always been used as tests of the traditions respecting the situations of the places to which they refer. They are not less exactly in harmony with the descriptions in other parts of the poem, and this in minor cases, where purposed fiction can hardly be supposed, not less than in the greater ones. For instance, the Arcadians of Il. vii. 134, are ἐγχεσίμωροι: those of the Catalogue are ἀγχιμάχηται (604), and ἐπιστάμενοι πολεμίζειν (611). The

Pelasgi of Il. x. 429 are δῖοι, those of the Catalogue (840) are ἐγχεσίμωροι. The Cephallenians of the Catalogue are μεγάθυμοι (631), those of Il. iv. 330 are στίχες οὐκ ἀλαπαδναί. The Crete of the Odyssey (xix. 174) has ἐννήκοντα πόληες, the Crete of the Catalogue (v. 649) is ἑκατόμπολις[o].

Single commands are in every instance assigned to who in those the rest of the poem appear as chiefs of the first order. In the case of Idomeneus alone is this in any way obscured; as the passage (645–51) runs: 'Idomeneus led the Cretans'..... Idomeneus led them, with Meriones. But it is very remarkable that Meriones holds just this sort of ambiguous relation to Idomeneus in the poem at large: sometimes he is called his θεράπων (xxiii. 113 *et alibi*), and his ὀπάων (x. 58 *et alibi*), while he stands among the nine first warriors of the army, who (vii.161), volunteer for single combat with Hector; and when Idomeneus leads the van, he manages the rear (iv. 251–4). Again, though the opportunities afforded by the Catalogue are of necessity narrow, yet Homer has contrived within its limits to mark distinctly the character and position of nearly every great chieftain: certainly of Agamemnon, Achilles, Menelaus, Telamonian Ajax (v. 668), and Ulysses.

The third portion, or epilogue, appears to be ascribable chiefly to the genial love of Homer for the horse. His arrangement of the army according to the number of ships, which conveyed each division, had shut out the mention of the chariots and the coursers who drew them, and he appears to have devised this closing in-

[o] The reasons for treating this as a coincidence will be found in a paper on Homer's use of number. (Studies on Poetry, sect. iii.)

vocation for the purpose of supplying the defect. It was certainly not necessary in order to fix the position of Achilles in the army, which the First Book had completely developed; and the passage is chiefly occupied with the horses of Eumelus, together with those of Achilles and his force.

It contains, however, two remarkable notes of historical veracity. The horses of Eumelus, a Thessalian, are proclaimed to have been by far the best ($μέγ'$ $ἄρισται$): and the Myrmidons, again a Thessalian contingent, are here spoken of as having a number of separate chariots and horses; we are told (773), 'the soldiers played at games.... The horses stood feeding, each near his own chariot, and the chariots were in their sheds.' This is never said of any other contingent in the army. In strict harmony with this picture, Thessaly was conspicuous throughout the historic times of Greece, for the excellence of its breeds of horses, and the high character of its cavalry.

If all this be so, we cannot wonder at the high estimation in which the Catalogue of Homer was held by the Greeks of after-ages, as the great and only systematic record of the national claims of the respective states.

This was not merely literary or private estimation: the Catalogue had the place of an authoritative public document. Under the laws of Solon, for example, it received the honour of public recitation on solemn occasions. It was also quoted for the decision of controversies. In the critical moment, which preceded the first Persian war, the Athenian and Spartan envoys apply on the part of Greece to Gelon for his aid. He claims the command. In resisting this claim and urging their own right to lead the fleet, unless that post be claimed by the Lacedæmonians, the Athenians found their pretensions on the magnitude of their fleet, their autochthonism, and, finally, the testimony of Homer to the merits of Menestheus [p].

The Trojan Catalogue has less of organic connection than the Greek with the structure of the poem at large.

In proceeding to this portion of his work, the poet does not renew his ornamental similes, or his invocation to the Muse. He evidently meant to lower the tone of his strain: and moreover he was not about to tax memory as he had done in the former operation, the proper names being only about one fourth in number of those used for the Greeks, and none of them being arranged in long strings like the towns of Bœotia.

He now begins in what may be called a natural order: taking first that section of the army, which was supplied by the Troic sovereignties, principal and subordinate; and among these giving the first place to the troops of Ilion itself, as the most considerable, and as those chiefly concerned. The next is given to the Dardan forces, which were connected with the original seat of the race, and the following ones to the contingents supplied by the subordinate sovereigns of the rest of Troas.

His pursuit of this order reminds us, that the geographical distribution was in the case of the Trojan list simple, and did not require the aid of mental geometry, as he had only to follow, almost throughout, a single line of States along the European and Asiatic coasts. It also strengthens the presumption that, when Homer chose an order so different, and so much less natural and obvious, in the case of the Greeks, he must have been governed by some peculiar reason.

It will be observed that, of the eleven divisions of

[p] Herod. vii. 161.

II. *Ethnology*.

the Allies, the two first are the Pelasgians and the Thracians. As the blood of these two races flowed likewise in the veins of the Greeks, the precedence given to them may have been founded on this relationship. But this presumption is qualified by our finding that, doubtless on the ground of geographical order, the Lycian contingent, which had, at any rate, strong Greek affinities, comes last of all.

For a reason given elsewhere, we must consider the numbers assigned to the Greek contingents as approximate representations of their respective force: but the omission to particularize numbers at all in the Trojan Catalogue is itself an evidence of its historical character. The Trojan army was of a miscellaneous character: we also know that the allied contingents went and came, and that their absence from home, not prompted by the same powerful motives as that of the Greeks, was shortened by reliefs. Thus we find Rhesus with his Thracians just arrived in the Tenth Book[q]: Memnon comes to Troy after the death of Hector[r]: and we are told of the sons of Hippotion (Il. xiii. 792), who ἦλθον ἀμοιβοί, had come as reliefs, on the preceding day. An army thus collected piecemeal, and thus fluctuating in its composition, could not leave behind it the same accessible traditions. Again, the destruction of Troy itself obliterated what alone could have been their depository; nor had Homer, as a Greek bard, either the same motives or the same means for gathering detailed information, as he would naturally possess with reference to his own countrymen.

Hence, as the Trojan Catalogue is shorter, so also its scope is more limited. It contains no specification of forces: no anecdotes going farther back than the

[q] Il. x. 434. [r] Od. xi. 521.

existing generation : scarcely any of what may be called specialties of character or position as to the chiefs. It shows a good deal of knowledge of the geography and products of the countries, but this knowledge is of a much more general and vague character, than that which he has displayed in almost every portion of the Greek Array. He gives here very few lists of towns at all, and never uses epithets requiring us to believe that he had a personal knowledge of their site and character. Only Ariste is δῖα, and Larissa is ἐριβώλαξ. In two or three cases he speaks of commercial products ; a characteristic which it is obvious that he might have learned without any personal experience of the countries. He does not use this particular kind of sign at all in the descriptions of the Greek Catalogue: and we may perhaps correctly interpret it, where it appears, as a token of his want of vivid and experimental knowledge.

He also occasionally names a mountain or a river. But there is a general avoidance of particular and characteristic epithets, such as, (to refer to the Bœotian list alone,) πετρήεσσα given to Aulis, πολύκνημος to Eteonos, εὐρύχορος to Mycalesos, ἐϋκτίμενον to Medeon and Hypothebæ, πολυτρήρων to Thisbe, ποιήεις to Haliartos, πολυστάφυλος to Arne, ἐσχατόωσα to Anthedon, with perhaps one or two other cases.

Another material inference is suggested by the very different texture of the Trojan Catalogue.

Upon the whole, this vagueness of description cannot, I think, but be regarded as much in conflict with the belief that Homer was a Greek of Asia Minor, if at least his comparative knowledge of the two countries on the opposite sides of the Ægean is to be taken as a sign, either positive or negative, of his nativity.

SECT. VI.

On the Hellenes of Homer; and with them,
Hellas; Panhellenes; Cephallenes; Helli or Selli.

We have next to inquire into the force of the Hellenic name in the poems of Homer.

It meets us not, like the Pelasgic, in a single form, but in a group of words; among which, the principal are as follows:

1. Ἕλληνες, Il. ii. 684. ⎫
2. Πανέλληνες, ibid. 530. ⎬ National or tribal names.
3. Σελλοί, Il. xvi. 234. ⎭

And, lastly, the territorial name of

4. Ἕλλας.

Observing the order of derivation as it has been pointed out by Mure[a], we shall naturally look to the word Ἕλλας as a guide to the meaning of its derivatives, Ἕλληνες and Πανέλληνες. It is itself drawn from Ἑλλοί or Σελλοί: but as that name is only once used in the Poems, and as by far the largest body of evidence tells upon the word Ἕλλας, the decision upon the whole group of words will turn mainly upon the inquiry we shall have to make into the use of that word by Homer. With it therefore we shall commence. Is there, we have to ask, clear proof, that it went beyond the dominions of Peleus? If it went beyond them, how far did it go? and did it include that division of Greece, in which Locris lay, whose inhabitants a particular line of the Catalogue classes with the Panhellenes? For no suspicion of spuriousness can justly arise out of the fact (if it be one),

[a] Lit. Greece. i. 39, note.

that Homer calls by the name of Hellenes the inhabitants of any country, which was itself within the scope of the territorial name Hellas: inasmuch as this is little more than, the word Yorkshire being given, to make use also of the word Yorkshiremen.

At the outset, however, it is essential to observe, that a certain elasticity in the use of geographical as well as political names could not but belong to the age, in which Homer lived: first, because of the successive movements of tribes, like wave on wave, so that the use of any such name would ordinarily be either growing or declining, but not stationary: secondly, because of the indeterminate forms which political authority assumed, as resting on a mixture, in unknown proportions, of the various elements of custom, compact, reverence, and force: and, thirdly, because of the want of well-defined geographical boundaries.

We are not entitled to assume that the territory, which we call Greece, was, in Homer's time, subdivided with precision between a given number of territorial names. We hear of Phthia, Ægialus, Elis, Arcadia: but these seem to be the exceptions rather than the rule. For many parts of it there are no local names whatever; and we must not look for any thing resembling the manner in which England is made up of its counties, France of its departments, or the later Greece of its individual states.

The passages in which the word Hellas is used by Homer stand as follows in the order of the Poems:

1. A verse in the Catalogue, Il. ii. 683:
οἵ τ' εἶχον Φθίην ἠδ' Ἑλλάδα καλλιγύναικα.

2. (Achilles *loquitur*), ix. 395:
πολλαὶ Ἀχαιΐδες εἰσιν ἀν' Ἑλλάδα τε Φθίην τε.

3. (Phœnix *loq.*), ibid. 447:
οἷον ὅτε πρῶτον λίπον Ἑλλάδα καλλιγύναικα.

4. (Phœnix *loq.*), ibid. 478:
φεῦγον ἔπειτ' ἀπάνευθε δι' Ἑλλάδος εὐρυχόροιο,
Φθίην δ' ἐξικόμην ἐριβώλακα.

5. (In the narrative), Il. xvi. 595:
Χάλκωνος φίλον υἱόν, ὃς Ἑλλάδι οἰκία ναίων
ὄλβῳ τε πλούτῳ τε μετέπρεπε Μυρμιδόνεσσιν.

6. (Penelope *loq.*), Od. i. 344:
μεμνημένη αἰεὶ
ἀνδρός, τοῦ κλέος εὐρὺ καθ' Ἑλλάδα καὶ μέσον Ἄργος.

7. (Penelope *loq.*), Od. iv. 724:
ἢ πρὶν μὲν πόσιν ἐσθλὸν ἀπώλεσα θυμολέοντα,
παντοίης ἀρετῇσι κεκασμένον ἐν Δαναοῖσι,
ἐσθλόν, τοῦ κλέος εὐρὺ καθ' Ἑλλάδα καὶ μέσον Ἄργος.

8. Penelope repeats the same lines, Od. iv. 814–16.

9. (Achilles *loq.*), Od. xi. 494:
εἰπὲ δέ μοι, Πηλῆος ἀμύμονος εἴ τι πέπυσσαι·
ἢ ἔτ' ἔχει τιμὴν πολέσιν μετὰ Μυρμιδόνεσσιν
ἦ μιν ἀτιμάζουσιν ἀν' Ἑλλάδα τε Φθίην τε.

10. (Menelaus *loq.*), to Telemachus, Od. xv. 80:
εἰ δ' ἐθέλεις τραφθῆναι ἀν' Ἑλλάδα καὶ μέσον Ἄργος,
ὄφρα τοι αὐτὸς ἕπωμαι, ὑποζεύξω δέ τοι ἵππους,
ἄστεα δ' ἀνθρώπων ἡγήσομαι.

Of these passages, there are some which admit for the word Hellas the contracted sense of the dominions of Peleus, or even of a simple portion of them. Namely the following:

In (1) we are reading part of the description of the country, from which the force of Achilles was drawn. Beginning from the line which precedes it, we may translate thus: 'the inhabitants of Alos, and of Alope, and of Trachin, and those who occupied Phthia, and the Hellas of fair women.' It is clear, on the face of the passage, that, whatever it may mean, the sense does not require it to mean more in this place than a particular district, forming part of the dominions of Peleus.

In (2), where Achilles says, there are many Achæan maids through Hellas and Phthia, any one of whom he can have for a wife.

In (5), where we are told that Bathycles, son of Chalcon, dwelt in Hellas, preeminent among the Myrmidons in prosperity and wealth.

And in (9), where the shade of Achilles asks whether his father Peleus is still in the enjoyment of kingly power in the populous country of the Myrmidons, or whether he is deprived and despised through the range of Hellas and Phthia.

But among these four passages there is a distinction. In (1), (5), and (9) Hellas is combined with Phthia. Now we have seen, that there were Phthians beyond the dominions of Peleus: if the territorial name Phthia was similarly extended, then the presumption would arise that Hellas also might mean something more than lay within those dominions. But there are many passages where Phthia is used without Hellas; and in them all it is used to express the district where Peleus reigned. It is not unlikely therefore, at first sight, that Hellas has the limited sense of a part of the kingdom in these passages. And in the passage relating to Bathycles, the son of Chalcon, the limited sense is yet more strongly suggested; yet, as we may hereafter see more clearly, it is by no means positively required either in that or in any of these four places.

And it is abundantly clear, from the remainder of the passages, that the name Hellas had already, in Homer's time, begun to bear a more extended sense.

In proof of this, let us take, firstly, the two passages in which it stands alone. In Il. ix. 444–8, Phœnix tells us that nothing would induce him to quit Achilles; no, not even if the gods, brushing off his old age, were to make him young and vigorous again, such as he was when first he left Hellas, the land of fair women, flying from his feud with his father Amyntor. Now this passage absolutely proves that the word Hellas was used by Homer, at least occasionally, for some limited district, and not (as in after times) for the entire country; inasmuch as Phœnix could not otherwise have said he *left* Hellas on this occasion. But on the other hand it demonstrates, that the limits of Hellas were not so narrow, as the passages heretofore considered might permit us to suppose. For Phœnix goes on to describe the cause of quarrel; and (478–80) says he took his course *through* broad open Hellas, and came *into* fertile Phthia, to Peleus the king. The supposition most consistent with the wording of these passages is, that Phthia comprised the principal district of the dominions of Peleus, while a portion of them may have fallen (as we elsewhere see was perhaps the case) under the name of Hellas: but they absolutely place the abode of Amyntor outside the realm of Peleus; and therefore, in saying that Phœnix left Hellas, and that he fled from his home through Hellas, they imply necessarily that Hellas, the region from which he fled, was, in part at least, outside of that realm to which he fled.

But these passages will harmonise perfectly with each other, and with those formerly examined, if we suppose that Hellas meant the whole of Northern Greece generally, but that a particular portion of it had been more definitely stamped with the name of Phthia, as the chief seat of Peleus and the Myrmidons. For then the original abode of Phœnix might be in Hellas, as he says (in ix. 447) that it was: and yet he would pursue his way through Hellas, as he says (ibid. 478) that he did: and he would also leave Hellas, namely by coming into Phthia: and moreover the dominions of Peleus might go beyond what was commonly known by the particular designation of Phthia, and might include some portion of Hellas, as, from Il. ii. 683, they evidently did.

This supposition is recommended to us, not only by its conforming to all the requisite conditions, and furnishing a convenient construction for all the passages we have examined, but by the fact that Phthia, and Phthia alone, is commonly mentioned in the poem as the home of Achilles and the Myrmidons: which shows that they had a more special relation to the territory known by that name, than to Hellas.

If any thing be still wanting, the proof is brought to completeness by two other passages: the one (Il. x. 261–7), which tells us that this Amyntor, son of Ormenus, dwelt in Eleon; dwelt there permanently, since Autolycus stole from him an helmet, by breaking into his substantial well-built house,

πύκινον δόμον ἀντιτορήσας[b]:

and the other the verse of the Catalogue[c], which places Eleon in Bœotia. These passages therefore clearly appear to carry the name Hellas as far as Bœotia, and to make it reach continuously from thence to Phthia. And if Hellas comes down to Bœotia, then it includes Locris; and the various tribes of these regions may be included in the general name of Hellenes, though to all appearance they were not as yet familiarly and ordinarily so called. And if Locris and Bœotia, with

[b] Il. x. 267. [c] Il. ii. 500.

part of Southern Thessaly (the dominions of Peleus), are included within the range of the name Hellas, we can have no difficulty in supposing that it included Northern Thessaly also, which must have been the pathway of the Helli to the South.

But we find Ἕλλας in another combination besides that with Phthia, in the four passages of the Odyssey, (one of them being a simple repetition of another,) which we have still to examine.

Now the line Od. iv. 726, repeated 816, is under suspicion, of which it is not worth while to scrutinise the justice: as the idea and force of it is just the same with that of Od. i. 344,

Ἀνδρὸς, τοῦ κλέος εὐρὺ καθ' Ἑλλάδα καὶ μέσον Ἄργος.

This passage describes the fame of Ulysses as spread through the breadth of Hellas and mid-Argos; (or, from the heart of Argos to its extremities, right through or *all over* Argos.) And again in Od. xv. 80, when Telemachus has proposed to return home forthwith from the court of Menelaus, his host gently dissuades him from haste, and counsels a more extended tour, καθ' Ἑλλάδα καὶ μέσον Ἄργος; offering to take charge of his horses, and to shew him 'the cities,' or secured dwellings, ' of men.'

The signification of the word Ἄργος will be considered hereafter: for the present purpose it is enough to observe that the word μέσον, as used by Menelaus, in combination with Hellas, of itself prevents our applying it simply to the narrow corner of the Peloponnesus in which the city of Argos was placed; and therefore that it can scarcely mean less than Peloponnesus. And it is not less plain, that whatever may be the force of the words when taken singly, their effect when taken together can hardly be less than this:

Menelaus must mean to point to Greece at large, as the scene of the proposed excursion. For there is no assignable portion of Greece to which, consistently with the words and the sense, he can be held to confine his meaning. If we could suppose him to mean Peloponnesus only by the two names Hellas and Argos, which he employs in this place, we should but enlarge thereby the Homeric capacity of the word Hellas; for we have already brought it down from the north to Bœotia; and we should, in the way now proposed, carry it through the isthmus, and over Peloponnesus, or, at the least, over some part of it. But even if Menelaus means Peloponnesus only, which is most improbable, it is plainly incredible that such should be the meaning of Penelope in Od. i. 344. As a Greek, she *cannot* mean to limit the renown of her husband to any sphere less wide than Greece.

We have already seen, that Hellas sometimes includes certainly the territory from Southern Thessaly to Bœotia, and probably Thessaly at large: and it is quite plain that, if it comes to Bœotia, it does not stop there, but applies to the whole of Middle Greece, the region between Thessaly and the isthmus: for the application of the term Hellas could not stop except at some great natural division of the country, and the isthmus is here the only one possible.

Now the name Argos is related to Thessaly[d], but much more specially related to the Peloponnesus, as we shall see from a number of passages. It has no relation at all in Homer to that division of the country in particular which we call Middle Greece.

Assuming it, then, to mean Peloponnesus, in that case Hellas means Middle with Northern Greece: and

[d] Il. ii. 681.

the two names of Hellas and Argos, taken together, completely and conveniently express the whole country. The only alterations are such as would assign to Hellas a larger sense; in no case can it, as to this passage, admit of a more restricted one.

The foregoing argument is supported to a certain extent by the fact, that while territorial names are frequent for the Peloponnesian part of Greece, (we have Achaic Argos, Iasian Argos, Elis, Arcadia, Lacedæmon,) the continent to the north of the isthmus is generally without territorial names: Phthia and Pelasgic Argos are, I think, the only exceptions. There is thus before us a gap, which the name Hellas, as it has been here construed, seems conveniently to fill.

This construction of certain passages, in which the word Hellas is contained, is not one which should be adopted by the reader unawares. But if, like myself, after examining into it strictly he assents to its justice and necessity, then he will find that it is of the utmost importance to the elucidation of Homeric history; for it supplies a key to other much contested uses of the Hellenic name.

In the first place, I submit that if we now review the ten passages in which Homer speaks of Hellas, and bear in mind that in some among them it cannot be construed as meaning less than, with a certain amount of indeterminateness as to boundaries, Northern and Middle Greece generally, we shall also find, that there is not one of all those passages, in which it will not at least admit of the same sense. I do not deny that it is open to us to hold that the Hellas, in which Chalcon dwelt, was a mere district of Thessaly, and that Homer attaches in different places different senses to the word. But if there is a sense, substantially one, which will suit the word in every place where it is used, it seems most reasonable to adhere generally to that sense. Such a meaning we have, I think, found for Hellas, in concluding that it is used to signify Northern and Middle Greece. In this sense it overrides and includes Phthia, as France overrides Alsace or Burgundy. But as there was a time when Alsace and Burgundy might, before the present state of incorporation, have been either said to be in France or not in France, without an outrageous license of speech either way, so perhaps the land of Phthia was for Homer either a part of Hellas, or a province carved out of Hellas by the special occupation of the Myrmidons, as occasion might chance to demand. Not that he did not conform to the facts, but that the facts were themselves indeterminate. To our habits, under which every inch of ground belongs to somebody, this indefiniteness is wholly strange; but in times when only spots here and there were appropriated, and there was no universal occupation, it was thoroughly natural, and the thing really strange would be the absence of it. Accordingly, when Phœnix says he left Hellas, he gives to Phthia, the name of the place he reached, its exclusive force. When he says Chalcon dwelt in Hellas among the Myrmidons, he probably means in Phthia, but now regards Phthia as covered by the larger designation. When Homer tells us the soldiers of Achilles were those who inhabited Alos, and Alope, and Trachin, and who occupied Phthia and Hellas, we understand by the three first, particular spots which the Myrmidons had settled, by Phthia a larger district which they had so far dotted with their occupancy as to make it peculiarly theirs, and by Hellas the surrounding country, into which they had more or less ramified.

Assuming then the sense of the word Hellas to be

now sufficiently ascertained, the next question is, how came this country, which has been described, to bear the name of Hellas? And the question admits of but one answer. It could only be called Hellas because tribes of Helli had become its masters, its governing race, the depositaries, through its various regions, of political and military power.

We must therefore understand that, according to Homer, tribes reputed to be of Hellic origin were so far distributed over this country, as to have begun at least to affix their name to it: though without having absolutely effaced every older name, like Πελασγικὸν Ἄργος, and though not precluding the introduction of names perhaps more recent, certainly more specific, such as Phthia.

We may now proceed to consider the force, according to Homer's use, of the names derived from Hellas. These are, as commonly understood,

1. Ἕλληνες,
2. Πανέλληνες,

    and to these I shall presume to add,

3. Κεφάλληνες.

The first of these is found only in Il. ii. 684. Here, after the description of the places from which the forces of Achilles came, the poet proceeds to give them their designation:

Μυρμιδόνες δὲ καλεῦντο καὶ Ἕλληνες καὶ Ἀχαιοί.

We find an exclusive use[e] of the word Myrmidons for the force of Achilles throughout the Iliad, except in this one place; notwithstanding that Phœnix, who was lord of the Dolopes, commanded one of the five divisions[f], and that we may therefore presume a certain part of the force to have been Dolopian. From this exclusive

[e] Iliad *passim*: and Od. iii. 182. iv. 9. and xi. 494.　　[f] Il. xvi. 171.

use, we cannot doubt that the name of Myrmidons was that which appertained to them in particular, as the ruling tribe among the subjects of Peleus.

Had we found reason to construe the word Ἕλλας in the preceding line as meaning only a district of his dominions, it would have followed, that Ἕλληνες meant the inhabitants of that district; and that a part of the soldiers of Achilles were Hellenes rather than Myrmidons, in virtue of a local name. But it follows from what we have already concluded about Hellas, that the name of Hellenes was applicable to all the Myrmidons as being themselves inhabitants of Hellas, that is, of Phthia, which belonged to Hellas.

And in passing it should be noticed that, although the Myrmidons inhabited Phthia, they are never called Phthians; nor do we ever hear of Phthians at all in Homer, except only in that passage where they are described as engaged with Locrians and others in repelling the Trojan assault [g]. They are there described as under the command of Medon and Podarces. But in the Catalogue Podarces and Medon [h], as substitutes for Protesilaus and Philoctetes respectively, command the second and fourth Thessalian contingents, which came from districts lying near the kingdom of Peleus. Either therefore the Phthian name extended beyond the limits of Phthia, or the Phthians were those whom the Myrmidons had recently driven out, and whose lands they had occupied.

We cannot conclusively settle the sense of the word Ἀχαιοὶ in this passage, except by anticipating the results of an examination, on which we have not yet entered. But it may be observed even at this point, that the bearings of the passage are somewhat adverse to a merely

[g] Il. xiii. 685–700. [h] Il. ii. 704. 727.

local construction for it. If Myrmidon was the strictly proper name, then Achæan must have been a designation which was not proper to the Myrmidons only, but which they enjoyed in common with others. And yet, on the other hand, not in common with all the Greeks, but in some sense more restricted than that, in which it is habitually applied to the whole army. For in that large and general sense every contingent of the army was Achæan, and Homer would certainly therefore not have mentioned the Achæan name with respect to one in particular. It can hardly escape observation that, studying great clearness and precision in the Catalogue, he systematically avoids the introduction of his general names for the army. We never read of Danaans or Argeians in it at all, and of Achæans only twice [h]. So far then as the passage itself guides us, it points to the supposition that those who were called Myrmidons properly, to distinguish them from all others, and Hellenes because they were (in common with others) inhabitants of Hellas, belonged likewise to a particular class or race of Greeks, to whom the name of Ἀχαιοὶ was applicable in some distinctive sense. The three appellations, accordingly, are not so many synonyms; but each has probably its own proper scope.

Thucydides [i] speaks with his usual accuracy, when he says that Homer has given the name of Hellenes to no portion of the army except the troops of Achilles from Phthiotis. He does not however go beyond the assertion that this word had not yet grown into an appellation for the Greeks universally, an assertion which, as far as Homer's evidence goes, is undeniable. But it does not require us also to deny that the Hellas of Homer extends beyond Phthia, and that the name of

[h] Il. ii. 530. 562. 684. [i] Thuc. i. 3.

Hellenes may even then have been beginning to attach to the inhabitants of other parts of Hellas, though perhaps less fixedly, as yet, than to the Myrmidons.

With these facts in view, I am wholly unable to follow those who have condemned, upon internal evidence, that verse òf the Catalogue in which we find mention of the Panhellenes.

Speaking of Oilean Ajax, commander of the Locrians, the poet says (Il. ii. 530),

ἐγχείῃ δ' ἐκέκαστο Πανέλληνας καὶ 'Αχαιούς.

It is not grammatically necessary that we should make these two words coextensive; and I do not believe that either of them separately, as here used, conveys the whole force of the two, though perhaps conjointly they may carry the assertion that he was the best spearman in the army.

If there was a Hellas in the time of Homer, which was inhabited by a variety of tribes, then, as these tribes dispersedly might be called with propriety Hellenes, even apart from the authority of constant use, so they might with equal propriety be combined into the term Panhellenes, which would mean all the tribes, including the Locrians, that inhabited Hellas, or Northern and Mid-Greece. Thus, as the Achæan name was at this time more prominent and distinguished in the Peloponnesus[j] than in any other part of the country, the poet may in this place by 'Αχαιοὶ mean the Southern or Peloponnesian Greece; so as, by the two epithets conjointly, to signify the whole army. Or he may mean all those who, in Hellas or beyond it, were of the pure Achæan race (assuming, for the moment, that such a race existed); and thus may here assert, that Ajax excelled all Hellas, and even all Achæans in or out of Hellas,

[j] Vid. inf. sect. viii.

II. *Ethnology.*

using the last of the two words by way of climax. I do not deny that he may also be construed to mean the whole host in the gross by Ἀχαιοὶ, agreeably to the common use of it; but this is less likely; as the name, so understood, would not be distinctive.

Nor do I see any reason to hesitate about treating the Homeric name Κεφάλληνες as one of his Hellenic group of names. As in the case of Πελασγοὶ, so here we have a name formed by a combination of different words. The word *head* seems to have been represented by a root of flexible structure. In Sanscrit it is *kapála*[k], in Greek κεφάλη, in Latin *caput*: but it also appears in the German *kopf*, and in the Greek κόπτειν, 'to butt,' and in κύβη, κυβιστάω, κυβερνάω. The word Κεφάλληνες seems, then, to be formed in the most direct manner from the root κεφ, signifying 'head,' and Ἕλληνες: and thus it both attaches Ulysses, with at least the dominant race among his subjects, to the Hellic stock, and indicates the tendency of the Hellenic name, even in Homer's time, to reproduce itself and to spread abroad.

Again, we observe in his rare use of Κεφάλληνες the same signs as in Ἕλληνες and Πανέλληνες, that the power of the name was only growing up from its infancy. For the word is used but twice in the Iliad, and no more than four times in the Odyssey, where there is constant occasion for addressing, or for speaking of, the subjects of Ulysses. We find in that poem Ἰθακήσιοι eleven times, and Ἀχαιοὶ constantly.

Having dealt with the Homeric derivations of Hellas[l],

[k] Donaldson's New Cratylus, p. 291.

[l] It is not necessary to trace in this place, with precision, the various applications of the name Hellas, after the time of Homer. Stanley (on Æsch. Suppl. 263) states, that what I have termed Middle Greece was the Hellas of Ptolemy: that with Strabo the word includes most of the islands of the Ægean: and, finally, that

let us now ascend to the word, from which it is itself derived; Hellas being evidently, in the Greek tongue, the country which had been occupied by the Helli.

Of the people who are so termed, either under the form beginning with the aspirate, or else under that of Σελλοί, we find obvious Homeric vestiges in the Hellespont, Ἑλλήσποντος; in various rivers termed Σελληείς; and in the invocation of Achilles to Jupiter, which places the Selli in the north of Thessaly, about wintry Dodona, and seems to stamp them as then still remaining a people of the rudest habits in their mountain home[m];

Δωδώνης μεδέων δυσχειμέρου· ἀμφὶ δὲ Σελλοὶ
σοὶ ναίουσ' ὑποφῆται ἀνιπτόποδες, χαμαιεῦναι.

The word Ἕλλοι would appear to be not the most probable reading of the text of this invocation; for it presumes an inconvenient loading of the sentence with the double pronoun σε and σοι. But there can be no doubt whatever as to its identity with Σελλοί. Independently of philological argument, there is the strongest presumption that in this place Achilles intends to name his own national ancestry, as being the ministers of the god; who give him, as it were, the right to invoke the aid of the Pelasgic indeed, but

it also came to include Asia Minor, and parts even of the African coast, as well as places elsewhere, which had been colonised by the Greek race. According to Cramer (Geogr. Greece, i. 2), at the epoch of the Peloponnesian war, Hellas meant everything south of the Peneus and the gulf of Ambracia. He considers that Herodotus also meant by it a portion of Thesprotia (Herod. ii. 56. viii. 47). It is interesting to observe how this domestic name, taken from the race which made Greece so great and famous, has retained its vitality through so many vicissitudes, and is now the national name of Greece, in opposition to that which was probably drawn from a Pelasgian source, and which, as proceeding from the Roman masters of the country, told its people the tale of their subjugation.

[m] Il. xvi. 234.

therefore genuine and original, Jupiter of Dodona. But no circumstance seems to be better established by philological research, than that in many cases of Greek words, which now begin with the aspirate, there was one (or more than one) initial letter, and that frequently that letter was the *sigma*. Much obscurity has hung about this subject, from the fact that discovery has proceeded piecemeal, and that for a length of time the word *digamma* was used to signify what had originally filled the void now existing in so many places of the Homeric versification. What this *digamma* might have been was disputed; but it was, almost insensibly perhaps, assumed to be some one letter or sound only. But as inquiry has made further advances, many forms of a lost letter or letters have been discovered: and it has also been made clear that the gaps ought to be filled up variously, and not by any one uniform expedient. To take very simple examples, there can be no doubt about the identity of ἐξ, ἕπτα, ὗς, with *sex, septem, sus*: nor any doubt about the essential identity of ὕδωρ and *sudor*, ἡδύς and *suavis*, ἑκυρός and *socer*: none therefore that the σ ought to be supplied, and not *f, w*, or *v*, in the passage φίλε ἑκυρέ[n]. While indeed a presumption arises[o] from the German words *schwieger* and *schwäger*, that a double or even treble loss may have occurred, and that the passage may have run φίλε σϜεκυρέ. Under these circumstances, in the case before us, where we have both forms represented, there can be no hesitation as to the identity of Ἑλλοὶ and Σελλοί: the first represented in Ἕλλας, Ἕλληνες,

---

[n] Il. iii. 172.

[o] I follow the acute and sagacious notes of Professor Malden to a valuable paper contributed by Mr. James Yates, during the year 1856, to the Philological Transactions: also Donaldson's *Cratylus*, p. 120.

Ἑλλήσποντος, and the Ἑλλοπία of Hesiod: the other and older one supported by Σελληεῖς.

There is another curious and instructive case, in which we have the older form of the word Σελλοὶ still remaining: besides that of Προσέληνοι, to which allusion has already been made in considering the case of the Pelasgian Arcadians. In the Birds of Aristophanes, the dramatist satirizes Athens and the Sicilian Expedition, under the name of a city in the clouds, called Νεφελοκοκκυγία; the object being to expose the arrogance of great pretensions, without adequate means to support them. There, he says, lie most of the goods of Theagenes, and all those of Æschines. This Theagenes was called κάπνος, smoke, because he promised much, and did nothing. Æschines was a pauper, who pretended to wealth. The Scholiast adds, ἦν δὲ Αἰσχίνης Σελλοῦ. Ἔλεγον δὲ ἐκ μεταφορᾶς τοιούτους Σελλούς· καὶ τὸ ἀλαζονεύεσθαι δὲ, σελλίζειν[p]. Cary thinks the term σελλίζειν came from a Sellus, the father of this Æschines. But in the first place, it seems difficult to rely on the Scholiast for knowing, still less for recording with accuracy, the name of the father of an obscure person, who had lived in the age of Aristophanes. In the second place, if Æschines was an obscure fellow, it is most improbable that his father's name should have become the root of a Greek word descriptive of a particular habit or propensity. Such words (for example) as hectoring and rhodomontading presuppose a great celebrity in the person on whose name they are based. Lastly, the derivation from the ancient Σελλοὶ seems a perfectly natural one, and also adequate to the case. It is in some degree characteristic of those who in reduced circumstances trace back their lineage to a very ancient stock, instead of

[p] In loc. Cary's Birds, p. 77.

relying simply on the substantial honour of their descent, still to affect the possession of the wealth which has passed away from them: to play for themselves the part, which Caleb Balderstone desires to play, on behalf not of himself, but of the Master of Ravenswood, in Scott's 'Bride of Lammermoor'; and altogether to be sensitive, or what is called touchy on the subject, and to lean on the whole towards a certain boastfulness, in common with the νεόπλουτοι at the other extremity of the scale. There is a broad distinction between treating the Scholiast as a witness to the existence and force of a current phrase, and the taking his word for the parentage of a nobody, like this Æschines, who had lived long before him. It may, however, not be necessary to construe σελλίζειν solely, or even specially, with reference to a pride in wealth which had passed away. If we shall hereafter show for the Selli[q] a Persian ancestry, then, even without any regard to change of circumstances, the phrase at once leads us back to the description given by Herodotus of the Persians their forefathers. Πέρσαι, φύσιν ἐόντες ὑβρισταὶ, εἰσὶν ἀχρήματοι[r].

I shall also have occasion to notice hereafter one or two other words apparently akin to Σελλοί.

[q] See sect. x.   [r] i. 89.

SECT. VII.

On the respective contributions of the Pelasgian and Hellenic factors to the compound of the Greek nation.

IN this attempt at an ethnological survey, we have now come down to the point, at which the Greek Peninsula passes over from its old Pelasgian character, and becomes subject to predominating Hellenic influences.

Now therefore, and before we examine the relations and succession of the great Homeric appellations for the Hellenes, appears to be the time for considering how the account stands between these tribes and the Pelasgians, and what were, so far as by probable evidence we can ascertain it, the respective contributions from the two sources to the integral character of the Greeks and of their institutions.

In the case of Greece, as it is known to us in history, we have the most remarkable disproportion between moral and physical power, and between the green and the full grown product, which is offered to view in the whole range of human experience. A circumscribed country, with a small population, throws forth, without loss of vital power, to the East and to the West, colonies greatly transcending itself, as would appear, in wealth and population; continues for many centuries to exercise a primary influence in the world; at one time resists and repels, at another invades and terrifies, at a third overthrows and crushes to atoms the great colossus of Eastern empire, and continues to exercise, through the medium of mind, a singular mastery, enduring down to our own time, and likely still to endure, over civilized man. And even the miniature organization of Greece presents to us, within its own limits, diversities of character almost enough for a quarter of the globe.

Many of these diversities connect themselves with the ethnological formation of the different communities. In the course of that process, so far as can be discerned, certain admixtures of foreign influence were supplied direct from Phœnicia, Egypt, or elsewhere: but the grand component parts or factors in this composite product are two, the Hellenic and the Pelasgic. To this dual combination, perhaps the double invocation of Achilles (Il. xvi. 233, 4) is a witness.

The development of the national character is the most large and varied in Attica, where the population, from successive immigrations of bodies of refugees, and from the free general resort and reception of strangers, presented also the largest and most varied ethnical compound.

In analysing that national character which thus resulted from the amalgamation of ingredients chiefly Hellic and Pelasgic, we have now to ask how far its different elements are referable to the Pelasgic or to the Hellic root respectively? We have traced in some degree the course and local circumscription of the races: can we affiliate upon them any of the contributions which they severally made to the varied manners and to the institutions of Greece?

The proof, as far as it is specific, can be only that which probable and conjectural evidence afford: but that evidence is supported by the fact, that it tends, as a whole, to an orderly result.

While they proceed from different sources, and present visible and even permanent distinctions of character, there is no violent disparity between the Hellic and the Pelasgic races: they afford a good material for coalescence. We are not to suppose that whatever the one had, the other had not. Of what belongs historically to the Pelasgi, much may stand as theirs only through their priority of entrance into the country.

I propose to inquire what evidence can be drawn, either from philological sources, or from the text of Homer, to throw light on the several pursuits and tendencies of these races, under the heads of Religion, Policy, War, the Games, Poetry, the Chase, and Navigation.

Under some of these heads, however, we must in a measure anticipate results which will be only obtained in full from later inquiries.

The Poems afford us no complete and decisive test for discriminating between the Hellene and the Pelasgian contributions respectively to the Greek religion.

We shall, however, hereafter find many details of evidence bearing upon this subject.

For the present I must confine myself to two very general propositions, which are founded on the relations of the Greek religion with those of Troy and of Italy.

First, there seems to be a presumption, which may weigh with us to a certain extent in the absence of counter-evidence, that those parts of the Greek religion which were common to the Greeks with the Trojans were Pelasgian, and that those which were not common, were not Pelasgian. But of the parts which were common, and therefore Pelasgian, many may have been originally Hellene too.

Again, a relationship subsists between Greece and Italy, as to the component parts of their respective populations, which, without being unduly strained, will throw considerable light upon the question of Hellic and Pelasgic attributes.

The Greek or the Italian of the classic times could not be expected to own relationship with what lay to the northward, on each of those two peninsulas. The Roman, therefore, whose investigations led him to suppose there were Pelasgians in Italy, would only derive them from Greece. For us the case stands far otherwise; and we must simply consider the Pelasgians of Greece, and the Pelasgians of Italy, as two among a variety of branches, which struck out at different times from the main trunk of an extended race, probably diffusing itself over many parts of Asia and Europe. In Greece and Italy respectively these Pelasgic tribes entered into new combinations, probably not wholly different, nor, on the other hand, by any means in exact correspondence.

We may perhaps be found not to go beyond the limits of the modesty which the case requires, when we simply lay down this rule: that correspondences in religion or in language between Greece and ancient Italy raise a presumption, that those features of each country, in which the correspondence is observed, are of Pelasgic origin.

1. Something of such correspondence we may perceive in regard to religion. The religion of Homeric Greece differs from that of Rome, not only as to minor deities, but in the names given to many of the greater deities, and especially in the far more imaginative character of its traditions.

Those parts of the religion of Greece and Rome which were common to both were probably Pelasgian.

Let us take first the names which correspond, and then those which are different.

(I.) Names of deities that correspond in the Greek and Latin tongues:

1. Ζεύς . . . . . . Deus.
2. Ζεὺς-πάτηρ . . . Jupiter.
3. Ἀπόλλων . . . . Apollo.
4. Ἱστιή . . . . . Vesta.
5. Λήτω . . . . . . Latona.
6. Περσεφόνη . . . . Proserpina.
7. Ἄρης . . . . . . Mars or Mavors.

(II.) Names of deities which do not in any manner correspond in the Greek and Latin tongues:

1. Ἥρη . . . . . . Juno.
2. Ποσειδῶν . . . . . Neptune.
3. Ἀιδωνεύς . . . . Pluto.
4. Ἀθήνη . . . . . Minerva.
5. Ἥφαιστος . . . . Vulcan.
6. Ἑρμῆς . . . . . Mercury.
7. Ἀφροδίτη . . . . Venus.
8. Ἄρτεμις . . . . . Diana.
9. Δημήτηρ . . . . Ceres.
10. Διόνυσος . . . . . Bacchus.

Two remarks may be made on the deities of the first list.

First, that it comprehends generally the gods whom we shall find to bear marks of being the most ancient among the Greek deities; with the marked exception, however, of Minerva[a].

Secondly, that in it we find no deity who takes part on the Greek, that is, the Pelasgian side, in the war of Troy. The only two names which do not appear on the Trojan side, are Vesta, who with Homer is not personified at all: and Proserpine, who from the seat of her dark dominion could not share in the wars waged upon earth.

[a] See Studies on the Theo-mythology of Homer.

On the other hand, when we turn to the second list of exclusively Greek names, we find that it contains all the deities who took part against Troy: and only two very secondary names of deities friendly to it.

Mars and Venus, both engaged on the Trojan side, and one standing in the first list, are the deities after whom, according to Ovid[z], the two first months of the Roman year were named in the first age of the city.

It would not, however, be safe to depend implicitly upon the apparent reappearance of certain names in the Latin language, without a fuller knowledge of the laws of discrimination between the early mythology of the Romans, and the form which their religious system assumed at the period when they came into free communication with Greece and its colonies, from which, as they certainly borrowed some names of deities, such as Pallas and Phœbus, so they may have assumed others too. We have no proof, for example, that Apollo was prominent, or even that he was known, in the earliest Roman worship. Cicero[a] says, *Jam Apollinis nomen est Græcum.* Still, a temple was raised to him in Rome[b] as early as 430 B. C.; and the Trojan sympathies of most of the deities in the first list tend in some degree to show both that they were well known in the Pelasgian religion, and that many of the older portions of the mythology were common to the Trojans, the early Romans, and the Pelasgians of Greece.

We may more boldly rely upon a general indication, which is offered to us by the religious systems both of Rome and of Troy, in comparison with that of Greece.

The large account of Roman deities furnished by Saint Augustine, in his 'De Civitate Dei,' constitutes for us the principal representation of the great work of

[z] Fasti, i. 39. [a] De Nat. Deor. ii. 27.
[b] Liv. Hist. Rom. iv. 25, 29.

Varro, now lost, on the 'Antiquitates Rerum Divinarum.' Notwithstanding the multitudinous development of the theurgic system, the '*De Civitate*' tends to support the belief that it was not vivified, like the system of the Greeks, by the intense pervading power of a vigorous and prolific imagination. The 'Fasti' of Ovid may perhaps be referred to as sustaining the same opinion. And Heyne in his commentary on Virgil has observed upon the comparative dulness and dryness of the early mythology of Rome: *Italici mythi longe a Græcæ fabulæ suavitate absunt; nec varietas grata inest*[c].

In a later portion of this work[d] I shall endeavour to show, that a similar character apparently attaches to the religious system of Troy: not so much a purity or simplicity, as a comparative poverty and hardness; and an indisposition in the inventions to assume those graceful forms, of which the Grecian Theo-mythology, as exhibited in Homer, is so full.

And again, when we pass from Homer to Hesiod, we find a great mass of religious fable, either added by the later poet, or grown up in the interval between the two. Hesiod's depositories are much more numerously peopled: but we have passed at once from the poetry of a theogony to its merest prose, when we compare his manner of touch or handling, and his ideas on these subjects, with those of Homer. And, as on other grounds we may consider Hesiod to represent the Pelasgian side of the Greek mind, we seem justified in referring the distinctive tone of his mythology in some degree to his Pelasgian characteristics.

[c] Exc. iv. ad Æn. vii. See Browne's History of Roman Literature, chap. viii. p. 129, and chap. iii. p. 41. Also Dunlop's Hist. Rom. Literature, vol. iii. p. 56.
[d] See 'The Trojans.'

But independently of confirmation from the case of Troy, and from the tone of Hesiod, the character of the old Italian mythology, so devoid of imagination, force, and grace, leads us to ascribe these properties, when we find them abound in the Greek supernaturalism, to its non-Pelasgian, that is, to its Hellenic source.

When, however, we turn to another form of development in religious systems, we find the case entirely different: I mean the development in positive observances of all kinds, and in fixed institutions of property and class. Here the religion of Rome was large and copious. Polybius has left upon record, in a most remarkable passage, his admiration of the Roman system of δεισιδαιμονία, which had, he says, been so got up, and carried to such a point, that it could not be exceeded. It was all done, in his opinion, on account of the multitude. Were States composed of the wise, the case would have been different: but as the people are full of levity and passion, λείπεται τοῖς ἀδήλοις φόβοις καὶ τῇ τοιαύτῃ τραγῳδίᾳ τὰ πλήθη συνέχειν[d].

Not less remarkable is the testimony of Dionysius; who, while he praises Romulus for the severe simplicity of what he caused to be taught and held concerning religion, and for the expulsion of immoral fables and practices, says that he arranged for his people all that concerned the temples of the gods, their consecrated lands, their altars, their images, their forms, their *insignia*, their prerogatives and their gifts to man, the sacrifices in which they delight, the feasts and assemblies to be celebrated, and the remissions of labour to be granted in their honour. In no other newly founded city could be shown such a multitude of priests and

---

[d] Polyb. vi. 56, sect. 6-12.

ministers of the gods[e], who were chosen, too, from the most distinguished families[f].

The Fasti of Ovid give an idea of the manner in which the Roman Calendar brought the ceremonial of religion to bear upon the course of life. For some centuries an acquaintance with the Calendar was the exclusive property of the sacred order[g]; and the priesthood turned to its own power and profit the knowledge, which afterwards filled the pages of that characteristic work.

Again, we shall have occasion, when considering the distinctive character of Troy, to notice that the political and ritual forms of religion appear to have been much more advanced there, than with the Greeks. This difference will naturally connect itself with the stronger Pelasgian infusion in the former case. We shall then find that of the two great kinds of sacred office, one only, that of the μάντις, and not that of the priest, seems at the time of Homer to have appertained to the Hellenic races.

And it is not a little curious to observe that, when Saint Paul arrives among the Athenians, the point which he selects for notice in their character and usages, after all the intermixtures they had undergone, is still this, that they are δεισιδαιμονέστεροι[h], peculiarly disposed to religious observances; and that, not contented with the gods whom they suppose themselves to know, they have likewise a supernumerary altar for 'the Unknown God.' Nor are we the less warranted to connect this peculiarity with the original and long preserved Pelasgian character of Athens, because that city had, for

[e] Dionysius, b. ii. 18–21.
[f] Id., b. viii. 38. See also Cic. Div. i. 2.
[g] Smith's Dict., Art. 'Fasti.'
[h] Acts xvii. 22.

centuries before, become a peculiarly apt representative of the full Greek compound: for a system of ritual observance has a fixity, which does not belong to mere opinion; and, when once rooted in a country, has powerful tendencies to assume such a solidity as survives vicissitude: perhaps in some degree on account of its neutral and pacific character, and of the power it leaves to men of separating between outward observance and inward act.

Although the opinion has been entertained, that from the earliest ages it was the exclusive privilege of the first-born to offer sacrifice, it appears most probable that the separate function of priesthood was, like other offices and professions, one of gradual formation. Whether the primitive institution of sacrifice was spontaneous or commanded, every man, that is to say, every head of a family, was, I shall assume, at first his own offerer or priest[i]. Then, as the household developed into the community, the priestly office, in the first stages of political society, as a matter of course appertained to the chief.

He, by the necessity of natural order, originally united in his own person the great functions of

1. Father.
2. Teacher.
3. Priest.
4. King.
5. Proprietor.
6. Commander.

The severance of these offices successively would arrive sooner or later, according as the progress made in numbers and wealth was rapid or slow. Concentration of employments in a single hand marks the primitive condition or retarded movement of society, while the division of labour is the sign of more speedy and more advanced development. Even the annals of the people

[i] Outram de Sacrif. b. i. ch. iv. sect. 3.

Order of Priests not Hellenic. 293

of Israel furnish instances in which we trace, at periods when these offices had undergone division under divine authority, vestiges of their former union. It appears that, besides Moses, who consecrated Aaron and his sons by divine command, Joshua, Samuel, and Saul [k] on certain occasions offered sacrifice. The exclusive character of priesthood has been impressed upon it, under Divine Revelation, by positive ordinance, and for a special purpose [l].

The Hellenes in Homer appear to exhibit it in its earlier state of union with the office of civil government; and the Pelasgians to display it as a function which has indeed become special and professional, but only on that self-acting principle which, in the progress of society, leads to division of labour.

If we suppose the case of two races, one of them inhabiting a rude and barren country in a state of perpetual poverty and warfare, and then recently, by a descent upon more fertile soils, brought into contact with civilised life: the other of them addicted from a much earlier period to pursuits of peace and industry, inhabiting plains, and accustomed to form agricultural settlements; there will be no cause for wonder upon our also finding that the latter of these races has a professional priesthood, while the former has none; but that the sacrificial office remains in the private dwelling with the father of the family, and on public occasions with the head of the civil government.

This appears to have been the state of facts as between the Trojans of Homer who had a priesthood, and the Hellenes who had none: and the difference may be

[k] Exodus xi. 12–16, and Levit. viii. 1–13. 1 Sam. xvi. 2, &c. See Calmet's Dict. Taylor's Edition, 1838. Art. Priest.
[l] Heb. v. 4.

principally referable to the different condition and history of the Pelasgian and the Hellic races: while other causes, belonging to the respective characters of the races, may have contributed their share towards the production of this curious result. Partly the greater personal energy and self-reliance of the Hellic tribes, but partly also the earlier and older ease, wealth, and fixity of the Pelasgians, are the probable reasons why, at the point of time exhibited in the writings of Homer, we find priesthood properly a Pelasgian, but not yet properly an Hellenic, and only to a limited extent an adoptive, institution.

Thus far, then, we have a presumption, to be greatly strengthened as I trust hereafter, that the Greek religion owed to the Hellenes its imaginative, and to the Pelasgians its sacerdotal and ceremonial development. And this presumption is, I think, in entire accordance with what we should reasonably anticipate, from relations otherwise known to have subsisted between the two races. I now pass on to the subject of language.

In attempting to illustrate the relations of Pelasgians to Hellenes through the medium of the affinities and contrasts between the Greek and Latin languages, I am aware that I venture upon ground which requires to be trodden with great circumspection. For the Latin nation may possibly have contained within itself some ethnical element not dissimilar to the Hellenic, as well as one substantially corresponding with the Pelasgian, factor of the Greek people. And again, there is a very extended relation of the two languages to a common root in the Sanscrit. The number of words traceable to such a root has recently been stated at 339 in the Greek, and 319 in the Latin tongues[1].

[1] Browne's Roman Classical Literature, ch. i. p. 13.

We must not then, it will justly be observed, infer from the simple fact of resemblance between a Greek and a Latin word, that the one has been borrowed or directly modified from the other.

Let us begin by considering the just effect of these remarks, and inquiring whether they do not still leave space enough for an useful examination.

I begin from the assumption, that there was a deep and broad Pelasgian *substratum* both in the Greek and the Roman nations. It is thought, and it may perhaps be justly thought, that a dominant tribe of Oscans, who were a nation of warriors and hunters, came among the Pelasgi of Italy, as the Hellenes came among the Pelasgi of Greece. But while we may properly assume the identity of the Pelasgian factor in the two cases respectively, it is quite plain that the compounds or aggregate characters are broadly distinguished, and represent an assemblage and admixture either of different qualities, or else of the same qualities in very different proportions. Therefore we are justified in laying it down as a general rule, that whatever is found in the language of the two countries alike was most probably Pelasgian: since, if that portion of the aggregate language had been supplied from those elements in which the nations differed, it is likely that a corresponding difference would have been found to prevail between their modes of speech.

Again, I think we must distinguish between the simple fact of derivation from an original source in common, and those degrees or descriptions of resemblance which show that any given words not only had one source at first, but that they continued together up to a certain point in the formative process, so as to be capable, from their shape, of derivation, not only from that root, but also one from the other. For instance, the Greek ἐγώ and the Latin *ego* are both stated to be derived from the Sanscrit *aham*. But here it is quite plain that they have not only set out from the same point, but travelled along the same road to their journey's end, as the Greek and Latin words are identical. On the other hand, if we take the Greek τέσσαρες, and the Latin *quatuor*, both are referred to the same Sanscrit root, *chatur:* but neither of them can well have been derived from the other, and each is more nearly related to the root than it is to the other. Or if we take the Latin *anser*, the Greek χήν, and the English 'goose,' these words scarcely appear to have a connecting link: but it is found, and a remote or mediate connection established, by means of the German *gans*. Instances might easily be multiplied.

In single cases, where the relationship of words is only of the kind last exemplified, it would not be safe to draw inferences to the effect of their being respectively due to this or that element in the composition of the nation.

But where there is such a similarity as to show either that the word has advanced nearly to its mature state before the Greek and Latin forms began to divaricate, or that the Latin form may have been derived from the Greek in an early stage of the history of the language, or *vice versâ*, then it seems just to refer the resemblance of terms to the existence of a powerful common element in the two peoples.

And further, if we shall find that the words standing in close kindred are capable of classification with reference to their sense, then, when we have once constituted a class of such words, it may be justifiable to add fresh words to it on the strength of a more remote affinity, in virtue of the presumption already created. For instance, if the names of the commonest objects and operations of inanimate nature are generally in close correspondence, we may infer a relation between other words which are in the same class as to meaning, though they may be not so nearly alike, with more confidence than if the reasoning as to this latter section were not supported by the former. On this principle I proceed in the collections of words given below.

Of course the utmost care must be taken to exclude those words which have been copied from Greek into Latin, after the literary ages of Rome had begun, and according to the practice which Horace has described and recommended [m].

Niebuhr was, I believe, the first person to draw from philological sources a conclusion as to the character and habits of the Pelasgians. He proceeded upon the threefold assertion, (1) that the words common to the two tongues are presumably Pelasgian, (2) that they for the most part refer to tillage and the gentler ways of life, and (3) that we may hence conclude that the Pelasgians were a people given to peace and husbandry. And conversely, that the words which widely differ in the two tongues are not Pelasgian, and that the pursuits which they indicate must have been more peculiarly characteristic of some other race, that contributed to make up the composition of the Roman nation. The principles thus assumed by Niebuhr [n] appear, when placed under due limitation, to be sound; and the only question is, whether they are supported by the facts of the case. If in a given language we find the words indicative of a certain turn of life to have been derived from

[m] Hor. de Art. Poet. v. 53.
[n] Hare and Thirlwall's Niebuhr, vol. i. p. 65.

a particular race, which forms part of the nation speaking that language, while other words, referable to other habits and pursuits, have been supplied by other races also numbered among its constituent parts, it is just to read the characters of those races respectively through the character of the words that they contribute to the common tongue. For the question is really one of forces which may have been adjusted with as much accuracy, as if they had been purely mechanical. The ordinary reason why a word of Pelasgian origin prevails over a word of Hellenic origin with the same signification, or the reverse, is that it is in more or in less common use: and the commonness of use is likely to be determined by the degree in which the employment or state of life, with which the word is connected, may belong to the one race or the other.

The survey taken by Niebuhr appears to have been rapid; and the list of words supplied by him is very meagre. Bishop Marsh [n] and other authors have, with a variety of views, supplied further materials. The most comprehensive list, to which my attention has been directed, is in the 'Lateinische Synonyme und Etymologieen' of Döderlein[o]. The subject is essentially one which hardly admits of a fixed criterion or authoritative rule, or of a full assurance that its limits have been reached. Mindful of the reserve which these considerations recommend, I should not wish to lay down inflexible propositions. But I venture to state generally, that those words of the Latin and Greek tongues, which are in the closest relationship, are connected

1. With the elementary structure of language, such as pronouns, prepositions, numerals.

2. With the earliest state of society.

[n] Horæ Pelasg. ch. iv.   [o] Sechster Theil. Leipzig, 1838.

3. With the pursuits of peaceful and rural industry, not of highly skilled labour.

Examples, numerous enough to show a most extensive agreement, will readily suggest themselves under the first head. To illustrate the other propositions, though it can only be done imperfectly, I will follow both the positive and the negative methods. The first, by comparing words which denote elementary objects, both of animate and inanimate nature, or the simplest products of human labour for the supply of human wants, or the members of the human body, or the rudiments of social order. The second, by contrasting the words which relate (1) to intelligence and mental operations, (2) to war, and (3) to the metals, the extended use of which denotes a certain degree of social advancement. It will I hope be borne in mind, on the one hand, that these lists are given by way of instance, and have no pretension to be exhaustive: and, on the other hand, that exceptions, discovered here and there, to the rule they seem to indicate, would in no way disprove its existence, but should themselves, if purely exceptions, be treated, provisionally at least, as accidental.

Class I.—*Elementary objects of inanimate Nature.*

ἔρα, terra
ἀήρ, aer
αἰθήρ, æther
αὔρα, aura
ἀστήρ } astrum
ἀστέρος } stella
 } sterula
κοῖλον, cælum
ἥλιος, sol
σε-λήνη, luna
νύξ, nox
(Ζεὺς) Διὸς, dies
πόντος, pontus
ἅλς } sal
θάλασσα } salum
πόλος, polus
λυκή in λυκάβας, } lux
λεύσσειν }

χείμων, hyems
ἔαρ, ver
ὥρη, hora
ἑσπέρα, vesper
νέφος } nubes
 } nebula
(νιψ) νίφος, nix, nivis
δρόσος, ros
ὑετος } fluvius
 } pluvia
ῥίγος, frigus
χάμαι, humus
πεύκη, pix
κῆπος }
σῆκος } sepes
λάκκος }
λάχυς } (*a pit*), lacus

ἄμπελος, pampinus
ὕλη, sylva
φύλλον, folium
ῥόδον, rosa
λαᾶς, lapis
ἄγρος, ager
ἄρουρα, arvum
ἄντρον, antrum
φῦκος, fucus
σπέος }
σπήλαιον } spelunca
ἴον, viola
σκόπελος, scopulus
ὕδωρ, sudor.

Class II.—*Elementary objects of animated Nature.*

θήρ, fera
λύκος, lupus
καπρός, aper
λέων, leo
ἔγχελυς, anguilla
ἰχθύς, piscis
ὠκύπτερος, accipiter
κύων, κυνός, canis
ὄϊς, ovis
βοῦς, bos
ταῦρος, taurus
ὗς, sus
ἵππος, equus
πῶλος, pullus
οὖθαρ, uber
ἀμνός, agnus
κριός, aries
ἀλώπηξ, vulpes.

Class III.—*Articles immediately related to elementary wants and to labour.*

1. DWELLINGS.
δόμος, domus
οἶκος, vicus
θύραι, fores
κληΐς, clavis
ἕδος, sedes
αἰθάλη, favilla
θάλαμος, thalamus
λέχος, lectus.

2. FOOD.
οἶνος, vinum
ἔλαια, olea
ἔλαιον, oleum
ᾠον, ovum

μῆλον, malum
σῦκον, ficus
τρύγη, fruges
ἀ-τρύγετος, triticum
σῖτος, cibus
γλάγος, } lac, lac-
γάλα, γάλακτος } tis
κάλαμος, calamus
κρέας, caro
μέλι, mel
δαίς, dapes
κοινή, coena.

3. CLOTHING.
ἐσθής, vestis
χλαῖνα, læna.

4. TOOLS AND IMPLEMENTS.
ἄροτρον, aratrum
ζεῦγος } jugum.
ζύγον }

5. NAVIGATION.
ναῦς, navis
λιμήν, limen
ἐρετμός, remus
κυβερνήτης, gubernator
ἀγκύρα, ancora
πούς, pes.

Class IV.—*The constituent parts of the human body, the family, society, and general ideas.*

1. THE HUMAN BODY.
κεφαλή, caput
κόμη, coma
ὦμος, armus[o]
μῆρον, fe-mur, moris
παλάμη, palma
πούς, pes
ὀδούς, οντος, dens, dentis
λάπτω, labrum
δείκνυμι, digitus
λάξ, calx
ἧπαρ, jecur
ἔντερον, venter
ἕλκος, ulcus
κέαρ } cor
καρδία }
γόνυ, genu
μυελός, medulla
ὀστέον, os (ossis)
ὤψ, os (oris).

2. THE FAMILY.
πατήρ, pater

μήτηρ, mater
υἱός, filius
φρήτηρ } frater
φρήτρη }
ἑκυρός, socer
χήρη } heres
χηρωστής }
γένος { gens
       { genus.

3. SOCIETY.
(ῥέζειν) ῥέξας, rex[p]
ἐλεύθερος, liber
τέκτων (στέγω), cf. tec-tum (tego)
φώρ, fur
παλλακίς, pellex.

4. GENERAL IDEAS.
νεύω, numen
θεός, deus

ὄνομα, nomen
μορφή, forma
ἴς, vis
ῥώμη, Roma, robur
κνίσση, nidor
ὀδμή, odor
φήμη, fama
φάτις } fatum
φάτον }
βίος, vita[q]
μόρος, mors
ὕπνος, somnus
ὀδύνη[r], odium
ἄλγος, algor
γεύω, } gustus
γεύσω }
ἦνις, annus
λήθη } lethum
λήτω }
δόσις, dos
δῶρον, donum
φυγή } fuga
φύζα }
αἰών, ævum.

[o] Applied principally to the shoulder of animals by the Latins.
[p] The link of ideal connection is to be found in the sacrificial office of the primitive *rex*. [q] Scott and Liddell *in voc.*
[r] Compare the Homeric derivation of Ὀδύσσευς from ὀδύσσομαι, Od. xix. 407.

Class V.—*Adjectives of constant use in daily life.*

μέγας, magnus	παχὺς, pinguis	ὄρθος, ordo[r]
παῦρος { parvus / paucus	βραχὺς, brevis	ὕπτιος, supinus
πλατύς, latus	βραδὺς } tardus / βαρδὺς	γραῦς, gravis
ἄγχος ⎱ ἄγκιστρον ⎬ { uncus / angustus or ⎰ ἄγοστος	χαὸς, cavus	λεπτὸς { levis / lentus
	τέρην, tener	λεῖος, lævis
	πλέος, plenus	γενναῖος, gnavus
	μείων, minor	δέξιος, dexter
κυρτὸς, curtus	μάσσων, major	ὅλος, solus
γῦρος, curvus	νέος, novus	ἡδὺς, suavis
πυρρὸς, furvus	ἄλλος, alius	πικρὸς, acris[s].
ἐρυθρὸς { ruber / rufus		

A very extensive list of perhaps one hundred or more verbs might be added, which are either identical or nearly related in the Greek and Latin languages: but it would not, I think, materially enlarge or diminish the general effect of those words which have been enumerated. We have before us about one hundred and eighty words in the classes of substantive and adjective only. They might nearly form the primitive vocabulary of a rustic and pacific people. Two exceptions may be named, which may deserve remark. It will be observed, that the senses are inadequately represented, only two of them, smell and taste, being included. The other three are also connected in the two languages as follows: touch, by the relation of θιγγάνω and *tango*: sight, by εἴδω and *video*: hearing, by the evident connection of the Latin *audire* with the Greek αὐδή, the proper name in Homer for the voice.

The other marked exception is that of religion. With slender exceptions, such as θεὸς = *deus*, the connection of *rex* with ῥέζω, of *numen* with νεύω, of λοιβή with *libo*, and that of ἀράομαι, ἀρητήρ with *orare, orator, ara*, there is a considerable want of correspondence in the leading words, such as ἱερὸς, ἄγιος, θύω, βῶμος, νῆον, ἄγαλμα, σέβω,

[r] Döderlein.   [s] Ennius.

μάντις, of the one tongue, and *sacer, sanctus, pius, templum, vates, macto, mola,* of the other. The greater part of the Pelasgian vocabulary must have been displaced on the one side or on the other: and as it is in Greece that we have much fuller and clearer evidence of the advent of a superior race, which gave its own impress to life and the mind in the higher departments of thought, we must conclude that this substitution probably took place in Greece, and was of Hellenic for Pelasgian words.

The proposition of Niebuhr with respect to terms of war, appears to me to be in the main well sustained by the facts. Let us take for example the following list: which appears to show that, in this department, with the exception of a pretty close relation between βέλος and *telum*, and a more remote one between πόλεμος and *bellum*, possibly also between *lorica* and θώρηξ, there is hardly in any case the faintest sign of relationship between the customary terms employed in the two languages for the respective objects.

telum	.... βέλος	prælium	}..{ ὑσμίνη
ensis }	{ ξίφος	pugna	}..{ μάχη
gladius } .... { φάσγανον		currus }	{ δίφρος
cuspis }		rheda } .... { ἅρμα
mucro } ...... αἰχμή		rota	.... κυκλός (Hom.)
acies }		temo	.... ῥυμός
galea	.... κυνέη	tuba }	
hasta	...... { δόρυ	classicum } .... σάλπιγξ
	{ ἔγχος	castra	.... κλισίαι
scutum[t] }	{ ἄσπις	tabernaculum[u]..κλισίη
clypeus } .. { σάκος	arcus	.... { βιός
lorica	.... θώρηξ		{ τόξον
ocrea	.... κνημίς	sagitta	...... { ἰόν
vagina	.... κολεός		{ ὀϊστός.
bellum	...... { Ἄρης		
	{ πόλεμος		

It can hardly, I think, be questioned, that this class of words presents on the whole a very marked contrast to those which were before exhibited. And as we see

[t] Perhaps connected with the Greek κεύθειν.   [u] Cæsar, b. iii. c. 96.

the highest martial energies of Greece manifestly represented in the Hellenes, we may the more confidently adopt that inference as to the habits of Hellenes and Pelasgians respectively, which the contrast between the two languages of itself vividly suggests.

Before quitting this head of the subject, let us notice the wide difference in the channels by which the two languages arrive at the words intended to represent the highest excellence. For 'better' the Greeks have βέλτερος, from βέλος, 'a dart,' and for 'best,' ἄριστος, from ἄρης, 'war;' while the Latins are contented with *optimus*, formed from a common root with *opes*, 'wealth.'

There is almost as remarkable a want of correspondence between the two languages in respect to the higher ideas, both intellectual and moral, as in regard to war.

In three words indeed we may trace a clear etymological relationship, but in two of the cases with a total, and in the third with an important change in the meaning.

1. The μένος of the Greeks becomes the Latin *mens;* so that a particular quality, and that one belonging to the πάθη rather than the ἤθη of man, comes to stand for the entire mind.

2. The Greek ἄνεμος is evidently the Latin *animus :* or, that word which remains the symbol of a sensible object in Greek becomes the representative of mind in Latin. The adjective ἀνεμώλιος is indeed capable of a metaphysical application: but it means 'of no account[x].'

3. The θυμὸς of the Greeks is the *fumus* of the Latins: and the case last described is exactly reversed.

The three great words in the early Greek for the unseen or spiritual powers of man's nature are νόος, φρὴν, and ψυχή. They perhaps correspond most nearly

[x] Il. xx. 123.

with the three Latin words *mens, indoles,* and *vita*[x]. There is not the slightest sign of conformity or common origin in any of the cases; although νόος is akin to *nosco*[y].

In two other very important words we find perhaps derivation from a common root, but nothing like a near or direct relationship. The Greek ἀρετή may proceed from the same stock with the Latin *virtus,* and in like manner ἄτη may have the same source as *vitium.*

Upon the whole we may conclude, that in this important class of words the resemblances are scanty and remote. It will be seen that under the head of general ideas there is not included any clear case of correspondence in a mental quality; and all the resemblances appear to rest, mediately or immediately, upon sensible objects and phenomena.

As respects the terms employed in navigation, it will have been observed, that they are all connected with its rudest form, that of rowing; and that they do not include the words for mast, yard, or sail, in all of which the two tongues appear to be entirely separated.

Again, it may be stated generally, that society in its very earliest stages has little to do with the use of metals. This rule will be of various application, according to their abundance or scarcity in various countries, and according to the facility with which they are convertible to the uses of man. As the objects of enjoyment multiply with the continuance and growth of industry, the precious metals become more desirable with a view to exchange. But the principal metal for direct utility is iron: and of that, the quantity known and used by the Greeks would appear, even in the time of Homer, to have been extremely small. The

[x] As in Æn. xii. 952.
[y] Buttmann's Lexil. in voc. κελαινός.

use of metal for works of art, and probably also for commercial exchange, would seem to have been derived from Phœnician, not Pelasgian sources; and we have no proof that when Homer lived they had acquired the art in any high degree for themselves.

The absence of any great progress in the use of metals may thus be set down as a sign of Pelasgianism. And now let us compare the Greek and Roman names for the metals respectively:

1. χρυσὸς, aurum.
2. ἄργυρος, argentum.
3. χαλκὸς, æs.
4. σίδηρος, ferrum.
5. μόλιβος, plumbus: in later Greek μόλυβδος, the form nearest to the Latin.
6. κασσίτερος, stannum.

Here also there is a great want of correspondence. Only in iron and lead, and possibly in silver, are there signs of relationship: but in all it is remote. In the other metals it is entirely wanting; and in those which are nearest, it amounts only to presumptive derivation from a common root. The want of community in this class of terms seems to show, that the race which was the common factor of the two nations, was probably not advanced in the use of metals beyond their elementary purposes.

I will only further observe, that while so many names indicative of social and domestic relations are akin, nothing can be more clearly separate than the Greek δοῦλος and the Latin *servus*. From this fact it would be no improbable inference, that slavery was unknown to the Pelasgians: and their ignorance of it would, on the other hand, be in the closest harmony with their slight concern in warlike and in maritime pursuits; since captivity in the one, and kidnapping through the other, were the two great feeders of the institution. It is also in close correspondence with the further hypothesis, which represents the Pelasgians as probably the race that first occupied the Greek soil, and found no predecessors upon it over whom to establish political or proprietary dominion[x].

It may, I think, deserve notice in confirmation of the general argument, that almost all those Greek words, which are in close affinity with the Latin, are found in Homer. For there can be little doubt that, after his time, the Greek tongue became more and more Hellenic: and the fact that a word is Homeric supplies the most probable token of a link with a Pelasgian origin.

And now let us sum up under this head of discussion.

It may be said with very general truth, that the words which have been quoted, and the classes to which they belong, have reference to the primary experience and to the elementary wants and productions of life: but that they do not touch the range of subjects belonging to civilization and the highest powers of man, such as war, art, policy, and song.

But if the evidence goes to show, that the Pelasgian tongue supplied both the Latin and the Greek nations with most of the principal elementary words, and with those which express the main ideas connected with rural industry, the inference strongly arises, 1. That they constituted the base of the Greek nation; and, 2. that, originally cultivators of the soil for themselves, there came upon them a time when other tribes acquired the mastery among them, so that thenceforth they had to cultivate it under the government of others. The case of the Pelasgian vocabulary in the

[x] Compare sup. p. 237.

Latin and in the Greek languages would thus appear to resemble the Saxon contribution to the English tongue: and it is likely that something like the general position, which we know to be denoted in the one case, is also similarly to be inferred in the other.

No inconsiderable light may, I think, be thrown upon the character and pursuits of the Pelasgian and Hellenic races respectively, from an examination of the etymology of the names of persons contained in the Homeric poems. For the names of men, in the early stages of society, are so frequently drawn direct from their pursuits and habits, that the ideas, on which they are founded, may serve to guide us to a knowledge of the character and occupations of a people.

By way of summary proof that a connection prevailed (whether the names be fictitious or not, I care not, for this purpose, to inquire,) between the Homeric names, and the pursuits and habits of those who bear them, I may refer to the names of Phæacians and Ithacans. Of the latter, which are numerous, not one is derived from the horse; and we know[y] that no horses were used in Ithaca. The former are chiefly composed of words connected with the sea: in conformity with the fact that the pursuits of the people are represented by Homer as thoroughly maritime.

The names of persons in Homer are extremely numerous, amounting to many hundreds. It would be hazardous, as a general rule, to assume for them an historical character, except in the cases of such individuals as, from general eminence or local connection, or from

[y] Od. iii. 601-8. The names of Ctesippus and Elatus among the Suitors are related to horses: but all the islands were not so rough as Ithaca, and some of the nobles may, like Ulysses, have had pastures on the continent. (Od. xiv. 100.)

some particular gift or circumstance, were likely to be held in remembrance. In some cases, as we have already seen[y], they bear the marks of invention upon them. But this question is little material for the present purpose: and indeed the probability that we ought, as a general rule, to regard the less distinguished names as fabricated for the purposes of the poem, makes it the more reasonable that we should turn to them to see how far they connect themselves with distinctions of pursuit, character, and race, and what properties and characteristics, when so connected, they appear to indicate as having been assigned by Homer to one race or to another.

We must not expect to arrive at anything better than general and approximate conclusions; for particular circumstances, unknown to us, may have varied the course of etymological nomenclature, and it may also happen, that in a great number of cases we cannot securely trace etymology at all.

Subject to these cautions, I would observe, first, that the evidence from other sources generally tends to show,

1. That the Trojans, except as to the royal house[z], and perhaps a few other distinguished families, were Pelasgian.

2. That the base of the Greek army and nation were Pelasgian: with an infusion of Hellenic tribes, not families merely, who held the governing power and probably formed the upper, that is, the proprietary and military, class of the community, in most parts of Greece.

3. That some parts of the Greek peninsula present little or no mark of Hellenic influences; particularly Attica and Arcadia.

4. That the Lycians appear to approximate more

[y] Sup. p. 256.   [z] Inf. sect. ix.

than the other races on the Trojan side to the high Greek type, and to present either the Hellenic element, or some element akin to it, in a marked form.

The investigation of individual names occurring singly would be endless, and often equivocal: but Homer frequently unites many names in a group under circumstances, which authorize us to assume a common origin and character for the persons designated: and others, though he may not collect them together in the same passage, are yet associated in virtue of palpable relations between them.

An examination of Homeric names, in the groups thus gathered, has brought me to the following results:

1. Where we have reason to presume an Hellenic extraction, a large proportion of those names, of which the etymology can be traced, appear to express ideas connected with glory, political power, mental fortitude, energy and ability, martial courage and strength, or military operations.

2. But where we may more reasonably suppose, in part or in whole, a Pelasgic stock, ideas of this kind are more rarely expressed, and another vein of etymology appears, founded on rural habits, abodes, and pursuits, or the creation and care of worldly goods, or on other properties or occupations less akin to political and martial pursuits, or to high birth and station.

It is at the same time worth remark that, among the slaves of the Odyssey, we find names of a more highborn cast than those most current among the Pelasgians. Such as Eumæus ($\mu\acute{a}\omega$, to desire eagerly and strive after), Euryclea, (who moreover is daughter of Ops the son of Peisenor,) Eurymedusa (in Scheria), and Alcippe (at Sparta[a]). There were two causes, to

[a] Od. ii. 347. vii. 8. iv. 124.

which this might be referable: first, that high-born slaves were often obtained both by kidnapping and by war; Eumæus, as we know, was of this class. And secondly, that the names of their lords may then, as now, have been occasionally given them. So that the high significations connected with servile names do not constitute an objection to the rules which have been stated.

There is another class of names, which requires especial notice. They are those which have reference to the horse. The rearing and care of the horse are in Homer more connected with the Trojans, than with the Greeks: and his standing epithet, ἱππόδαμος, is more largely employed on the Trojan side[b]. The horse was not exclusively, perhaps not principally, employed in war and games. He was used in travelling also: he may have been employed as a beast of burden: he certainly drew the plough, though Homer informs us that in this occupation the mule was preferable.

The points at which we may expect to find names chiefly Pelasgian, besides those which are expressly given us as such, will be these three:

1. In connection with some particular parts of Greece, especially Attica or Arcadia.

2. Among the masses of the common Greek soldiery.

3. Still more unequivocally among the masses of the Trojan force, and of the auxiliaries generally; except the Lycians, whom we have seen reason to presume to have been less Pelasgian, and more allied, or at least more similar, to the Hellic races.

On the other hand we may presume Hellic blood, or what in Homer's estimation was akin to it, among the Lycians, and likewise wherever we find, especially on the Greek side, any considerable collection of names

[b] See Mure's Hist. Lit. Greece, vol. ii. p. 86.

appertaining to the higher class or aristocracy of the army, or of the country.

The Homeric names, which are given us as expressly Pelasgian, are four only; and they belong to the Pelasgian force on the Trojan side.

1. Hippothous.   2. Pulæus.
3. Lethus.   4. Teutamus[e].

The etymology of the three first names seems obvious enough: and, though the persons are all rulers among their people, not one of them unequivocally presents the characteristics which we should regard as appropriate in Hellic names: although, from their being of the highest rank, we should be less surprised if the case were otherwise.

As regards the first of the four, upon examining the class of names relating to the horse in the poems, we find, as far as I have observed, only Hipponous[f] among the Greeks. This rank does not clearly appear: but νόος, the second factor of the word, supplies the higher element.

On the other side, in addition to Hippolochus, a name meaning horse-ambush, who was both Lycian and royal, we have Hippasus, Hippodamas, Hippodamus, Hippocoon, Hippomachus, and Hippotion. We have likewise,

Melanippus, (Il. xvi. 695.)
Echepolus, (Il. xvi. 417.)
Euippus, (Il. xvi. 417.)

Take again Pulæus, from πύλη. This name may mean porter or gate-keeper: it is scarcely susceptible of a high sense. In connection with the character of the Pelasgians as masons and builders of walled places, it is appropriate to them. Homer has three other names, and no more, which appear to be founded simply upon

[e] Il. ii. 840-3.   [f] Il. xi. 303.

the term gate: Πύλων, Πυλάρτης, and Πυλαιμένης. They are all on the Trojan side.

Next, we have a larger class of names, where a strong infusion of the Pelasgic character may be expected: namely, those connected with Attica.

Among these, three belong to its royal house, and in them we find no certain features of the Pelasgian kind. They are,

1. Erechtheus,
2. Peteos,   } From Il. ii. 547–52.
3. Menestheus,

The last of the three, however, seems, if derived from μένος, to belong to the higher class of names.

Besides these three there are,

4. Pheidas,
5. Stichius,   } Il. xiii. 690, 1.
6. Bias,

7. Iasus,
8. Sphelus,   } Il. xv. 332, 7, 8.
9. Boucolus.

Now the whole of these are commanders or officers; and yet four of them, Pheidas (φείδω), Stichius (στείχω), Sphelus (σφάλλω), and Boucolus (βούκολος), are in a marked manner of the Pelasgian class: Bias (βίη), may perhaps belong to it, as meaning mere physical force: and on the etymology of the ancient name Iasus I do not venture to speculate. Boucolus, like Boucolion, which we shall meet presently, deserves particular attention: we find nothing at all resembling it among the names which are (on other grounds) presumably Hellic.

Other names in the poems, which there may be some reason, from their local connection, to presume Pelasgian, are,

Names of the Pelasgian Class.

1. Lycoorgus, ⎫ From Il. vii. 136, 149, where
2. Ereuthalion, ⎭ they are described as Arcadians.
3. Dmetor, Lord of Cyprus, from Od. xvii. 443.
   And perhaps we may add,
4. An Ion or Ian, as head of the Ἰάονες.
5. An Apis, the early eponymist of the Peloponnesus, or a part of it[c].

Now, though these are all rulers and great personages, the name Dmetor is the only one among them which seems in any degree to present Hellenic ideas: nor need that mean a subduer of men; it may as well mean simply a breaker of horses. Apis, we have every reason to suppose, means the ox. Lycoorgus, from Λυκὸς and ἔργον or its root, has all the appearance of being characteristically Pelasgian.

Let us now inquire if the rules laid down will bear the test of being applied to the lower order of the Greek soldiery.

In the Fifth Iliad Hector and Mars slay a batch of apparently undistinguished persons[d]. They are,

1. Teuthras.   4. Œnomaus.
2. Orestes.   5. Helenus (son of Œnops).
3. Trechus.   6. Orestius.

And again in the Eleventh Iliad Hector slays nine more;

1. Asæus.   6. Agelaus.
2. Autonous.   7. Æsymnus.
3. Opites.   8. Orus.
4. Dolops (son of Clytus).   9. Hipponous.
5. Opheltius.

Now out of the seventeen names here assembled,
Four, namely, Autonous, Clytus, Agelaus, and Æ-

[c] See inf. sect. viii.   [d] Il. v. 705-7.

symnus (from its connection with the word αἰσυμνήτης, ruler), belong to what I term the Hellic class.

Three, namely, Teuthras, Asæus, and Helenus, do not immediately suggest a particular derivation.

Of Hipponous I have already spoken. The other nine appear to conform to the Pelasgian type. Œnomaus corresponds with the Latin Bibulus.

Again; the names of ordinary Trojans appear to belong generally to the same type.

When Patroclus commences his exploits in the Sixteenth book, he slays in succession,

1. Pronous.
2. Thestor, son of
3. Enops.
4. Erualus.
5. Erumas.
6. Amphoteros.
7. Epaltes.
8. Tlepolemus, son of
9. Damastor.
10. Echios.
11. Puris.
12. Ipheus.
13. Euippus, and
14. Polumelus, son of
15. Argeas.

Of these only Tlepolemus and Pronous can with certainty be assigned to the higher class. Damastor is doubtful, like Dmetor; but perhaps from its connection with Tlepolemus, we ought to place it in the same category. Still it must be observed that Homer takes care to bring into action against Patroclus and the Myrmidons his favourites the Lycians, as well as the Trojans[e]: and that therefore we are to presume in this list an intermixture of Lycian names.

The names of ordinary Trojans are for the most part of the same colour. But we must bear in mind that we cannot so easily trace the Trojan as the Greek commonalty. Homer rarely allows a Greek of high station

[e] Il. xvi. vv. 369, 393, 419, 422.

or distinction to be slain: whereas the Greeks continually destroy Trojans of eminence. We may therefore be prepared to find names of the higher type somewhat more freely sprinkled among the Trojan than among the Greek slain.

In the Sixth Iliad[f] a number of the Greek heroes dispatch consecutively a list of Trojans, which supplies the following names:

1. Dresus.
2. Opheltius.
3. Æsepus
4. Pedasus

These two were sons of Boucolion, an illegitimate son of Laomedon, who apparently never was acknowledged, but was brought up in the lower class by his mother Abarbaree.

I add these names to the list:

5. Boucolion.
6. Abarbaree (mother of Boucolion).
7. Astualus.
8. Pidutes.
9. Aretaon.
10. Ableros.
11. Elatus.
12. Phylacus.
13. Melanthius.
14. Adrestus.

Among all these names there is not one which we can with confidence place in the higher category except Aretaon. Dresus (compare $δρήστηρ$, a domestic servant), Opheltius, Boucolion, Melanthius (from its use in the Odyssey, supported by Melantho, and both belonging to servants), are unequivocally of the Pelasgian class:

[f] Il. vi. 20–37.

probably Elatus (which however is found among the Ithacan suitors), Phylacus, Adrestus, should be similarly interpreted. Astualos ($ἄστυ$, $ἅλς$) has no contrary force: and of the rest the derivation is not obvious.

If we take the second batch of Trojans slain by Patroclus, it gives a somewhat different result. They are[g],

1. Adrestus.
2. Autonous.
3. Echeclus.
4. Perimus, son of Megas.
5. Epistor.
6. Melanippus.
7. Elasus.
8. Moulius.
9. Pulartes.

Of these Autonous and Epistor would seem clearly to belong to the higher class; to which we may add Echeclus, if it is derived (like Echecles, a Myrmidon chieftain) from $ἔχω$ and $κλέος$: but even this is not a large proportion.

Now when we turn to the Lycians[h] slain consecutively by Ulysses, we find a material change. These are,

1. Koiranos.
2. Alastor.
3. Chromius.
4. Alcandros.
5. Halios.
6. Noemon.
7. Prutanis.

All of these seven visibly belong to the higher or Hellenic order of names, except $Χρόμιος$, which I presume may be akin to $χρῶμα$, and $Ἅλιος$, 'mariner.' But this last named designation is also somewhat Hellic: I doubt if we find among Pelasgian names any taken from maritime ideas or pursuits.

Again, when Achilles comes forth, there is provided for him a list of victims bearing distinguished names[i], though practically unknown as characters in the poem. At the end of the Twentieth book he slays,

[g] Il. xvi. 694. [h] Il. v. 677, 8.
[i] Il. xx. 455-87.

1. Druops.
2. Demouchus, son of
3. Philetor.
4. Laogonus, and
5. Dardanus, sons of
6. Bias.
7. Tros, son of
8. Alastor.
9. Moulius.
10. Echeclus, son of
11. Agenor.
12. Deucalion.
13. Rigmos, son of
14. Peiroos, one of the Thracian leaders.
15. Areithous.

Now of these fifteen names none, if judged by the rules which we have laid down, would clearly fall into the Pelasgian, or more plebeian, class, except Dryops, perhaps Laogonus, and Bias: three only. Peiroos and Rigmos (probably akin to ῥῖγος) are Thracian, and may be put aside. Six, viz., Demuchus, Philetor, Alastor (contrast with this Lethus), Echeclus, Agenor, and Areithous, are of the Hellic class. The others, Dardanus, Tros, Moulius (Il. xi. 739), and Deucalion are repeated from eminent historical personages.

In this set of names we observe, in conjunction with a new instance of Homer's ever wakeful care in doing supreme honour to Achilles, unequivocal evidence, as I think, that the poet did distribute his names with some special meaning among his minor, and, (so we must suppose,) generally or frequently, non-historical personages.

And the further inference may perhaps be drawn of a probable affinity of race between the highest Trojans and the Hellic tribes.

This inference may be supported by another example. The numerous sons of Antenor, whose names are collected from different parts of the poem, are as follows:

1. Agenor, Il. xi. 59.
2. Acamas, ii. 823. xi. 60. xii. 100, *et alibi*.
3. Archelochus, ii. 823. xiv. 464.
4. Coon, xi. 248.

5. Demoleon, xx. 395.
6. Echeclus, xx. 474.
7. Helicaon, iii. 123.
8. Iphidamas, xi. 221.
9. Laodamas, xv. 516.
10. Laodocus, iv. 87. and
11. Pedæus (νόθος), v. 70.

I apprehend Laodocus should be construed, after the manner of Demodocus, to signify having fame or repute among the λαός. If so, then of the ten legitimate sons, eight have names with an etymology that directly connects them with the higher signification. The name of the Bastard only is more doubtful.

Among the Suitors in Ithaca, who are the princes and chief men of the island, with their connections, and others of the same class, we have the following list of names of the high class:

Mentor.	Leiocritus.
Elatus. (cf. Il. xi. 701.)	Leiodes.
Euryades.	Agelaus.
Eurydamas.	Damastor.
Eurymachus.	Demoptolemus.
Eurynomus.	Euryades.
Amphinomus.	Mastor.
Peisander.	Euenor.
Eupeithes.	Phronius.
Antinous.	Noemon.

Nor are the names which have not been placed in this list of an opposite character. They are chiefly such as have not an obvious etymology. Two of them, Ægyptius and Polybus, were, as we know, great names in Egypt, and they probably indicate a Pelasgian or an Egyptian extraction. Others are, Halitherses, Melaneus, Ctesippus, Nisus, Antiphus, Peiræus. Of these,

Of the higher or Hellenic Class.

the two, or even the three, first may perhaps be regarded as properly Hellic.

Take again the six sons of Nestor:

1. Antilochus.
2. Stratius.
3. Thrasymedes.
4. Echephron.
5. Perseus.
6. Aretus (akin to ἀρέ-σκω, ἀρετή, and the Arete of Scheria).

Of these only Perseus would not at once fall within the class; and this is evidently a most noble name, taken from a great Greek hero. Indeed it must itself stand as a conspicuous example of the rule, if we shall hereafter be able to show[k] a relationship between the Hellic races and Persia as their fountain-head.

Lastly, let us take the Myrmidon leaders and commanders. These were,

1. Patroclus; { and after him the heads of the five son of { divisions.
2. Menœtius.
3. Menesthius.
4. Eudorus.
5. Peisander, son of
6. Maimalus, from μαιμάω.
7. Phœnix. This name may represent, (1) Phœnician extraction or connection; (2) The palm tree; (3) The colour of red or purple, akin to φόνος, and to blood, which the colour φοῖνιξ is supposed to betoken. In any of these three aspects, it will fall into the Hellic class.
8. Alcimedon, son of Laerces.
9. Automedon.

All these names belong to the higher categories. It is therefore the general result of our inquiry, that wherever we have reason on other grounds to presume

[k] Inf. sect. x.

a Pelasgian origin, we find in the proper names of persons, unless they chance to be merely descriptive of the country they inhabited, a decided tendency to represent peaceful, profitable, and laborious pursuits, or the lower qualities and conditions of mankind. But wherever from other causes we are entitled to presume an Hellic relationship, there, so far as a simple etymology will carry us, the personal appellatives appear to run upon ideas derived from intellect, power, command, policy, fame, the great qualities and achievements of war; in short, apart from religion, which does not appear to enter into the composition of nomenclature at all, all the ideas that appeal most strongly to those masculine faculties of our race, in which its perfection was so vividly conceived by the Greeks to reside.

One among the most remarkable features of the Homeric Poems is, their highly forward development of political ideas in a very early stage of society[l]. It seems hardly necessary to argue that these were of Hellic origin; because the fact is before us, that they make their appearance in Homer simultaneously with the universal ascendancy of the Hellic over the Pelasgian tribes wherever they were in contact; and because, in comparing the two nations together, we shall have occasion to note the greater backwardness, and indocility, so to speak, of the Trojans[m] in this respect. I assume, therefore, without detailed argument, the peculiar relation between the Hellic stock and the political institutions of Greece.

For similar reasons I shall touch very briefly the relation of the Hellic tribes to the martial character of Greece.

We may consider the whole Iliad, which represents

[l] See 'Studies on Policy.'   [m] See Studies on 'The Trojans.'

a conflict between less Pelasgic and more Pelasgic races, and which gives a clear superiority to the former, as a general but decisive testimony to this fact.

We find another such testimony, with a well established historical character, in the comparison between the secondary military position of Athens in the Iliad, and its splendid distinctions in later times. It is true indeed, that the Athenian troops are mentioned specifically in the attack upon the ships, together with the Bœotians, Locrians, Phthians, and Epeans [m]. Of these the two latter are called respectively $\mu\epsilon\gamma\acute{a}\theta\nu\mu\omicron\iota$ and $\phi\alpha\iota\delta\iota\mu\acute{o}\epsilon\nu\tau\epsilon\varsigma$; the Athenians are the Ἰάονες ἑλκεχίτωνες, an epithet of most doubtful character as applied to soldiers. It seems to me plain that Homer by no means meant the particular notice of these five divisions for a mark of honour: they fought to be defeated, and he does not use his prime Greeks in that manner. No Peloponnesian forces are named as having been engaged on this occasion. Those probably were the flower of the army; and it is mentioned in the Catalogue that the troops of Agamemnon were the best [n]. Again, it will be seen, on reference to the Catalogue, that the whole force of Middle Greece is here in battle except the Ætolians, the contingent of Ulysses, and the Abantes (for whom see 542–4). These three are all distinguished races, whom he seems purposely to have excluded from a contest, where honour was not to be gained. The military contrast, then, between the earlier and the later Athens, may be taken to be established: and with it coincides that very marked, though normal and pacific, transition of Attica from the exclusively Pelasgic to the fullest development of the composite Greek character [o].

The passage of the seventh Iliad, which describes

[m] Il. xiii. 685.   [n] Il. ii. 577.   [o] Herod. i. 56.

the war of the Pylians with the Arcadians, suggests a like conclusion.

Upon the whole, however, the *de facto* Hellic ascendancy in Greece at the time is, with reference to war and the strong hand even more than to policy, a full presumption of their title to be regarded as having given birth to the splendid military genius of Greece.

When, for the business of the Trojan war, Homer divides the two great traditive deities [p], and assigns to the Greeks Pallas, the more political, energetic, and intellectual of the two, to the Trojans Apollo, we may take this as of itself involving an assertion, that the high arts of policy and war were peculiarly Hellenic.

We come now to the principle of what may be called corporal education, which found a development among the Greeks more fully than among any other nation; first, in gymnastic exercises, generally pursued, and, secondly, in the great national institution of the Games.

"There were," says Grote [q], "two great holding points in common for every section of Greeks. One was the Amphictyonic Assembly, which met half yearly, alternately at Delphi and at Thermopylae; originally and chiefly for common religious purposes, but indirectly and occasionally embracing political and social objects along with them. The other was, the public festivals or games, of which the Olympic came first in importance; next, the Pythian, Nemean, and Isthmian: institutions, which combined religious solemnities with recreative effusion and hearty sympathies, in a manner so imposing and so unparalleled. Amphictyon represents the first of these institutions, and Aethlius the second."

This passage places in an extremely clear light the relative position of the Games and the Amphictyonic

[p] See Studies on Religion, sect. 2. [q] Hist. of Greece, vol. i. p. 137.

Assembly. The Council represented a religious institution, partaking also of a political character. The Games, on the other hand, were a gymnastic celebration, made available for national gatherings: placed, as a matter of prime public moment, under the guardianship of high religious solemnities, and referred for greater effect, in the later tradition, to some person of the highest rank and extraction, as their nominal founder. As the objects of the Games and the Council were distinct, so were their origin and history different; and this difference mounted up into the very earliest ages. This is clearly proved by the extra-historic and mythical names assigned to their founders, whose faint personality does not even serve to repress the suggestion of fiction, conveyed with irresistible force by etymological considerations. But the legend, though a legend only, conformed to the laws of probability, by assigning to Amphictyon a Thessalian birth, and by vindicating at the same time to Aethlius the higher honour of the immediate paternity of Jupiter; while, by placing him in Elis it secures his function as the institutor of the oldest, namely, the Olympic Games. In this legend, too, we see Hellenic imagination providing for its own ancestral honours in competition, as it were, with those of the sister institution, which may have been Pelasgian.

The foundation of Games *in genere* appears to be traceable, with sufficient clearness and upon Homeric evidence, to the Hellic tribes.

The lengthened detail of the Twenty-third Iliad is of itself enough to prove their importance, as an institution founded in the national habits and manners. We must not, however, rely upon the absence of any similar celebrations, or even allusions to them, among the Trojans; since their condition, in the circumstances of the war, will of itself account for it. But we may observe how closely it belonged to the character of the greatest heroes to excel in every feat of gymnastic strength, as well as in the exercises of actual warfare. The kings and leading chiefs all act in the Games, with the qualified exception of Agamemnon, whose dignity could not allow him to be actually judged by his inferiors, but yet who appears as a nominal candidate, and receives the compliment of a prize, though spared the contest for it; and with the exception also of Achilles, who could not contend for his own prizes. Again, it is a piece of evidence in favour of the Hellic character of public Games, that, though there were three Athenian leaders alive during the action of the Twenty-third Book, none of them took any part. They were Menestheus, Pheidas, and Bias. Again, the speech of Ulysses to Euryalus, the saucy Phæacian[r], with the acts which followed it, strengthen the general testimony of the Iliad upon the point. So does the prosecution of these exercises, to the best of their power, even by the Phæacians, the kindred of the gods.

So much for the general idea of Games in Homer; but, to draw the distinction with any force between what is Hellic and what is Pelasgic, we must refer to those passages which afford glimpses of the earlier state of Greece, and see what light they afford us.

According to the Homeric text, Elis and Corinth were the portions of the Peloponnesus, where the early notes of the presence of the Hellenic races are most evident. Now of these Elis had the greatest and oldest Greek Games, while the Isthmian festival at Corinth was held to stand next to them.

The invention of these gymnastic exercises was

[r] Od. viii. 179.

ascribed in the later mythology to Mercury, who is in Homer a Hellenic, as opposed to Pelasgian, deity.

> Mercurî, facunde nepos Atlantis,
> Qui feros mores hominum recentum
> Voce formasti catus, et decoræ
> More palæstræ[s].

It has been observed, that the Hermes of Homer bears no trace of this function: but we have no proof in Homer of the formal institution of Games at all, although we have clear signs of them as a known and familiar practice; and the Mercury of the poems is even yet more Phœnician than he is Hellenic. Aristophanes[t] produces the Ἑρμῆς Ἐναγώνιος, and supplies a fresh link of connection by referring to ἀγῶνες in music, as well as in feats of corporal strength and skill. So does Pindar[u].

In truth, these Games were the exercise and pleasure of the highest orders only. For we see that, in Homer's Twenty-third Book, not a single person takes a part in any of the eight matches that is not actually named among the ἡγεμόνες and κοίρανοι of the Catalogue, with three such exceptions as really confirm the rule. They are Antilochus, the heir apparent of Pylos, Teucer the brother of Ajax, and Epeus, (only however in the boxing match,) who appears from the Odyssey[x] to have been a person of importance, as he contrived the stratagem of the horse. Even the σόλος αὐτοχόωνος, the iron lump, part of the booty of Achilles, had formerly been used for the sport only of a king[y].

> ὃν πρὶν μὲν ῥίπτασκε μέγα σθένος Ἠετίωνος.

The Greek Games presuppose leisure, and therefore the accumulation of property, or the concentrated pos-

[s] Hor. Od. i. 10. 1.
[t] Plutus 1162.
[u] Pyth. ii. 18. Nem. x. 98.
Isthm. i. 85.
[x] Od. viii. 493. xi. 592.
[y] Il. xxiii. 827.

session of lands: but this comports much more with Hellenic than with what we know of Pelasgic society, in which we do not find the same signs as in the former, of an aristocracy occupying the middle place between the people at large, and the royal house. Let us now examine another part of the Homeric evidence.

In the Eleventh Iliad, Nestor's legend acquaints us that, at the time of the war between Pylians and Elians, Neleus the king appropriated a part of the Pylian spoil, in respect of a 'debt' owed him in Elis, the nature of which he explains[z]:

τέσσαρες ἀθλοφόροι ἵπποι αὐτοῖσιν ὄχεσφιν,
ἐλθόντες μετ' ἄεθλα· περὶ τρίποδος γὰρ ἔμελλον
θεύσεσθαι· τοὺς δ' αὖθι ἄναξ ἀνδρῶν Αὐγείας
κάσχεθε, τὸν δ' ἐλατῆρ' ἀφίει, ἀκαχήμενον ἵππων.

There were then, it is plain, chariot races regularly established (for the Games are here spoken of without explanation, as a matter familiarly known) in Olympia: and this was during the boyhood of Nestor, or about two generations before the Trojan war. The tribes, which we here see concerned in these Games, are first, the Pylians, and next the Elians, of whom Augeas was king. It will be seen in a subsequent part of this inquiry[a], that both of these tribes were Hellic, and not Pelasgian. Yet certainly there is nothing here to show directly the non-participation of Pelasgians in the games.

There is however another passage of our useful friend Nestor in the Twenty-third Book, which supplies in some degree even this form of evidence. 'Would,' says he in his usual phrase, 'would I were young and strong[b],'

ὡς ὅποτε κρείοντ' Ἀμαρυγκέα θάπτον Ἐπειοὶ
Βουπρασίῳ, παῖδες δ' ἔθεσαν βασιλῆος ἄεθλα·

Here is a distinct testimony to the custom of funeral Games in Elis, nearly two generations before the *Troica*.

[z] Il. xi. 699-702.   [a] Vid. inf. sect. viii.   [b] xxiii. 629.

They embraced, as we find further down in the record,
1. Chariot races, with the best prize; 2. Boxing;
3. Wrestling; 4. Running; and 5. Hurling the spear.
But we have a further most valuable passage. There
was no person present, says Nestor, equal to myself;
and then he adds an exhaustive enumeration of the
races that furnished the company:

οὔτ' ἄρ' Ἐπειῶν,
οὔτ' αὐτῶν Πυλίων, οὔτ' Αἰτώλων μεγαθύμων.

For the Epeans (or Elians) and Pylians, I repeat the reference already made. Nor can I doubt that the Ætolians, the subjects of Œneus and his illustrious family, belonged to the same stock. I do not inquire whether, as they were always in later times held to belong to the Æolian branch of the Greeks, so their name may have been radically akin to, or identical with, the name of Æolus, which is often with Homer Αἴωλος. But we find Meleager (independently of the reference to him, evidently as a great national hero, in the Catalogue [c],) selected by Phœnix for the subject of an episode of great length, and held out as a warning and example to Achilles[d]. It may safely be assumed he would have chosen no character for this purpose, except that of an hero of pure Hellic origin. And the description of Tydeus, the father of Diomed, by the epithet Αἰτώλιος[e], again serves to identify the Ætolian name with the Hellic races.

The tribes present, then, at the Games were all Hellic, and they were all conterminous: the Epean inhabitants, the Pylians, neighbours on the South, the Ætolians from the other side of the narrow strait, which was the most frequented passage into Peloponnesus. In fact, it was evidently an assemblage of the neighbouring tribes; but with a most remarkable exception, that of the

[c] Il. ii. 642.   [d] Il. ix. 529-99.   [e] Il. iv. 399.

eastern neighbours of Elis, those same Arcadians, whom by many signs we are enabled to conclude to have been Pelasgian.

A third instance in which Homer notices gymnastic exercises, is in Il. iv. 389. Here Tydeus, having gone to Thebes, finds a solemn banquet proceeding in the palace of Eteocles. Alone among many, and on questionable terms with his hosts, he nevertheless at once challenges them to gymnastic games, and beats them all.

ἀλλ' ὅγ' ἀεθλεύειν προκαλίρετο, πάντα δ' ἐνίκα
ῥηιδίως· τοίη οἱ ἐπιρρόθος ἦεν Ἀθήνη.

Achæan, that is Hellene, himself, he is, if not among Hellenes, yet among the members and adherents of that Phœnician dynasty which had established itself, to all appearance, in Bœotia, at a somewhat early date: even as, at a period slightly later[f], Minos established from Phœnicia a Throne in Crete, which soon became wholly Greek in character.

And again, in Il. xxiii. 678-80, we are told, that Mecisteus, on the death of Œdipus, went to Thebes to the even then customary funeral Games, and there was victor over all the Καδμείωνες who opposed him, by the aid of Minerva. Euryalus, the son of Mecisteus, was an Argive, and was the colleague of Diomed and Sthenelus. The same observations are applicable here, as in the last case.

There is therefore nothing in any one of these cases to connect the gymnastic celebrations with the Pelasgian, but every thing to associate them with the Hellic races.

Of the Greek Games, the Pythian are those which, as being under Apollo, might most be suspected of

---

[f] Sup. pp. 167, 242, and see 'The Outer Geography of the Odyssey.'

Pelasgic origin. But these did not apparently begin as a national gymnastic festival until about 586 B. C.[g] The Olympic contests had then been regularly recorded for nearly two hundred years, since 776 B. C. And in the laws of Solon there was a reward of 500 drachms for every Athenian who should gain an Olympic prize, of 100 only for an Isthmian: while of the Nemean and Pythian Games, as being merely local, they take no notice. So these Games, besides being secondary, belonged to times much later, and also purely Hellenic.

The Panathenaic Games are apparently of similar date. And with this evidence from the earlier historic times before us, no importance can attach to a tradition so late as that of Pausanias, who makes Theseus found the Panathenaica, and Lycaon, son of Pelasgus, the Λύκαια[h]. But it is well worthy of remark, that in reporting this tradition he adds, that the Olympic Games were much older, that they mounted to the very highest antiquity of the human race, and that Κρόνος and Jupiter were said to have contended at them for prizes. Again, great fame attached to the Games said to have been celebrated by Acastus on the death of his father Pelias. Stesichorus, who lived in the seventh century, wrote a poem upon them; but Pelias, the brother of Neleus, and son of Tyro, (having Neptune for his father,) was of undoubted Hellic origin[i].

Minor instances of the addiction of the Hellic races to Games may be found in the constant practice of the Ithacan Suitors, and in the resort of the Myrmidons before Troy, during the seclusion of Achilles, to this method of beguiling their time[j].

The case stands only a little less distinctly as to song.

[g] Grote's Hist. ii. 322.   [h] Paus. viii. 2. 1.
[i] Grote's Hist. Greece, i. 160.   [j] Il. ii. 773.

There is an ἀοιδός in the palace of Priam, as well as in that of Ulysses; one in that of Agamemnon, and one in that of Alcinous. The Muses are Olympian Muses. Olympus geographically was quite as much Hellic as Pelasgian, and in every other sense, as I believe, far more. We may perhaps most fairly estimate its national character, by contrasting the Jupiter of Olympus with the Jupiter of Dodona, and the home of the large and varied group of Grecian gods with the solitary grandeur which affords a trace of the old Pelasgian worship. In this view Olympus and the Muses will be clearly Hellic. Further[j], Thamyris in his boast supposes the Muses to be contending against him at the public matches. If I have been correct in tracing such matches to an Hellic source, Thamyris must have regarded the Muses as Hellic when he made this supposition. Again, Thamyris himself is a Θρῆξ, that is to say, a highlander: this connects him with the Helli of the hills, not with the Pelasgians of the more open country. The place, too, where the punishment is inflicted upon Thamyris, is in the dominions of Pylus: which, at any rate for a term equal to three generations before the *Troica*, had been Achæan, that is, Hellic[k].

Apollo was doubtless an object of Pelasgian worship: the Apollo of Homer however is not confined to the Pelasgians, but is by many signs, scattered throughout the poems, placed in close as well as friendly relations with the whole Greek nation. Among these may be reckoned his acceptance of the propitiation and prayer offered by Calchas. In truth, though it is his business, as the organ of Jupiter, to assist the Trojans, he no where shows any of that hostility to their opponents, which Neptune and Juno show to them.

[j] Il. ii. 597, 8.
[k] On Pelasgian music see Müller's Dorians, i. p. 367 (transl.)

In later times, the traditions of Orpheus, Musæus, and Eumolpus, always Θρῆκες, supported the tradition which derives Greek song from the mountain tribes.

Why has Arcadia a muse of her own, but because the Pelasgian poetry is not the Hellic? and does not the reputed character of that muse oblige us to assign a Hellic origin to the higher national poetry?

Hesiod, as author of the Works and Days, is so enormously different from Homer in his frame of mind, as well as his diction, that it is hard to trace, even in the most general form, a complete national affinity between them. The Theogony, by its subject, brought him nearer to Homer, but it is quite destitute of the heroic power and fire: a calm and low-toned beauty, as in the legend of the Ages, is all to which Hesiod ever rises. To my conjecture, he seems to personify the one-stringed instrument which might suffice for Pelasgian song: while the Diapason of Homer, embracing with its immeasurable sweep things small and things great, things sublime and things homely, all objects that human experience had suggested, and all thoughts that the soul of man had imagined or received, presents to us that Greek mind, full, varied, energetic, lively, profound, exact, which was destined to give form for so many ages to the genius of the world.

I cannot however part from this subject, and leave the Hellenic races in possession of the honour of having principally contributed to mould the powerful imagination of the Greeks, without noticing the opposite conclusion of Mr. Fergusson, in his admirable 'Handbook of Architecture.'

He treats the Greek nation as made up chiefly of two ingredients, the Dorian and the Pelasgian. He takes the Greeks of the Trojan Epoch to have been Pelasgian, and so to have continued until the return of the Heraclidæ. Then, according to him, began the Hellenic, which he treats as synonymous with the Doric, preponderance; and, having Sparta before him as the one great Hellic type, he observes that the race was far better adapted "for the arts of war and self-government, than for the softer arts of poetry and peace [k]."

But the supposition of a Pelasgic supremacy in Homeric Greece, is contrary to all the evidence afforded by the text of Homer, and, I think we may add, to the belief alike of ancient and of modern times. Even the limited part of the Homeric evidence which is connected with the names Ἕλλας and Ἕλληνες, seems large enough to overthrow any such hypothesis. Though the Dorian race was Hellenic, it was apparently a late outgrowth from the stock, and has no pretension whatever to be considered as the universal type of its products. In Sparta, the excessive development of policy was doubtless unfavourable to human excellence in other forms; among others, to poetry and art. Still, neither verse, music, nor architecture are disconnected from the Dorian name and race. It seems quite impossible to refer the war-poetry of the Iliad, the grandest in the world, for its origin to a people so unwarlike, in reference especially to the changeful, romantic, and poetic side of war, as the Pelasgi.

The adventurous tone and tenour of the Odyssey, and its wide range over the world, and over the sea, are as little in keeping with what we can see of Pelasgic habits in the heroic age. Above all, that largeness and unimpaired universality of type, which belongs to human character as drawn by Homer, and especially

[k] Fergusson's Illustrated Handbook of Architecture, book vi. chap. i.

to Achilles and Ulysses, demonstrate (I cannot use a weaker word) that all the materials of Grecian greatness were in his time fully ripened.

At the same time it is not necessary to deny, that the Pelasgians may have been endowed with a high sense of beauty. Not that Homer appears to have had a vivid conception of beauty in connection with architecture, their great reputed accomplishment; for he seems, on the contrary, to have had little idea of ornament in buildings, beyond the blaze of plates of polished metal: far different here from what he shows himself to be in dealing with dress, or armour, or the forms of men and horses. But we have before us the fact that through Athens itself preeminently, and likewise through its colonies to the east, the Greek race earned in aftertimes the very highest honours in poetry and the fine arts. On the one hand, however, a large share of these honours, especially in early times, fell to the share of the race called Æolian, which was clearly Hellic, and a principal part of the Hellic family. On the other hand, Arcadia, which remained more purely Pelasgian, while Athens received all sorts of mixtures, never attained to high distinction in art, nor rose above a modest and tranquil strain of verse. The great tragedians and the great artists were of a race the most composite in all Greece. The natural inference would seem to be, that whatever the Pelasgians may have contributed to the general result, however they may have afforded for poetry and art (as also they did for war) a good raw material, it was only when in combination with other elements from other sources, that they could attain to great practical excellence. A lively sense of beauty is, doubtless, not only a condition, but even a foundation: yet a great organising power is as necessary for the production of the great works of imagination, as it was to Lycurgus for the Spartan constitution, or to Aristotle for philosophical analysis and construction; and this was the commanding and sovereign faculty in a mind such as that of Homer.

The connection between the Homeric Greeks and the traditions of huntsmen is, I think, sufficiently evident from Homer. His hunting legends, and the multitude of his hunting similes, are so many signs of it; and many indications, I think, concur towards forming a belief that the Greeks owed their fondness for the chace to their Hellic, not to their Pelasgic habits and blood.

I take first the relation between Achilles and his instructors. Chiron was the teacher of Achilles in the surgical art, while Phœnix had charge of his higher education. Surgery and war would obviously go together. But Chiron too gave his father the ashen spear from Pelion, which none but Achilles could wield: he was the most civilized ($\delta\iota\kappa\alpha\iota\acute{o}\tau\alpha\tau\sigma\varsigma$) of the Centaurs, the one to whom the ideas of right, on which society is founded, were most congenial. But he seems to dwell on Mount Pelion, not like Phœnix, in the court of Peleus; he is, therefore, without doubt, a huntsman, and is in fact a link between the old and rude, and the new and more civilized life of the Hellic tribes.

Again. Of the Hellic legends of Homer, which are not in all very numerous, two have hunting for their subject: as,

1. That of the Calydonian Boar in Il. ix.

2. That of the visit of Ulysses to the court of Autolycus, in Od. xix.

Now these two legends are the only ones in the poems, that do not relate to war. Though the Trojans dwelt by Ida, we never hear of their hunts: but their princes feed sheep upon its slopes, or tend horses in the plain below.

Even apart from particular evidence, we might presume that, if the nation derived its warlike turn from a Hellic source, so it must likewise have been with hunting, which was next of kin to war.

Lastly, if this supposition be correct, it helps to account for what is otherwise an anomaly in the poems. Diana fights on the Trojan side: yet we find no evidence that she was worshipped among the Trojans, or even known to them in the character, in which she has the greatest mythical celebrity. She is mentioned but once, I think, among them; it is by Andromache, and that is as having put a period to her mother's life [l], nowhere in her character as a huntress. But among the Greeks she constantly appears otherwise than as in connection with death. Her epithets, $\dot{\alpha}\gamma\rho o\tau\acute{\epsilon}\rho\eta$, $\kappa\epsilon\lambda\alpha\delta\epsilon\iota\nu\grave{\eta}$, $\iota o\chi\acute{\epsilon}\alpha\iota\rho\alpha$, are far more suitable to the huntress, than to the more solemn function of the ministry of Death among human beings. Again, Helen is compared to her in appearance. The calamities of the Kalydonians came upon them in consequence of their neglect as to her worship on a particular occasion [m]; and the particular punishment inflicted is the sending a wild boar upon them. Nausicaa [n] is elaborately compared to her, and in this simile she is described as hunting in Taygetus and Erymanthus. Thus while among the more Pelasgic Trojans, she appears only in virtue of the relation to death which (we shall find) she holds from a traditive source [o]; it is the Hellic influence, which superadds the mythical and imaginative attributes of the beautiful

[l] Il. vi. 428.   [m] Il. ix. 533.   [n] Od. vi. 102.
[o] See infra, Studies on Religion, sect. ii.

huntress: and which, in so doing, supplies a marked proof of the addiction of the Hellic tribes to that pursuit.

It is not easy to judge whether the turn of the Greeks for navigation ought to be referred in any degree to a Pelasgian source. Plainly, if there was such a source, it was not the main one. We have seen that only the most elementary words connected with propulsion by rowing, appear to bear any sign on them of proceeding from that stock. We cannot argue from the maritime excellence of the Athenians at a much later date to their nautical character in the time of Homer, on account of the important ethnical changes, which in the mean time they had gradually, but most thoroughly, undergone. On the other hand, our finding the pure Pelasgian population of Arcadia resorting to the inland country, and wholly destitute of ships, affords a negative indication. A stronger, and indeed very remarkable one, is supplied by the total want of ships among the Trojans, notwithstanding that their situation was one highly favourable to the acquisition of maritime power. Yet Paris needed to have ships built for him in order to effect his tour[p], and the building of them appears in the Iliad as having been an event of much note in Troy. On the other hand, Homer is full of indications of the locomotive tendencies of the Hellic races. Among these may be mentioned, the wide circle embraced in the adventures of Hercules: the offer of Menelaus[q] to accompany Telemachus on a journey about Greece: the sojourn of Neoptolemus[r] in Scyros: the frequent visits of Idomeneus[s] to Sparta before the war: the marriage of Theseus[t] to a daughter of the king of Crete: the journey of Nestor[u] into Thessaly: the pleasure

[p] Il. v. 62.   [q] Od. xv. 80.   [r] Od. xi. 506.
[s] Il. iii. 232.   [t] Od. xi. 322.   [u] Il. i. 269.

visits of Autolycus to Ithaca, and of the young Ulysses[x] to Autolycus: the evident familiarity of the Poet with the idea of travelling to recover debts[y]: the existence of places of wide resort for Games and Oracles[z]: the custom of assembling from a group of districts at the funerals of great men[a]: nay, the very choice of the voyages of Ulysses for the subject of so great a part of the Odyssey, and the lengthened tour of Menelaus. And while the Pelasgians appear to be akin to the land-loving Egyptians, we have found the Hellenes to be strongly sympathetic in character with the Phœnicians, the great masters of navigation in the heroic age.

From the speech of the Pseudo-Ulysses in the Fourteenth Odyssey, we have the strongest evidence that navigation and agricultural pursuits, which were those of the Pelasgians, stood in sharp opposition to one another. He could not bear tillage, but loved ships and war[b].

ἔργον δέ μοι οὐ φίλον ἦεν,
οὐδ' οἰκωφελίη, ἥτε τρέφει ἀγλαὰ τέκνα·
ἀλλά μοι αἰεὶ νῆες ἐπήρετμοι φίλοι ἦσαν
καὶ πόλεμοι καὶ ἄκοντες ἐΰξεστοι καὶ ὀϊστοί.

It is also plain, from two circumstances at least, that Homer regarded travelling as one great means of mental and practical culture. One is, that he describes this benefit as attained in the case of his great hero Ulysses;

ὃς μάλα πολλὰ
πλάγχθη . . . . . .
πολλῶν δ' ἀνθρώπων ἴδεν ἄστεα, καὶ νόον ἔγνω[c].

The other is that, in the very remarkable simile of the

[x] Od. xix. 399, 413.
[y] Od. iii. 267. xxi. 16.
[z] Il. xi. 698–702. Od. vi. 364. xiv. 327.
[a] Il. xxiii. 629–43.
[b] Od. xiv. 222.
[c] Od. i. 1–3.

z

Thought, he treats travelling as the great stimulus to the growth of the mind of man:

ὡς δ' ὅτ' ἂν ἀΐξῃ νόος ἀνέρος, ὅς τ' ἐπὶ πολλὴν
γαῖαν ἐληλουθὼς φρεσὶ πευκαλίμῃσι νοήσῃ·
ἔνθ' εἴην, ἢ ἔνθα· μενοινήῃσί τε πολλά [d].

Both as to navigation then, and as to locomotion, which stand nearly related to each other, it would seem that we ought probably to regard the Hellic stock as the parent of the Greek accomplishment.

After this laborious and microscopic investigation, we may now be justified in taking a survey more at ease of the ground which we have traversed so slowly, and in endeavouring to embody our general results in a rude sketch of the succession, places, and functions of the two great races of early Greece.

Relying, therefore, upon what has been produced in the way of proof, I will proceed to fill up its interstices with such conjectures as probable reasoning will supply.

The Greek nation was originally formed of two great coefficients, the Hellic and Pelasgic races respectively: and there is no evidence, that any other race entered largely into its composition, or modified it sensibly: although individual foreigners or companies of emigrants, which left little impression on the names of districts or races, may notwithstanding have exercised a powerful influence from time to time. We may consider the Leleges, Caucones, and other pre-Hellenic tribes as branches of the Pelasgian family, or as akin to it rather than to the Hellic stem.

There is Homeric and post-Homeric evidence, which seems to shew us the Pelasgians established through

[d] Il. xv. 80.

Greece from Macedonia in the north, to Crete in the south: as well as in Italy, and elsewhere beyond the borders of Greece.

It is on the whole most probable, that the Pelasgians principally entered Greece from the south by Crete; but they may have entered it in both directions. In either case, there is no other people to dispute with them in continental Greece the title of its first regular settlers. They chose their habitations in the plains, and were essentially a lowland people. It is even likely that they derive their name from this characteristic, and that it marks them at once as agriculturists.

As respects the religion of Greece, its most essential features were probably common to the two races: a principle illustrated by the fact that the Helli, by a kind of natural succession, become the wardens and interpreters of the great Pelasgian shrine of Jupiter at Dodona.

The first form of the religion of Greece was probably due to the Pelasgians; and moreover it would appear to be from them that it received, in the main, its ritual and hierarchical, as contradistinguished from its imaginative, development. They appear to have incorporated it in visible institutions, and to have given social order to the country; probably in that form in which men live sparsely, and not in the large aggregations of considerable cities. But social order in any form implies some means of defence against the lawless: and we must view the Pelasgians as having introduced the construction of works of this class, which were then of prime necessity to the existence of communities. Their standing pursuit was evidently that of agriculture: the only link of connection established by Homer between them and the beautiful in art, is the doubtful one of the epithets περικαλλέα and καλὰ[e] applied to the architecture of the palaces of Priam and Paris respectively.

In general, the Pelasgian race, though without the vivid temperament of the Hellic tribes, yet would appear to have been both brave and solid in character.

The stream of Pelasgic immigration, flowing chiefly northward, is met by the counter-stream of Hellic tribes, proceeding from the highland nation of the Helli, which had taken its seat in the mountains to the north of Thessaly.

They in their southward course overspread the same countries which the Pelasgi had already occupied; successive tribes of immigrants going forth from the parent stock at different times, as the pressure of population on the means of subsistence required it, and under different names, taken in all likelihood from their leaders.

In the nest of mountaineers, barbarism, or at least rudeness, continues: but as the young broods go forth, and make their way into more favourable conditions of physical and social life, their great capacities for development find scope, and they rapidly assume a new character.

By their greater energy and activity, they became everywhere the dominant race. Policy and war fell into their hands: they supplied the more vigorous, intellectual, and imaginative element in the wonderful composition of the Greek mind. Of the Pelasgian imagination it is difficult to speak in a definite manner: but it probably had not that masculine tone, and energetic movement, when alone, which marks the mind of Greece.

Far more expansive than their Pelasgian antecessors,

[e] Il. vi. 242, 315.

the Hellic tribes availed themselves of the great advantages which the country offers for extended navigation, which was so essential as a means both of communication, and of attracting the elements of civilization from abroad. They were apt pupils under apt instructors, the Phœnician mariners. They developed the Pelasgic religion into their more enlarged and diversified mythology: they idealized the visible world together with human nature, and established those peculiar and pervasively poetical relations between the seen and the unseen spheres of existence, which are the basis of the Greek mythology. Their keen sense of the beautiful led them to adorn both the body and the mind of man with the attributes of deity, while their imaginative power continually prompted them both to clothe celestial objects in shapes borrowed from the visible world, and to equip the gods with sentiments and passions drawn from the sphere of every day experience.

They likewise brought with them the gymnastic element of the Greek system, the education of the body; and they made provision for this education, in conjunction with a powerful means of national union, in the Games which became so famous through so many ages.

The same qualities which found employment in fashioning the relations of earth to heaven, were likewise busy in uniting the past with the present, by the agency of history in the form of song.

Of this race were the Achæans, who by their power and extension through Greece, gave to it and to its people their first famous designation, that which they bore in the Homeric times. From the same source proceeded all the Hellenes, derivatively so called, and the Myrmidons. Under the great Achæan name, understood

II. *Ethnology.*

in its special sense, are probably included with the Pelopids, the Pylians, Cephallenians, Epeans, Myrmidons, Locrians. Nor can we be certain that it did not also include those Æolid families whose power and extension subsequently impressed large portions of Greece with the Æolian name.

While imperial cares and aims, and the refinements and enjoyments, together with the stir, movement, and solicitude of life, fell to the Hellic portion of the Greek societies, and took its form from them, the Pelasgian element, though depressed below the surface, continued to live and act with vigour; it predominated in the classes which form the solid *substratum* of society, those on which rural industry, if not those on which mechanical pursuits depended, and from which the upper surface, when exhausted by the prolonged performance of its functions, may draw in every society successive stocks of new materials to renovate its vital forces.

While Homer himself seems to represent the unbounded wealth and fulness, and the manifold and versatile power, of the composite Greek mind, we appear to have, in the rural strains of Hesiod, if not in the unenlivened theogonic traditions ascribed to him, the just and natural exemplification of all that we might expect in a Pelasgic poet.

In later, as well as in Homeric times, the Arcadians seem in the most marked manner to have exhibited the Pelasgic aspect of the Greek mind and life: and they show it much in the same relation to the Hellic races, as that of the Saxons to the Norman chivalry. Like the Saxons, it was not in bravery that they failed: they were ἐγχεσίμωροι and ἐπιστάμενοι πολεμίζειν: but in energy and passion, and likewise in governing and organizing powers, they were beneath the competing race, and therefore they gave way: while, from their enduring and solid qualities, they were well qualified in after generations to supply the greater waste caused by a more vivid temperament and keener action in the soil above them.

Among the Spartans we find developed, in a very peculiar degree, two of the imperial elements of the Greek character. The first is that political faculty of the Hellic races, by which, as Strabo says, they perserved their ἡγεμονία from the time of Lycurgus, down to the fifth century.

And the second is, the idea of the education of the body, as an essential and main part of human training: a sentiment which to us may seem narrow, but we must remember that the Greeks kept fully in their view what we have dropped from our theories, though it may be hoped, not wholly from our practice, namely, the influence of bodily exercise and discipline in forming mental qualities and habits.

It was to Attica, however, that was reserved the office of exhibiting in the fullest degree the manysidedness of the Greek character: and the efficient cause, by which she was fitted to fulfil this function, probably may have been that constant infusion of new blood by the successive immigrations of the different Greek races, without the absolute displacement of any of them on a large scale, which, as we have seen, Thucydides remarks to have been her special characteristic. Hence she always exhibited both the ancient and the fresh; both, too, in the highest degree; urging, like Arcadia, the autochthonic origin of her population, which must refer to its Pelasgic element; contending with that state, and with Argos[f], for the honour of the traditions

[f] Paus. i. 14. 2.

touching Pelasgus and the worship of Ceres; but richer at the same time than any other Greek State, in the varied aggregate of the qualities, which the composite or entire Greek mind appears to have owed to Hellic infusion. Hence the breadth of the transition which, according to Herodotus[g], she had made from the Pelasgic to the Hellenic character: and yet she had made it without any visible breach in the continuity of her social and political traditions.

Though Thessaly was the country in which, to all appearance, the Hellic tribes, coming down from the poverty and rudeness of their highland life, first began to develope their amazing powers, and to acquire civilization, yet it was rather, so to speak, their caravansera or halting house, than their abode.

The Helli, thus travelling through Hellas, give it a name, and receive from it one in return; so that when they pass on to the southward, they are no longer Helli but Hellenes, and have only a secondary and derivative relation to their original home and stock. It is intelligible, that they should not wish to claim too close a kindred with the ἀνιπτόποδες χαμαίευναι of Homer[h], although most ready to own the relationship in solemn appeals to the ancient seat of Jupiter. Even in Homer's time, they had advanced very far ahead of the habits thus ascribed to them: for when the Greek chiefs return from the Doloneia, they first wash in the sea, then pass into the bath, and thirdly are anointed, before they begin their well-earned meal[i].

The rapidity of their growth in numbers, and of their propagation southwards, might be due to their having settled on a fertile plain; while necessities, arising from the vicissitudes of climate, would be the probable and

[g] Herod. i. 56.   [h] Il. xvi. 235.   [i] Il. x. 537–9.

less copious cause of migration from the hills. But in any case, whether from the rapidity of their passage through Thessaly, or from their having actually occupied no more than a small portion of it, they left it in the Homeric, and apparently also in the Hesiodic period, still partly impressed, as they must have found it, with the Pelasgic name [k]. The prolonged existence of this appellation indicates in part perhaps the predominance of the Pelasgic element in this country, in part the fugacious character of the Hellic settlement, of which only the Achæan portion lived through the historic times in such a degree of force as to maintain its visible identity: this, too, according to post-Homeric tradition, was peopled by the Myrmidons from the south, and not directly from the region of the Helli.

Thessaly, then, was the nursery or cradle of the Hellic or Hellenic races, but it was no more. Consequently with the lapse of time, as it wanted the true mixture of ingredients, Thessaly became less and less Greek in its essential habits and sympathies: while from its preserving a federal consitution, under a federal head, the τάγος, we may also refer to its more Pelasgian character the apparent fact, that it was not so liable to political change, or νεωτέρισις, as were the less Pelasgian parts of Greece. When, after centuries of vicissitude, the outward notes of its original blood were almost gone, Pelasgian feeling still survived: for Thucydides relates that, when Brasidas entered Thessaly at the head of the Lacedæmonian army, he found the mass of the people attached by affection to the Athenian cause, and had to rely on aristocratic influence to furnish him with guides[l].

[k] Hes. Fragm. xviii.   [l] Thuc. iv. 78.

SECT. VIII.

On the three greater Homeric appellatives.

a. Danaans. *b.* Argives. *c.* Achæans.

WE now come to the great Homeric appellatives, Danaan, Argive, and Achæan. As Thucydides has said (i. 3), Δαναοὺς δὲ ἐν τοῖς ἔπεσι, καὶ Ἀργείους, καὶ Ἀχαιοὺς ἀνακαλεῖ. Why has the great historian arranged the three names in this order? It cannot be with reference to the comparative frequency of their use: for the first is employed the smallest number of times, and the third is by far the most frequent. For the present let us postpone seeking after the cause; and simply note it as probable, even if no more than probable, that there *is* a cause.

Let me, by way of preface to the examination of these names, consider the various ways in which, so far as we have the means of tracing them (which is but to a limited extent), the names attached by Homer to the inhabitants of particular countries are derived.

They appear to come either

1. From an eponymist directly, who is also an original founder, as Δαρδανοὶ, Τρῶες, from Dardanus, and Tros, in relation to Dardania and Troja respectively.

2. From the land they live in: and thus from an eponymist, if there has originally been one for the territory.

For example, we find Ἰθακήσιοι from an island Ἰθακὴ, which again was derived from Ἰθακός. In a case like this, when the appellation of the people comes not directly, but mediately from the name-giver, a territorial designation intervening, we can draw no inference as to the oneness of race between them and him. Thus in the case before us, Ἰθακήσιοι, though connected with Ἰθάκη, has not as of necessity, any connection whatever with Ἰθακὸς personally.

3. From the land they live in, as described by its most prominent physical characteristic.

For example, the Thracians (Θρῇκες), must evidently be so called from the roughness of the country, as a cognate word to τρηχύς, which is thus applied to Ithaca,

τρηχεῖ᾽, ἀλλ᾽ ἀγαθὴ κουροτρόφος.   Odyss. ix. 27.

Again, from Αἰγίαλος, the district afterwards called Achæa, we have, in later Greek [a], the name Αἰγιαλεῖς for the inhabitants. This does not occur in Homer, but we have what is equivalent to it in the name of Αἰγιάλεια, who was wife of Diomed, and daughter of Adrastus, the former king of Sicyon in Ægialus. This is an instance of the application of the principle, not to the inhabitants at large, but to an individual inhabitant.

4. The name of a population may be derived secondarily from that of another population. Thus while we must derive Ἕλληνες from Ἕλλας, this in its turn can only be drawn from the Ἕλλοι.

5. In the single case of the Athenians, we find the name of a population derived from that of a deity.

6. It is presumable, though not certain, that entire populations took their name from ruling individuals or races. It seems hardly possible to explain, for example, the name Καδμεῖοι, which nowhere connects itself with any of the foregoing sources of eponymism,

[a] Strabo, pp. 37 2, 383.

otherwise than by reference to an individual Cadmus, whom Homer mentions in Od. v. *333*.

The idea prevails extensively, at least by sufferance, that these three great names are in Homer mere synonyms, and have no reference to any actual and historical differences, either existing when Homer wrote, or known by him to have existed at a previous period.

This question it is proposed now to examine. I commence by making a broad admission. It is this.

Upon the face of the poems, and on almost all ordinary occasions, Homer seems at first sight to use, and he very frequently does use, as equivalent and interchangeable, those three principal designations which he applies to the Greeks in common.

It is a very important question, however, whether Homer knew of and observed any distinctions between these names. For if he did, then these mere commonplace words, as they are taken to be, may involve in them the germ of much early history.

In this investigation, we have the advantage of dealing in great part, not with mere traditional assertion, but with facts. The use of particular names, at particular epochs, for particular tribes, affords (if the text can be trusted for genuineness) a class of evidence analogous to that supplied by coins and inscriptions for history, or that afforded by geological phænomena with respect to the formation of the globe.

The poems of Homer, particularly the Iliad, abound in passages relating to prior occurrences. These passages are not in general of a high order of poetical beauty, as compared with the rest of the poem; they often cause the action to hang rather heavily; many of them make up the speeches of old men, whose natural leaning to loquacity it appears that the Poet has, with his usual skill, made to minister to the accomplishment of his own marked historic aims. But they are repositories stored, we may almost say packed, with the most curious and suggestive information.

Some of them may be without date: but the time is generally fixed within limits sufficiently close, either by genealogies, or by the period in the lives of the narrators, to which the tales belong. The war of the Elians and Pylians in the Eleventh Book took place in the boyhood of Nestor: probably from fifty to sixty years before the war of Troy. The birth of Eurystheus, related in the Nineteenth Book, was probably earlier still by ten or twenty years. The other legends fall into the interval between these events and the *Troica*. Now if we can trace a difference in the application by Homer of his appellatives, either as to the times or the places, he may hereby conclusively, though unconsciously, tell us a good deal about his view of the succession, and the local distribution, of ruling races in Greece.

Such a rule of difference is easy to be traced.

For example. In the Catalogue[b] and elsewhere, if in the course of the action he refers to the soldiers who proceeded from the country afterwards called Bœotia, he calls them Βοιωτοί. But where Agamemnon has, or rather makes, occasion to tell a story of the same people acting in prior history, he calls them, not Βοιωτοὶ, but once Καδμεῖοι, and once by the equivalent name Καδμείωνες[c]. The tale is an account of the mission of Tydeus from Thebes to Mycenæ, in company with Polynices, which had occurred under the Pelopid dynasty.

In this story it appears, that Tydeus and Polynices,

[b] Il. ii. 494. xiii. 685. vid. sup. p. 243. [c] Il. iv. 385. 191.

first obtained a promise of the help they wanted; but that, after they had departed, there was a change of resolution. Hence messengers were sent to acquaint Tydeus, and apparently to recall the force. The expression is (Il. iv. 384),

ἔνθ' αὖτ' ἀγγελίην ἐπὶ Τυδῆ στεῖλαν Ἀχαιοί.

An allusion to this occurrence is again put into the mouth of Minerva in Il. v. 800–7. The resemblance in the names used is so precise as to be almost *precisian*. Again, the Mycenians are named once, and named as Ἀχαιοί. Again, the Thebans are named twice, and once it is as Καδμεῖοι, once as Καδμείωνες.

These two instances fortify one another to such a degree by their concurrence, that, as I would submit, they would, even if they stood alone, amount to a demonstration that Homer had regard to the times and circumstances under which the several races prevailed, in those passages of his work which refer to particular incidents of prior history, personal and local. But there is no lack of other evidence.

First, we have other pieces of prior history, which affect the same portion of Greece. The first of these probably preceded the *Troica* by only two, or, at the utmost, two and a half generations. It is the account of the birth of Eurystheus, given by Agamemnon himself in the Nineteenth Book. The scene of it is described as Ἄργος Ἀχαιικόν. He calls it indeed by the name, which it still bore at the time when he spoke, and which was understood by the hearers, for it remained the same country as it had been in former times. But the same people, who in the time of Tydeus, living under the Pelopids, were Ἀχαιοί, in the time of Eurystheus, and therefore before the predominance of the Pelopids, are described as Ἀργεῖοι. In

Il. xix. 122, Juno thus speaks of the birth of Eurystheus

ἤδη ἀνὴρ γέγον' ἐσθλός, ὃς 'Αργείοισιν ἀνάξει.

And again, v. 124, the same term is used.

Again, it appears from the Sixth Iliad that Prœtus, who expelled Bellerophon about the same time, was king of the 'Αργεῖοι (Il. vi. 158);

ὅς ῥ' ἐκ δήμου ἔλασσεν, ἐπεὶ πολὺ φέρτερος ἦεν
'Αργείων.

According to extra-Homeric tradition, Prœtus was the brother of Eurystheus. According to Homer, his power extends over Ephyre, and over the Argives: and as Æolid dynasties were then ruling in the west, it is the country afterwards called the Argos of the Achæans, within some part of which he must have ruled. But in telling both the story of Prœtus, and the story of Eurystheus, with reference to the same side of Peloponnesus, and entirely out of connection with one another, the text of Homer, true to itself, calls the subjects of each at that period, only by the name 'Αργεῖοι, never Δαναοὶ or 'Αχαιοί.

Thus, one generation before the *Troica* he calls people Achæans, and calls them by that name only, whom one or two generations earlier he describes, and repeatedly and uniformly describes, as having been Argives. There can hardly be stronger circumstantial evidence of the fact, that to each term he attached its own special meaning.

And yet it is not simply that Homer has made the Argive the more ancient, and the Achæan the more recent, name. On the contrary, he uses both the one and the other with marked respect to place as well as to time. For at the great Argive epoch he has Achæans: and at the great Achæan epoch, that of the poems, he has Argive associations, and a local Argive designation, still remaining.

In the Eleventh Book, Nestor detains Patroclus with a speech of great length. In the beginning of this harangue, he refers to the circumstances of the moment, and, having ended his preface, he travels back to his own early youth, indeed almost his childhood, to give the story of a war, or foray, between the Epeans and the Pylians. When he has ended this tale, he returns to the actual position of affairs before Troy.

In the narrative of this raid[d], he commonly terms the one side Epeans, and the other Pylians. But he once calls the Epeans, who were inhabitants of Elis, Elians. This is natural enough: for as the Elian name afterwards (and so soon as in the time of Homer) prevailed in that race and country, it might very well have been already beginning to come into use. But he also calls the Pylians Achæans; and he uses the name distinctively, for it is where he is speaking of them as the conquering party[e]. For this there is clearly no corresponding reason. It is equally clear that Homer does not call the Pylians Ἀχαιοὶ, simply in the sense of being Greeks, for then the name would not have been distinctive; the enemy too would have been included with them, which would turn the passage into nonsense. Homer, then, (there is no other alternative) means to say that the Pylians were, in some particular sense, of the Achæan race.

This is the more worthy of remark, when we look to the preamble and peroration of the speech. For in both of these, which refer to the whole body of the Greeks and to the Trojan epoch, he employs his usual names, and calls them both Danaans (Δαναῶν οὐ κήδε-

[d] Il. xi. 670–761.   [e] v. 759.

ται, v. 665, also vid. 797), and Argives ('Ἀργείων ἀέκητι, v. 667): finally Achæans (υἷες Ἀχαιῶν, 800).

Thus then he calls the Pylians Achæans at the time of the Argive predominance: for this local war could hardly have been more than ten or twenty years after the birth of Eurystheus, and must therefore have been before, or else during his reign; that is to say, at a time when his own subjects are called Ἀργεῖοι.

Again. Homer uses the word Ἀργεῖος in the feminine singular fifteen times. Twice it is with reference to Juno. Of course this application of the term is figurative. But though it be figurative, the figure is evidently founded on her close and intimate relation, not to the Greeks at large only, but to the Argive name; and to the persons, but more particularly to the place, that was so specially associated with it[f].

In all the other thirteen places, the epithet is joined with the name of Helen. Does it for her mean simply Greek, or something special and beyond this? Now if it meant simply Greek, it would be strange that she is never called, I will not say Δαναή, because the Danaan name has no singular use in Homer, but certainly Ἀχαιή or Ἀχαιΐς. Especially as the word Ἀχαιός is used as an epithet, be it remembered, many times oftener, than is Ἀργεῖος: and it alone is used to describe the women of Greece generally.

Again, if the epithet Argive, as applied to Helen, meant simply Greek, it might be suitable enough in the mouth of a Trojan speaking among Trojans, but it would have been weak and unmeaning, and therefore most unlike Homer, in the mouth of a Greek or a friend of Greeks; or when, as in the Odyssey[g], Helen is no longer among strangers, but at home. Yet it is used

[f] Inf. p. 392. [g] Od. iv. 184, 296.

in the following passages among others, (1) by Juno to Minerva, Il. ii. 161, (2) by Minerva to Ulysses, Il. ii. 177; and here in a near juxtaposition with the Achæan appellative, which goes far to prove of itself that 'Αργείη has a meaning more specific than merely Greek. The passage is,

'Αργείην Ἑλένην, ἧς εἵνεκα πολλοὶ Ἀχαιῶν
ἐν Τροίῃ ἀπόλοντο.

I doubt whether Homer ever places in such proximity the two epithets with the same meaning for each [g]. The tautology would be gross, if Achæan and Argeian each meant neither more nor less than Greek : but if 'Αργείη have the local sense, nothing awkward remains. (3) It is used by Agamemnon, Il. iii. 458, in addressing the Trojans; (4) Il. iv. 174, in addressing Menelaus; (5) Il. ix. 140, in addressing the Greek Council. It seems quite clear, from even this enumeration, that 'Αργείη, as applied to Helen, must mean something different from the mere fact that she belonged to the Greek nation at large.

Nor is it difficult to find a meaning. Homer indeed leaves us but narrow information as to the extraction of Helen. He calls her sometimes εὐπατέρεια [h], and many times Διὸς ἐκγεγαυῖα [i]. In the Third Iliad he shows her to be the sister of Castor and Pollux, and in the Eleventh Odyssey he shows them to be the children of Tyndareus and Leda [j]. Who Tyndareus was we do not know from him. But the common tradition, which makes him a sovereign in Eastern Peloponnesus, is thoroughly accordant with the slight notices in Homer. For, as we see from the cases of Eurystheus and Prœtus, it was in Eastern Peloponnesus that the Argive

[g] See inf. sect. ix.
[h] Il. vi. 292. Od. xxii. 227.
[i] Il. iii. 199 et alibi.
[j] Il. iii. 236. Od. xi. 298.

power and name prevailed; and Helen, the daughter of Tyndareus is, as we have also seen, characteristically with him the Argive Helen. Thus then it may now be lawful to say, we are supplied with a meaning for the name which makes it especially appropriate in the mouth of Agamemnon, the head of the Pelopids. For they were the race who, coming in at the head of the Achæans, had from the West overpowered and superseded the Argive power of the East, while they also held as heirs to it by marriage: and if a royal Argive house at the epoch of the war survived only in Helen and her sister Clytemnestra, she in part at least represented its title, and, as a lawful wife of Menelaus, added to his throne whatever authority the name and rights of her race were capable of conferring.

Having, I trust, seen enough to justify the belief that some at least of these names in the mind of Homer had a definite as well as a more general meaning, let us now, taking them in succession, proceed to examine what that meaning is.

Among the three great Homeric appellatives, let us direct our attention first to the one, which is presumably the oldest. The word Δαναοὶ, from the comparative paucity of the signs and indications connected with it, evidently answers to this description.

We will take first the Homeric, and then the later, evidence respecting it. Of the former, the greater number of particulars are negative. Indeed we have but two positive notes to dwell upon; both of these, however, are of great importance.

1. The Danaan name is with Homer a standing appellation of the Greeks. I think, however, it can be shown that it never means the Greek nation, but always the Greek armament or soldiery.

II. *Ethnology.*

It is used in the Iliad one hundred and forty-seven times. The name Ἀργεῖοι is employed oftener, namely, one hundred and seventy-seven times in the plural, besides eleven times in the singular as a personal epithet: and Ἀχαιοὶ much more frequently still.

If we observe the shadings, attached to these words respectively by means of the epithets which Homer annexes to them, we shall find they establish perceptible distinctions.

The epithets of Δαναοὶ are exclusively military epithets:

1. ἥρωες.
2. θεράποντες Ἄρηος.
3. φιλοπτόλεμοι.
4. αἰχμηταί.
5. ἀσπισταί.
6. ἴφθιμοι.
7. ταχύπωλοι.

The epithets of Ἀργεῖοι are as follows:

1. ἰόμωροι, Il. iv. 242. xiv. 479.
2. ἀπειλάων ἀκόρητοι, Il. xiv. 479.
3. θωρηκτοί, Il. xxi. 429.
4. φιλοπτόλεμοι, Il. xix. 269.
5. ἐλεγχέες, Il. iv. 242.

Upon these we may observe, first, that they are few in number; secondly, that they are used with extreme rarity; being only applied in four passages altogether, whereas the word Δαναοὶ has epithets in twenty-two. Thirdly, this word only twice in the whole of the poems has a military epithet attached to it. For I must follow those, who do not translate ἰόμωροι as corresponding with ἐγχεσίμωροι: (1) because the Greeks were not archers, (2) because the derivation from ἴα, 'the voice,' giving the sense of braggart, harmonises exactly with the accompanying phrase ἀπειλάων ἀκόρητοι: as well as (3) for the presumptive, but in Homer

His epithets for the three designations. 357

by no means conclusive, reason, that ἴον in composition is long.

The epithets of Ἀχαιοὶ are numerous, highly varied, and of very frequent use. They are these:

1. ἀπειλητῆρες.
2. μάχης ἀκόρητοι.
3. ἀνάλκιδες.
4. δῖοι.
5. ἑλίκωπες.
6. ἐϋκνήμιδες.
7. ἥρωες.
8. καρηκομόωντες.
9. μεγάθυμοι.
10. μένεα πνείοντες.
11. χαλκοκνήμιδες.
12. χαλκοχίτωνες.
13. ὑπερκύδαντες.
14. ἀρηΐφιλοι.
15. φιλοπτόλεμοι.

These epithets are used in nearly one hundred and thirty passages, and they may be classified as comprising,

(1) One or two words of sarcastic reproach, very rarely used.
(2) Words descriptive of courage and spirit: such are μεγάθυμοι, μένεα πνείοντες.
(3) Words indicating that disposition to brag, which is more or less traceable in the military conduct of the Greeks, as well as glaringly palpable among the Trojans.
(4) Words descriptive of personal beauty: ἑλίκωπες and καρηκομόωντες.
(5) The word δῖοι, which signifies generally the possession of some kind of excellence.
(6) Words relating to well made and well finished armour: ἐϋκνήμιδες, χαλκοκνήμιδες, χαλκοχίτωνες.

And of the epithets of the three appellatives respectively we may say,

(1) Those of Ἀχαιοὶ are highly diversified, extended, and elevated in meaning: and are not suitable for soldiers exclusively.

(2) Those of Ἀργεῖοι are so slight and rare that they may be passed over.

(3) Those of Δαναοὶ are most properly neither those of chiefs, nor of a nation at large, but of a soldiery.

In the Odyssey the Danaan name is used thirteen times: but it never signifies either the Greeks contemporary with the action of that poem, or the Greek nation in its prior history: it is employed always retrospectively, and always of the soldiery in the Trojan war.

It will be observed by readers of the poems, that Homer often brings two of the three great appellatives, or even all the three, into juxtaposition so near, as would be inconvenient upon the supposition that they are purely synonymous. For instance, in Il. i. 71, we have Ἀργεῖοι and Ἀχαιοὶ in the same line, and in Il. i. 90, 91, Δαναοὶ and Ἀχαιοὶ in two successive lines. It is, I think, obvious, that this inconvenience will be mitigated or removed, if it can be shown that each of these three names, though they were most commonly applied to mean the same body of persons, nevertheless had its own shade of meaning. And we shall presently have to examine cases, where a determination of this kind appears to be required by the sense[k].

All the rest of the Homeric evidence connected with the name Δαναοὶ is of a negative character.

It is never used in the singular number, either as an adjective, or as a substantive. Nor is it ever applied to women: a point not immaterial, in connection with the question, whether with Homer it does not mean the Greeks of the army exclusively. There is, again, nothing in his use of it which associates it with a par-

[k] Inf. pp. 410, 11.

ticular class of the army, either the lower or the higher; but it appears to be essentially general, comprehensive, and, I may add, likewise invariable in its meaning.

Still less should we expect to find it, nor do we find it, connected with the inhabitants of any particular part of the country: it has not, like the Cadmean or Cephallenian name, a local habitation within Greece. Nor has it in itself any root, or any derivative, which would associate it with any territory, as $Αἰγιαλεῖς$ refers us to $Αἰγίαλος$, or even as $Ἄρκαδες$ is related to $Ἀρκαδίη$.

Its use in the Iliad is in exact harmony with that in the Odyssey: it is never associated with the history of the Greeks or any part of them: in short, there is no clear evidence of its existence or application beyond the limits of the camp.

Neither has it any thing related to the physical character of the country, or to any of the races known to have inhabited it, or to any employment or habit of life, or to any deity. It floats before us like Delos on the Ægæan, without any visible or discoverable root. And the only question is, whether the slight positive evidence at our command is not so limited, and so hemmed in on all sides by negatives, as to determine the hypothesis that may be drawn from it to one particular form, by forbidding us to move, except in one particular direction.

It is quite plain that the Danaan name must have had some root, lying very deep in the history or legends of Greece: since it would not have been possible for Homer, as a poet of the people, handling a subject the most profoundly national, to describe the Greek army under any name, except one associated with some of the most splendid, or the most venerable, traditions of the country.

In one way alone could this name fulfil the required condition. If its root was not territorial, nor tribal, nor religious, it could only be personal. Was there, then, a Danaus known to the early history of Greece, who founded a dynasty in its centre of power, at a period anterior to the Hellenic history of the country, so as not to be in competition with the honours of that race? If so, then it is intelligible that the Greeks might be called Δαναοὶ by Homer. If that dynasty had passed away, we can well understand why Δαναοὶ should not be a name of contemporary Greeks as such: just as Καδμεῖοι was not an admissible designation for contemporary Bœotians. Further, if it had never been an historical appellative at all, but was the mere reflection cast by the figure of a great primitive personage, and incorporated, for the Poet's purpose, in a designation made national by him, then we can see how natural it was, that he should limit the word altogether to an heroic and martial sense ; just as Cambrian for Welshman, or Caledonian for Scotchman, or Gael for Highlander, or son of Albion for Englishman, would be an appellation naturally appropriated to romance, or war, or any strain impregnated with a strong vein of imagery or passion, but yet would not be suitable for the purposes of pure history.

In this inquiry concerning the Danaan name, we must, I think, carry along with us, as a cardinal element in the case, that which we know from other sources respecting the manner in which Homer was wont to veil all traces of the entry from elsewhere of races, persons, or influences into Greece. It must never be forgotten, that, throughout the whole of the poems, there is apparently not one single statement, made to us with the intention of conveying information respecting the colonization of Greece from abroad. It seems to be the Poet's intention that we should assume all Greek manners, institutions, and races, to have sprung out of the very soil: and it is only accidentally that he imparts to us any information or suggestion on this subject, when he is in quest of some other purpose, and unawares lets fall a gleam of light upon some foreign settlement or immigration.

All this is conformable to the course of natural feeling. Shakespeare found it worth his while to sing of Lear, but not of Hengist and Horsa; of the English in France, not of the Normans in England. And though Danish invasions have not robbed our great Alfred of his fame, yet for a long time, in order to guard its brilliancy, it may have been that we coloured in our own favour the military history of the period. Arrivals from abroad, in the early periods of the life of a nation, are usually the conquests, in one form or another, of foreigners over natives: of what is strange to the soil over what is associated with it. It can hardly be, that such narratives should be popular. An abnormal instance to the contrary may be found in the fable, which deduced the Julian line in Rome from Æneas: but this was for poetry composed a thousand years after the date of its narrative; composed when the line of national continuity with those, whom Æneas was taken to have conquered, had been completely broken; and composed for the ears of a court, when the pulse of national life had become almost insensible. Even the process, by which Hellenes mastered Pelasgians, is nowhere professedly related by Homer; whose purpose it was to unite more closely the elements of the nation, and not to record that they had once been separate.

Except in the one point, that the name Καδμεῖοι had had a clear and undeniable place in prior history, there is a marked analogy between the modes in which Homer treats the Cadmean and the Danaan stories. In each of the two cases, general tradition tells us of a foreigner, who enters Greece and founds a dynasty. This dynasty, after acting powerfully on the destinies of the country for some generations, in the course of time disappears, the name dying with it. All this, in the first of the two instances, we have seen to be sufficiently supported by inference and suggestion from Homer. Yet Homer never mentions Cadmus, except as it were by chance, in the act of giving the extraction of Leucothee[1]; nor states that he came from abroad; nor that he founded a dynasty at all. He gives us Cadmus, father of Leucothee, and Cadmeans, and lets us make of them what we can. So here he gives us Danaans, and not indeed a Danaus, but a Danae, who is presumably related to Danaus.

2. In Iliad xiv., Jupiter renders an account of his passion for various women, all of them persons in the very highest positions; and among these for Danae[m].

Δανάης καλλισφύρου Ἀκρισιώνης,
ἣ τέκε Περσῆα, πάντων ἀριδείκετον ἀνδρῶν.

In this passage we have Danae exhibited as the head of a line of sovereigns through Perseus, who occupied the most ancient and most distinguished seat of power in Greece, that of the Eastern Peloponnesus. From her, indeed, the derivation of sovereignty is locally continuous down to the time of Homer. Perseus is the father of Sthenelus[n], and Sthenelus of Eurystheus. Next to him, we find Pelops in possession of the throne, with a new sceptre, betokening a new sovereignty. That is to say, he was no longer a merely local sovereign, whose highest honour it was to be first in that class, *primus*

[1] Od. v. 333.   [m] Il. xiv. 319.   [n] Il. xix. 116.

inter pares; but he had also acquired an extensive supremacy, reaching beyond his own borders, or those of the Achaic Argos, and embracing all Greece, with a multitude of islands[o].

Such is the line of Danae downwards: beginning with a son, whose paternal extraction we shall consider hereafter[p]. And her epoch, as we shall see, is six generations before the Trojan war. For tracing her upwards, we have no means from Homer, except such as are afforded by the word Ἀκρισιώνη. The use of a patronymic which describes Danae as the daughter (most probably) of Acrisius, in some degree makes it likely that Acrisius either was the brother of Danaus, or otherwise collaterally related, rather than directly descended from him. For, had Danae herself been descended from Danaus, it seems improbable that she would have drawn her patronymic from the less distinguished Acrisius, unless Danaus was a very remote ancestor. But this is very improbable: for seven generations before Troy form the utmost limit of Homer's historical knowledge; and where all besides falls within that line, it is improbable that there should be a single exception reaching greatly beyond it. And again, from the course of migration, it is likely that we should find his oldest traditions in Asia, and not in Europe. On the other hand, that Homer should stop short in tracing the lineage onwards, just before he came to the foreign immigrant, is in exact conformity with what he has done in omitting to connect Œdipus and Epicaste[q] with Cadmus, or Pelops with Tantalus. In the former of these two cases, the omission all the more cogently suggests design, because Epicaste is the only woman introduced in the Νεκυΐα without mention of her husband, among all those, eight in number, of whose cases

[o] Il. ii. 108.   [p] Inf. sect. x.   [q] Od. xi. 271.

he gives us the detail. It is most probable, therefore, that Homer meant the genealogy to stand as follows: and at the least, it must not be thought that the text of Homer gives countenance either directly or indirectly to those later fables, which throw back the first Greek dynasties into a very remote antiquity.

1. Danaus=Acrisius
    |
    2. Danae
    3. Perseus
    4. Sthenelus
    5. Eurystheus (=Hercules)=Pelops
        6. Atreus=Thyestes
        7. Agamemnon=Ægisthus.

According to these presumptions, Danaus is contemporary with Dardanus[r]: and also is just such a person as Homer's poetic use of the name Δαναοὶ would lead us to expect; one who came from abroad, and is on that account kept in majestic shadow; one who founded a throne, but did not introduce a race: one who may have given his people the name of Δαναοὶ, as Cadmus gave that of Καδμεῖοι, for the time while his dynasty was in power, but whose name disappeared, together with its sway. We have, it will be remembered in Homer, no Homeric legends of the period of the Danaids, so that we do not know whether the name Δαναοὶ was then in any degree national or not.

According to the post-Homeric tradition, Danaus was an Egyptian[s], brother of Ægyptus. He migrated into Greece, and became king of Argos. Acrisius and Prœtus were reputed to be his great-grandsons.

[r] See inf. sect. ix.

[s] Fragm. of the Danais, Düntzer, Fragm. der Epischen Poesie, p. 3. It has been argued by E. Curtius (*Ionier vor der Ionischen Wanderung*, pp. 11—13), that there were settlers on the Egyptian sea-board, belonging to the Ionian race, and to the same stock with the Hellenes. From among such settlers, whether Ionian or not, it seems likely that the immigrants from Egypt to Greece might have proceeded.

In Homer, too, we have an Acrisius and a Prœtus: but Prœtus is contemporary with Bellerophon, two generations before the *Troica*, so that he is later by four generations than Acrisius, and later by at least four than Danaus.

The more recent tradition, contradicting Homer positively in this, as in so many instances, carries Prœtus back to the time of Acrisius, and then, paying some respect to the interval between Prœtus and Danaus, gives compensation by thrusting Danaus himself three generations further back.

Of the posterity of the Homeric Prœtus we hear nothing, and with him the Danaid line, prolonged in a junior branch, may have expired. Tradition places him on the throne of Tiryns. His holding a separate sovereignty in Argolis is not of itself in conflict with the Homeric account of the Perseids, who reigned at Mycenæ; because we find in Argos itself a separate sovereignty under Diomed at the epoch of the *Troica*. But the terms used are peculiar. Prœtus ruled over Ἀργεῖοι;

πολὺ φέρτερος ἦεν
Ἀργείων· Ζεὺς γάρ οἱ ὑπὸ σκηπτρῷ ἐδάμασσεν [t].

The account of Eurystheus in the Nineteenth Book may, however, imply that he was king of all the Ἀργεῖοι: and at first sight there is some conflict here, because both Eurystheus and Prœtus may be said to date two generations before the *Troica*. The solution is probably as follows. The passion of Antea, wife of Prœtus, for Bellerophon, suggests that her husband was more advanced in life than Bellerophon, whom, as the grandfather of Glaucus, we may take as justly representing in time the second generation before the war. On the other hand, as Eurystheus was the contemporary of

[t] Il. vi. 158.

Hercules, and Hercules had a son, as well as grandsons in the war, we may assume Eurystheus to have been junior to the generation, as Prœtus was its senior; so that they need not have been contemporary princes.

The historic place assigned to Danaus, either as we might fix it from Homer, or as the later tradition would determine it, keeps him clear of the earliest Hellic traditions in southern Greece. None of these can well be carried back beyond Sisyphus; and Sisyphus stands at five generations before the war, while Danaus cannot be less than seven. Had Homer made Danaus synchronise with the earlier Hellic sovereignties, it would have been, in my view, a presumption against his Egyptian origin, or his existence altogether. For an Egyptian stranger was little likely to attain to power, where Hellenes were already in the field: the more energetic genius would subdue the less vigorous. The expulsion of the Hellenic Bellerophon, and the plot against his life, may really have been connected with the political jealousies of the Danaids towards the formidable newcomers of the Æolid stem: nor do I read the fable of Jupiter with Danae otherwise than as a veil, used to give dignity to the commencement of an Hellic sovereignty, which, in the person of Perseus, partly succeeded, partly supplanted, the Danaid throne.

Danaus has been mentioned by Hesiod, the first among the later authorities. This poet states, that he relieved Argos from drought: an operation which harmonises well with the tradition that brings him from a country dependent on the irrigation of the Nile, as the conditions of cultivation there could not but lead at an early date to care in the management of water. He likewise calls Perseus by the name of $\Delta a\nu a\iota\delta\eta s$, and also terms him the son of Danae[u].

[u] Hes. Fragm. lviii. and Scut. Herc. 216. 229.

The only point of connection between the Danaids and the Argive or Argeian name is, that Prœtus, the last of the Danaids, reigns over Argeians. But this is at a period when the Perseid house, which was evidently Hellenic, has already become the first in rank among the Greek thrones, and has given, as is probable, the Argeian name to the people of Eastern Peloponnesus. The whole evidence, therefore, throws the Danaan name, with all its incidents, back to a period anterior to that of Argeians and of Achæans.

But if the Danai were thus before the 'Αργεῖοι and before the 'Αχαιοὶ, whom did they follow?

The evidence of Æschylus in the Supplices supports the tradition which makes them immediately follow the Pelasgi[v], or which, more strictly, represents their name as the first of those borne by the Greek nation after it had ceased to be simply Pelasgic.

By Euripides was conveyed a kindred tradition, that Danaus, having come to Argos, colonized the city of Inachus; and that the Peloponnesians, previously called Pelasgiotes, were thereafter called Danai[x].

Πελασγιῶτας δ' ὠνομασμένους, τὸ πρὶν
Δαναοὺς καλεῖσθαι νόμον ἔθηκ' ἀν' Ἑλλάδα.

These traditions, received through the tragedians, coincide with the evidence of the Homeric text. For this text, in the first place, clearly throws the Danaan line farther back than that of any of the Hellic tribes. Secondly, by negative evidence, no where employing the Danaan name in the pre-Troic legends, he leaves us to infer that it must have been the oldest, and the most remote from common use, of his three great appellations. Thirdly, Homer supplies us with no other name which there is

[v] Sup. sect. iii.   [x] Eurip. Ar. Fr. ii. 7.

the smallest ground for inserting between the Danaans and the ancient Pelasgi, of whom we have found traces, direct and indirect, in so many places of the poems.

Thus, then, although we can plead little but conjecture from Homer with respect to the person Danaus, we seem to be justified in concluding from his testimony, that the appellation was dynastic, that the dynasty was pre-Hellenic, and that it stands in chronological order next to the Pelasgic time.

The name 'Αργεῖοι is the next with which we have to deal: and this name, applicable to persons, is so evidently founded on the name "Αργος, applicable to territory, that with this latter word we must of necessity begin the investigation; just as in order to arrive at the meaning of the term Hellenes, we were obliged to begin with Hellas.

And the word "Αργος is so important, and as it were central, in the geography of Homer, that we had better first consider what are the various forms of expression which Homer uses when he wants to express in words the entire territory of the Greek nation:

1. We have already seen that he appears to use for this purpose the combined force of the names Hellas and Argos;

ἄνδρος, τοῦ κλέος εὐρὺ καθ' Ἑλλάδα καὶ μέσον "Αργος [y].

2. He employs other combinations for the like purpose. The first is that of "Αργος, extended by the epithet πᾶν, and joined with the islands. These words taken together embrace the whole Empire of Agamemnon:

πολλῇσιν νήσοισι, καὶ "Αργει παντὶ ἀνάσσειν [z].

3. And again, with the proper name 'Αχαιΐς,

"Αργος ἐς ἱππόβοτον, καὶ 'Αχαιΐδα καλλιγύναικα [a].

[y] Od. i. 344.   [z] Il. ii. 108.   [a] Il. iii. 75, 258.

Applications of the name Argos.

This is spoken by the Trojan herald of the possible adjustment of the quarrel, upon which, he says, we shall dwell quietly in Troy, and *they* will return to Argos and Achæis. By "they" he means all the Greeks, therefore the country to which they return means all Greece.

4. It may be a question whether Ἄργος, in combination with μέσος, includes the whole of Greece, as in the speech of Diomed to Glaucus:

τῷ νῦν σοι μὲν ἐγὼ ξεῖνος φίλος Ἀργεῖ μέσσῳ
εἰμὶ, σύ δ' ἐν Λυκίῃ [b].

5. It is also a question, what is the geographical force of Argos, even when standing alone. It is manifestly wide in certain passages. Thus Paris mentions the κτήματα,

ὅσσ' ἀγόμην ἐξ Ἄργεος ἡμέτερον δῶ [c]:

and Polydamas, speaking of the possible destruction of the Greek army,

νωνύμνους ἀπολέσθαι ἀπ' Ἄργεος ἐνθάδ' Ἀχαιούς [d].

a line repeated elsewhere. On the other hand, the word in some places has undoubtedly a limited meaning only.

6. Again, we find the word Ἀχαιΐς γαῖα, used apparently with the intention of signifying the whole Greek country; as in the first Iliad by Nestor;

ὦ πόποι, ἦ μέγα πένθος Ἀχαιΐδα γαῖα ἱκάνει [e].

7. And we have the same word Ἀχαιΐς without γαῖα, both in the Iliad and the Odyssey.

For instance, when Nestor and Ulysses were collecting the Greek forces, they were

λαὸν ἀγείροντες κατ' Ἀχαιΐδα πουλυβότειραν [f].

And Ulysses, addressing his mother in the Shades beneath, says,

[b] Il. vi. 224.   [c] Il. vii. 363.   [d] Il. xii. 70.
[e] Il. i. 254, and vii. 124.   [f] Il. xi. 770.

370   II. *Ethnology.*

οὐ γάρ πω σχέδον ἦλθον Ἀχαιΐδος, οὐδέ πω ἀμῆς
γῆς ἐπέβην [g].

To proceed first with what is most clear, I think it may be taken for certain that Ἀχαιΐς, with or without the affix γαῖα or αἶα [h], means nothing less than the whole of Greece in the passages where Homer uses this appellative alone. One passage, indeed, taken alone, affords decisive proof for itself that even the islands are included. Telemachus [i] thus describes his mother as unrivalled in Greece:

οἵη νῦν οὐκ ἔστι γύνη κατ᾽ Ἀχαιΐδα γαῖαν
οὔτε Πύλου ἱερῆς, οὔτ᾽ Ἄργεος, οὔτε Μυκήνης,
οὔτ᾽ αὐτῆς Ἰθάκης, οὔτ᾽ ἠπείροιο μελαίνης.

For here are clearly enumerated as among the parts of Ἀχαιΐς, several Peloponnesian states, the island of Ithaca, and the continent, evidently meaning that to the North of the Corinthian gulf.

And yet it may remain true that, though commonly meaning Greece at large, Ἀχαιΐς may still have a more special connection with the South, as the whole of this island is called Britain, whereas the name has been derived especially from its southern inhabitants.

But in the passages numbered (1) and (3) we find the whole of Greece designated by the use, not of one, but of two expressions: in the first case they are,

    1. Ἕλλας.   2. μέσον Ἄργος.

In the second they are,

    1. Ἄργος.   2. Ἀχαιΐς.

And with these we may compare the expression, evidently meant to cover all the Greeks, in Il. ii. 530, under the names

    1. Πανέλληνες.   2. Ἀχαιοί.

---

[g] Od. xi. 166 and 481. See also Od. xxiii. 68.
[h] Od. xiii. 249. [i] Od. xxi. 107.

Applications of the name Argos.

Now there are here three ways in which the words may be used so as to convey their joint sense, which I assume to be that of Greece *entire*: viz.

1. That each word should cover a part, the two parts together making up the whole, *i.e.* that the words should be used distributively.

2. That each should cover the whole, and that the words should be used cumulatively.

3. That one of the words should apply to a part of Greece only, and should be overlapped as it were by the other, that other meaning the whole.

Now as 'Αχαιΐς uniformly means all Greece in eight passages where it stands alone, this will naturally govern its sense in the two passages, where it is joined copulatively with "Αργος. We shall also hereafter see the local use of the 'Αχαιοὶ so diffused, that it would hardly be possible to suppose any other meaning. Thus, then, we have one point fixed, from which to operate upon others.

But what does the "Αργος ἱππόβοτον mean?

It is demonstrable that in Homer the word "Αργος has several meanings.

1. It is a city, as in Il. iv. 51,

ἤτοι ἐμοὶ τρεῖς μὲν πολὺ φίλταταί εἰσι πόληες
"Αργος τε, Σπάρτη τε, καὶ εὐρυάγυια Μυκήνη.
τὰς διαπέρσαι κ. τ. λ.

2. It is a limited territory, probably such as was afterwards the State of Argolis. For when Telemachus is quitting Sparta, Theoclymenus joins him[k], φεύγων ἐξ "Αργεος. And again, when Melampus quitted Pylos, he came to Argos:

ὁ δ' ἄλλων ἵκετο δῆμον
"Αργος ἐς ἱππόβοτον[1].

[k] Od. xv. 223.

The first proves that Sparta was not included in the geographical name Ἄργος: the second proves the same of Pylos: and this too is the Ἄργος ἱππόβοτον.

The same phrase is used in Od. iii. 263, of Ægisthus, who endeavours to corrupt Clytemnestra,

μυχῷ Ἄργεος ἱπποβότοιο,

Here Mycenæ is plainly meant by the μυχὸς, and the Ἄργος ἱππόβοτον is Argolis, or something like it.

This district, including Mycenæ, was the head quarter of the Greek power. Now we find that the whole dominion of Priam was named Τροίη, while including many cities and much territory, and the name Τροίη was also sometimes applied to the capital, of which the proper name was Ilion. So Venezia at the present day means both a city and a territory, even though the city is outside the territory; the only distinction lying in the use or non-use of the article. Therefore it was sufficiently natural, that the Trojan herald should name the whole from the most excellent part, and so identify them: and on the other hand, it would not be otherwise than natural, were he to name the most excellent part, and likewise to name the whole, without verbally distinguishing them.

So that in Il. iii. 75, 258, the phrase Ἄργος ἐς ἱππόβοτον, according to what has preceded, may either mean,

1. The part of the Peloponnesus containing Argos and Mycenæ as its head quarter, (and then the line must be interpreted in the third of the modes above pointed out; as we might now say, 'we visited Rome and Italy.')

2. Or it may mean the whole of Greece, by transfer from its capital part, and then the line must be inter-

[1] Od. xv. 238.

preted in the second mode, as might now be said, 'to our Green Erin, our Ireland mother of the brave.'

The English 'and' would indeed mar the sense: but the Greek καὶ is much more elastic, and may be equivalent to the Italian *ossia*, or to the sign =.

I doubt if there be any passage in Homer where the word Argos stands alone, or with a characteristic epithet such as ἱππόβοτον, and where it requires any other sense than one of the three just given—the city—the north east of Peloponnesus—and (by metonymy) all Greece.

When Nestor (Il. ii. 348) denounces those Greeks who should think of returning home before the mind of Jupiter is known, and calls returning Ἄργοσδε ἰέναι, it seems indisputable that we must construe Ἄργος Greece.

When Paris says he brought the κτήματα from Argos, the most natural construction is, as the place was Sparta, and therefore not Argos in the narrow sense, from which he took them, that he means by Argos to signify Greece.

When Sisyphus dwells at Ephyre, μυχῷ Ἄργεος ἱπποβότοιο, the word means the north eastern district Peloponnesus[m].

The word Ἄργος in the Catalogue (ii. 559) most probably means the city only.

As it is plain that in some passages it cannot mean the Peloponnesus, and as that meaning does not appear to be supported by superior probability in any place, such a meaning ought not to be admitted.

It is another question how we ought to construe the phrases μέσον Ἄργος—Ἀχαιϊκὸν Ἄργος, used four times —and Ἴασον Ἄργος.

[m] See also Il. xiii. 378. Od. xv. 224, 239.

II. Ethnology.

The two latter are evidently analogous to Πελασγικὸν Ἄργος, which we have already found to mean Thessaly.

Of the four passages where we read the phrase Ἀχαιικὸν Ἄργος, the two first[n] relate to the return of Agamemnon and the Greeks, and appear to admit therefore either of the limited sense of a portion of Peloponnesus as the most eminent part, or of the extended one of all Greece, better than of the intermediate one of Peloponnesus itself, with which neither Agamemnon, nor the whole body of the Greeks, had any separate and defined relation, as they had with the dominions of Agamemnon in the capacity of their supreme Chief, and perhaps with those of the Pelopid family jointly, so as to include Menelaus.

In the third case it is used of Juno, as she goes to hasten the birth of Eurystheus[o],

καρπαλίμως δ' ἵκετ' Ἄργος Ἀχαιικὸν, ἔνθ' ἄρα ἤδη
ἰφθίμην ἄλοχον Σθενέλου Περσηϊάδαο.

This passage evidently admits the sense of the city, or a limited district, better than that of the Peloponnesus at large. Indeed, as the seat of the Perseid dominion is evidently intended, and as that dominion did not reach over all Peloponnesus, we may say that this could not be the meaning of the words.

But the fourth passage requires a larger signification for this phrase. It is the question of Telemachus, asking where Menelaus had been during all the time that Ægisthus was about his crime[p];

ποῦ Μενέλαος ἔην;
ἦ οὐκ Ἄργεος ἦεν Ἀχαιικοῦ, ἀλλὰ πῇ ἄλλῃ
πλάζετ' ἐπ' ἀνθρώπους;

This seems clearly to include Sparta in Achaic

[n] Il. ix. 141, 283.   [o] Il. xix. 115.   [p] Od. iii. 249.

Argos; and, this being so, no meaning is so suitable to it in this place as Eastern Peloponnesus. This construction is also eminently suitable to the relation between Eastern Peloponnesus and the Achæan power, which had its central seat there.

Undoubtedly Strabo treats Ἀχαιϊκὸν Ἄργος as meaning the whole of Peloponnesus (viii. 5. p. 365, ibid. 6. p. 369), but the argument from Homer's text seems to be against him: and even he admits from Od. iii. 249, that the term applied also to Laconia in particular: ἀλλὰ καὶ ἰδίως τὴν Λακωνικὴν οὕτω προσαγορευθῆναι[q].

As then it appears that the sense of Eastern Peloponnesus will suit the phrase Ἄργος Ἀχαιϊκὸν in all the four passages where it is employed, while the more extended meaning of the whole Peloponnesus is required by none, and could only be even admissible in one (Od. iii. 249), we may conclude that Eastern Peloponnesus is the proper meaning of the phrase.

We now come to Ἴασον Ἄργος.

In Od. xviii. 245, Eurymachus the Suitor, in paying a compliment to the beauty of Penelope, says to her, you would have more suitors than you have,

εἰ πάντές σε ἴδοιεν ἀν' Ἴασον Ἄργος Ἀχαιοί.

Now it must first be admitted, that this does not refer to any country out of the Peloponnesus. For in the first place, that was the most distinguished part of the country, and the chief Achæan seat; so that the intention of this speech therefore most naturally bears upon it. But also we have nothing in Homer to connect any local use of the word Ἄργος with Middle Greece.

[q] It is curious that Strabo should say in viii. 6, that Homer often marks Ἄργος by the epithet ἵππιον, as well as ἱππόβοτον, when the former word does not occur at all in the Homeric Poems.

376   II. *Ethnology.*

But if Eurymachus means nothing to the North of Peloponnesus, it is again most probable that he refers to that part of Peloponnesus with which Ithaca had most intercourse, where lay its relations of business, and of hospitality. Now this part was Western Peloponnesus, as we see from the journey of Ulysses to Ephyre (Od. i. 260); from the journey of Telemachus which, as it were, spontaneously takes that direction; from the course of public transactions implied in his speech (Od. iii. 82, cf. 72); from the χρεῖος, which Ulysses went to recover in Messene (Od. xxi. 15); from Nestor's being the person to visit Ithaca in the matter of the great Trojan quarrel; and from the apprehension felt by the party of the Suitors, that Ulysses would forthwith repair to Elis, or to Pylos for aid. (Od. xxiv. 431.)

Just so the relations of Crete were with Eastern Peloponnesus; and therefore Helen at Troy recognises Idomeneus, because she has often seen him in Sparta. And this, I may observe in passing, is probably the reason why Ulysses, in the fictitious accounts which he gives of himself in Ithaca, is so fond of making himself a Cretan, namely that he may avoid any risk of detection, by placing his own proper whereabout at a distance beyond the ordinary range of intercourse.

Nor are we wholly without information from Homer on the subject of the original Iasus himself, from whom the name appears to be derived; and whose name we find still subsisting in Attica at the time of the *Troica*[r].

For a passage in the Eleventh Odyssey informs us that Amphion, son of Iasus[s], was a powerful prince in

[r] Il. xv. 332.
[s] Od. xi. 281. E. Curtius ('Ionier,' p. 22 et seqq.) connects Iasus, Amphion, Iaolkos, Jason, with the Ionian race.

Minyeian Orchomenus: that his youngest daughter, the beautiful Chloris, was queen of Pylos: and that Neleus, marrying her, founded there the dynasty of the Neleids. Thus through Pylos we connect a powerful Iasid family with Western Peloponnesus, possibly five generations before the Trojan war, and at a time when we find from Homer that the Danaids or Perseus must have been reigning in Eastern Peloponnesus. This seems enough to justify putting the sense of Western Peloponnesus upon the phrase Ἴασον Ἄργος in the speech of Eurymachus.

We may justly inquire whether it is so certain, as seems to be taken for granted, that the Minyeian Orchomenus, where Amphion reigned, was the Orchomenus of Bœotia. For his daughter Chloris was sovereign of Pylos, and we must suppose that sovereignty to have been not acquired by herself, but inherited from her father. Now it is very improbable that Amphion could have been sovereign at the same time of Pylos and of the northern Orchomenos: between which intervened an Æolid family settled at the Isthmus, another race of Hellenic chiefs, the line of Portheus, in Ætolia, and perhaps also the dynasty of Cadmus in Bœotia. We have no instance in Homer of the possession by the same prince of territories not continuous. Now there was there a river Minyeius, between Pylos and Elis; in Arcadia as well as in Bœotia there was an Orchomenos at the period of Homer; it seems then probable, that the name of that town should be combined with the Minyeian name in Peloponnesus as well as in Bœotia. If it were so, the political connection with Pylos is natural, and the application of the Iasian name to Western Peloponnesus becomes still more easy of explication. But even though the Orchomenos here named be Bœotian, the case remains sufficiently clear. For it was once, or formerly (πότε) that Amphion reigned in Orchomenus; and the meaning may well be, that having in earlier life reigned there, he had afterwards accompanied the southward movement of the time, perhaps being expelled from his fat soil; and that he established, or reestablished the connection between Western Peloponnesus and the Iasian name.

Lastly, the place μέσον Ἄργος seems to be equivalent to the English expression, 'through the breadth of Argos,' or *all over* Argos; and though we may think that Ἄργος alone means one side of the Peloponnesus, μέσον Ἄργος may very well mean the whole. In the speech of Diomed[t] to Glaucus, it cannot mean less than this: on the other hand, from its being the counterpart of Lycia, it may perhaps not less probably signify the whole of settled Greece, and thus be the equivalent of πᾶν Ἄργος in Il. ii. 108. But the more convenient sense for Od. xv. 80 is plainly the Peloponnesus, because then it squares precisely with Hellas in the same passage, and the two together make up the whole of Greece. But without disturbing the signification of the word Hellas, as meaning Northern and Middle Greece, we might still give to μέσον Argos the force of 'all Greece.' The words of Menelaus would then stand as if an inhabitant of London said to his friend a foreigner, 'I will take you through Scotland and all Britain.' It is difficult, however, to decide absolutely between these two senses of μέσον Ἄργος. What we see plainly is, that the word Ἄργος had taken the deepest root, and a very wide range, in connection with Greek settlements, and with such settlements only.

[t] Il. vi. 224.

And now with respect to the line so much criticised,

ἐγχείῃ δ' ἐκέκαστο Πανέλληνας καὶ Ἀχαιούς [u].

The word Πανέλληνες may, we have seen, either mean the tribes of Greece beyond the Isthmus, or those of all Greece: in which latter and more likely sense it is coextensive with Ἀχαιοί. I here finally touch upon this verse along with those properly geographical, on account of the important combination which it involves.

We find in Il. i. 270, iii. 49, and in Od. vii. 25, xvi. 18, the expression ἀπίη γαίη, which some of the grammarians, and the common opinion mentioned by Strabo [x], have explained to mean the Peloponnesus, while modern scholars render it simply distant [y]. In the two passages of the Iliad, the former construction is certainly more suitable: and the combination with τηλόθεν in Il. i. 270, is tautological, flat, and un-Homeric, if ἀπίη mean merely distant. In Od. xvi. 18 either sense will serve the passage. In Od. vii. 25 (when we again have τηλόθεν) Ulysses states himself to have come ἐξ ἀπίης γαίης. As he had not come from Peloponnesus, it is assumed that this is not the meaning. I question the reasoning. Ulysses everywhere, when questioned, shows an immense fertility in fiction about himself: in every case, however, carefully reporting himself to be come from a distant spot. I see no reason therefore why we should not construe Ἀπίη γαῖα to mean the Peloponnesus; in conformity with the tradition which Æschylus [z] reports concerning Apis, and with the undoubted usage of the tragedians. As I interpret the Outer or Romance-geography of the Odyssey, the Peloponne-

[u] Il. ii. 530.
[x] Strabo viii. p. 371.
[y] Heyne on Il. i. 270. Buttmann Lexil. in voc. Crusius ad locc.
[z] Suppl. 277.

sus would be understood by the Phæacians of Homer to be extremely remote from their country. The difference of quantity is no sufficient reason against this construction. Plainly 'Απίη γαίη, if it be a proper name at all, means the whole Peloponnesus, and not a part of it, for Nestor in Il. i. 270 uses it so as to include the Western side, and Hector, Il. iii. 49, so as to include the Eastern.

I will now sum up the conclusions to which this inquiry has brought us, either by certain or by probable evidence, with respect to Homer's geographical nomenclature for Greece at large, and for its principal members.

1. 'Αχαιΐς
   'Αχαιΐς γαῖα } invariably mean the whole of Greece.
   'Αχαιΐς αἶα

2. "Αργος either alone, or with epithets other than those which concern geographical extension, means

   (1) The city only, as in Il. iv. 52, and probably in Il. ii. 559.

   (2) The immediate dominions of Agamemnon in the north and north-east of Peloponnesus, as in Od. iii. 263.

   But it is possible, though by no means certain, that "Αργος in this sense should be held to include the whole Pelopid dominions, which were looked upon as having a certain political unity, and thus to be the equivalent of "Αργος 'Αχαιϊκόν.

   (3) By metonymy from this supreme and metropolitan quarter of Greece, it means the whole country.

3. The phrase πᾶν "Αργος in Il. ii. 108 means the whole of Continental Greece.

4. The phrase μέσον Ἄργος means most probably the whole of Greece, or Greece at large; possibly the Peloponnesus only.

5. Πελασγικὸν Ἄργος is Thessaly, from Macedonia to Œta.

6. Ἀχαιϊκὸν Ἄργος means the Pelopid dominions of the Troic time, or in general words, Eastern Peloponnesus.

7. Ἴασον Ἄργος means Western Peloponnesus.

8. The word Ἑλλας means
   (1) probably a portion of the dominions of Achilles, as in Il. ii. 683, ix. 395;
   (2) certainly the country outside them to the southward of Phthia, down to the Isthmus of Corinth, and probably reaching northward through the rest of Thessaly: Il. ix. 447 and elsewhere;
   (3) it is possible that Ἑλλας may mean all Greece in Od. i. 344, and xv. 80; but more likely that the sense is the same as in (2).

9. The phrase Ἀπίη γαίη most probably, though not certainly, means the entire Peloponnesus.

What then was this name Ἄργος, which Homer uses so much more frequently, and with so much more elasticity and diversity of sense, than any other territorial name whatever?

In the first place let us remark how rarely it is used for a city; in the strict sense of the word, we cannot be said to find it more than once. Its proper meaning is evidently a tract of country.

From this it is limited to the city to which the tract of country belonged: or it is extended to the country at large, of which the particular tract was the capital or governing part. Both these significations are what are termed improper: the latter is also political, and has no relation to race, or to an eponymist, or to any physical features of soil or scenery, whether the word Ἄργος may have had such reference or not, when used in its original, proper, and usual application, to mean a district.

As previously with populations, let us now set out the various descriptions of source, to which the Homeric names of countries and places owe their origin.

They appear to be derived either

1. From an individual eponymist, as Ithaca from Ithacus, Od. xvii. 207; Dardania from Dardanus, Il. xx. 216; Ascanie from Ascanius, Il. ii. 863; while we see the intermediate stage of the process in the name Ἀπίη, joined with γαῖα, supposed to indicate the Peloponnesus, and to be derived from Apis.

2. From a race in occupation: as in the case of Ἀχαιὶς γαῖα, and Ἀχαιὶς simply, from the Achæans; Ἕλλας from the Ἕλλοι; Κρήτη or Κρηταὶ (Od. xiv. 199) from the Κρῆτες.

3. From its physical features or circumstances directly, such as Αἰγίαλος from being a narrow strip along the shore of the Corinthian gulf, between the mountains and the sea: there is also a town Αἰγίαλος of the Paphlagonians, Il. ii. 855. Probably we may add Εὔβοια, Eubœa, from the adaptation of that fertile island to tillage, which afterwards made it the granary of Athens.

4. From some race occupying it: and in the cases where that race has been named from any feature of the country, then, not directly but derivatively, from the country itself.

For instance, Θρῄκη from Θρῆκες, Thracians, which word again must come from a common root with τρᾱχύς. The name Τρηχῖν has obviously a similar origin.

So again in the later Greek we find the old Αἰγίαλος named Αἰγιάλεια from the intermediate formation Αἰ-

Etymology of the word Argos.

γιαλεῖς: and perhaps Ἀργολις from the Ἀργεῖοι, who inhabited it, and took their name from Ἄργος.

And so in Homer we have Φθίη; from that apparently comes Φθῖοι, and from this again, in the later Greek, Phthiotis.

Such then are the ordinary sources, as far as we know, of the territorial names of Homer.

The three aids which we have for judging of the meaning of the name Ἄργος are, the Homeric text, etymology, and the later tradition.

None of these in any manner connect the name Ἄργος either with an eponymist, or with a race of inhabitants, either mediately or immediately, as its root. We can only therefore look for its origin in something related to the physical features of the country, or countries, to which it was applied.

The word ἄργος itself is frequently found in Homer otherwise than as a proper name. It is used as an adjective in the following combinations:

1. κύνες ἀργοὶ Il. i. 50.
2. βόες ἀργοὶ Il. xxiii. 30.
3. ἀργὴν χῆνα Od, xv. 161.

So also we have the compounds ἀργὴς (κέραυνος) ἀργικέραυνος, ἀργεστὴς (Νότος), ἀργενναὶ (ὄϊες, ὀθόναι), ἀργινόεις (Κάμειρος), ἀργιόδοντες (ὕες), ἀργιπόδες (κύνες). Ποδάργης (horse of Achilles).

And it is usual to give to the word ἀργὸς[a] in these several forms the several senses of

1. Swift, as in swift dogs, swift thunderbolt.
2. White, as in white goose, white (chalky) Cameirus.

---

[a] See Scott and Liddell, in voc. Damm Lex. Hom. in voc. Crusius Il. xxiii. 30. Nitzsch on Od. ii. 11, and Hermann quoted by him.

3. Sleek, shining, as in sleek oxen, with glistening coats.

It is said truly, that what is swift in motion gives an appearance of shining: and what shines is in some degree akin to whiteness. But it is neither easy to say, in this view of the matter, which is the primary, and which the secondary, meaning of the word, nor what is its etymology. Nor does it show the slightest resemblance to the local name Ἄργος, which, from the variety of its applications, apart from any question of race or political connection, must have had some etymological signification.

Nor, as regards the βόες ἀργοὶ in particular, is it very easy to believe in the sleekness of the oxen in Homer's time, (this seems to be rather an idea borrowed from the processes and experience of modern times,) or of the camp oxen of any time. Nor is the matter mended by two forced attempts, one to construe βόες ἀργοὶ as oxen having white fat within them, or again, as slow oxen. From these sources, then, we can at present obtain no light.

Now I submit that the just signification of the proper name Ἄργος is to be found by considering it as akin to the word ἔργον, which plainly appears in Homer to have agricultural labours for its primary object. And it seems pretty clear, that by the transposition of letters which so commonly occurs in popular speech, especially during the infant state of languages, the word ἄγρος, 'a field,' is no more than a form of Ἄργος.

K. O. Müller, as we have seen, considers that Ἄργος with the ancients means a plain[b]: I would add a plain, not as being a flat surface, but as being formed

---

[b] Orchomenus und die Minyer, p. 119. See also E. Curtius 'Ionier,' p. 17.

Etymology of the word Argos.

of cultivable ground, or else it means a settlement formed upon such ground.

In speaking of the word *plain* as applied to Greece, we use it relatively, not as it would be employed in reference to Russia or Hungary, but as meaning the broader levels between the hills, and commonly towards the sea: such as those valleys of Scotland which are called *carses*, or those called *straths*.

Now in the first place I know no other meaning of the word Ἄργος which will suit its various uses in Homer as Pelasgic Argos, Achaic Argos, Iasian Argos. What is the one common physical feature of the several regions that accounts for the common factor in these three compound expressions, if it be not that of plain, that is to say, cultivable, and cultivated, or settled country?

Again, look at the relation of Ἄργος to Ἀργεῖοι. What except a physical and geographical meaning, still adhering to the word, and holding it somewhat short of the mature and familiar use of a proper name, can account for the fact that we have in the history and geography of Greece so many cases of an Argos, without Argives, that is local or provincial Argives, belonging to it? Achaic Argos indeed has Ἀργεῖοι belonging to it, but Pelasgic and Iasian Argos have none. Just so we might speak of the Highlands of Saxony, or of the Lowlands of Switzerland; but the inhabitants of the first are not known as Highlanders, nor those of the latter as Lowlanders [c].

I believe there are no phrases, which more nearly translate the words Ἄργος and Ἀργεῖοι, than Lowlands

[c] Strabo found in his own time, and has reported it as the custom of the 'moderns,' that the Argive plain passed by the name of Ἄργος, and not the city only.

and Lowlanders respectively. For the word Lowlands means land not only lying low, but both lying low, and also being favourable for cultivation: and these ideas more truly represent the land fitted for the sort of settlement called ''Άργος, than the mere idea of level plains.

If this be the idea of the word Argos, we see the propriety of its application to the city of Argos and its district. For this city stood, as a city of the town and more open country, in a certain opposition to Mycenæ, which nestled among the hills; and which bore geographically much the same relation to Argos, as Dardania to Ilion. It afterwards fell also into the same political analogy.

In the phrase 'Αχαιϊκὸν ''Άργος, Homer deals with a case where, as it is sometimes applied without an epithet, ''Άργος may justly be called a proper name, like the European *Pays-bas*; but there is no evidence of this in his 'Pelasgic Argos,' and 'Iasian Argos,' and it seems likely that he rather intends in those phrases to employ the term Argos as a word simply descriptive, and to speak of the Pelasgian Lowlands, and the Iasian Lowlands. The difference of sense is just that which we should indicate in English by the absence of the capital letter.

There is evidence that the name had not exhausted its elasticity even after Homer's time. In later ages we find an Argos of Orestis in Macedonia; an Argos of Amphilochia in Western Greece; an Argos near Larissa in Thessaly[d], and other cases more remote. Nothing but a geographical force still adhering to the word will account for this extension.

[d] Cramer's Greece, i. 197. 385. ii. 10. Strabo ix. p. 440.

Etymology of the word Argos.

The same is the inference to be drawn from the epithets and quasi-epithets, or descriptive phrases, applied to it by Homer. With the exception of one passage, where he gives it the political epithet[e] κλυτὸν, they are all physical; being ἱππόβοτον, πολυδίψιον, πολύπυρον, and οὖθαρ ἀρούρης. Of these four epithets, the first is in Homer peculiarly connected with the specific form and character of the country: accordingly, while it is the standing epithet of Argos, being used with it eleven times out of only fifteen in which the word has any epithet or quasi-epithet attached to it, it is never found with Achæis, or with Hellas. And the proof of its physically descriptive character lies in the passage where Telemachus gives to Menelaus an account of Ithaca;

ἐν δ' Ἰθάκῃ οὔτ' ἄρ' δρόμοι εὐρέες, οὔτε τι λειμών·
αἰγίβοτος, καὶ μᾶλλον ἐπήρατος ἱπποβότοιο[f].

The ἱππόβοτος of Homer, again, does not point merely to fertility, but also to labour and its results; not merely to pasture, but also to grain, for the horses of Homer are fed on this as well as on herbage,

κρῖ λευκὸν ἐρεπτόμενοι καὶ ὀλεύρας[g].

Now, in referring the word Ἄργος to a common root and significancy with ἔργον, we are not bound to hold that it attains its initial vowel by junction with the particle ἀ used in its intensive sense. For we have the word, and also its derivatives, in this form, coming down to us from the old Greek. Among the four tribes of Attica which subsisted until the time of Cleisthenes[h], one was that of the Ἀργάδες or husbandmen: and in the Elian inscription supposed to date about the For-

[e] Il. xxiv. 437.
[f] Od. iv. 606.
[g] Il. v. 196. viii. 560.
[h] Grote's Hist.

tieth Olympiad[i], or more than 600 years B. C., we have the very word ἔργον in the form ἄργον, with the digamma, in a passage which I copy,

ΑΙΤΕϜΕΠΟΣ ΑΙΤΕϜΑΡΓΟΝ

This inscription, says the Article in the *Museum Criticum*, is of older date than any other which has either been brought in copy from Greece, or is to be found on the marbles. The matter of it is a public treaty, between the Elians and some of their neighbours, concluded for an hundred years.

Another good example of the interchange of the vowels α and ε is in the word ἀρόω, which it is obvious to derive from ἔρα, the earth. In the Latin we see both forms preserved, the one in *aro* to plough, the other in *sero* to sow. And this latter suggests the derivation of the Greek σπείρω from a similar source.

If then the meaning of Ἄργος be an agricultural settlement, and its root the same with that of ἔργον, we need not now discuss at large whether that root be the old word ἔρα or terra, which however appears to be probable, and which accounts both for the especial reference of the word ἔργον in Homer to tillage, the oldest industry, and for the subsequent extension of its meaning to labour and its results in general.

Now, having this view of the words Ἄργος and ἔργον, we shall find, in the fundamental idea of labour itself, a meaning which will furnish a basis for the Homeric adjective, and for all its compounds in all their varied applications. That idea is always in relation with what is earnest, and (so to speak) strengthful; sometimes this takes the form of keenness, and then

---

[i] See *Museum Criticum*, vol. i. p. 536, and Marsh's Horæ Pelasgicæ, p. 70.

comes in the idea of swiftness in conjunction with labour: sometimes, again, it takes the form of patience, and then labour suggests slowness. The labour of a dog is swift, that of an ox is patient: hence the κύνες ἄργοι are laborious dogs, therefore swift; and hence too the βόες ἄργοι are laborious oxen, therefore slow; the office of the one being to cover space, and of the other to overcome resistance. We may bring the two senses near without any loss in either case, by calling the oxen sturdy or sedulous, and the dogs strenuous or keen.

The third sense of whiteness legitimately attaches to the effect of rapid motion upon the eye.

The sense of sleekness does not appear to be required in Homer: but it may be a derivative from that of whiteness.

By one or more of the three first senses, or by the original sense of labour in its (so to speak) integral idea, all the Homeric words may be justly rendered. Some of them will bear either the sense of swift, or that of white: for instance, ἀργής with κεραυνός. In Aristotle[k], de Mundo, c. 4, we have τῶν κεραυνῶν...οἱ ταχέως διάττοντες, ἀργῆτες λέγονται. And again, ἀργεστής with Νότος. This may mean the fleet Notus: it may also mean white, as carrying the light white cloud from over the sea, in the sense taken by Horace, who appears to have been an accurate and careful observer of Homeric epithets; and who says,

> Albus ut obscuro deterget nubila cœlo
> Sæpe Notus[l].

This sense of the word Argos will suit other uses of it which have not been yet named.

For instance, it will suit the ship Argo, which we may

---

[k] Steph. Lex.   [l] Carm. I. vii. 15.

consider as swift, or, and perhaps preferably, as stout, strong, doing battle with the waves: as we now say, a good ship, or a gallant ship. Again, it suits the noble dog Argus of the Odyssey, whose character would be but inadequately represented by either patient, swift, or white. Considering this word as the adjective of the word which describes what has been well called by a writer of the present day, "noble, fruitful labour," we at once see him before us, swift as he had been, and patient as he was, but also brave, faithful, trustful, and trustworthy. Argus the spy, named in the 'Αργειφόντης of Homer, represents one side of the early meaning of the word[m]. The adjective ἀργαλέος, exaggerating as well as isolating that element of difficulty which the root comprises, represents another: and the later word ἀργοῦντες[n], the idle, catching the idea of slowness at the point where it passes into inertness, similarly represents yet another.

Such being the case in regard to the name Ἄργος, we shall now have an easy task in dealing with 'Αργεῖοι.

Homer employs this word in four places (to speak in round numbers) for three in which he uses Δαναοί.

He employs it as an epithet, sometimes with the name of Juno, and frequently with the name of Helen.

In the Odyssey[o] we have this singular and rare juxtaposition of the words:

'Αργείων Δαναῶν ἠδ' Ἰλίου οἶτον ἀκούων.

Nitzsch[p] observes, that we might almost suppose the word 'Αργείων to be an epithet, and this observation is quoted by G.Crusius. Eustathius, the Scholiast, Barnes,

---

[m] See Nitzsch on Od. i. 38 for his etymology of Argeiphontes; but not for his etymology of Argus, which he simply refers to Argos.
[n] Soph. Fr. 288.
[o] Od. viii. 578.
[p] In loc.

Payne Knight, do not notice it. It seems to me more agreeable to Homeric laws to treat Ἀργείων as the substantive, and Δαναῶν as the adjective. For as Homer knows of an Achaic, an Iasian, a Pelasgic Argos, so he may consistently speak of Danaan Argives, with the latent idea that there might be, and were, other Lowlanders out of Greece. But there were not, so far as we know, any other Danaans than a single Greek dynasty.

Homer also in other places uses Δαναοί[q] as an adjective, with the substantives ἥρωες and αἰχμηταί. He has no corresponding use of Ἀργεῖοι: thus the old idea of a *colonus* or farming settler seems still to colour the word, and lingers in it, even after it has grown to be in common use a proper name.

In the application of the word Ἀργείη as an epithet to Juno and Helen, he appears not to mean simply Greek but Argive Juno, Argive Helen, so that the word here is not properly the singular of Ἀργεῖοι the national name, but simply the adjective formed from Ἄργος, in the sense of that part of Peloponnesus which formed the Pelopid dominions. To these Helen belonged: and for that family, as previously for the Perseid race, Juno felt her chief anxiety, evidently because they were the political heads of Greece.

Thus the use of Argeian as an adjective seems to be quite clearly limited to a local sense of the word: and this being the case, it seems remarkable that the attention of the commentators before Nitzsch should not have been directed to the line in the Eighth Odyssey, and that Nitzsch, with ἥρωες Δαναοὶ and αἰχμηταὶ Δαναοὶ to guide him, should suggest the sense of Argive Danaans, instead of Danaan Argives.

[q] Il. ii. 110, 256. xv. 733. xii. 419.

The local use, however, of the Argeian name must not be dismissed without a more full investigation. Let us first dispose of its use for Juno and Helen.

The proof that Helen is meant to be described as not merely Greek, but as connected with Achaic Argos or Eastern Peloponnesus, has already been sufficiently [q] set forth.

As respects Juno, we shall find that her affections always centre in the house that was paramount in the chief seat of Hellenic power, the Eastern Peloponnesus. Her tenacious attachments are constantly directed to the nation, and they survive dynastic changes. Hence her keen and venturesome feeling for Eurystheus; her never dying, never sleeping hatred to his rival Hercules; her esteem for Agamemnon equally with Achilles[r], though they were so unequal in fame and valour: perhaps suggesting that Achilles was regarded by her either because he was necessary for the purposes of Agamemnon, or because he was closely allied to the chief Achæan stock[s]. Hence it is that, when he has assumed his arms[t], she thunders in his honour: and hence her especial love for the three cities, which were the symbols of Greek power, Argos, Sparta, and Mycenæ[u]. So intense is her attachment, that she could wish to be the actual mother of the Greeks, even as she would readily devour the Trojans upon occasion[x]. Hence, once more, even in the Odyssey, where she is almost a mute, it is mentioned, that Agamemnon[y] came safe across the sea, for Juno protected

[q] Sup. p. 353, 4.
[r] Il. i. 196.
[s] Inf. p. 417.
[t] Od. xi. 45.
[u] Il. iv. 52.
[x] Od. iv. 35.
[y] Od. iv. 515.

Transition from Argeians to Achæans.

him. This is quite enough to fix the sense of Ἀργείη, when it is applied to Juno, as a local sense.

In fact, Homer's use of this word with a restrained and local sense is not only clear, but most carefully defined, both as to time and as to place.

While in the army before Troy he freely interchanges Danaan, Argive, and Achæan, as they are near enough to identity for his purpose, he never applies Danaan at all to the Greeks at home, and employs the other two names with the most accurate discrimination.

The Argeian name is confined in place to the Eastern Peloponnesus, and in time to the Perseid epoch. Upon the transfer of the sovereignty to the Pelopid house, the Argeian name ceases to be applied to their immediate subjects. Let us now examine passages which may illustrate the case.

1. Two or nearly three generations before the *Troica*, in the time when Bellerophon was young, Prœtus ruled over the Ἀργεῖοι,

πολὺ φέρτερος ἦεν
Ἀργείων· Ζεὺς γὰρ οἱ ὑπὸ σκήπτρῳ ἐδάμασσεν[z].

Now Prœtus was certainly not lord of Greece. There was no lord paramount of Greece before the Pelopids: and near the time of Prœtus we have Eurystheus, Œneus and his line, Cadmus and his line, Neleus and his line, Minos and his line, as well as probably other thrones, each in its own place. But Prœtus falls within the period of the Perseids, and within the local circumscription of the Eastern Peloponnesus where they reigned.

[z] Il. vi. 158.

2. But neither is Eurystheus spoken of by Homer as sovereign of Greece; though he is king of the Argives [a],

ὃς Ἀργείοισιν ἀνάξει.

For when Juno fraudulently asks and obtains from Jupiter the promise that the person to be born that day shall enjoy a certain sovereignty, it is not over the Argives, but over the περικτίονες:

ἦ μὲν τὸν πάντεσσι περικτιόνεσσιν ἀνάξειν
ὅς κεν ἐπ' ἤματι τῷδε πέσῃ μετὰ ποσσὶ γυναικός.

Thus the promise is the babe shall reign over περικτίονες, a word clearly inapplicable to the whole of that straggling territory, which was occupied irregularly by the Greeks. But when the fulfilment is claimed, it is that he shall reign over Ἀργεῖοι. Therefore the two names are coextensive, and accordingly Ἀργεῖοι does not mean all Greeks; for example, it does not include the line of Cadmus then ruling in Bœotia.

3. But we come down to the time of Tydeus, who was lord of Argos during the epoch of the Pelopid sovereigns. And now we find that his subjects cease to be called Ἀργεῖοι (see Il. v. 803. iv. 384) in the legends, where Homer observes a peculiar nicety in the application of these important words.

4. Still the Argeian name continues to preserve its local application to the inhabitants of Argos and its district, or of Achaic Argos.

At the games on the death of Patroclus, Idomeneus thinks he discerns Diomed coming in as the winner, and he describes him thus:

[a] Il. xix. 122.

δοκέει δέ μοι ἔμμεναι ἀνὴρ
Αἰτωλὸς γενέην, μετὰ δ' Ἀργείοισιν ἀνάσσει[b].

It is plain that here Idomeneus means among Argives, and not among Greeks.

1. Because not Diomed was lord among the Greeks, but Agamemnon.

2. Because Diomed was lord over a part of the Argives.

3. Because the word is used in evident contradistinction to, and correspondence with, the foregoing word Αἰτωλὸς, which is undoubtedly local.

Again, when we are told that Orestes made a funeral feast for the Ἀργεῖοι[c], we may probably presume that we have here again the local sense.

Thus we see plainly enough the history of the rise of the Argive name. Belonging to the subjects of the ruling part of Greece, it grows so as to be applicable to all Greeks, in cases where no confusion can arise from its being thus employed. Thus the Roman name became applicable to Campanians or Calabrians as subjects of Rome, in contradistinction to Germans, Dacians, or Parthians; but if the subject in hand were domestic and Italian, the domestic distinction would naturally revive. Even so Homer's Greeks are all Argeians in the *Troica:* but at home they have their local meaning, like Cadmeans, Ætolians, Pylians, Elians, Epeans, Arcadians, Locrians, and also, as we shall find, Achæans.

It is at the very period of the local prevalence of the Argive name, that we find also from Homer unequivocal appearances of a Cretan empire, circumscribing it by sea, and possibly more or less by land, though per-

[b] Il. xxiii. 470. [c] Od. iii. 309.

haps the Minoan power and dynasty may not at once have acquired its Grecian character. If then, with respect to the word Ἀργεῖοι, we see that it was originally of limited and local application; we have no reason whatever to suppose that the Danaan name could ever have been of wider scope. Two questions then arise.

First, why does Homer use the Danaan and Argive names as national, when they were only local?

Secondly, the priority of the Danaan name being clear, as we see that the Danaan dynasty preceded that one whose subjects were called Argives, why did the Argive name supplant or succeed the Danaan?

The first question will be resumed hereafter, but I will now touch upon the second.

The name Danaan, in all likelihood, was that of a dynasty originating beyond seas; and if so, it could not well, until softened by the mellow haze of distance, be more popular with the Greeks, when they had awakened under Hellic influence to a full consciousness of national life, than it would have been with the English in the last century to be called Hanoverians or Brunswickers.

The Danaid line ceased, when Perseus came to the throne, as he was descended on the father's side from another source.

Nothing could be more natural, than that with this change of dynasty an old and merely dynastic name should disappear. But why should it be succeeded by the name Ἀργεῖοι?

I hope it will not be thought too bold, if, founding myself on the probable, perhaps I might say, plain resemblance of meaning between Πελασγοὶ and Ἀργεῖοι, I conjecture that on the disappearance from use of the name Δαναοί, instead of falling back upon the old agricultural name Πελασγοὶ, which had by a Danaan conquest become that of a subordinate, if not servile class, the people may have come to bear the name Ἀργεῖοι; borrowed, like the other, from the region they inhabited, and from their habits of life in it, and of equal force, but without the taint which attached to the designation of a depressed race.

In this view, the name Ἀργεῖοι may be defined to be the Hellic equivalent of the old Pelasgic appellation of the people of the country: and it naturally takes root upon the passing away of the Danaan power, within the dominions of those to whom that power had been transferred.

I shall hereafter have occasion to consider further, what was the first historic use of the Argeian name.

There are signs in the later Greek of the affinity, which I have here supposed, between the Pelasgian and Argeian names, and of the assumption of the functions of the former by the latter. I do not enter on the question of etymological identity, but I refer to similarity of application alone.

In Suidas we find the proverb Ἀργείους ὁρᾷς, with this explanation; παροιμία ἐπὶ τῶν ἀτενῶς καὶ καταπληκτικῶς ὁρώντων. Now we know nothing of the Argives, that is, the inhabitants of Argolis, which would warrant the supposition that they were of particularly savage and wild appearance. But if Ἀργεῖοι, as has been shown, originally meant settlers in an agricultural district, and if in process of time the population gathered into towns, in lieu of their old manner of living κωμηδὸν, then, in consequence of the change, Ἀργεῖοι would come to mean rustics, as opposed to townspeople, and from this the transition would be slight and easy to the sense of a wild and savage aspect, as in the proverb.

II. *Ethnology*.

Let us compare with it the Latin word *agrestis*. This I take to be precisely similar, indeed identical, etymologically, with Ἀργεῖος. The point of divergence is when Ἄργος by transposition becomes ἀγρὸς, whence are *ager* and *agrestis*. Materially this Latin word is in still closer correspondence with ἀργηστής, a Greek derivative of ἄργος. Ideally, it passes through the very same process as has been shown in the case of Ἀργεῖος, and here it is strongly supported by the common Homeric word ἄγριος, rude or savage, which comes from ἄγρος, made ready by transposition to yield such a derivative.

This name we find not only as an adjective, but likewise as a proper name. It is applied to a brother of Œneus and Melas, a son of Portheus[d]: and in these names we appear to see described the first rude Hellic invaders of Ætolia, at an epoch three generations before the *Troica*. The *agrestis*, or agricultural settler, next comes to mean the class of country folk, as opposed to the inhabitants of towns or *urbani*; and then, while *urbanus*, with its Greek correlative ἀστεῖος, passes on to acquire the meaning of cultivated and polished, *agrestis*, on the other hand, following a parallel movement with Ἀργεῖος, and in the opposite direction, comes to mean uneducated, coarse, wild, barbarous. Thus Ovid says of the river Achelous, when he had been mutilated by the loss of his horn in the combat with Hercules,

> Vultus Achelous agrestes
> Et lacerum cornu mediis caput abdidit undis[e].

Thus Cicero, in the Tusculans, after a description of the battles of the Spartan youths, carried on not only with fists and feet, but with nails and teeth, asks, *Quæ*

---

[d] Il. xiv. 115. [e] Ov. Met. ix. 96.

barbaria India (al. *barbaries Indica*) *vastior atque agrestior ?*

We also find in Suidas the phrase Ἀργεῖοι φῶρες, and this explanation: Ἐπὶ τῶν προδήλως πονηρῶν· οἱ γὰρ Ἀργεῖοι ἐπὶ κλοπῇ κωμῳδοῦνται. Ἀριστοφάνης Ἀναγύρῳ.

No part of this play remains, so that we are left to general reasoning: but it seems a most natural explanation of this proverb or phrase, that the word Ἀργεῖος, meaning wild and savage, should be applied to banditti: theft in the early stages of society, always frequenting solitary places, as in the later ones, it rather draws to the most crowded haunts of men.

Again, Æschines, in the Περὶ Παραπρεσβείας, brings the grossest personal charges against Demosthenes, for offences, which he says had brought upon him various nicknames. Among these, he thus accuses him: Ἐκ παιδῶν δὲ ἀπαλλαττόμενος, καὶ δεκαταλάντους δίκας ἑκάστῳ τῶν ἐπιτρόπων λαγχάνων, Ἄργας ἐκλήθη. This passage is noticed by both Suidas and Hesychius under Ἀργᾶς, and it is explained ὄνομα ὄφεως. A serpent, either generally or of some particular kind, had, it seems, the name of Ἀργᾶς, which we can easily derive from ἄργος, taken in the same sense as that in which it became the name of Argus the spy. 'Now the serpent was more subtil than any beast of the field[f].' But this does not seem to satisfy the intention of the highly vituperative passage in Æschines. This imputation of extreme cleverness or craft would not have been perhaps a very effective one in Greece. I think he more probably means to call Demosthenes a swindler or plunderer, *homo trium literarum*, from whom his guardians were trying to

[f] Gen. iii. 1.

recover, and who was likely to be exposed, not like the serpent, to get off: and in this sense the word 'Αργὰς at once attaches itself to the reported passage in Aristophanes, and through that to the old meaning of *agrestis* or 'Αργεῖος. Nor is 'Αργεῖος, a thief, more remote in sense from 'Αργεῖος, a rural settler, than is *paganus*, an idolater, from *paganus*, a villager.

I will take yet one more illustration, Hesychius under 'Αργεῖοι gives this explanation; ἐκ τῶν Εἱλώτων οἱ πιστευόμενοι οὕτως ἐλέγοντο, ἢ λαμπροί. Now the sense of λαμπροί might easily be derived from the primitive sense, in the same way as that of whiteness. But it is quite distinct from the explanation respecting that select and trusted class of Helots, who were called 'Αργεῖοι. This usage both serves to explain history, and is explained by it. 'Αργεῖοι was the name of the Greek citizen in Eastern Peloponnesus under the Perseids; it appears in part to have retained its local force throughout the period of the Pelopids; for though in the legend of Tydeus the inhabitants of Argolis we at least find the name 'Αχαιοὶ among them, yet in the Twenty-third Iliad, and in the Third Odyssey, they are called 'Αργεῖοι. In the local usage, then, the Helot meaning a serf, the emancipated Helot would be a citizen, an 'Αργεῖος. But neither serfship nor citizenship were in those days rigidly defined, and the one ran into the other. What could under such circumstances be more natural, than that any Helot who was separated from his brethren, by being taken into the confidence of his master, and living on easy terms with him, should acquire the name of 'Αργεῖος, and that the class who had thus obtained it in a somewhat peculiar sense, that is to say, the sense of a free rural settler, or (so to speak) freeholder, should continue to bear it as descriptive of their own position, even when it had ceased to be generally applicable to the free Greeks of that particular district? which of course it could no longer be when the family and dynastic tie between Argolis and Lacedæmon came to be dissolved.

And if I am right in supposing that even in Homer[g] the name 'Αργεῖοι evidently leans towards the masses, and that of 'Αχαιοὶ towards the select few or chiefs, such a distinction is in marked harmony with the whole of this inquiry respecting the force of the former phrase.

According to the view which has been here given, we must carefully distinguish between the sense of 'Αργεῖοι, as a national name in Homer, and that of ῎Αργος, in this respect. The name 'Αργεῖοι was raised to the distinction of a national name apparently in consequence of the political ascendancy of a house that reigned over territories specially named ῎Αργος, and over subjects named from the region 'Αργεῖοι. I say this without undertaking to determine whether there actually was a period in which the Greeks were as a nation called 'Αργεῖοι, a supposition which seems to me improbable: or whether it was a name which Homer applied to them poetically, like the name Δαναοὶ, because it had once been the proper designation of those who held the seat of Greek supremacy. In either view, however, the case of the name ῎Αργος is different. That name had not its root in political power, actual or remembered: it kept its place, as being founded in a good physical description, so far as it went, of the general character of the principal habitable parts of the peninsula which the Hellic tribes, swarming down-

[g] See inf. p. 410.

wards from their hills, successively and gradually occupied. Hence the substantive was, as we see, capable of spreading beyond the adjective in space, since, while we have an Iasian and a Pelasgian Ἄργος, we have no Iasian or Pelasgian Ἀργεῖοι. Thus they were detached one from the other. In Homer the epithet has a larger range of clear signification than the substantive. But apart from Homer the substantive appears from etymology to have been the older, and from history either to have reached points at which the adjective never arrived, or to have long survived its desuetude.

The Achæans.

The lights, which we have already obtained in considering the Danaan and Argive names, will assist the inquiry with respect to the Achæans. At the same time, the fullest view of that name and race cannot be attained, until we shall have succeeded in fixing what we are to understand by the Homeric ἄναξ ἀνδρῶν.

I now proceed, however, to show from the text of the poems,

1. That of the three great appellatives of the nation, the name Ἀχαιοί is the most familiar.

2. That the manner of its national use indicates the political predominance of an Achæan race, in the Homeric age, over other races, ranged by its side in the Troic enterprise, and composing along with it the nation, which owned Agamemnon for its head.

3. That, besides its national use, the name Ἀχαιοί has also an important local and particular use for a race which had spread through Greece, and which exercised sway among its population.

4. That the manner of its local and particular use points out to us, with considerable clearness, the epoch

at which it acquired preponderance, namely that when Pelops and his family acquired ascendancy in Greece.

As respects the first of these propositions, the numerical test, although a rude one, yet appears to be conclusive. We find that Homer uses the name 'Αργεῖοι in the plural two hundred and five times, of which twenty-eight are in the Odyssey; besides fifteen passages in which the singular is used. And the name Δαναοὶ about one hundred and sixty times, of which thirteen are in the Odyssey. But we find the name 'Αχαιοὶ employed from seven to eight hundred times: that is to say, five hundred and ninety-seven times in the Iliad, and one hundred and seventeen times in the Odyssey; all these in the plural number, besides thirty-two places of the poems in which it is used in the singular, or in its derivatives 'Αχαιΐς or 'Αχαιϊκός.

The particulars next to be stated will bear at once upon the first and upon the second proposition.

Homer very rarely attaches any epithet to the name 'Αργεῖοι, more frequently by much to Δαναοὶ, and still oftener to 'Αχαιοί. To the first only six times in all: to the second twenty-four: and to the third near one hundred and forty times. It is not likely that metrical convenience is the cause of this diversity. We have already seen that 'Αργεῖοι is susceptible of a substantive force, which will carry one at least of the other names by way of epithet, as if it indicated an employment, and not properly the name of a race. A like inference may be drawn from the greater susceptibility of carrying descriptive epithets, which we now find the Danaan and Achæan names evince. For example, the name of the Scotts, Douglasses, or Grahams, four centuries ago, would have afforded larger scope for characteristic epithets than such a name as Farmers or Colonists, when used to point out a particular people, or than such a name as Lowlanders, while it still retained its descriptive character, and had not yet become purely titular or proper. We must probably look, then, to political significance for the basis of the use made by Homer of the Achæan name.

When we examine the character of the epithets, this presumption is greatly corroborated. Homer uses with the word 'Αχαιοὶ, and with this word only, epithets indicating, firstly, high spirit, secondly, personal beauty, and thirdly, finished armour[h]. I take these to be of themselves sufficient signs, even were others wanting, to point to the Achæans as being properly the ruling class, or aristocracy, of the heroic age.

The Achæan name, again, attains with Homer to a greater variety of use and inflexion than the Danaan or Argeian names.

He has worked it into the female forms 'Αχαιΐδες, 'Αχαιιάδες, 'Αχαιαὶ, as on the other side he has done with the names Τρῶες into Τρωὲς, Τρωάδες, and Τρωαὶ, and Δάρδανοι into Δαρδανίδες: but he has not made any such use of the names 'Αργεῖοι and Δαναοί. The female use of the former appears indeed in the singular with the names of Juno and of Helen, but never as applicable to Greek women in general, or to a Greek woman simply as such.

He uses it in the singular to describe 'a Greek' 'Αχαιὸς ἀνηρ, Il. iii. 167, 226: which he never does for the two other names. In the same manner he uses Δάρδανος ἀνηρ, Il. ii. 701. This form seems to indicate the full and familiar establishment of a name; and the

[h] Sup. p. 357.

Dardanians had, we know, been Dardanians for seven generations before the *Troica* (Il. xx. 215-40).

In the opening passage of the First Iliad, not less than in that of the Odyssey, Homer has, as it is generally observed by critics, intentionally given us a summary or 'Argument' of his poem. But I doubt whether sufficient notice has been taken of the very effective manner in which he has given force to his purpose, by taking care in that passage to use the most characteristic words. Achilles is there the son of Peleus, for his extraction, as on both sides divine, but especially as on the father's side from Jupiter, is the groundwork of his high position in the poem. Agamemnon is likewise here introduced under the title which establishes the same origin for him, and more than any thing else enhances the dignity of his supremacy before men[i]. And the Greeks too, if I am correct, are not without significancy here introduced to us, as is right, under their highest and also their best established designation, that of Achæans. Nor is it until they have been five times called Achæans[k] that he introduces the Danaan name[l] at all. The Argive name, as if the weakest, when it is first employed, is placed in an awkward nearness to the title of Achæans, perhaps by way of explanation:

ὃς μέγα πάντων
Ἀργείων κρατέει, καὶ οἱ πείθονται Ἀχαιοί[m].

Again the paramount force of the Achæan name may justly be inferred from its being the only territorial name which had clearly grasped the whole of Greece at the epoch of the *Troica*[n].

Turning now entirely to what indicates more or less of peculiar character in the Achæans, I would observe,

[i] See inf. sect. ix.   [k] Il. i. 2, 12, 15, 17, 22.
[l] Il. i. 42.   [m] Il. i. 81.   [n] See sup. p. 380.

that the adjective δῖοι appears to be the highest of all the national epithets employed by Homer; and this he couples, as has been observed by Mure[o], (who recognises a peculiar force in the term,) with the Achæan designation alone among the three. He also applies it to the Pelasgi; for whom, as we have found, he means it to be a highly honourable epithet. Probably the Achæans are δῖοι because of preeminence, the Pelasgians because of antiquity. To no other nation or tribe whatever does he apply this epithet. His very chary use of it in the plural is a sign of its possessing in his eyes some peculiar virtue.

Of its feminine forms one has been selected to convey the most biting form of reproach to the army, in the speech of Thersites. Now it is remarkable that in that speech, of which an inflated presumption is the great mark, the Achæan name is used five times within nine lines, and neither of the other names is used at all. I do not doubt that the upstart and braggart uses this name only because it was the most distinguished or aristocratic name, as an ill-bred person always takes peculiar care to call himself a gentleman. And doubtless it is for the same reason that he takes the feminine of Ἀχαιός, instead of using Δανααὶ or Ἀργεῖαι for his interpretative epithet, when he wants to sting the soldiery as 'Greekesses and not Greeks.'

Somewhat similar evidence is supplied by the Homeric phrase υἷες Ἀχαιῶν, which has nothing corresponding to it under the Danaan or Argive names. This is an Homeric formula, and the form υἷες seems to belong exclusively to the Achæan name. To the Greeks who always asked the stranger who were his parents, this phrase would carry a peculiar significance.

[o] Hist. Gr. Lit. xv. 5. vol. ii. p. 77.

What addressed them as the sons of honoured parents would be to them the sharpest touchstone of honour or disgrace. And what the patronymic was to the individual, this form of speech was to the nation, an incentive under the form of an embellishment. It is a principle that runs throughout Homer; it is every where μηδὲ γένος πατέρων αἰσχύνεμεν. The poet could not say sons of Danaans, for their forefathers were not Danaan: nor sons of Argeians, for this would recall the ploughshare and not the sword: though the army are addressed from time to time as ἥρωες Δαναοὶ, and ἥρωες Ἀχαιοὶ, they are never ἥρωες Ἀργεῖοι. But to be sons of the Achæans was the great glory of the race, even as to degenerate from being Achæan warriors into effeminacy would have been its deepest reproach: and the fact that he calls a mixed race sons of the Achæans is conversely a proof that the Achæan element was the highest and most famous element in the compound of their ancestry.

But, unless I am mistaken, we have many passages in Homer where the use of the simple term Ἀχαιοὶ is shown from the context to have a special and peculiar, sometimes perhaps even an exclusive reference to the chiefs and leaders of the army. I think it may be shown that the word has in fact three meanings:

1. That of a particular Greek race, which extended itself from point to point, acquiring power everywhere as it spread, by inherent superiority.

2. That of the aristocracy of the country, which it naturally became by virtue of such extension and assumption.

3. That of the whole nation, which takes the name from its prime part.

We have now to examine some passages in support

of the second meaning: and I know not why, but certainly these passages appear in the Iliad to be most abundant near the opening of the poem.

Chryses solicits 'all the Achæans and most the two Atridæ[p].' All the Achæans assent, except Agamemnon. Now the priest could not solicit the army generally except in an assembly: and there is no mention of one, indeed the reply of Agamemnon[q] is hardly such as would have been given in one. It is likely, then, that those whom he addressed were Agamemnon's habitual and ordinary associates; in other words, the chiefs.

When Calchas proceeds to invoke the vengeance of Apollo, which is to fall upon the army at large, it is no longer the Ἀχαιοὶ of whom he speaks, but his prayer is,

τισείαν Δαναοὶ ἐμὰ δάκρυα σοῖσι βέλεσσιν[r].

Although I do not concur with those, who find no element of real freedom in the condition of the Greek masses, whether at home or in the camp, yet it seems plain enough, from the nature of the case, that the questions relating to the division of booty, as being necessarily an executive affair, must have been decided by the chiefs. Now whenever questions of this class are handled, we generally find such an office ascribed to Ἀχαιοί. Agamemnon says[s], 'Do not let me alone of the Argeians go without a prize;' and in conformity with this we find Nestor stimulating the host at large with the expectation of booty[t]. But Achilles replies to Agamemnon, 'that the *Achæans* have it not in their power to compensate him there and then, for they have no common stock:' but 'when Troy is taken,

[p] Il. i. 15, 22.   [q] i. 26–32.   [r] i. 42.
[s] i. 118.   [t] ii. 354.

then we the Achæans will repay you three and four fold[u]. The same subject is again touched in i. 135, 162, 392. ii. 227: and both times with reference to the 'Αχαιοὶ as the distributors of the spoil. In Il. ii. 255 it is allotted by the ἥρωες Δαναοί.

In the same way we find a decided leaning to the use of the word 'Αχαιοὶ, when reference is made to other governing duties.

For instance, in the adjuration of Achilles by the staff or sceptre. 'It has been stripped of leaf and bark, and now the υἷες 'Αχαιῶν, who are intrusted by Jupiter with sovereign functions, bear it in hand[x].' It is hardly possible here to construe the phrase without limiting it to the chiefs.

I have referred to the passage where Homer introduces the word 'Αργεῖοι for the first time, under the shadow, as it were, of 'Αχαιοί. Now, if we examine that passage, we shall perceive that unless there be some shade whatever of difference in the meaning, the words are tautological, an imputation which Homer never merits. But if we admit in the Achæan name a certain bias towards the nobles of the army, then the sense and expressions are alike appropriate.' 'I fear the resentment of him, who mightily lords it over (all) the Greeks, and to whom even the Achæans (or chiefs) submit themselves[y].'

Again the phrase 'Αχαιὸς ἀνήρ[z], twice used by Homer, and both times in the mouth of Priam from the Trojan wall, both times also refers to noble and chieftainlike figures, which his eye, keen for beauty, discerns among the crowd. The second case is particularly worthy of notice:

[u] Il. i. 123, 127.   [x] i. 237.   [y] i. 78.
[z] iii. 167, 226.

410   II. *Ethnology.*

τίς τ' ἄρ' ὅδ' ἄλλος Ἀχαιὸς ἀνὴρ ἠΰς τε μέγας τε,
ἔξοχος Ἀργείων κεφαλὴν ἠδ' εὐρέας ὤμους;

Of which the effect seems to be expressed in these words:

> Who is th' Achæan Chieftain
> So beautiful and tall?
> His shoulders broad surmount the crowd,
> His head outtops them all.

Here again, if Achæan and Argeian be synonymous, the use of the latter word is in the highest degree insipid, but if the reference be to the chief, excelling in height the mass of the soldiery, a perfect propriety is maintained.

I need not extend these illustrations to other passages, such as Il. ii. 80, 346. ix. 670. And, on the other hand, it is easy to point to passages where the force of the Achæan and Argeian names is obviously identical, such as Il. ix. 521: or again where Achæan and Danaan must agree, as in Il. ix. 641, 2. The most frequent use of the Achæan name is, I believe, for the nation, and not the race or class: yet a number of passages remain to show the native bias and primitive meaning of the word.

I will however point out two more places, one in each poem, where that shading of the sense, for which I contend, will either greatly facilitate the rendering of the text, or even may be called requisite in order to attain a tolerable construction.

1. It deserves particular notice, that Homer sometimes places the words in very close proximity, as in the following passage;

νηῶν ἐπ' ἀριστερὰ δηιόωντο
λαοὶ ὑπ' Ἀργείων· τάχα δ' ἂν καὶ κῦδος Ἀχαιῶν
ἔπλετο· τοῖος γὰρ Γαιήοχος Ἐννοσίγαιος
ὤτρυν' Ἀργείους·

This is in Il. xiii. 676–8, and Δαναῶν follows in 680. The nearness of the words, and the place of 'Αχαιοὶ, between the twice used 'Αργεῖοι, is highly insipid and un-Homeric, if they are pure equivalents. But now it seems by no means impossible, that the Poet may in this passage have in view a distinction between the leaders and the mass. He may have meant to say, 'Hector had not yet learned that his men were suffering havock on the left from the Greek troops. But so it was; and the chiefs might now perhaps have won fame, such was the might with which Neptune urged on their forces,' but that, &c.

2. It is difficult, except upon the supposition of a different shade of meaning in these appellatives, to construe at all such a passage as

ἐξερέεινεν ἕκαστα,
Ἴλιον, Ἀργείων τε νέας, καὶ νόστον Ἀχαιῶν[a].

Here the juxtaposition of the words, if they are synonymous, becomes absolutely intolerable. But the sense runs easily and naturally, if we render it 'he inquired (of me) all about (the fall of) Troy, and the fleet (or armament) of the Greeks, and the adventures of the chiefs while on their way home.'

The Odyssey, however, appears to offer a larger contribution towards our means of comprehending the Homeric use of Ἀχαιοὶ, than can be supplied by the mere citation of particular passages.

There is considerable evidence of a division of races in Ithaca: and also of the application of the Achæan name to the aristocracy of the country.

The length of time during which Ulysses had been absent, will account for much disorganization in his

[a] Od. x. 14.

dominions: and their lying chiefly in separate insular possessions would tend to aggravate the evil. Still not only Nestor, Idomeneus[b], Philoctetes, Neoptolemus, but also Menelaus, who was absent almost as long as Ulysses himself, appear to have resumed their respective thrones without difficulty; so that we are led to suppose there must have been much peculiarity in the case of Ithaca. Part of this we may find in the fact, that the family of Ulysses may but recently have attained to power, and that the consolidation of races was imperfect. Besides his force of character, he had accumulated[c] great wealth, following in the footsteps of his father Laertes, who was both a conqueror and an economist[d]. His power, thus depending on what was personal to himself, could not but be shaken to its very base by his departure, and by his long detention in foreign parts.

So far as we can learn from the text of Homer, the family of Ulysses had come, like the other Hellic families, from the north: and it had only reigned in Ithaca at most for two generations. His extraction is not stated further back than his paternal grandfather Arceisius[e]. But his connections all appear to be in the north. His maternal grandfather, Autolycus[f], lived by Parnesus, or Parnassus, in Phocis, near to Delphi. And his wife's father, Icarius, had a daughter Iphthime, who was married to Eumelus[g], heir-apparent of Pheræ in the south of Thessaly: a circumstance which affords a presumption of proximity in their dominions. Thus it is probable that Laertes may have married in Thessaly; and, as we have no mention of the sovereignty of Arceisius, it is highly probable that Laertes was the

[b] Od. iii. 188,9.   [c] Od. xiv. 96.   [d] Od. xxiv. 377, and 205-7.
[e] Od. xvi. 118.   [f] Od. xix. 394.   [g] Od. iv. 798.

first, either to acquire the Ithacan throne, or at least to hold it for any length of time.

The fountain near the city, which supplied it with water, and which probably marks its foundation, was constructed, as we are told, by Ithacus, Neritus, and Polyctor[h].

The first must have been the Eponymist of the island: the second of its principal mountain[i].

Peisander, called ἄναξ and Πολυκτορίδης[k], is one of four principal Suitors, whose gifts to Penelope are specifically mentioned in the Eighteenth Odyssey. Thus he would appear to have been most probably nephew to the Eponymist of the island. Sometimes indeed the patronymic is derived from a grandfather, or even, as in the case of Priam (Δαρδανίδης, Il. xxiv. 629, 631), from a remote ancestor; but then he must apparently be a founder, or one of the highest fame. But Peisander at the least may have been the son of Polyctor; and he was probably the representative of the family, which had been displaced from the Sovereignty by the house of Laertes. He afterwards appears among the leaders in the struggle of the Suitors with Ulysses[l].

The names applied to the subjects of Ulysses in the Odyssey are three: Κεφαλλῆνες, Ἰθακήσιοι, and Ἀχαιοί. In accordance with its use in the Iliad, the first of these, which is but four times[m] used, appears to be a name of the whole people of the state; and, judging from what we have seen of the force of the word, it implies that the Hellenic element was dominant. The difference in the use of the other two is very marked.

In the first place, the Suitors are commonly called

[h] Od. xvii. 205-7.   [i] Od. ix. 22.   [k] Od. xviii. 299.
[l] Od. xxii. 243.   [m] Od. xxi. 210. xxiv. 354. 377. 428.

Ἀχαιοὶ[n], never Ἰθακήσιοι, nor ever Δαναοὶ or Ἀργεῖοι. Either, being the aristocracy, they were an Achæan race; or else, without all being of Achæan race, they were called Achæan, because they were the aristocracy. Of that class they are stated to have constituted the whole[o].

The more probable of these two suppositions is, that they were by no means exclusively of Achæan blood, but took the name from their birth and station. It is most natural to suppose that the displaced family of Peisander, and probably others, were not Achæan, but belonged to an older stock. This stock may have been Hellenic; for, as we know, there were Hellenic, and in particular Æolid, families in Greece long before we hear of the Achæans there.

The house of Ulysses still indeed had friends in the island, like Mentor, like Noemon, son of Phronius, (or the class represented by these names, if they be typical only,) or like Peiræus, who took charge of Theoclymenus at the request of Telemachus[p]. But the bulk of the people were neutral, or else unfriendly. The best that Telemachus can say is, that the *whole* people is not hostile[q]. And in the last Book, whilst more than one half the Assembly take up arms against Ulysses the rest simply[r] remain neutral: so that he has no one to rely upon but his father, his son, and a mere handful of dependents.

While the Achæan name is thus exclusively applied to the Suitors, and apparently to them because they formed the aristocracy, the people, when assembled,

[n] Od. i. 394. 401. ii. 87. 90. 106. 112. 115. xviii. 301, et alibi.
[o] Od. ii. 51. xvi. 122.   [p] Od. ii. 386. xv. 545.
[q] Od. xvi. 114.   [r] Od. xxiv. 463.

are invariably addressed as Ἰθακήσιοι. It is said indeed, that the Achæans[s] were summoned by the heralds to the Assembly of the Second Book: but it seems to have been customary to send a special summons only to principal persons, as we find in Scheria[t]; though all classes were expected to attend, and did attend.

I do not, however, venture to treat it as certain, that the word Ἀχαιοὶ is not applied to the population of Ithaca generally. When Euripides addresses the Assembly, and incites the people to revenge the death of the Suitors, we are told that οἶκτος δ᾽ ἕλε πάντας Ἀχαιούς. This may mean the aristocratic party in the Assembly, as we know that there were two sections very differently minded. At any rate, if the whole people be meant, it is by the rarest possible exception. The name is applied, as we should expect, to the soldiers who sailed with Ulysses to Troy: but within Ithaca it seems clear that the name properly denotes the nobles. And upon the whole it seems most probable, that these Ἀχαιοὶ, in the Twenty-third Book, are the party of the Suitors, with reference rather to their position in society than their extraction: while the minority, who do not join in the movement against Ulysses, are probably the old population of the island, who have no cause of quarrel to make them take up arms against him, and yet no such tie with him, either of race or of ancient subordination, as to induce them to move in his favour.

Ithaca was ill fitted for tillage, or for feeding anything but sheep and goats. And Ithacus, its eponymist, being a very modern personage, it seems highly probable that, whether Achæan or not, he and his race were Hellenic, and gave to the population that peculiar

[s] Od. ii. 7.   [t] Od. viii. 11.

name of Cephallenes, under which Laertes describes them as his subjects. But there were probably anterior inhabitants of the old Pelasgian stock, submerged beneath two Hellenic immigrations, caring little which of their lords was uppermost, and forming the supine minority of the final Assembly.

The use of the Achæan name in Ithaca, in broad separation from the Ithacesian, must then prove either its connection with a race, or its bias towards a class, and may prove both. But quitting the latter as sufficiently demonstrated, I now proceed to trace the local use of the Achæan name.

And, first of all, we find it locally used in the North; in that Thessaly, where the name of Hellas came into being, and from whence it extended itself to the Southward; therefore in the closest connection with the Hellic stem.

We are told in the Catalogue, with respect to the division under Achilles, after the names of the districts and places from which they came,

Μυρμιδόνες δὲ καλεῦντο, καὶ Ἕλληνες, καὶ Ἀχαιοί [u].

Now we find throughout the Iliad, that the local or divisional name of this body is unchanging: the troops of Achilles are uniformly denominated Myrmidons. Therefore Homer does not mean that one part were Myrmidons, another Hellenes, another Achæans, but that the three names attached to the whole body, of course in different respects. They were then Myrmidons, whatever the source of that name may have been, by common designation. They were Hellenes, because inhabitants of Hellas, of the territory from whence the influence and range of that name had

[u] Il. ii. 624.

Local uses of the Achæan name. 417

already begun to radiate, more properly and eminently therefore Hellenes, than others who had not so positively acquired the name, though they may have been included in the Πανέλληνες. And manifestly they could only be called 'Αχαιοί, because known to be under leaders of the pure Achæan stock, who were entitled to carry the name in their own right, instead of bearing it only in a derivative sense, and because it had spread all over Greece. Of this peculiar and eminent Achæanism in the Peleid stock, we have, I think, two other signs from the poems: one in the possible meaning of the love of Juno, which we have seen extended to Achilles in an equal degree with Agamemnon; the other in the marriage of Hermione to Neoptolemus, which was founded upon a promise given by Menelaus her father while before Troy. Doubtless the eminent services of Neoptolemus might be the sole ground of this promise: but it may also have had to do with kin, as some special relation, of neighbourhood or otherwise, appears commonly to accompany these matrimonial connections. In conformity with this passage, the name 'Αχαιίδες is applied by Achilles in the Ninth Book to the women of Hellas and Phthia.

It is wonderfully illustrative of the perspicacity and accuracy of Homer, to find that, in this very spot, which he has so especially marked with the Achæan name, it continued to subsist as a local appellation, and to subsist here almost exclusively, all through the historic ages of Greece. On this subject we shall have further occasion to touch.

2. Of the five races who inhabited Crete at the time of the *Troica*, one was Achæan[x]:

[x] Od. xix. 175-7.

ἐν μὲν Ἀχαιοὶ
ἐν δ' Ἐτεοκρῆτες μεγαλήτορες, ἐν δὲ Κύδωνες,
Δωριέες τε τριχάϊκες, δῖοί τε Πελασγοί.

The presence of an Achæan tribe in Crete may have been due to its constant intercourse with Eastern Peloponnesus[y], where the Achæans had for some time been dominant: or to those relations with Thessaly, to which the name of Deucalion in Homer bears probable witness. In any case, the passage clearly establishes the local virtue of the name. It also exhibits to us Achæans as distinct from Dorians, and shows us that there were a variety of branches, known to Homer, of the Hellenic tree. And the enumeration of the Achæan and Pelasgian races with others in this place, compared with the uniform description in the Iliad of the whole force of Idomeneus as Cretan, shows us how careful Homer was to avoid such confusion as the juxtaposition of Achæans and Pelasgians would have caused with reference to the main ethnical division in the Iliad.

3. In the Pylian raid of the Eleventh Book, Nestor carefully distinguishes between the parties, as Epeans, also called Elians, on the one side, and Pylians, also called Achæans, on the other[z]. This raid took place in his early youth, perhaps forty or fifty years before the *Troica*, and within the Achæan epoch. And as he withholds the Achæan name from the other party, they plainly were not Achæan in the limited sense. And yet they were Hellenic: for, among other Hellenic signs, Augeas, the king of the Epeans, was an ἄναξ ἀνδρῶν. Thus again we have Achæan fixed as a subdivision, though probably the principal subdivision, of the Hellenic race.

[y] Il. iii. 232.   [z] Il. xi. 671, 94, 732, 7. xi. 687, 724, 37, 53, 59.

Local uses of the Achæan name.

4. A fourth case, in which the Achæan name appears clearly to have a limited signification, is in a second passage of the Greek Catalogue, where a part of the forces of Diomed are described as those,

οἵ τ' ἔχον Αἰγίνην, Μάσητά τε, κοῦροι Ἀχαιῶν[a].

Although Mases has been taken to be a town, yet its junction here with Ægina perhaps rather points to it as an island. It appears to be admitted that its site is unknown. And an extra-Homeric tradition[b] reports, that the small islands off the Trœzenian coast were called after Pelops. It is impossible not to observe the correspondence between this tradition, and the indirect traditions afforded us by Homer's language in this verse. For in the Catalogue he seems carefully to avoid repeating the general Greek appellatives in connection with the inhabitants of particular places, and to give them local and special names only. It follows irresistibly, that therefore he must be understood here to speak of the distinct race and local name of Achæans: to which race and name would naturally belong any settlers brought by Pelops into Southern Greece.

And, as Homer does not discontinue altogether the application of the Argeian name to the inhabitants of Argolis, he probably in this place means to distinguish Achæans not only from other Greek races, but even from other subjects of Tydeus and of Diomed, who would most properly be called Argeians.

It thus appears, that twice in the Catalogue Homer has occasion to use the Achæan name locally, and in its original or, so to speak, gentile sense. And accordingly he has been careful not to risk confusion by employing it in its wider signification either at the com-

[a] Il. ii. 562.   [b] Pausanias ii. 321.

mencement of the Catalogue or at the close. In both cases he uses the word Δαναοί; the only one of his great appellatives which nowhere takes a local or otherwise varied meaning. When he begins he invites the Muse to tell him, v. 487,

οἵτινες ἡγεμόνες Δαναῶν καὶ κοίρανοι ἦσαν.

So also at the close, v. 760, he sums up in these words,

οὗτοι ἄρ' ἡγεμόνες Δαναῶν καὶ κοίρανοι ἦσαν.

5. As Nestor applies the Achæan name to the inhabitants of Pylos, so from the time of the Pelopid sway it becomes applicable to those of Eastern Peloponnesus generally, in a sense wider than that of Il. ii. 562, but yet narrower than the national one. In Il. iv. 384, and Il. v. 803, those, from among whom Tydeus set out for Thebes, are called 'Αχαιοί. So also in the colloquy with Glaucus, Diomed calls the comrades of his father on that occasion by the same name (Il. vi. 223). He repeats the name in his prayer to Minerva, Il. x. 286, 7; and here he is careful to distinguish them from the Thebans of that epoch, who are Καδμεῖοι (288).

6. In further prosecution of the same subject, we have yet to consider the force of the kindred Homeric word Παναχαιοί.

This is undoubtedly a term that challenges particular notice. No writer is so little wont as Homer to vary his expressions without a reason for it. But since the word 'Αχαιοὶ is used many hundred times as the simple equipollent of Greek, it cannot require the prefix παν to enable it to convey this sense effectually. Therefore to suppose that Παναχαιοὶ means Greeks and nothing more, would render the prefix unmeaning, and I conclude that such cannot be an adequate explanation of its purpose. But if we construe the word as having

The name Παναχαιοί.

a specific reference not only to the aggregate, but to the parts of which it is made up, then the prefix παν becomes abundantly charged with meaning. The word Παναχαιοὶ will in this view mean what we should call 'all classes of the Greeks,' 'the Greeks from the highest to the lowest.'

It is used, in all, eleven times. Of these eleven passages, seven times it appears in the expression ἀριστῆες Παναχαιῶν. Here the preceding word ἀριστῆες at once directs the mind to this notice of the different classes, and receives much force from the distinctive particle παν: as we may judge from the fact that Homer never but once (ἀριστῆες Δαναῶν, Il. xvii. 225) appends the appellative in its simple form to ἀριστῆες. The prefix παν seems to strip the idea of conventionality, and to make it real: the chiefs are the pick and flower of the whole Greek array.

Only in one other passage of the Iliad do we find Παναχαιοί; it is in the peroration of the speech of Ulysses to Achilles[c]:

εἰ δέ τοι 'Ατρείδης μὲν ἀπήχθετο κηρόθι μᾶλλον,
αὐτὸς καὶ τοῦ δῶρα, σὺ δ' ἄλλους περ Παναχαιοὺς
τειρομένους ἐλέαιρε κατὰ στρατόν.

'Still, if you detest (the king) Atrides from your heart ever so much, him and his gifts, yet pity the Greeks throughout the army, now suffering from the highest to the lowest.' The force of the Παναχαιοὶ κατὰ στρατὸν is here very marked.

Lastly, in the Odyssey we find the line thrice repeated,

τῷ κέν οἱ τυμβὸν μὲν ἐποίησαν Παναχαιοί,

and always in the same connection with the death of some select and beloved hero of the army. Its obvious

[c] Il. ix. 300.

sense is, 'all classes of the Greeks would have joined to do him honour, by lending a hand to raise his funeral mound.'

In every one of these cases therefore the word Παναχαιοὶ seems to express the combination of all classes, and thus to point distinctly to the word Ἀχαιοὶ as capable of signifying something less than all classes, namely, one, that is, the ruling class.

The construction thus put upon Παναχαιοὶ is in conformity with Homer's usual mode of employing such words as the adjective πᾶς and the preposition σὺν in composition. We have previously seen the intensive force of πᾶς in πᾶν Ἄργος and Πανέλληνες. And πᾶς itself receives additional power from σύν. As in Il. i., where Achilles, having just before reminded Calchas of his office as Seer to the Δαναοὶ, proceeds to assure him that no one of the Greeks shall hurt him for doing his duty, it is now no one, not of the Δαναοὶ merely, but of the σύμπαντες Δαναοί; no, not even if he name Agamemnon himself as the guilty person[d].

It is hardly necessary to point out how accurately all this coincides with the general results to which we have been already led. According to these, the bulk of the Greeks were a Pelasgian population, under the sway of ruling tribes and families, belonging to another race; among which the most powerful were those belonging to the Achæan stock; and whose Argeian name was etymologically, and perhaps practically, a sort of substitute for the older Pelasgian one.

Nor is there difficulty in conceiving how, if the Achæans became the dominant race in the most important parts of Greece, they might, without constituting a numerical majority, give their name to the mass

[d] Il. i. 85–91.

of the people, and to the country itself, as Britain and Britons became England and English from the Angles, or as Lombardy took its name from the Lombards, and, unhappily, European Turkey, once the civil head of Christendom, from the Turks.

It has been customary to speak of the question whether Homer was an Æolian Greek: to give the Æolian name to the forms of the Greek language prevailing in his time: and to describe the Achæans as a branch of the Æolians. With certain exceptions, says Strabo[e], the Æolian name still prevails outside the Isthmus; and it also covered the Peloponnesus, till a mixture took place. The Ionians from Attica had occupied Ægialus; and when the Heraclids, with the Dorians, became masters of many Peloponnesian cities, the Ionians were expelled in their turn ὑπὸ 'Αχαιῶν, Αἰολικοῦ ἔθνους, after which two ἔθνη only remained in Peloponnesus, the Æolian and the Dorian.

Again, as respects the *digamma*, Heyne[f] most justly observes that it may much more justly be called Pelasgic than Æolic; since the Æolians, as far as we know, only retained it, after having found it in use with the Pelasgi. But in general, to those who ground their judgments on the Homeric text, the whole view of the relation of Achæans and Æolians, as it is commonly given, will appear a false one. In the first place the Æolians as a nation or tribe are wholly post-Homeric: unless we are bold enough to find some modification of their name in the Αἰτωλοί. The Æolid families, indeed, of Homer have evidently a great position, which we shall further discuss[g]: but they simply fall for the time under the general name of Achæans, as much as any

[e] B. viii. c. 1. p. 333. [f] Hom. Il. vol. vii. p. 711.
[g] See inf. sect. ix.

other families, and more than families like the Æacidæ, who were in close political relations with a race bearing a designation of its own, namely, the Myrmidons. This nowhere appears to have been the case with the Æolians. On the contrary, the Neleids, though they were of illegitimate birth, may perhaps be considered as belonging to the Æolidæ; but their subjects actually bore the name of Achæans, besides their territorial name of Pylians[h]. With respect to the epoch of the *Troica*, instead of calling the Achæans an Æolic race, it would be more reasonable to call the Æolids (as there was nothing more extensive than a patronymic connected with that name) Achæan houses. I do not however mean that they were properly such: for the Æolid name appears in Southern Greece before the Achæan, and was probably an older branch from the same trunk.

The subsequent prevalence of the Æolian as compared with the Achæan name, (the Hellenic, however, overlying and soon absorbing both,) appears to point to one of two suppositions. Either there was an original Æolian tribe, which has escaped notice altogether in Homer, as the Dorians have all but escaped it: or else, and more probably, it may have happened that part at least of these Æolian houses held their ground in Greece, while the Achæan name, which had been elevated by the political predominance of the Pelopid sovereigns, collapsed upon the loss of that predominance. It was to be expected that the name should share in the downfall of the race, when the Heraclid and Dorian invasion expelled the bearers of it from the seat of their power, and reduced them first to be fugitives, and then to settle in a mere strip of the Pelo-

[h] Sup. p. 352.

ponnesus; a single region of narrow scope, and, as is remarked by Polybius[i] after many centuries, of small weight and influence, which from them was called Achæa. The fact that the Dorian name is all but unknown to Homer, while the Achæan one is at its zenith, not only heroically, as in the Iliad, but in the every day familiar use of Ithaca throughout the Odyssey, is to me one of several strong presumptions, not countervailed by any evidence of equal strength, that Homer could not have lived to see that great revolution, which so completely effaced the ethnical landmarks, and altered the condition, of Southern Greece.

There is certainly a striking analogy between the relation of the Æolid houses named in Homer to the afterwards prevalent and powerful Æolian race, and that of the Heraclid families, also named by him, to the Dorian race, which in like manner grew from obscurity in the Homeric period to such great after-celebrity. Hercules himself appears before us in the ancient legend as the great Dorian hero, 'everywhere paving the road for his people and their worship, and protecting them from other races[k].' The only Heraclids mentioned nominally by Homer are Tlepolemus, Pheidippus, Antiphus; and there are others without names specified[l]: none of these, or of the Greeks of the expedition, are called Dorians, while, again, none of the Heraclids of Homer are called by the Achæan or Æolid names. They may have been Dorian houses, like the Æolid houses; and the name may have become tribal afterwards, when they rose to power. The tradition of the reception of certain Heraclids in Attica appears to have been recognised by

[i] Polyb. b. ii. c. 38.   [k] Müller, Dorians, ii. 11. 6.
[l] Il. ii. 653. 665. 678. v. 628.

the Lacedæmonians in the historic ages[m], and in the supposition of a friendship thus established, we may perhaps find the true explanation of the Decelean privilege mentioned by Herodotus[n].

In arranging chronologically the **Danaan, Argeian,** and **Achæan** names of Homer, we give the first place to Danaan, and the next to Argeian, so as to bring the Danaans nearest to the Pelasgi. But the real meaning of this is simply that the three names were suggested to Homer by three periods of Greek history, which stand in the order given to the names. If, however, instead of tracing the purpose of the Poet, we are to look for ethnical history, then we must state that the Danaan name does not denote a change of race, but it is a mere foreign affix to the closing portion of the Pelasgian period. Nor does the Argeian name, if we suppose it to have been a sort of translation or reconstruction of the Pelasgian, directly indicate the Hellenic infusion; but the mere fact of its substitution for a preceding appellation appears to presuppose a cause. Homer, indeed, gives us no Greek stories of the Danaid period, so that we do not certainly know that he might not have described the Greeks of that period also as Argeian. All we can say positively is, that his use of the Argeian name *de facto* begins with the epoch of the first Hellenic throne in Greece, that of the Perseids. I hope to show that the Achæan name and that of Perseus belong in truth to the same stock and origin[o]: but it is with the Pelopids only that the Achæan name appears, and it denotes the second stage of the Hellenic preponderance, as the Argeian name marks the first, and the Dorian the third. The first, or Argeian, stage belongs partly, as I believe, to the house of Perseus, but

[m] Müller ii. 11. 10.   [n] Sup. p. 88.   [o] Inf. sect. x.

partly, as is clear from the Homeric text, to the houses descended from Æolus.

Æolus himself is nowhere mentioned in Homer. The oldest Αἰολίδαι given to us as such are Sisyphus and Cretheus. The patronymic does not of itself enable us to determine whether these were sons of Æolus, or were more remotely descended from him. But indirectly we may perhaps be enabled to fix his date, as follows:

1. Bellerophon the grandson of Sisyphus[p], is called by the contemporary Lycian king, the offspring of the deity, that is, of Jupiter:

γίγνωσκε θεοῦ γόνον ἠῢν ἐόντα[q].

The meaning of this can only be that the person, whom Homer has indicated as the founder of the race, namely Æolus, was a reputed son of Jupiter.

2. In the Νεκυΐα of the Eleventh Odyssey we are introduced to Tyro, the daughter of Salmoneus, and the wife of Cretheus[r]. She is decorated with the epithet εὐπατέρεια, never given elsewhere by Homer except to Helen, and apparently an equivalent with him for Διὸς ἐκγεγαυῖα.

It is by no means unlikely, I would venture to suggest, that a similar force may lie in the epithet Salmoneus, who is here called ἀμύμων. That epithet is indeed sometimes applied on the ground of personal character. But Homer also gives it to the villain Ægisthus, which appears quite inexplicable except on the ground of the divine descent of the Pelopids[s]. The later tradition has loaded Salmoneus with the crime of audacious profanity: and it has also, beginning with Hesiod[t], made him a son of Æolus. The

[p] Il. vi. 154, 5.   [q] Ibid. 191.   [r] Od. xi. 235-7.
[s] Inf. sect. ix.   [t] Fragm. xxviii.

word ἀμύμων, combined with the εὐπατέρεια of Tyro, leaves little room for doubt that perhaps both, and certainly the latter of these representations are agreeable to the sense of Homer. If so, then Tyro was a granddaughter of Æolus; and we can at once fix his date from Homer, as follows:

1. Æolus.
2. Salmoneus, Od. xi. 235-7.
3. Tyro = Cretheus, ibid.
4. Pheres, Od. xi. 259.
5. Admetus, Il. ii. 711-15, 763.
6. Eumelus, ibid. and Od. iv. 798.

From which last cited passage I set down Eumelus as the contemporary of his brother-in-law Ulysses, and half a generation senior to the standard age of the war.

We have also the collateral line of Sisyphus from Æolus as follows: 1. Sisyphus; 2. Glaucus (1); 3. Bellerophon; 4. Hippolochus; 5. Glaucus (2), contemporary with the war[u]. According to this table Sisyphus might be either the son or the grandson of Æolus.

And again, Cretheus, who like Sisyphus is Αἰολίδης, may have been either the uncle or the cousin of his wife Tyro. The Fragment of Hesiod would make both him and Sisyphus sons of Æolus, and therefore uncles to Tyro.

These genealogies are in perfect keeping with what Homer tells us of the Neleid line. Tyro, he says, fell in love with Enipeus. In the likeness of that river, Neptune had access to her, and she bore to him two sons, Pelias and Neleus. Neleus is the father of Nestor: and Nestor stands one generation senior to Eumelus; for he was in his third tri-decadal period[x],

[u] Il. vi. 154, 197, 206.   [x] Il. i. 250.

if the expression may be allowed, during the action of the Iliad. Thus we have (as before), 3. Tyro; 4. Neleus; 5. Nestor; 6. Nestor. The maternal genealogy of Eumelus brings us exactly to the same point: for Alcestis, the daughter of Pelias, was married to his father Admetus[y].

Thus the Æolid genealogies are laid down by Homer with great clearness, except as to the first interval, and with a singular self-consistency. Perseus[z], as we have seen, belongs to the fifth generation before the war. This is nearly the same with Sisyphus, and with Cretheus: and we are thus enabled to determine with tolerable certainty the epoch of the first Hellenic infusion into Greece. It precedes the arrival of Portheus in Ætolia by one generation, and that of Pelops by two.

Of Sisyphus we know from Homer, that he lived at an Ephyre on or near the Isthmus of Corinth. It is not so clear whether Cretheus ever came into the Peloponnesus. There is an Enipeus of Elis: but there is also one[a] of Thessaly, which was doubtless its original. The name, however, of the Thessalian stream appears to have been written Eniseus. Nitzsch[b] determines, on insufficient grounds as far as I can judge, that the passage of Od. xi. cannot mean the Enipeus of Pisatis. I can find no conclusive evidence either way: but Sisyphus was certainly in Southern Greece at or before this time, so that we need not wonder if Cretheus, another Æolid, was there also. His reputed son Neleus founded, without doubt, the kingdom of Pylos. Post-Homeric tradition places even Salmoneus, the father of Tyro, in Elis.

[y] Il. ii. 714.   [z] Sup. p. 364.   [a] Thuc. iv. 78.
[b] On Od. iii. 4.

We have now before us an outline of the first entrance of Hellic elements into Greece, south of Thessaly. It seems to have been effected by five families;

1. The house of Perseus.
2. That of Sisyphus.
3. The illegitimate line of Cretheus, or the Neleids.
4. Probably the legitimate line of Salmoneus, represented in Augeas.
5. Next to these will come Portheus, the head of the Œneidæ in Ætolia: and only then follows the great house of the Pelopids, not alone, but in conjunction with a race, to whose history we now must turn.

Of the Danaid and Perseid princes we have no reason to suppose, that they enjoyed the extended power which was wielded by Agamemnon. Not only would they appear to have been circumscribed, latterly at least, by the Minoan empire founded in Crete, but Homer gives us no intimation that their dominion at any time included the possession of a supremacy over a number of subordinate princes beyond their own immediate borders, or reached beyond the territory which may be generally described as the Eastern Peloponnesus.

A direct inference bearing on this subject may be obtained from the passage concerning the sceptre of Agamemnon[c]: for the Pelopids do not succeed to that of Eurystheus and the Perseids, but they hold from Jupiter: which seems to imply that they acquired much more, than had been under the sway of their predecessors. Probably therefore we shall do well to conclude that Eurystheus, for example, had a limited realm, and that by land only: Agamemnon, a certain supremacy by land and sea, within the range of which

[c] Il. ii. 101–8.

the old Minoan empire had now fallen. Still the kingdom of Eurystheus was probably in its own day the greatest, and was also probably the oldest, of all properly Hellenic kingdoms.

If, then, neither of the prior dynasties of Danaus and Perseus reigned over all Greece, it is unlikely that either of them could give a name to the whole nation: though they might give a name to the part of the country which, having in their time been particularly famous and powerful, became under the Pelopids a metropolis, supreme throughout the rest of the country; and whose people then not only took the name of 'Αχαιοὶ for itself, but extended it over the whole of Greece.

It is thus more than probable that the scope of the name Danai, (if we are to assume that it was then a name in actual use,) under the Danaids, and of the name 'Αργεῖοι under the Perseids, was local, and confined in the main to Eastern Peloponnesus, where those princes ruled; with the addition of any other parts of the country, over which they might for the time have extended their power. And if so, then we have to suppose that Homer, having received the traditions of the Danaan and Argeian princes as having been at the head in their own time of Greek history or legend, gave to the nation by way of a poetical name, but of a poetical name only, the appellation which their subjects respectively had borne, and which had never before been, and never became by any other title than his poetical authority, applicable to all the Greeks.

The Achæan name, on the other hand, differs from these, first, in denoting the extension of a particular race, though not over the whole country, yet through very many of its parts, and secondly, in the fact that the ruling house of those who bore the name enjoyed a real political supremacy over both the continent and the islands. So that it became the most legitimate exponent of Greek nationality, until it had lost both its extension and its power; the one by compression of its principal tribes into a narrow space: the other by the transfer of its political prerogatives to the great Dorian family of the Spartan kings, after the conquest of the Heraclidæ.

When the Achæans had ceased to predominate, there could be no reason why their name should remain stamped upon their brethren, who boasted of the same descent, and who had attained to greater force.

As in the Homeric times, while the Achæans were the leaders of Greece, they might claim to represent the whole Hellenic stock, so, when the Dorians had dethroned them and occupied the seat of power, when the Æolian name was widely diffused, and, again, when Athens with its mixed race became great, and claimed, along with its vaunts of antiquity and continuity, to pass over, as Herodotus says, to the Hellenic class, but without an Achæan descent, then the Achæan name could no longer adequately represent the title to nationality, and the various races naturally fell back on the designation which gave no exclusive right or preeminence to any of them, and which they were all entitled to enjoy in common. They apparently however chose to be connected with the rich plains of Thessaly, where they first learned civilization, and organized their collective or national life, rather than with the rude and coarse manners of their more remote ancestors in the hills. They were therefore not Helli, but Hellenes.

This may be considered as the *rationale* of the common and palpably manufactured tradition respecting

Hellen and his family, of which we have the earliest form in Hesiod.

Our conclusions respecting the names by which Homer describes the inhabitants of Greece may now be summed up as follows:

1. We set out from the point at which Greece is, probably for the first time, settled by a race given to tillage and pacific habits, under the general name of Pelasgians, with subdivision under minor names of particular tribes, or partially and locally intermixed with fragments of other races.

2. A dynasty of foreign origin, in a portion of Greece which then became, and ever after continued to be most famous, leads the march of events; and, apparently without displacing the Pelasgians themselves, yet seems to have displaced, in a certain quarter, the Pelasgic by the Danaan name; at any rate, it attains to such celebrity, that its history, in the eye of Homer, fills the whole breadth of its own epoch, and its name stands in after time, poetically at least, for a national title.

3. An Hellenic dynasty of Perseids, belonging to the Greek Peninsula, follows this dynasty; and, effacing the trace of foreign rule, governs its subjects under the Argeian or Argive name; which, without reviving the title of the Pelasgi, a word now becoming or become subordinate, yet like that title is founded on the physical character of the regions in which the population was settled, and upon the employments suited thereto.

4. Next appears upon the scene the Achæan name, which bears no mark of relationship to the soil, or to any particular employment, or to any particular eponymist, but appears to be the designation of a race, not indeed foreign, yet new to the Peloponnesus.

5. A warlike and highly gifted race gradually per-

vade different parts of Greece under this name: the Pelopids, its ruling family, possessing themselves of the throne of the Perseids, attain, perhaps through the extended sympathy of Achæan blood, to a national supremacy. The Achæans are, in fact, become the Greeks of the Troic age. They include Æolids and Æacids, Argives, Bœotians, Ætolians, Epeans, Abantes, Dorians, Arcadians, Ionians, and all the other local tribes, as well as the mass of old Pelasgians, who constitute the working population (so to speak) of the country; some of them by virtue of blood, and the rest by that political union, in which the Achæans had an undisputed ascendancy.

6. All the characteristics of this race, social and religious, and its close geographical proximity to, if not indeed its identity with, the first-named or Myrmidon Hellenes of Homer, appear to derive it from the North, to dissociate it from the Pelasgic, and to unite it with the Hellic stock.

7. Time passes on; we lose the guiding hand of Homer; but universal tradition assures us that the Dorians, emerging, like those who had preceded them, from the cradle of the nation, lead another and the last great Hellenic migration southward; the Pelopids are driven from the throne of that which may be termed the metropolitan region of Greece; they migrate to an inferior seat, with their followers, and become the obscure heads of a secondary State: and the name of Hellenes, belonging to all the great Greek tribes in common, whether of Achæan, Æolid, or Dorian blood or connection, becomes the grand historical designation of the nation at large.

8. After perhaps eight hundred years of fame and freedom for Hellas, the iron hand of Roman power descends upon her at a time when the old Achæan

name has revived by means of a democratic confederacy, and has once more overspread[e] the Peloponnesus. From this time, Hellas takes her place in history only as a minor portion of the Roman empire, even while, by an inward process, she is asserting her intellectual supremacy[f], and moulding the literature and philosophy of her conquerors. But to them politically she is no more than an appendage of the *Magna Græcia*, whose glory it is to be a part of imperial Italy, and whose name the land of Homer's song must now assume in virtue of a double relationship; the first, that of their common social base, the old Pelasgi, of whom the Greeks (Γραϊκοὶ) were probably a part; and the second, that of a more recent colonization. Thus the Graic or Greek name, having existed, but never having emerged to what may be called visibility in Hellas, travels round to it again by the route of Italy, and finally becomes predominant in this its earliest seat.

Of this intermixture and succession of names dependent on the fusion of races, and on political supremacy, we have sufficient example in our own island. It has been inhabited by Britons, Romans, Angles, Saxons, Jutes, Danes, and Normans. All came more or less as conquerors, one following upon the other. But two names only have left their mark, Britons and Angles: all the others, including the last or Norman conquerors, are submerged. So it has been with the succession of Pelasgians, Achæans, Hellenes, Greeks. Each of these names historically superseded the one before it. Apart from them, by the high privilege of Poetry, stand their names in another combination: the Iliad

[e] Polyb. ii. c. 38.
[f] Hor. Ep. II. i. 156. *Græcia capta ferum victorem cepit.*

and Odyssey shew us Danaans, Argeians, and Achæans, as in the main synonymous before Troy: yet each with its own leaning, which makes Δαναοὶ most properly and by preference 'the soldiery,' Ἀργεῖοι, 'the masses,' and Ἀχαιοὶ, 'the chiefs.'

It still remains to observe the immediately subsequent literary history of these three great appellatives, which the *fiat* of Homer made so famous.

Hesiod and the minor Greek poets afford us the only satisfactory illustration of actual usage, because the tragedians may probably have sought, in treating heroic subjects, to employ the nomenclature of the heroic age. The other poets spoke, of course, according to their own respective ages.

In Hesiod we do not find Δαναοὶ at all: Ἀργεῖος only in the singular for Juno: Ἀχαιοὶ is once used for the Greeks collectively, in a retrospective passage referring to the assembly at Aulis[g]. He uses Πανέλληνες[h] in the same poem with the same sense. An important passage of Strabo[i] testifies, that both Hesiod and Archilochus were acquainted with the use of the names Ἕλληνες and Πανέλληνες for the Greeks at large; and refers to works of theirs, now lost, by way of example as to the latter term. Both Ἑλλάς and Ἕλληνες are freely used in Simonides, who also has Ἀργεῖοι for the Argives only. And generally these old writers, coming next after Hesiod, knew nothing of the use of Ἀργεῖοι, or even of Ἀχαιοὶ, for the whole nation, while the word Δαναοὶ is not found in them at all.

This is strongly confirmatory, as it appears to me, of the propositions I have endeavoured to establish.

Among the tragedians the name Ἀχαιὸς, with its

---

[g] Ἔργα, ii. 269.   [h] Ibid. ii. 146.
[i] Strabo, viii. 6. p. 370.

Its value as primitive history. 437

derivatives, used to some extent by Æschylus, progressively declines: the Danaan name holds its ground rather better, and 'Αργεῖος better still; though all are eclipsed by the great historical name of Hellenes, which probably had enjoyed an undisputed prevalence from the time of the Dorian conquest. Thus, for poetical use, dealing with the events and characters of the heroic age, they properly fall back upon the names which Homer employed.

From these successions of name, whether the particular appellation be founded upon lineage or upon physical incidents, it is not unreasonable to hold that we may draw the outlines of a primitive history, at least with more confidence and satisfaction than by efforts to compound and piece together the miscellaneous and promiscuous traditions of many ages and places, set wide apart from one another; in respect to which, even where we have not to lament the gnawing power of Time, we, at least, know that the faculties both of exaggeration and of invention, stimulated by vanity, rivalry, and self-interest in many other forms, have been at work. It is better to deal with slighter relics, of which we know the *bona fides*, than with an abundance of such as have been falsified. Besides, when we have effectually exhausted the power of the first, we may much more profitably use the subsidiary lights which the second will afford us. And the tendency of an attempt to invest the Homeric text with an unequivocal supremacy, is to substitute for complete and symmetrical systems, in which the hewn stone and the trash are not distinguishable one from another, very slight and partial indeed, but yet authoritative fragments and outlines, all the intervals of which are filled up by avowed conjecture. This conjecture is without a pretence to authority properly so called, but it is, at any rate, both kept visibly apart from what is authoritative, and likewise founded upon the suggestions which even fragmentary testimony, when genuine and near the source, is well qualified to make.

And the succession of names is in effect of itself almost a political history. For the names of nations are not arbitrarily changed, though such things have been done to particular cities within the dominion of particular states. The names of races, especially of races disposed, like the Greeks, to knit themselves closely with the past, are cherished as a material portion of their patrimony. When they alter, it is for some great and commanding political reason. Such as, for example, if some tribe or family, previously not advanced beyond its fellows, in some great national exigency becomes invested with the responsibility of acting for the whole body, and thus grows to be as well its representative and organ in all external relations, as also the representative of its inward life: or when some conquering dynasty and host have by the strong hand entered in upon prior occupants of the soil, and, reducing them to dependence or to servitude more or less qualified, or narrowing the circle of their possessions, have taken into their own custody, together with the best lands of the country, the whole range of public affairs, and have imposed laws upon the vanquished, and imparted to them manners. In this case, the different elements are welded into a political unity, by a power proceeding from that race which among them has possessed the greater physical and martial force. But unless there be more than the merely convulsive effort of conquest, unless deep roots be struck into the soil, and sharper furrows drawn upon it than the spear alone can carve, or than the wave of a mere deluge traces, unless, in a word, there be a predominant organizing faculty, the effect will not be permanent; and the crude mass of mere strength will sink down amid the surrounding milder, but more enduring and more prevailing impulses. In some instances it has been so: the body, which has been stronger in the hand, has proved weaker in the intellectual and moral, that is to say, the enduring, elements of power. The undying yet daily influences and sympathies of peace wear down the convulsive vibrations, which the shock of war and conquest have communicated to the social fabric., Victory must end in possession, like toil in sleep. Possession implies the dispersion of the conquerors, and, in such cases as these, their free intermixture with the vanquished. Ties of neighbourhood, of commerce, of marriage, ties belonging to all the transactions of life, are gradually multiplied between the new comers and the old; and by a gentle process, experience and opinion gradually decide, not imperiously in the spirit of party, but insensibly for the benefit of all, what laws, what manners, what language [k], what religion shall predominate. The fate of the name follows that of the institutions and habits with which it was connected; and the old designation prevails ultimately over the new, or the new over the old, in proportion as the older inhabitants have contributed a larger or a smaller share towards the common national life resulting from the combination; in proportion as the newly arrived receive more of impression than they impart, or impart more than they receive.

[k] The mode of this process, with reference to language, is beautifully exhibited for the case of Spain, in Ticknor's Spanish Literature, Appendix A. (vol. iii.)

SECT. IX.

On the Homeric title ἄναξ ἀνδρῶν.

BOTH in modern society, and in the forms of modern language, the distinction is a familiar one, which separates between descriptive affixes or epithets, and titles properly so called.

A descriptive affix, be it substantive, like Δαναοὶ αἰχμηταὶ, or adjective, like Δαναοὶ φιλοπτόλεμοι, describes a quality, and challenges from the reader, like any other phrase conveying an idea, assent to the justice of its description. These descriptive affixes have a tendency, from repeated use, to grow into *formulæ*, and then at length they approximate to the nature of titles.

But a title is quite a different thing from a descriptive affix. A title is the current coin of language, which is intended to pass from mouth to mouth without examination. It is like a pronoun, having for its office simply to indicate, or to stand for, a particular person. It is the index of a rank or office, a thing determinate in its nature, like an unit of number: and it has no relation, when once fixed as a title, to personal character, though in its origin it may have been founded on the real or presumed existence of personal qualities. Like a descriptive affix, a title may be either adjective, as 'most noble,' or substantive, as 'marquis.'

Titles evidently presume a certain progress in the organization of political society; while descriptive epithets must be used, in order to meet the purposes of human speech, even in its first stages.

This degree of progress must have been attained in the time of Homer; for the use of titles in the poems, as well as of descriptive epithets, can be clearly made out.

Among the descriptive epithets of Homer we find, of substantives, ἡγεμόνες, ἀριστῆες, and also βασιλεῖς, ἀοιδοί. Of adjectives, applied to classes, σκηπτοῦχοι (βασιλῆες), ὑπερμενέες (βασιλῆες), θεῖοι (ἀοιδοί): and applied to persons, ἐχέφρων Πηνελόπεια, Τηλέμαχος πεπνυμένος, πολύμητις Ὀδυσσεύς: and many more.

In modern phraseology, duke, earl, baron, knight, esquire, are titles: nobles, clergy, freeholders, burgesses, are descriptive phrases. Of a descriptive epithet or affix which has grown to be a title, we may find instances among those just cited; knight (*knecht*) meant originally a servant, then a person performing particular service to the king; and esquire (*scudiero, écuyer*) meant a person who bore the arms of a knight, particularly his shield. In process of time these became titles. Again, words may hang doubtfully upon the confine between title and epithet; as the much criticised expressions of the English Common Prayer Book, '(our) most religious and gracious (king).'

We find in Homer that the word βασιλεύς, a king, had already begun to pass from the function of a mere descriptive word towards that of a title; for, though rarely, he attaches it to the names of individuals, besides freely using it without them; and it is an usual note of titles properly so called, that they can, even if substantives, either be combined with the name of the person, or, in addressing them, substituted for it. In the Iliad we find Ἀλεξάνδρῳ βασιλῆι, and in the Odyssey Ἔχετον βασιλῆα. Again, we find βασίλεια used in the Odyssey in the vocative[a], which in like manner marks it as a title.

[a] Od. iv. 697.

II. *Ethnology.*

The word ἄναξ, again, in Homer, which must on no account be confounded with βασιλεύς[b], is commonly a descriptive epithet, nearly equivalent to our word *lord*, and, like it, having an extraordinary elasticity of sense; for as a person may now be lord, so he might then be ἄναξ, of a kingdom, a people, a field, a mine, a slave, a horse, or a dog. Instances are countless. Sometimes the meaning is lord, or master, relatively to a particular object, as of the horses of Nestor,

οἱ δὲ ἄνακτος ὑποδδείσαντες ὁμοκλήν......[c]

Sometimes it means in the abstract a class of persons,

οἷοί τε ἀνάκτων παῖδες ἔασιν[d]·

where the ἀνάκτων παῖδες nearly corresponds with our 'children of the higher orders,' i.e. the masters of slaves.

On the other hand, in reference to the immortals, ἄναξ is sometimes a title: as in Il. xvi. 233,

Ζεῦ ἄνα, Δωδώναιε, Πελασγικέ.

There are, however, in Homer various words which are undoubtedly and uniformly titular. Such are in particular the adjectives Διοτρεφής and Διογενής, which are very nearly equivalent in power to the phrase 'Royal Highness' of the present day. They commonly accompany the name of the individual, or of the class, to which they belong: and they are confined, with one single exception, in the Iliad, to persons of the highest known rank, that of βασιλεύς or king. The exception is Phœnix, who is in one place addressed by Achilles

---

[b] This caution is not needless, as the error is a common one. Damm, indeed, most strangely says, ἄναξ *ex multo augustius nomen quam* βασιλεύς (in voc. ἄναξ). The English translators, Chapman, Pope, Cowper, and others, render ἄναξ ἀνδρῶν, king of men. Voss, with his usual precision, though probably without a very specific meaning, translates it, '*der herrscher des volks.*'

[c] Il. xxiii. 417.

[d] Od. xiii. 223.

Examples of titles.   443

as γέραιε Διοτρεφές. But Achilles says this χαριζόμενος, when petting and coaxing the old man, and therefore the instance does not destroy the force of the general rule.

In one place we have ὁ Διογενὴς[e] used for Achilles in the third person without his name: which still more strikingly marks the word as a title. Also Διοτρεφὴς is not unfrequently used in the vocative, without, as well as with, the name of the person to whom it is addressed. It may possibly be worth notice, that these words, Διοτρεφὴς and Διογενὴς, are never applied to Agamemnon, as if they had, again like the phrase 'Royal Highness,' a limit upwards as well as downwards, and were not applicable to the supreme head of the nation. There is indeed one passage where Agamemnon is addressed as Διοτρεφὴς, but it is in the universally suspected[f] νεκυΐα of the Twenty-fourth Odyssey. Plainly this fact cannot be referred to metrical considerations, even as to Διοτρεφὴς, because either in the genitive, or in the vocative, it would easily have been made available: especially in the latter inflexion, for Agamemnon is addressed vocatively some five and twenty times in the poems. I admit that Ulysses may allude to him in the line,

θυμὸς δὲ μέγας ἐστὶ Διοτρεφέος βασιλῆος[g].

But the phrase here is more abstract than personal: it is perhaps as we should say, 'our royal master.'

The word βασιλεὺς may have borne originally a merely descriptive character. But it has only partial traces of that character still adhering to it, as it is used in the Iliad. The chief note of such a sense, that I can find, is, that it is used in the comparative and superlative to distinguish the Pelopid house from the other kings.

[e] Il. xx. 17.   [f] V. 121.   [g] Il. ii. 196.

Agamemnon is βασιλεύτατος, Il. ix. 69, and Menelaus is evidently intended in the βασιλεύτερος of Il. x. 239; where Diomed is bidden to choose the best man, irrespectively of rank, and not to tie himself to the βασιλεύτερος.

As the Odyssey represents a period of political disorganization, brought about by the long absence of the chiefs, it is not surprising that we find the word βασιλεύς, and its proper epithet Διοτρεφής, used in this poem with greater laxity. The βασιλῆες and the Διοτρεφεῖς[h], are here not the kings but the aristocracy of Scheria, and of the dominions of Ulysses: and it is a compliment paid to Telemachus by Theoclymenus, when he says[i],

ὑμετέρου δ' οὐκ ἔστι γένος βασιλεύτερον ἄλλο
ἐν δήμῳ Ἰθάκης.

Yet even here the special and official sense of βασιλεύς remains: no one is ever called individually a βασιλεύς unless he is on the throne, though Antinous is said to resemble one of the king-class,

βασιλῆϊ γὰρ ἀνδρὶ ἔοικας[k].

And the same Antinous sarcastically expresses his hope, that Jupiter will not make Telemachus βασιλεύς in Ithaca, notwithstanding his right of succession by birth[l]. If βασιλεύς only indicated a certain station, Telemachus without doubt was βασιλεύς already.

The sense proper to it in Homer is that in which, for some thousands of years, it appears to have maintained a world-wide celebrity.

And now as respects the constructions which have been put upon the phrase ἄναξ ἀνδρῶν. It is not noticed by Heyne or by Crusius. Of the translators I

---

[h] Od. i. 394.　　　[i] Od. xv. 533.　　　[k] Od. xvii. 416.
[l] Od. i. 386; cf. 401.

have already spoken. As regards the Lexicographers, Scott and Liddell say 'Agamemnon *as general-in-chief* is specially ἄναξ ἀνδρῶν, while Orsilochos is called ἄναξ ἄνδρεσσιν in Il. v. 546;' but the phrase is πολέεσσ' ἄνδρεσσιν ἄνακτα, which I take to be simply equivalent to ἀνάσσοντα, and to have no relation to a phrase or *formula*.

Damm[m] says it indicates supreme dignity united with military command.

Again; Mure[n] remarks, that in common with ποιμὴν λαῶν and κρείων, 'it denotes the office of any king or chieftain, but more particularly that of a supreme ruler or commander.'

That these explanations are entirely beside the mark, I am convinced after a somewhat minute consideration.

In answer to Damm, I would observe that the phrase was applied to Æneas, who was a commander, but not a sovereign: it was applied to Anchises, who was a sovereign, but not a commander; it was applied to Eumelus, who was neither a sovereign, nor a warrior of any note, and who commanded no more than eleven ships.

It does not then depend upon the highest degree either of military or of civil elevation.

Nor does it in all cases attach to divine descent, even though that descent be from Jupiter; nor even if it be immediate or next to immediate: as among the living, Sarpedon the son of Jupiter has it not, neither has Polypœtes his grandson (Il. ii. 740). So, among the dead, it is not given either to Hercules or to Rhadamanthus[o], sons of Jupiter. If, as is probable, reputed extraction from Jupiter in all cases attached

[m] In voc. ἄναξ.   [n] Lit. Greece, vol. ii. p. 78.   [o] Il. xiv. 322.

II. *Ethnology.*

to it, it was a remote and not a near extraction, and thus the title was the ornament of an antique lineage; certainly divine descent was not the immediate qualification for the particular dignity.

I do not dispute, that an idea of divine descent attaches generally and immediately to sovereigns as such, at least in the Iliad. But this is represented by the words Διοτρεφὴς and Διογενὴς, as they bear witness by their etymology, and not by ἄναξ ἀνδρῶν. Indeed we seem to find the word Διοτρεφὴς used for heaven-born, without reference to political power, in that line of the Odyssey (v. 378), where Neptune applies it to the Phæacians:

εἰσόκεν ἀνθρώποισι Διοτρεφέεσσι μιγείης.

But of those Homeric titles which are specifically Greek, by far the most remarkable is the title of ἄναξ ἀνδρῶν.

It is used by the Poet fifty-two times: fifty times in the Iliad, twice only in the Odyssey.

It is applied forty-six times to Agamemnon, and six times to five other persons, once for each in four cases, and twice in one. The persons are,

Eumelus, a living Greek.

Augeias, } dead Greeks.
Euphetes, }

Anchises, } living Trojans.
Æneas, }

It appears and perishes with Homer, not being found in the writings of any other Greek author.

It is never used in any of the cases, except the nominative: never separated from the proper name of the person to whom it is applied, except once (Il. i. 7), and then only by the particle τε: it always precedes the name except in that single passage: it always ends with the first half of the fifth foot of the verse, except in that same passage: and again, the word ἄναξ is never separated from the word ἀνδρῶν, except once in the Odyssey by the word δέ.

It is applied to no person whose name does not begin with a vowel, and to no person whose name is not of the metrical value necessary to enable it to form the last foot and a half of the hexameter: as, Agamemnon, of two short syllables and two long ones; Euphetes, three long ones; Eumelus, two long and one short. Circumstances, these last, which, if they stood alone, would raise a presumption that the use of it was determined by metrical considerations only.

That metrical considerations had some degree of influence on the use of phrases in Homer, we may sufficiently judge, by observing that while Homer uses the name of Achæans four times for that of Argeians once, he uses the forms Ἀχαίοισι and Ἀχαίοισιν but twelve times, whereas he uses Ἀργείοισι and Ἀργείοισιν more than sixty times.

But we may observe that no metrical considerations could have prevented Homer from applying the phrase to Diomedes, Polypœtes, or others, whose names differ from that of Agamemnon only in having a consonant at the beginning of them: and yet he has not done this: the names of all his six ἄνακτες ἀνδρῶν begin with a vowel. Thus as he restrains himself beyond what metre requires, he may have had some reason other than metre to govern his use of the title.

The question is, whether there are, evidently or probably, other conditions of substance, which, besides these of sound, meet in the persons designated by the title, and which enable us to trace and fix its purport?

With reference to Mure's explanation I observe,

that it does not appear to take account of the difference between descriptive words in general, and titles, as applicable to Homer; but rather to assume that the Homeric phrases are simply of the former class.

It is plain that the word κρείων is a term of that class only: which, *pro tanto*, is indicated by its relationship to the established and ordinary epithet of comparison κρείσσων. It clearly describes the class of those, who bore single-handed rule, in the address to Jupiter, ὕπατε κρειόντων[p]; and it answers to the epithet princely in Il. xxiv. 538.

ὅττι οἱ οὔτι
Παίδων ἐν μεγάροισι γονὴ γένετο κρειόντων.

'For he had not as yet a princely offspring in his home.'

Lower than Βασιλεύς, which corresponds to the rank implied by our term 'majesty,' and less wide in sense than ἄναξ, which corresponds very nearly with 'lord,' it is generally the equivalent as to rank of prince or princely, according to the English sense of the terms; but it is in Homer always a descriptive word only, and never a title. Accordingly it is found in the later Greek writers, when both ἄναξ ἀνδρῶν, and even ποιμὴν λαῶν have disappeared.

The phrase ποιμὴν λαῶν is more largely used than κρείων, and with more appearance of approximation to that substantive character, and susceptibility of individual application, which belongs to a title. Thus in

Οἱ δ' ἐπανέστησαν, πείθοντό τε ποιμένι λαῶν,
σκηπτοῦχοι βασιλῆες[q],

the βασιλῆες are the members of the Greek βουλή, and ποιμὴν λαῶν means Agamemnon. Like κρείων, it was applicable to those who held secondary sovereignties, the feudatories, so to speak, of the principal chiefs: as

[p] Il. viii. 31. Od. i. 45.   [q] Il. ii. 85.

for instance, we find among the secondary commanders of the Pylian division,

Αἵμονά τε κρείοντα, Βίαντά τε, ποιμένα λαῶν[r].

It reaches down to persons, of whom we know and can infer nothing, but that they may probably have held small fiefs (so to call them) with derivative sovereignty of some kind, such as were, among the Trojans[s], Bienor, Hypeiron, Apisaon, Hypsenor: and it is also applied to the sons of the greater chiefs, for example, Thrasymedes and Agenor[t], as well as to the chiefs themselves, including Agamemnon. It is likewise given to Ægisthus, when he was, *de facto,* in possession of the throne of Agamemnon[u]. It is therefore applicable to the idea of political rule in the very widest sense, differing however from ἄναξ in so far that, while it is assigned to personages of smaller note politically, it is confined to the expression of that kind of superiority, and has nothing whatever to do with property.

I find it, on the whole, impossible to detect in this phrase any thing of a definite character, except that it expresses political rule at large, and expresses it under the form of a figure adapted to the early and patriarchal state of society. I hesitate then to call it with confidence a title, because the class to which it applies is somewhat indeterminate, and therefore it is wanting in specific meaning: yet it may partake somewhat of that character. We must, however, distinguish broadly between the element of subordination to Agamemnon, such as we see it in Nestor and Diomed, and that of the class to which the lower ποιμένες λαῶν belonged. These were as widely separated as the great feudatories

[r] Il. iv. 296. [s] Il. ix. 92. v. 144. xi. 578. xiii. 411.
[t] Il. ix. 81. xiii. 600.   [u] Od. iv. 528.

II. Ethnology.

of mediæval France, from the petty lords who so much abounded in this island.

In its form, the phrase bears an external, rather than a real resemblance to ἄναξ ἀνδρῶν. For ποίμην figuratively used expresses no more than the office of a ruler in his political relation to his subjects; while ἄναξ ἀνδρῶν is much more peculiar in character, since ἄναξ exhibits the idea of master as well as ruler, and he is not merely ἄναξ of a people, but ἄναξ of individual men, in respect to something appertaining to man as such, of which he is the possessor or usufructuary. The ποιμὴν λαῶν expresses a relation, which implies that political society is already formed, for λαός means a body united in that form.

Again, we are scarcely entitled to presume that ἄναξ ἀνδρῶν denotes the office of 'any king or chieftain,' when, though it is used in some fifty passages, it is only applied to six persons: nor is it less hazardous to say that it means especially the office of a supreme ruler or commander, when out of these six persons only one at all answers to that description, and when at least three are persons of insignificant power, as well as individually obscure.

Once more, it is the manner of Homer, where he applies an epithet or phrase characteristically to one of his greater personages, to give them the exclusive use of it, such as the ποδώκης δῖος for Achilles, κορυθαίολος for Hector, πολύμητις and πολυτλὰς δῖος for Ulysses. For example, κορυθαίολος is used thirty-eight times for Hector, never for any other hero: though it is used once for Mars, in Il. xx. 38. It would be strange if he departed from this usage in the case before us. But if ἄναξ ἀνδρῶν be a mere phrase of description, as Mure supposes, he does depart from it in the strangest manner; for while he applies it forty-six times to Agamemnon, he likewise gives it to the very insignificant Eumelus. If it be a phrase simply serving the purpose, as an epithet would, of denoting the great political position of Agamemnon, how can its force be more utterly shattered than by bestowing it not only upon Eumelus, who does nothing except drive a chariot, but upon Euphetes, who is mentioned but once in the poems of Homer, without any epithet or circumstance whatever except this to distinguish him, and who is named nowhere else at all? If it describes a ruler as supreme among rulers, why is it thus debasingly, as well as loosely, applied? But if it describes a ruler generally, then why is it employed so restrictedly? The actual mode and conditions of its use require us to examine whether it does not in fact cover some specific idea, derived from a form of society which, even in the days of Homer, had become, or, at the least, was becoming obsolete; perhaps already in some part a monument of the past, and cutting across, rather than fitting into, the arrangements and usages of his time.

The peculiar formula 'lord of men' appears well adapted to mark the period of transition from the patriarchal to the political construction of society; in the family, sovereignty and the possession of property are united, and the βασιλεύς naturally follows after and grows out of the ἄναξ. Authority is here clothed in a form more extended than that of a mere family connection, yet the idea of it remains indeterminate: there is no distinct formation of *class*; superiors are not yet viewed under the formal political notion of kings, nor (as in λαός) have *men* yet come to conceive of themselves as subjects. There are human beings with a superior: but there is no society with a head. In that state of things, power, if less secure and rooted, was more absolute:

witness the projected sacrifice by Abraham of his son Isaac.

To sum up, however, what we have said upon the other phrases, it appears that we have in Homer four words commonly used to express the ruling office, from the highest form of that office downwards: they are,

1. βασιλεὺς, the most limited: confined in the Iliad to those who both were practically supreme, and ruled over considerable territory, or else were of primary importance from personal prowess or other qualities.

2. κρείων, the next; embracing the very highest, but descending to secondary princes, though commonly confined to the more considerable.

3. ποιμὴν λαῶν, which, also capable of application to the highest, yet, as expressing political dominion in the widest form, embraces the subordinate, derivative, and petty principalities even of persons who do not appear to have been in any sense independent sovereigns.

4. More varied in its application than any of these, perhaps older, and related to the time when the only known form of sovereignty implied indeterminate, and so far absolute powers of disposal, the word ἄναξ involves the double idea of political authority and of ownership; it accompanies them both, like our word *lord*, when they separate, and it adheres to each of them in all its forms.

I admit that the construction which it is now proposed to put upon ἄναξ ἀνδρῶν has not, so far as I am aware, been heretofore propounded; and that this is, *pro tanto*, a presumption against it. But in lieu of *pro tanto*, I would in this case crave to write *pro tantillo*; for it seems to be the fact, that, as only of late has Ethnology been systematically studied, so only of late have the text and diction of Homer been subjected to minute investigation; and it is reasonable to expect, that the further application of critical attention to it may yet disclose to our view much, which has heretofore been unsuspected. It is the more allowable to proceed upon this view in the case of ἄναξ ἀνδρῶν, because so few readers of Homer appear even to have observed that it is ever applied to any person besides Agamemnon, and therefore the common opinion rests upon an inaccurate impression as to the elementary facts. My purpose, accordingly, may more justly be described as an attempt to open a new question, than as an attack upon a critical verdict regularly delivered.

Let us now proceed to examine what the facts really are respecting the use of the phrase ἄναξ ἀνδρῶν in Homer.

It is applied to Agamemnon in the following passages:

Il. i. 7, 172, 442, 506.	x. 64, 86, 103, 119, 233.
ii. 402, 434, 441, 612.	xi. 99, 254.
iii. 81, 267, 455.	xiv. 64, 103, 134.
iv. 148, 255, 336.	xviii. 111.
v. 38.	xix. 51, 76, 146, 172, 184, 199.
vi. 33.	xxiii. 161, 895.
vii. 162, 314.	Od. viii. 77.
viii. 278.	xi. 396.
ix. 96, 114, 163, 672, 677, 697.	

It is also applied to Anchises, Il. v. 268.
     Æneas, Il. v. 311.
     Augeias, Il. xi. 701, 739.
     Euphetes, Il. xv. 532.
     Eumelus, Il. xxiii. 288.

Now although, as we have seen, the term is in fact employed only with names nearly akin to one another in point of metrical value, yet the Poet has given us the most distinct evidence that the employment of it was not a mere metrical expedient to assist him in the use of names otherwise unmanageable. This we learn in the two following forms:

1. The name Eumelus is one of those to which he applies the phrase: but the metrical conjunction of it with this name is by no means particularly convenient, for out of five places in which Homer mentions Eumelus in the nominative case, he only once gives him his title of ἄναξ ἀνδρῶν. Again, it is evident that he has no preference for the end of the verse as a place for the name of Eumelus; for he places it elsewhere, at the beginning, and in τὴν Εὔμηλος ὄπυιε (Il. ii. 714. Od. iv. 798), on the only two occasions when he uses the nominative without a title annexed. He only puts it at the end of the verse in order to couple it with ἄναξ ἀνδρῶν, and with κρείων (Il. xxiii. 288, 354). So far then from being a metrical convenience, this phrase rather forces him out of his way in order to introduce it. So it is with Æneas. Homer uses his name very many times, but never once places it at the end of a verse, except in the single case in which he attaches it to the title ἄναξ ἀνδρῶν. Again, then, the phrase compels him to adopt a position which he is uniformly careful to avoid elsewhere for Æneas, and this in little short of forty instances.

2. Besides the names to which Homer applies the phrase, he employs a great number of names, of persons having high or the very highest rank, which possess exactly the same metrical value as one or another of the six names above quoted; but yet to none of these does he at any time give the title of ἄναξ ἀνδρῶν. Of such names I have observed the following: and I exclude from the list the merely local characters of the Odyssey, and all persons in inferior station.

Persons to whom it might have been applied. 455

(1) Of the same metrical value with Eumelus:

Patroclus.	Ægisthus.
Pheidippus.	Admetus.
Euneus.	Amphius.
Eudorus.	Euphorbus.
Euphemus.	

And of the dead,

Isandros.   Adrestus.

(2) Of the same metrical value with Augeias, Euphetes, Æneas, Anchises:

Antenor.	Hercules (Heracles).
Sarpedon.	Eurystheus.
Pyræchmes.	

(3) Of the same metrical value with Agamemnon:

Diomedes.	Agapenor.
Polypœtes.	Euphenor.
Megapenthes.	Prothoenor.
Thrasymedes.	Hyperenor.
Eteoneus.	

(4) Of the same metrical value with Agamemnon, except having the last syllable short:

| Menelaus. | Melanippus. |
| Echepolus. | Polydorus. |

And of the dead,

Rhadamanthus.   Meleagros.

Here are thirty-five names as susceptible of conjunction with the phrase ἄναξ ἀνδρῶν as the six to which he attaches it. How comes it to be attached, significant as it is *primâ facie*, to the six, and never to the thirty-five? Did it come and go by accident, or had Homer a meaning in it?

Moreover, I would by no means be understood to

admit, that metrical obstacles would have sufficed to prevent Homer from applying almost any title to almost any name: such were the resources of his genius and his ear, and such the freedom that the youthful elasticity of the language secured to him.

It must be remembered too that he has given us an instance (in Il. i. 7) of a second site, so to speak, for ἄναξ ἀνδρῶν in the Greek hexameter, which would have enabled him at once to combine it with all such proper names as come within the compass of a dactyl and trochee, or a spondee and trochee. Such as Πουλυδάμας γὰρ.... Καὶ Πρίαμος μὲν.... Καὶ γὰρ Τευκρὸς.... Θησεὺς αὐτὸς.... Δάρδανος αὐτὸς.... And even without altering its usual position in the verse, by a break of it, or a *cæsura*, which is not unfrequent with him, he might have given us (for example) ἄναξ ἀνδρῶν γὰρ Ἐρεχθεύς. Or he might by *tmesis*, more liberally used, have further widened the field for its employment.

Or again, he would have been free, by the rules of his own usage, to have said in the vocative, ἀνδρῶν ἄνα.

His abstinence from inflexion absolutely, and from *tmesis* almost entirely, in the use of ἄναξ ἀνδρῶν, I think deserves remark. We might be struck, even in another author, by finding a word fifty-six times in the nominative singular, and never in any other form: but in Homer these slight circumstances have a value and significance, which in ordinary cases it would be more dangerous to assign to them. It seems to me possible, that this restraint in the use of the name, which always assigns to it the most commanding place in the sentence, was not unconnected with a sense of reverence towards it. I think that if we were to examine the correspondence, for example, between British Ministers and their Sovereign, we might find that the phrase

'Your Majesty' was placed, under a sort of natural and unconscious bias, by the writers, in the nominative case, in a proportional number of instances far exceeding that which the pronoun 'you' would supply in an ordinary letter.

It is difficult to define this delicate and subtle sentiment: but it may perhaps be illustrated by the feeling on which is founded the prevailing usage of addressing among ourselves the very highest ranks, and in some languages all persons of consideration, in the third rather than the second person. And again, it is the same description of sentiment, which, when carried into the sphere of religion, has led Dante invariably to forbear, when he introduces the name 'Cristo' at the close of a verse, from placing any other word in rhyme with it, so that he makes it its own echo (so to speak), and repeats it thrice, in no less than four passages, to meet the full demand of his metre[x].

Or again, as Homer appears to have possessed a fineness of ear which is not only wonderful, but by us in some part inappreciable, it may be that he attached an importance, which we cannot measure, to preserving a perfect uniformity in this dignified and sonorous title, as a means of producing popular impression, not less than of satisfying his own taste.

Other instances might be given from Homer, bearing upon the case.

Ἐνοσίχθων is used forty times, and only once out of the nominative, though metrical reasons could not hamper the poet with respect to any of the cases of this noun. Διογενὴς is used in the nominative and vocative only. Κύδιστος is used sixteen times, and in the vocative alone. The feminine form however is

[x] Paradiso, xii. 71. xiv. 104. xix. 104. xxix. 11.

found in the nominative, but only in two passages (one of them with a rival reading) applied to Minerva. Εὐρυκρείων is found twelve times, and only in the nominative.

Perhaps again the rarity and slightness of his use of *tmesis* may be accounted for, not by euphony alone, but by the circumstance that these two words had grown by titular use almost into one.

The fact that the phrase ἄναξ ἀνδρῶν should have disappeared with Homer himself, while his heroes were incessantly sung by later poets, of itself raises a presumption that it belonged to a state of things which, when after a wide interval the race of his successors began, had wholly ceased to exist.

That stage of society, in the closing stages of which Homer lived, and which we know through him alone of classical authors, was the patriarchal stage in its last phasis. By the patriarchal stage of society, I mean the stage in which rights on the one hand, and powers and duties on the other, were still indeterminate, and were gradually passing from the state of *nebula* into that of body. Now, if the phrase ἄναξ ἀνδρῶν belonged to it, without doubt it must at the outset have exhibited its unvarying characteristic, the union of sovereign political power not only with hereditary descent, but with a reference to some original stock as an object of deep veneration, if not to a relationship of blood more or less remote between the royal family and their subjects, or to the dominant race among them.

The chieftaincies of the Celtic tribes in our own island, such as they existed until within only one century back, afford us a partial analogy. The primary idea is that of the headship of an extended family, sometimes approximating to the character of a nation;

sometimes more limited, so that many of such families or tribes may be regarded as belonging to the same nation. One marked characteristic of these chieftaincies is that the preeminence and power, which they attached to birth, is separable from, though capable of union with, sovereignty strictly so called, that is, an absolute political supremacy, and subsists in its main particulars even after the division; neither does it become ambiguous or indefinite, where the field for its exercise is a narrow one. The splendour of the name increases with the range of dominion, but its integrity subsists even in the most contracted sphere, so long as the organization on which it is dependent remains.

It is at least conceivable, that the Greek and the Celtic chieftaincies thus far agree. They differ in this, that the Hellenes, whenever we hear of them, appear more or less clearly as the subjugators of some race in prior occupancy of the soil, and as the masters of slaves: so that, while the relation of the Highland Chief to his clan was elevated and softened by union in blood, a Greek chieftaincy rather affected the relation between the head of the tribe and, not the whole, but only a privileged part, of the community.

The fundamental idea of this chieftainship would lie in the possession of the powers of government, patriarchally organized, by lineal descent, and traced up to the point which was the recognised fountain-head of the traditions of the race.

Where the idea of succession by primogeniture was well defined, there probably would be but one line in existence at a time that could hold the title for any one race. But there might be cases where the rule of primogeniture was unknown, or not consistently applied, or where the fact of elder descent was contested, or where common descent from some one acknowledged race and period might confer the title on a variety of families, situated at remote points from one another, in each of which it might afterwards be confined to the lineal heir. In such cases there would be a plurality of lines, all running up into the stem of a common ancestor, and all bearing in their own separate successions the title of chieftainships.

Again, among these chieftains one might be politically supreme over the rest within a given country. Such were the Macdonalds, Lords of the Isles, in Scotland, who claimed to be kings as well as chieftains: and such in Ireland were the Kevanaghs, O'Ruarcs, and O'Briens.

If therefore I am right in interpreting the phrase ἄναξ ἀνδρῶν to mean properly (together with something more) *Chieftain,* in a sense including the main elements of Celtic chieftaincy, or *Patriarch,* (but the latter phrase is less applicable from its conventional connection with advanced age), then it need excite no surprise if we find an ἄναξ ἀνδρῶν on each side, and not in the supreme command. At the same time, though there are vast differences in power between one Homeric ἄναξ ἀνδρῶν and another, they are all, so far as we see, strictly in the position of princes ordinarily independent within their dominions, though owning, it might be, the prerogatives of a qualified political supremacy lodged in other hands.

Case of Agamemnon.

It is very worthy of remark, that Homer scarcely ever describes Agamemnon by personal epithets. In a few passages (I see seven noticed) he uses the word δῖος in connection with the name: but this is one of the least specific among the Homeric epithets for individuals, and is employed not only for Achilles, Hector, Ulysses, Nestor, and others, but for a crowd of inferior personages, so that, as a word of the most general purport, it has little or no defining or individualizing power. It means preeminence in some particular kind, among a class, and it is applicable to any class; to Agamemnon greatest among sovereigns, and to Eumæus worthiest among swineherds. A few times Homer calls him ἥρως, a word which he also applies to the entire Greek army (Il. ii. 110). In all other places, (I omit, of course, the invectives of Achilles,) he is characterised only by words taken from his position or descent. The principal of these are 'Ἀτρείδης, which he enjoys in common with Menelaus: κρείων, applied to him and to various other chiefs: ποίμην λαῶν, yet more largely and loosely used: εὐρυκρείων, which is exclusively his own among men, and which is the epithet used by Homer as properly descriptive of his wide-reaching sway. It is also applied to Neptune among the immortals, because vastness was with Homer a principal feature of the θάλασσα, his domain. Lastly, Agamemnon is ἄναξ ἀνδρῶν, which, as I hold, describes his position by birth as the head or chieftain of the Achæans properly so called.

There are two remarkable passages, which are evidently intended to supply the key-note, as it were, for our conception of the material power of Agamemnon: the first, Il. ii. 108, respecting the sceptre: the second, in the Catalogue, Il. ii. 576–80: in both of these he is called κρείων, in neither ἄναξ ἀνδρῶν. This fact entirely accords with the supposition that neither a determinate form of political power, nor military command, is the vital idea of the phrase.

II. *Ethnology.*

On the other hand, although the Poet does not seem to connect this phrase with imperial power, yet that he intended to use it as one highly characteristic, we may at once deem probable from his having employed it in that remarkable passage[y] with which the poem begins, and which so succinctly, yet so broadly opens the subject of it. For here he has taken the phrase ἄναξ ἀνδρῶν out of its usual, and elsewhere its only place in the verse, and has subjoined it, contrary in this likewise to his uniform practice elsewhere, to the name of the person described by it. The line is

Ἀτρείδης τε, ἄναξ ἀνδρῶν, καὶ δῖος Ἀχιλλεύς.

Evidently this is done for greater emphasis: as 'great Alexander' is less emphatic than 'Alexander the Great,' and 'king Darius' than 'Darius the king.' It may be admitted that the epithet δῖος, used in this place for Achilles, is not one of the most characteristic: but Achilles had already been described (in v. i.) by that distinguished patronymic which formed his chief glory[z], as it connected him, through his father and his grandfather, with Jupiter.

All these presumptions drawn from the case of Agamemnon converge upon a point: they tend to show, that ἄναξ ἀνδρῶν means preeminence indeed, but yet a particular kind of preeminence; and one distinct from, and more specific than, the general idea of sovereignty.

The so-called genealogy of Agamemnon differs from every other one given by Homer in this, that it does not describe the descent in a right line. For as Thyestes, one of his three predecessors on the Pelopid throne was the father of Ægisthus, who was the contemporary, but yet not the brother of Agamemnon, he

[y] Il. i. 1–7.   [z] See Il. xx. 106.

must without doubt have been brother to Atreus, Agamemnon's father. It is in fact not a genealogy simply, but rather a succession in dignities. The dignity of ἄναξ ἀνδρῶν may have combined with that of the political supremacy to lead Homer into this unusual course. If, as I suppose, ἄναξ ἀνδρῶν required the double derivation both of lineage and of sovereignty, this was the way, and the only way, in which Homer could attain his end. And his having pursued this method seems to imply that such *was* his end.

I cannot therefore under the conditions of the definition given above, explain the application of the phrase to Agamemnon by mere reference to his political supremacy. It will be necessary to prove, either by direct or by presumptive evidence, his lineal connection with the primitive Grecian or Hellenic stock, the trunk of the tree from which other Achæan families were branches and offshoots only.

I propose to do this by showing,

First, that no appreciable value is to be attached to the notions which represent him as the grandson of an Asiatic immigrant; while even if this descent could be made good, we should not on that account be justified in at once proceeding to deny that the Pelopids were of pure Hellenic blood.

Secondly, that he was not merely at the moment the political head of Greece, but that he was also the hereditary chief of the Achæans, then the ruling tribe of the country.

Thirdly, that this Achæan tribe was in all likelihood derived from Thessaly, where it was especially rooted and distinguished: as Thessaly was itself fed from the Helli of the mountains, and constituted the secondary and immediate source from whence the Hellenic races successively issued, and spread themselves over the peninsula.

I do not pretend to carry the proof of a patriarchal position or lineal chieftaincy in the case of Agamemnon further. We do not know what was the strictly original royal stock of the Hellenic tribes. The current tradition of Hellen and his sons would be very convenient, but it is too obviously accommodated to after-times, and too flatly at variance with the earliest, that is to say with the Homeric accounts, to be in the slightest degree trustworthy as an historic basis. We may take the Hesiodic tradition as affording evidence of the belief that there was a primitive royal stock, and that the ruling families had been derived from it, since within these limits it does not contradict Homer; but we can justly build upon it nothing further. Undoubtedly the very employment of the phrase ἄναξ ἀνδρῶν, if the proposed construction of it can be made good, will greatly fortify this belief. But this can only be made good in a presumptive manner: as by showing that the phrase was only given in ruling families: and only in the representative lines of ruling families: and only in families which ruled over tribes of the dominant race; and which had so ruled from time immemorial—that is to say, they must be families of which it cannot be shown that at any time they had acquired their position in their own tribe. If a first ancestor, apparently the channel of the title, is indicated, he must be one from whom history begins: there must be nothing before him, nothing to show that he or his line had ever been less than what he came to be. Lastly, the tribes, over which the ἄναξ ἀνδρῶν rules, must be in visible or presumable connection locally with the original seat or cradle of the nation; and it will be a further confirmation of the argument if, as we ascend the lineal lines, we find in them a tendency to converge towards an unity of origin, which we shall find poetically expressed as the divine parentage of Jupiter, and thus covered with the golden clouds of a remote antiquity, that not even the sun can pierce[a]. Perhaps we may even find reason to suppose it likely that descent from Jupiter was an essential qualification for the title of ἄναξ ἀνδρῶν.

First, then, let us deal with the negative or adverse presumptions, which would go to prove that Agamemnon was not Hellenic at all.

It may be urged,

1. That we see, even from Homer, that Pelops was a recent hero, only two generations before the *Troica*, so that Agamemnon has no antiquity to boast of.

2. That, according to extraneous tradition, there is no connection between Agamemnon and the Hellic stock: as Pelops is reputed to be the son of Tantalus, and Tantalus the king of Phrygia.

To the first I answer, that the list of names in Il. ii. 101—8, is not simply a genealogy, for it includes Thyestes, who is not in the right line; but it is a succession of kings on a common throne, and can only therefore begin with Pelops, as the first who sat upon that throne.

But, further, even if it were a genealogy, yet Homer seems usually to begin his genealogies not with the first known ancestor of a person, but with the first ancestor of his who settled in the place where he exercises power. Thus Nestor, though we acquire indirectly a knowledge of his earlier descent through the Νεκυῖα, has no genealogy beyond Neleus his father,

[a] Il. xiv. 343.

because he was the ancestor that migrated into Peloponnesus, or, at least, that first acquired the Pylian throne, by marriage into a prior, and perhaps a Pelasgian house[b]. Ulysses has none beyond Arceisius; and it is plain, from the records of the earlier dynasty in Ithaca, that there could have been no king of that house before him. Dardanus and Minos, heads of genealogies, were also the founders of sovereignties. Again, Portheus is given us as the head of the Œneid line in Ætolia: and we have found it probable that he was the first of his race[c] who migrated into that country. The same considerations, in all likelihood, hold good with regard to Pelops.

Now with respect to the second objection.

We are to remember that Homer has nowhere asserted the connection between Pelops and Tantalus, or between Tantalus and Phrygia.

But not even the latter connection, and far less the former, would disprove the title of Agamemnon to represent lineally the character of ἄναξ ἀνδρῶν. For, as we have seen, that title subsisted in the line of Dardanus, and the causes which planted it there might also have planted it in Phrygia; which is not irrationally supposed to have been the line of march for the Hellic race in its original movement westwards[c]. Moreover, Phrygia is not a name confined to Asia.

There are, however, many indirect Homeric indications, as well as much extra-Homeric tradition, which tend to connect Pelops both with Tantalus and with Greece.

First, even if Tantalus were known to Homer as the father of Pelops, he could not have been named in

[a] Od. xi. 281.
[b] Sup. p. 398.
[c] See E. Curtius, Ionier vor der Ionischen Wanderung, p. 9.

Connection of Tantalus with the Greeks. 467

the tradition of Il. ii. 101—8, unless he had occupied, like Pelops, the throne to which Agamemnon succeeded.

From the appearance of Tantalus in the Νεκυΐα, it is probable that Homer regarded him as Greek, either by birth or by what we may call naturalization. This he might be in the Poet's view, if the traditions concerning him, without assigning to him Greek birth or even residence, made him the father of one who became a great Greek sovereign. If, for instance, we take the name of Æolus; it is the source of some of the most famous Greek houses, yet Homer never mentions it, except in the patronymic, and gives us no means of absolutely attaching it to any part of Greece. Æolus may have been known only as the father of Greeks. So Minos was not of Greek birth; but was naturalized, and therefore appears in the Νεκυΐα as the judge of the nether world. All the other personages, without exception, who are introduced there, are apparently Greek: Sisyphus, Hercules, Tityus, Theseus, Pirithous, from clear marks of residence: even Orion, since he is made the hero of a scene in Delos[d], appears, whatever his origin, to have been already Hellenized by tradition. Nor is it easy to avoid the same assumption with respect to Tantalus.

Again, we may be quite sure, that Tantalus was a person of the highest rank and position. None others seem to have been distinguished by an express notice of their fate after death. Orion was the object of the passion of Aurora (Od. v. 121). Tityus was an offender so lofty, that he became the occasion of a voyage of Rhadamanthus himself to deal with his crime[e]. Sisyphus was, as we have found reason to believe[f], of the most exalted stock.

The punishment of Tantalus in the nether world is

[d] Od. v. 121. also see Il. xviii. 436.   [e] Od. vii. 323.
[f] Sup. sect. viii. pp. 427, 8.

probably, as in other cases, the reflection of a previous catastrophe, certainly of a previous character, upon earth. The nature of his punishment is a perpetual temptation, of irresistible force, presented to the appetites of hunger and thirst, while the gratification of it is wholly and perpetually denied. This shews that his offence on earth must have been some form of πλεονεξία, of greediness, presumption, or ambition. It is therefore not unlikely that by restless attempts at acquisition, he may have convulsed his dominions, and caused his son to migrate.

Now this supposed vein of character in Tantalus would thoroughly accord with that of the Pelopid line. He is punished for covetousness or acquisitiveness. His son gains a kingdom through Mercury, who is the god of increase by fair means or foul. His grandson Thyestes gathers wealth (πολύαρς, Il. ii. 106): his great-grandson Agamemnon is deeply marked by the avarice everywhere glanced at in the Iliad: and finally we have the reckless and guilty cravings of the ambition of Ægisthus.

We are by no means without reasons from the poems for placing Tantalus, as the later tradition places him, among the heroes of the stock of Jupiter. One ground is afforded us by the text of the Eleventh Odyssey for supposing that he was, I do not say a son, but at least a descendant of Jupiter. It is this; that apparently all the heroes, to whom we are thus introduced, were at least of divine extraction. They are, besides Tantalus, as follows :—

1. Minos, who was a son of Jupiter. (Od. xi. 568.)
2. Orion: he was of divine extraction according to the later tradition. In Homer he has no parentage, but he had at least attained to divine honours, inasmuch as he was translated into a star. (Od. v. 274 et alibi.)

3. Tityus, son of Γαῖα. (Od. xi. 596, and vii. 324.)

4. Sisyphus, son of Æolus; therefore descended from Jupiter.

5. Hercules, son of Jupiter (ibid. 620.)

But I rely specially upon the passages towards the end, where these are all called ἄνδρες ἥρωες, and where Ulysses says he might have seen others, namely, Θήσεα Πειρίθοόν τε, θεῶν ἐρικύδεα τέκνα, illustrious children of the gods: as if to be a child of the gods were a condition of appearing in this august, though mournful, company.

Hereas, a Megarian author of uncertain age, is quoted by Plutarch[g] as having declared that the last cited verse was among the interpolations of Pisistratus. But Hereas was as likely to be wrong in this statement, through Megarian antipathy, as Pisistratus to have interpolated the verse in favour of Athenian vanity. The internal evidence is, I think, in its favour. For the phrase θεῶν ἐρικύδεα τέκνα is, according to the view here given, really characteristic. It is, at the same time, characteristic through the medium of an idea which, though it can be deduced fairly from the text, is not obvious upon its surface; namely the idea that all the heroes of the Νεκυῖα were divine. The verse is therefore supported by something in the nature of a spontaneous or undesigned coincidence.

The post-Homeric tradition makes Niobe the daughter of Tantalus; and, if this be so, then we may derive from her very high position a further support to the presumption that Tantalus was of the race of Jupiter, as also to the hypothesis of his personal connection with Greece. For that the tradition of Niobe is Greek we see, from its being cited by Achilles; and that she was a sovereign is clearly implied by the

[g] Thes. 20.

combined effect of various circumstances. The first is her being compared by Achilles with Priam. The second, that the vaunt of an inferior person would hardly have been noticed by the direct intervention of the gods. The third is the singular extent and dignity of that intervention: Apollo slays the sons, Diana the daughters; Jupiter converts the people to stone; the Immortals at large bury the dead. The fourth is the use of the term λαούς, which means plainly the subjects of the kingdom where Niobe was queen.

We cannot now carry farther the presumptions that Tantalus was the descendant of Jupiter, and Agamemnon of Tantalus: but if, in considering the cases of the other members of his class, we shall sufficiently shew that they were all descended in common repute from Jupiter, we shall then perhaps be warranted in relying more decidedly upon the connection, which is suggested by the text in the case of Agamemnon through his presumed ancestor Tantalus.

It is difficult to find more than slight traces of the seat of the power of Tantalus from Homer.

He mentions a mountain called Sipylus[h], near the Achelous, and thus near the principal passage from Northern and Middle into Southern Greece. Here it is that he places the mourning Niobe. But Pausanias places the tomb of Pelops on the summit of Mount Sipylus, meaning, apparently, the hill of that name in Lydia[i]. Again, the Phryges, over whom the later tradition reports him to have reigned, are also made known to us as a Thracian people[k]: a designation quite capable of embracing any of the hill tribes in the neighbourhood of Thessaly. We have another sign of the extension of this name in the Phrygians of Attica,

[h] Il. xxiv. 615.   [i] Pausan. ii. 22. 4.
[k] Strabo, xii. p. 579. xiv. p. 680.

mentioned by Thucydides (ii. 22): and the Phrygian alphabet is closely akin to that of Greece.

Strabo, however, observes, that the state of these traditions is so greatly confused, so as to make them scarcely tractable for the purposes of history[1].

The connection of Pelops with Southern Greece is well supported by the ancient name of Peloponnesus. No notice of this name is found in Homer; but we need not be surprised, if Pelops was the first of his race in that part of the country, at finding him sparely recognised by the Poet: it is the uniform manner of the poet with strangers or *novi homines*.

The Homeric notices of Pelops are not more liberal than of Tantalus. 1. We find him called $\pi\lambda\acute{\eta}\xi\iota\pi\pi\sigma$[m] in such a way as shows that something connected with the driving of a chariot must have been attached either to the known habits, or to some great crisis of his life, or to both. In either mode, it agrees with the common tradition, according to which, by success in the chariot race, he won the hand of Hippodameia, daughter of king Œnomaus, and therewith the throne of Pisa. We have another fact from Homer which tends to support this tradition, namely, that in the earliest youth of Nestor there were, as we have seen, public games, which included chariot-races, in Elis.

2. The common tradition is also further supported by the passage in the Second Iliad, which gives us the line of Pelopid sovereigns. For we are there told that Vulcan wrought the Pelopid sceptre for Jupiter: that Jupiter gave it to Mercury, and Mercury to Pelops the horse-driver, who handed it on to Atreus and the rest. From this statement two things clearly appear. First, that the throne of Pelops was gained either by craft, or at least by enterprise, of his own. Secondly, that it

[1] Strabo xii. 572, 3. [m] Il. ii. 104.

was a new power which he erected, and that he was not merely the transferee of the power of the Perseid line.

Nor is it difficult to discern wherein the novelty consisted. This sceptre carried the right of paramount lordship over all Greece—

πολλῇσιν νήσοισι καὶ Ἄργεϊ παντὶ ἀνάσσειν[n]—

whereas the Perseids had been local sovereigns, though probably the first in rank and power among their contemporaries of Continental Greece.

Now this sovereignty, thus extended, was plainly an Achæan sovereignty. For we have seen that, contemporaneously with its erection, Homer drops the marked and exclusive use of the word Ἀργεῖοι for the inhabitants of that quarter, and calls them by preference Ἀχαιοί, the older name falling into the shade. Thus, then, the Achæans rose with the house of Pelops: and this being the case, we can the better understand why it was that that house rose to so great an elevation. It was because the Achæan race had now acquired extension in the North and in the South of Greece, in Eastern and Western Peloponnesus, and because it usually predominated wheresoever it went. Thus the house of Pelops had an opportunity of gaining influence and power, which had not been enjoyed by the preceding dynasties, though they ruled from the same sovereign seat. They were families only: the Pelopids were chiefs of a race.

What we have thus seen from Homer, with respect to the high position attained by Pelops, is confirmed by the later tradition.

Pausanias notices the local traces of Tantalus, as well as of Pelops, in Elis. A harbour there bore the name of Tantalus[o]: and Pelops was worshipped in a sanctuary

[n] Il. ii. 108.   [o] Paus. v. xiii. 1-4.

hard by the temple of Jupiter Olympius. It was on the right hand, in front of that temple, a very marked situation in all likelihood: and Pausanias says, that the Elians reverenced Pelops among heroes, like Jupiter among gods. It was probably on this account, and as a memorial of the worship from high places, that the θρόνος, or seat of Pelops, was, as he says, not only in Sipylus, but on the summit of the mountain.

Another tradition makes Pelops the original king of Pisa, the rival town to Elis, which at length succumbed to it. And a further tradition reports, that he became the son-in-law of Œnomaus, king of Pisa, by conquering him in the chariot-race: and together with this, that he restored the Olympian Games. Another tradition reports him to have come from Olenos in Achaia: and as the Dorians, with the Heraclids, came into Peloponnesus by that route, probably as the easiest, so, and for the same reason, may Pelops probably have done. Lastly, while Homer places Achæans in Ægina and in Mases, (of which the site is unknown,) Pausanias (b. ii. c. 34) states that nine islands (νησίδες) off the coast of Methana, which lies directly opposite Ægina, were in his time called the Islands of Pelops.

Before quitting the subject of Pelops, I would observe, that his worship in Olympia with such peculiar honours is connected with a tradition, that he raised the Olympian Games to a distinction which they had never before attained. Now if we view him as the principal chief who brought the Achæans into Peloponnesus, this tradition tends to support the view which has been taken in a former section of the relation between the Hellic race and the institution of public Games. Nor is there any thing more intrinsically probable, than that a chief from the great breeding region of Thessaly should have either founded the chariot or horse-races of Olympia, or should have raised them to an unprecedented celebrity, and secured for them the truly national position that they for so long a time maintained.

We have seen thus far,

1. That the title of ἄναξ ἀνδρῶν is employed by Homer as the chief distinction of Agamemnon.

2. That most probably Agamemnon was descended from Tantalus, as well as from Pelops, that the line was a line of sovereigns all along, and Tantalus in all likelihood a reputed descendant of Jupiter himself.

3. That the Achæans emerge in company with the Pelopids, from the cavern of pre-historic night, and that the Pelopids are therefore to be taken as in all likelihood the chief and senior house of the Achæan tribe.

But we have still to ask, whence came the Achæans themselves? and how are we to prove their connection with the Hellenic name and stock?

And first, as to Homeric evidence.

We have already seen, in considering Homer's account of the contingent of Achilles, and also from Il. ix. 395, that the Achæan race appears to have been the dominant one in the proper and original Hellas of Thessaly: which appears to place it beyond doubt, that the Achæans were they who first carried with them extensively into Greece the Hellenic name, a name always following in the wake of the Achæan one, and in Homer extending to all Greece, unless we except that part which was the sovereign seat of Achæan power.

The first form of the name is with the Helli of Northern Thessaly: the second is developed into the Hellas proper of Southern Thessaly; we find the third in the more large and less determinate use of the word for Greece to the northward of the Isthmus. The name gains this extension apparently just during the period while the Achæans are moving southward, as the house of Ulysses to Ithaca, the house of Neleus, perhaps with an Achæan train, to Pylos, the Pelopids to Mycenæ and Sparta, Tydeus from Ætolia to Argos.

And again, we must observe this distinction. We see the Achæans come into the Peloponnesus, and we can, from the text of Homer, point out the time when they were not there. But we do not see them come into Thessaly from among the Helli of the mountains. We simply find their name prominent there; from which we must conclude, that Homer meant to point them out as the first representatives on an adequate scale of Hellas in that country.

All this is strongly confirmed by the later tradition as to the connection of Pelops with the Achæans of Thessaly, and by the clear historical proofs in our possession of the profound root which the Achæan name had taken there.

Strabo, in a passage where he chooses a particular tradition from among many, as peculiarly worthy of record, says[p],

'Αχαιοὺς γὰρ τοὺς Φθιώτας φασὶ συγκατελθόντας Πέλοπι εἰς τὴν Πελοπόννησον, οἰκῆσαι τὴν Λακωνικὴν· τοσοῦτον δ' ἀρετῇ διενεγκεῖν, ὥστε τὴν Πελοπόννησον, ἐκ πολλῶν ἤδη χρόνων Ἄργος λεγομένην, τότε 'Αχαϊκὸν Ἄργος λεχθῆναι.

Thus he at once asserts the connection of Pelops with the Achæans, and of the Achæans with Thessaly. He proceeds to say, that Laconia was considered to have a peculiar title to the name of Achaic Argos[q]; that some construed Od. iii. 251 as supporting it, and that the Achæans, driven by the Dorians out of Laconia, in their turn displaced an Ionian race from Achaia, and took possession of the district.

[p] Book viii. 5, 5. p. 365.   [q] See sup. p. 381.

II. *Ethnology*.

Herodotus[r], in treating of the Peloponnesus, describes the Arcadians and Cynurians as αὐτόχθονες, who had never changed their habitation; four other races, including the Dorians, as ἐπήλυδες, and the Achæans as having migrated about the Peloponnesus, but never left it. He does not explicitly place the Achæans in either class; and this tradition does not throw much light on the origin of the Achæans, which would seem not to have been within his knowledge, but only deals with matter subsequent to their entry into Peloponnesus.

Pausanias[s], again, would seem rather to draw the Thessalian Achæans from Peloponnesus than *vice versa*. He tells us that, after the death of Xuthus, Achæus went with an army from Ægialus, and established himself in Thessaly. But with Homer before us, we may boldly say, that there was no such person as either the Xuthus or the Achæus of the later tradition, and that there were, on the other hand, Achæans in Thessaly long before the time assigned to this Achæus, namely, the epoch when the race took refuge in Ægialus. This tradition, then, is late and worthless, and, even if it directly contradicted that of Strabo, which it does not, could not be put in competition with it.

The tradition which made Phthiotis in Southern Thessaly the cradle of the Achæan race, where it first grew into conscious life, seems to have been an undying one.

Here again history comes in to our aid. Throughout the historic times of Greece, and down to the era of Polybius, there were Achæans of Phthiotis. When, 205 years before Christ, Quintius, the Roman general, examined into the origin of the Greek cities, and made

---

[r] Herod. viii. 7, 73.   [s] Pausan. vii. 1.

a classification of them[t], the Achæans of Phthiotis were declared to be Thessalians: and he appears to use the name for all Phthians, since he calls Phaxidas[u] an Achæan, seemingly for no other reason than that he was an inhabitant of Melitea, a city of Phthiotis.

I take it then to be sufficiently proved, that Agamemnon and his house were the proper heads of the Achæan race, which rose with them. The proof is doubled by the fact that they fell with it: for in the post-Homeric literature, all of which follows the Dorian conquest, the Achæan name has ceased to be a living name for the nation of the Greeks.

And as the Pelopids were the leaders of the Achæans, so I now assume it to be sufficiently shown from Homer, that the Achæans were in his time at the head of all the Hellenic families and tribes; of the Dorians, the Æolids, the Cephallenes, and whatever others came from the same stock, and were in fact, for their age, the proper type of Hellenism itself.

That most remarkable supremacy of Agamemnon over the Greek nation, which is so strongly marked on the page of Homer, and to the force of which Thucydides ascribes the wonderful movement of the Trojan war, left behind it a tradition which it was thought worth while by the ruling race of Dorians to appropriate, even after the shipwreck of the old political system.

Orestes came to the throne of Agamemnon, and Tisamenus to that of Orestes. He was cast out by the Heraclids with the Dorians, and they made Sparta the chief seat of their power. Thus established in the primacy of Greece, they held it, under the name of Ἡγεμονία, contested sometimes, but only after the lapse of several ages, by ˙Athens: never absolutely

[t] Polyb. xviii. c. 30.   [u] v. 65. 3 and 11.

taken away, until it passed, as Polybius says, unexpectedly, into the hands of the Thebans, in the fourth century before the Christian era.

Tisamenus and his Achæans went into Ægialus, and gave it their own name. But the imperial Spartans found it for their interest to put in their claim to the old Agamemnonian title. So, as Pausanias[x] informs us, even down to his day, the Tomb of Tisamenus was shown in Sparta, and hard by it the Lycurgian feast of Pheiditia was kept; with a tradition that their fathers, admonished by an oracle, had fetched the remains of the last Pelopid sovereign from Helice in Achæa. On the other hand, the Achæans, who in the time of Polybius[y] had not yet ceased to keep the image of their legendary ancestor Achæus, and whose claim to that image was recognised by the Roman general, likewise cherished a tradition that the family of Tisamenus had been continued, and had reigned among them down to the time of Ogygus[z], when their League was formed upon the basis of democratic institutions.

Now it is no more than we might expect, that the Achæans should, in their depressed fortunes, fondly cherish the recollections of their glory, by preserving and honouring the memory of the last of that race, who, through being their sovereigns, were also the heads of the Greek nation. But why did the Dorians exhibit an anxiety of a kind in their position so remarkable? Such a feeling could hardly have existed, had there not been a special character attaching to the Pelopid race, as possessed not only of an actual supremacy, but of some peculiar title by descent, to which it was worth the while of the Dorian sovereigns to lay claim, as a kind of heirs by adoption. We do not find that when the Pelopids came in with their

[x] Paus. vii. 1. 3. [y] Polyb. xl. 8. 10. [z] Polyb. ii. 41. 4. iv. 1. 5.

Achæans, they had shown any corresponding solicitude to connect themselves with the memory of Danaids or of Perseids: on the contrary, Homer expressly disconnects the dynasties, by assigning to the Pelopids a new sceptre, fresh by the hands of Mercury from Jupiter. It seems to follow, that in all likelihood the Pelopids had something which neither Danaids nor Perseids possessed before them, and which the Dorians too did not hold at all, or did not hold by so clear a title: the honour, namely, not of Hellenic blood alone, but of being ruled by a family which represented an original and primitive sovereignty over the Hellenic nation, through its foremost, or Achæan tribe.

This is the more remarkable, because the Dorian sovereigns of Sparta claimed Hercules, and through him Jupiter, for their progenitor. But the patriarchal chieftaincy, though not more directly connected with a divine stock, had superadded to it that accumulation of dignity, which depends upon the unbroken transmission of power from the most remote historic origin: and Hercules was modern in comparison with those to whom some of the Hellenic families were able (as we have seen) to trace their ancestry.

Were we to give credit to the common tradition respecting Hellen and his sons, I admit that it would raise a new difficulty in the way of the construction, which I propose to attach to the $\ἄναξ\ ἀνδρῶν$. Instead of seeing Agamemnon invested with it because he is head of the Achæans, and highly favoured by a special, nay by an almost exclusive appropriation of it, because they are the foremost Hellenic tribe, we should have to own in them the youngest of all the branches from that stem, with Dorians, Æolians, and Ionians too, taking precedence of them: and we should have to look, and look in vain, for any trace or presumption

II. *Ethnology.*

whatever of his descent from that Achæus, whom the tradition feigns to have existed.

But with the acknowledgment of Homer's historical authority, the credit of that tradition falls; as indeed it is etymologically self-convicted by the formation of its cardinal name Hellen.

The Achæan prominence in Homer rests on grounds sufficiently clear: over the Ionians, who appear to be not even an Hellenic race; over the Dorians, latent in the Pylian town of Dorion, or among the sister races of Crete, where they are as yet wholly undistinguished: over the Æolids, (for there are no Æolians,) because these are single shoots only, while the Achæans are a branch, a principal section of the Hellenic race; and also, as I think may be shown[a], because of all Hellenes they appear really to have had the most normal connection with the true fountain-head of their race.

Nowhere among the Dorians, and (of course, if the Ionians are Pelasgian,) nowhere among the Ionians, have we any trace of the name ἄναξ ἀνδρῶν, or of the thing indicated by it. May not this be the reason that the Dorian kings of Sparta sought (so to speak) to serve themselves heirs to the house of Agamemnon?

I may observe in passing, as to the Ionians, that it has recently been held that they are not only Hellenic, but the oldest Hellenes: that they parted from the rest of the race in Asia, came into Greece by the islands, and were its great sea-faring race. This theory, ably as it has been supported, is but doubtfully agreeable to the positive or negative evidence of Homer: still it is not less fatal to the current tradition of Hellen and his family, than that which views the Ionians as more nearly connected with the Pelasgians[b].

[a] See sect. x.
[b] Die Ionier vor der Ionischen Wanderung: von E. Curtius, Berlin, 1855.

Only among Achæans, Æolids, and Dardanians, do we find the patriarchal title of ἄναξ ἀνδρῶν. The Dardan house fell with the Trojan war. The throne of Augeias had given way even before that great crisis. It is probable that the line of Euphetes was then no longer in existence; else we must have heard of it in the Catalogue, or during the action. The realm of Eumelus was remote and small, and if it had been wrecked in the convulsions of the period, it would leave nothing upon which the Dorians could lay hold as a point of junction with the past. But they had come into the very dominions of the family of Pelops, though with a transfer of the metropolis from Mycenæ to Sparta. Here was the true Greek Patriarchate, of which for purposes of policy they might well desire to become the ostensible representatives.

The legend of the Hellenidæ might probably be meant to cooperate towards the same end. Its determinate form I have ventured to discard: but its spirit and intention have their importance in connection with the subject of the extraction of the Greeks. It affords early witness to the general belief in the derivation of the Greek races from Thessaly: and though it does not suffice of itself to prove that a Dorus or an Ion came from thence, yet it is of great importance as a testimony to their general connection with Thessaly, and it powerfully corroborates evidence such as Homer affords to that effect in the case of the Achæans. Nor are we entirely without Homeric evidence of a connection between the Dorians and the Achæans, and thus between the Dorians and Thessaly. For the Dorians are found in Crete together with the Achæans (Od. xix.), and in the dominions of Nestor peopled by Achæans we find the town called Δώριον, Il. ii. 594. As, however, the great

Dorian mass came into Peloponnesus not under a family of Dorian rulers, but under Heraclids, their connection with the old Hellas was not maintained by any regal tradition, and hence perhaps the need of the legend of Hellen to revive the memory of it.

Let us now endeavour to gather together the threads of the argument.

It is plain that Agamemnon was not called ἄναξ ἀνδρῶν on account of his great monarchy; because other great monarchs want the title, and, again, other insignificant lords hold it.

Nor did he possess it on the ground of autochthonism: for the Achæans were immigrants into the Peloponnesus, and not autochthons, and they had been preceded by other races.

Neither was it borne by him on the ground of a divine descent more direct or more illustrious than that of others: for his divine descent would in that case at least have been specifically stated, instead of being left to remote and hazardous inference. Nor is the title borne by Achilles, who was the great grandson of Jupiter, or by Hercules or Minos, who were his sons.

If sovereignty and antiquity be connected with the title, they are not of themselves sufficient to confer it: and if divine descent be a condition of it, this must be joined with other conditions.

These negatives, established in the case of Agamemnon, leave room, I believe, for but one supposition; namely, that the ἄναξ ἀνδρῶν must indicate chieftaincy, or in other words, the lineal headship, passing by seniority, of one among the ruling or royal houses, who represent the stem of a particular race, in his case the Achæan branch of the Hellenic family; and who govern, and have continuously governed, those of their

Summary of the Evidence.

own name or branch. Of these royal houses there might be many, allied together by common derivation, at the same or different epochs, from a common stem.

In sum, the Homeric picture appears to be as follows.

First we have the remote and wintry Dodona of Thessaly, the most ancient and most awful seat of the religious worship of the Greeks; in connection with which Achilles invokes Jupiter for the success and safe return of Patroclus.

Around Dodona dwell the Selli or Helli. The special veneration paid to the place points it out as the oldest site of the national worship; and the possession of this oldest site again points out the tribe as the mother-tribe of that wonderful Greek race, whose fame is graven ineffaceably upon the rock with a pen of iron.

From among the Helli of the mountains, who nowhere appear among the contingents of the Greek army, must have proceeded the migratory bands who gave to the Thessalian plain the name of Hellas. Their descendants fix themselves as settlers there. Beguiled into civilization, they become Hellenes; they spread, by their inborn elastic energies, towards the south, and carry with them, only a little in their rear, the very title of their Hellenic origin, as well as their own peculiar name.

The ruling families of their septs or clans give each to its actual head, if not to its heir, the dignity of ἄναξ ἀνδρῶν, and this title they carry forth with them to the southern provinces in which they plant themselves.

One of these ruling families, the head of the great sept of the Achæans, carries the right to this title in the case of Agamemnon: and inasmuch as it betokens what is both oldest and highest in descent and in civil authority in the whole group of the Hellenic tribes, it forms an appropriate and characteristic designation for their chief ruler and leader.

Having thus considered the case of Agamemnon, the great Achæan chieftain, in this view, we may proceed to the other cases of Anchises and Æneas, of Augeias, Euphetes, and Eumelus.

In none of these cases, however, have we the same right to assume *in limine* the character of chieftainship by known lineage from an Hellenic family, as in the case of the Achæans. The cases of Anchises and Æneas may indeed be treated on grounds of their own. In the other instances, we must inquire what ground Homer furnishes for especially connecting these persons with the headship of ruling families, and with Hellas or Thessaly.

This I shall do, subject to the general rule, that if in any particular case there can be found a special mark of connection with Thessaly or Hellas in or about a particular spot, it is thereupon to be inferred that in that particular place the connection was known and commemorated. If, for example, we find at a given point an ἄναξ ἀνδρῶν, reason binds us to presume that, as the local name might show the derivation from the first seat of the race, so by this title the lineal descent from a ruling family there was meant to be commemorated and marked.

The Cases of Anchises and Æneas.

But first for Anchises and Æneas.

Homer is the historian as well as the poet of Greece: but he is neither the poet nor the historian of Troy, further than as it was necessary for him to describe generally to the Greeks the race with whom they had been engaged in a death-struggle.

The strong resemblance between the two nations, and especially their partaking, to a certain extent, of a common lineage, seems to have constituted a difficulty in his way. Already in his time the sentiment of Greek nationality was strong. Whether he chiefly found or made it so, is nothing to the present purpose. This sentiment of nationality required to be circumscribed by a clear line, marking the extent of the Greek political organisation; and if it was unfavourable to the acknowledgment of relationship to any race beyond that line, especially was it so in the case of a race that the Greeks had conquered. Probably therefore the purpose of Homer required that he should instinctively as it were keep in special obscurity the notes of kindred between the two countries.

In the case of the Greeks, Homer has intelligibly pointed out the origin of the race among the hills of Northern Thessaly round the ancient Dodona, and near Olympus, its poetical counterpart, and the residence of Jupiter with his gorgeous train. Yet more clearly has he in the case of the Trojans enabled us to trace them to their fountain-head, again in the mountains, and beside the roots, of Ida, where they worshipped the Idæan Jove[c]. We have here the race without predecessors, residing in the very spot where they were planted by their divine progenitor, and coming down by a clear line of seven generations to the cousins Hector and Æneas.

But although the conditions of chieftaincy are thus obviously fulfilled in the race of Dardanus, yet difficulty presents itself in a new form. Why is the term ἄναξ ἀνδρῶν applied to Anchises and to his son Æneas, but never to Priam, or to his son Hector, or to any of his family?

[c] Il. iii. 276. vii. 202. ix. 47, 8. xvi. 605. xxiv. 290, 308.

II. *Ethnology.*

The answer to this question opens a curious chapter of Homeric history and speculation. In going through it I shall endeavour carefully to separate between positive statement, and interpretation or conjecture.

These facts then are on the face of the poem.

1. Anchises nowhere personally appears in it. And yet there was at Troy an assembly of $\delta\eta\mu o\gamma\acute{\epsilon}\rho o\nu\tau\epsilon s$ (Il. iii. 146-8). Of the persons there mentioned, Lampus, Clytius, and Hiketaon were brothers of Priam; others, for example, Panthus and Antenor, were in the exercise of at the very least a subaltern sovereignty. They were present at Troy, while their sons fought in the Trojan ranks. The reason, therefore, of the absence of Anchises is not to be sought in his being represented by Æneas. Nor in the immunity of his dominions, through their being placed among the mountains, from war: for Æneas himself, before he came to Troy, had only been rescued by divine interposition from the hands of Achilles[e]. Why then does Anchises never appear? Either surely because of the high rank of his sovereignty, or because of some unexplained rivalry between the families.

2. It does not appear that Æneas took any part in the councils of the Trojans. But still he is always represented as a personage of the greatest importance. It is said of him, as of Hector, $\theta\epsilon\grave{o}s\ \delta'\ \grave{\omega}s\ \tau\acute{\iota}\epsilon\tau o\ \delta\acute{\eta}\mu\omega$. Yet his character would seem to be wholly unmarked by any great or striking quality, such as we find in Sarpedon and in Polydamas. Something peculiar then in his birth and position must have been the cause of the importance attached to him, as it is not to be found in his personal qualities.

3. Accordingly, there are clear indications of a

[d] Il. ii. 58. [e] Il. xx. 90-3, 128-31.

jealousy between Æneas himself and the Trojan royal family. In the great battle of B. x. 118, Deiphobus, wanting aid, goes to seek Æneas (459–61).

τὸν δ' ὕστατον εὗρεν ὁμίλου
ἑστάοτ'· αἰεὶ γὰρ Πριάμῳ ἐπεμήνιε δίῳ
οὕνεκ' ἄρ', ἐσθλὸν ἐόντα μετ' ἀνδράσιν, οὔτι τίεσκεν.

Now this aversion is wholly foreign to the character of Priam, which was genial and kindly: nor can it be accounted for by any thing in the very neutral character of Æneas. There is an opinion of some critics, that he and Anchises had given offence by advising the restoration of Helen. This, however, seems (B. iii. 159) to have been the general wish of the δημογέροντες, to whom it is expressly ascribed; and it is Antenor, who proposes it in the Assembly; why then should it not, if it existed, be mentioned by Homer in the case of Æneas and Anchises? Yet there is not the faintest reference to it. It would still, however, appear insufficient to account for the feeling imputed to Priam. Coupling it with the high position of Æneas, and the absence of Anchises, I cannot but think there is most probably a reference here to the headship of the family, which is designated by the term ἄναξ ἀνδρῶν. Nothing could be more natural than this jealousy between the recent and wealthy city of the plain on the one hand, and the ancient but comparatively poor city of the hills on the other, if the ruling family of Dardania claimed by seniority the chieftaincy of the race.

4. Another remarkable indication of the peculiar position of Æneas is afforded by the taunt of Achilles (Il. xx. 179–83),

ἦ σέ γε θυμὸς ἐμοὶ μαχέσασθαι ἀνώγει
ἐλπόμενον Τρώεσσιν ἀνάξειν ἱπποδάμοισιν
τιμῆς τῆς Πριάμου;

'But you will not get it,' he proceeds, 'for Priam has children of his own, and is no fool.'

To this taunt Æneas makes no reply, except by stating his genealogy, for which Achilles had not asked. Is not this very like justifying his expectation of the throne? or what other connecting link can be pointed out between the taunt of Achilles, and the genealogy given in answer to the challenge it conveyed?

5. While Ilion, the city of Priam, was later by several generations, probably having been founded in the reign of Ilus, Anchises reigned in Dardania, the original seat (Il. xx. 216) of the race. The fact of his sovereignty there seems to be indicated by our finding Æneas in command of the Dardanians, with two sons of Antenor, who probably served as his lieutenants (ii. 819–23): by the connection which that passage establishes between Anchises and the hill country, inhabited (Il. xx. 216) by the Dardanians; by the division of the royal line at the point where the Ilian name first appears (Il. xx. 231); and by a number of places showing the high position in the army which Æneas held, as head of the Dardanian force.

6. The rank of Æneas was without any rival or parallel in the Trojan army, except Hector. Though strictly speaking Dardanian, he is addressed as

Αἰνεία, Τρώων βουλήφορε·

His name is often combined with that of Hector, and when so combined frequently precedes it. Thus we have (vi. 75),

εἰ μὴ ἄρ' Αἰνείᾳ τε καὶ Ἕκτορι εἶπε κ. τ. λ.

To this are subjoined, by Helenus, words which assign to Æneas a parity of command with Hector:

Αἰνεία τε καὶ Ἕκτορ, ἐπεὶ πόνος ὔμμι μάλιστα
Τρώων καὶ Λυκίων ἐγκέκλιται g.

If it be thought that metrical considerations had to do with putting Æneas in these places as well as in xx. 240, before Hector, so they might have to do with placing Ilus before Assaracus in the genealogy.

It is asserted of him by Mars in the person of Acamas, Il. v. 467,

κεῖται ἀνὴρ ὄντ' ἶσον ἐτίομεν Ἕκτορι δίῳ,
Αἰνείας, υἱὸς μεγαλήτορος Ἀγχίσαο.

Lastly, we have the prophecy of Neptune that the sceptre of Dardanus should continue in the line of Anchises (Il. xx. 302–8).

And, as regards the application to Æneas of the title which properly belonged to Anchises, this seems to connect itself with the practice of the heroic age as to a devolution of sovereignty, either partial or total, by aged men upon their heirs. We seem to find another example of this in the case of Eumelus; and the instances of Achilles, and especially of Ulysses, are also in point.

7. As the character of Æneas does not account for the jealousy felt towards him, so neither does his conduct. He nowhere thwarts Hector by opposition, or tries him by advice that he is not inclined to take. Of this course of proceeding we have an instance; but it is in Polydamas. If, then, neither the character nor the conduct of Æneas supply the explanation, we must look for it in some claims that he was entitled to make in virtue of lineage, and that consequently attracted jealousy towards him.

8. Although it has been assumed that Priam was the head of the Trojan race and federation, this is not stated by Homer. In Il. xxiv. 544 it is only said that

g Il. vi. 77.

he excelled the other princes of that region, (1) in his wealth, and (2) in the number, or possibly it may mean the excellence of his sons. On the contrary, it is doubtful, by the mere words of the poem, whether Priam represented the senior or the junior line, and when we compare and draw inferences from the text, we may arrive at the conclusion that it was the junior line, quite as easily as at an opposite one; especially if we shall find, that the rights of seniority itself were less determinate in Troas, than in Greece.

In the genealogy of the Twentieth Book, we find no assistance towards elucidating this question, except in the precedence given to names. The three sons of Tros stand in the following order:

  1. Ilus. 2. Assaracus. 3. Ganymedes.

Then (1) the fate of Ganymedes is described;

  (2) the line of Ilus is traced down to Priam;

  (3) that of Assaracus is traced to Anchises.

Here the line of Priam has precedence: but on the other hand, lastly, Æneas proceeds to state his own birth from Anchises, before that of Hector from Priam,

  αὐτὰρ ἔμ' Ἀγχίσης, Πρίαμος δ' ἔτεχ' Ἕκτορα δῖον[e].

9. In the Fifth Iliad we learn, that Jupiter presented some horses of a particular breed to Tros, as a compensation for the loss of his son Ganymedes. Anchises brought his mares to them in the time of Laomedon without leave, and thus got possession of the breed. And it is in this place that Homer calls him ἄναξ ἀνδρῶν[f]. It may also be observed that this was the act of a young man; for Laomedon, on whom he played this trick, was one generation higher in the family tree. It is here shown undoubtedly that the horses of Tros, the common ancestor, descended to the line of Priam; which

[e] Il. xx. 240. [f] Il. v. 268.

was the more wealthy and powerful, and occupied the plain country, where the horses fed in great numbers (xx. 221); but again, does it not seem as if this very proceeding of Anchises may have had reference to a rivalry between the two houses, and a claim on his part to the headship of the family? especially from the use in this very narrative of the phrase ἄναξ ἀνδρῶν for Anchises (v. 268), and shortly after for his heir Æneas (v. 311).

To sum up the evidence. We find the phrase ἄναξ ἀνδρῶν applied to two persons only among the Trojans. Those two are a father advanced in years, and his heir apparent. The father is plainly enough the sovereign of Dardania, as well as descended from Dardanus; and Dardania, though secondary in power, was the original seat of the race. We cannot say positively whether Anchises represented the elder or the younger branch of the family: for precedence of name is sometimes given to one, and sometimes to the other line. But as Troy was powerful, and Dardania poor, we can understand the precedence of the Trojan line, even although it be supposed junior: whereas it seems difficult to account for the fact that the precedence is sometimes given to Æneas, or for the jealousy felt both towards him, and by him, except on the supposition that his family in its humbler circumstances either were the rightful representatives of Dardanus, whose sceptre, after the fall of Troy, Æneas and his sons were undoubtedly to transmit[h]; or at least were in a condition, whether by primogeniture in Assaracus, or whether by holding the original seat of the race, to make fair and plausible pretensions to the distinction.

It is important to bear in mind, that we have not

[h] Il. xx. 303.

the same clear assertion of the right of the elder branch to succeed to power in Asia, which the cases of Agamemnon, Protesilaus, Thrasymedes, and perhaps others, supply in Greece. On the contrary, we shall find Sarpedon first leader of the Lycians, though of a junior branch to Glaucus, and likewise representing only the female line. We shall also find great reason to question whether Hector, even if he was the heir expectant of the succession, was not, nevertheless, junior to Paris. This want of definiteness in the rule of succession is exactly what would bring it into dispute, and perhaps into prolonged dispute. And if the right of seniority was not fully acknowledged in Asia, this would at once explain, why Homer did not observe an uniform order in the genealogy: perhaps it might also explain his not being historically aware what that order was.

If this be so, the apparent anomaly of the application, on the Trojan side, to secondary persons only of the title so constantly given to the highest Greek, disappears, and becomes the consistent application of a rule. And Anchises with Æneas may then offer the most perfect model of the ἄναξ ἀνδρῶν, as uniting with continued sovereignty not only known lineal descent from the first ancestor, and from Jupiter, but also the continued possession of the original seat.

It may however be asked, why, even if we allow that ἄναξ ἀνδρῶν is among the Greeks a title of patriarchal chieftaincy, should we therefore assume that it had the same defined meaning among a people of different blood and institutions?

Let me briefly answer this question.

It is to the Helli that we have looked back as the most probable source of those ideas and institutions of clanship, which gave rise to the title of ἄναξ ἀνδρῶν. But the Helli were a mountain people, (for they were around the wintry Dodona,) and so were the Dardanians: and the institutions of highlanders in different parts, even at wide intervals of space and time, often present strong mutual resemblances. The limited means and pursuits of man in such a physical position check development, and tend to maintain uniformity.

The Dardan highlanders worshipped Jupiter on Ida, as the Helli worshipped him at Dodona. That it was the same Jupiter, we may infer with the greatest confidence, from the fact that Homer makes one formula of invocation common to his Trojans and his Greeks[i].

ὧδε δέ τις εἴπεσκεν Ἀχαιῶν τε Τρώων τε·
Ζεῦ πάτερ, Ἴδηθεν μεδέων, κύδιστε, μέγιστε, κ. τ. λ.

The bulk of the religion was nearly the same on both sides, as far as the principal deities were concerned.

As the first among the proofs of affinity in blood, I should be inclined to cite that very visit of Paris to Menelaus, which gave occasion to the war. We have no other instance recorded in Homer of a foreign prince, received as such in domestic hospitality by a Greek chieftain. Nor can we, inversely, find that Greek chieftains were similarly entertained by foreigners. We have indeed an account of gifts received by Menelaus in Egypt[k]; and we have the kindly reception by the Egyptian king and his people of the Pseudo-Ulysses as a suppliant[l]; and the similar entertainment of Ulysses, again as a suppliant, in Scheria. But these cases fall greatly short of the case of Paris. Again, Homer calls the Egyptians ἀλλόθροοι ἄνθρωποι[m]: and that phrase is an usual one with him, evidently representing a familiar idea. But he never calls the Trojans ἀλλόθροοι, nor

[i] Il. iii. 297, 320.   [k] Od. iv. 125-35.   [l] Od. xiv. 276-86.
[m] Od. iii. 302.

speaks of them as having different manners or religion from the Greeks. The strongest word applied to them is ἀλλόδαπος[n]. But this word seems to mean simply 'from another place,' and does not convey the proper and full idea of a foreigner. For not only the Lycian Sarpedon is an ἀλλόδαπος to the Trojans, but Greek pirates are usually said to attack ἀλλόδαποι, whereas they evidently were wont to plunder those of their own nation, even down to the time of Thucydides: and above all Eumæus, disgusted and worn out with the profligate misdeeds of the Suitors, thinks of moving off ἄνδρας ἐς ἀλλοδάπους, together with his oxen (ἰόντ' αὐτῇσι βόεσσιν), by which he could not have meant more than a short passage to the Greek continent[o]. On the whole, I think that all this permits the supposition that the Trojans were admitted to be a kindred, though they were not a Greek people.

But further, the poems are full of testimony to the affinities between the Trojans and the Greeks. It is true they also bear witness to considerable differences: but both nations had been settled in the plain country for several generations before the Trojan War; and, with the growth of agriculture and trade, arts and wealth, they might well have diverged from the close parallelism of a ruder age.

At this point, however, we must call to mind some matters, which have been more largely discussed already.

Among these resemblances of a general character it may be observed, that there evidently are Pelasgi on both sides of the great quarrel. The Πελασγοὶ of the Trojans are among the ἐπίκουροι (Il. ii. 840): the Πελασγοὶ of the Greeks appear as one of the Cretan races, distinct from the Dorians and Achæans, and

[n] Il. iii. 48. xix. 324.   [o] Od. iii. 48. xx. 219. Il. xvi. 550.

probably as the first founders of those lowland settlements in Thessaly (ii. 681), over which the Hellenic and Achæan names seem principally to have prevailed. Thus the Pelasgian name forms a decided bond of union between the two races: though, from the Poet's mentioning it on the Trojan, and suppressing it on the Greek side, we at once infer that the Pelasgian element was stronger and more palpable among the Trojans.

Next, it may be recollected that, according both to antecedent probability and to tradition, those Helli who colonized the tract about Dodona must have come from, that is, come by way of, Dardania. There is thus every likelihood of a similarity, either of race or of manners, between those who passed onwards, and those who dropped off the movement, and remained behind.

Nor are there wanting some indications, small in amount, but trustworthy in their nature, of primitive identity between the Dardans, or some portion of them, and the Helli.

The Trojan Catalogue divides itself into two principal parts. The latter of these (840–877) recites the names of the allied nations. The former (816–39) mentions no names of races but the Trojan and Dardanian; which were really one, and were even in name sometimes treated as identical: for Æneas is addressed, though commander of the Dardans[p], as

Αἰνεία, Τρώων βουλήφορε.

This division of the Catalogue is clearly indicated by the verse which introduces it,

ἔνθα τότε Τρῶές τε διέκριθεν ἠδ' ἐπίκουροι·

where the word Τρῶες evidently includes the Dardanians.

[p] See also Dolon's description, Il. x. 418–21.

And that every thing is Trojan, or Dardan, which lies within the division, vv. 816–839, may further be inferred from Dolon's description of the bivouac of the ἐπίκουροι in Il. x. 428–31. He enumerates nine nations, some of whom appear among the eleven described in Il. ii. 840–77, but not one among those portions of the force which are described 816–839. I therefore gather, that every thing in this part of the Catalogue is strictly Trojan or Dardan. But here we have

Ἄσιος Ὑρτακίδης, ὃν Ἀρίσβηθεν φέρον ἵπποι
αἴθωνες μεγάλοι, ποταμοῦ ἀπὸ Σελλήεντος.

The mention of this river is repeated in Il. xii. 96, 7.

Now the name of a river Selleeis at once suggests a connection with the tribe of Selli or Helli: and further on we shall find, that Ephyre is a sign of the Helli, as Larissa is of the Pelasgi, and that one at least of the Ephyres of Greece, probably one situated in Thessaly, was by a river Selleeis. In later times Sicyon[q], and in Homer Elis, if not Thessaly, show each their Ephyre with a river Selleeis.

It has been already noticed, that in the Games of the Twenty-third Iliad, Homer tells us that the σόλος, or ball of iron given by Achilles as a prize, had previously been hurled by the strong arm of king Eetion. And as all the traces of gymnastic exercises in Homer lead us to refer them to Hellic families, we may perhaps be justified in taking this as an indication that Eetion, the father of Andromache, belonged to this stock.

Another trace of the name of the Helli is found in the grammatical structure of the ancient Homeric word Hellespont. Its composition declares it to be the

[q] Strabo, p. 338.

sea of Helle. Helle would be the descriptive name of a woman of the tribe of Helli. Nor could any thing be more natural, than that the Strait and neighbouring water should take its appellation from the tribe of Helli, or even from a person of that tribe, when we have every reason to believe they made the passage in the course of their migration westward.

In later times, the name Hellespont has been restricted to the narrow strait between the Sea of Marmora and the Archipelago. In Homer it bore this sense, at least oocasionally or inclusively, because he calls it ἀγάρροος [r]. At other times he calls it πλατὺς, and the commentators have been much puzzled to show how a narrow strait could be a broad one, while the interpretation *salt* has also been suggested for the epithet. It is just possible, that this adjective might apply to what was afterwards known as the Hellespont, and might describe it as broad, in comparison with the bay in which lay the Greek ships: but it is much more natural to construe it more freely, and to understand by it the broad Hellespont, in opposition to the narrow Hellespont; that is, the open sea, in opposition to the ἀγάρροος, which signifies the Strait. The expression πλατὺς Ἑλλήσποντος is used but thrice; once [s] for the water near the part of the camp occupied by Achilles, which we know was by the open sea [t], and twice [u] with reference to the sepulchral mounds which were to be erected there, and for which the most conspicuous spot would of course be chosen. What πλατὺς suggests, another epithet, ἀπείρων [x], surely requires: for it is incredible that this word should be applied to the mere Strait. And in truth, independently of epithets, it is

[r] Il. xii. 30. [s] Il. xvii. 432. [t] Il. i. 350.
[u] Il. vii. 86. Od. xxiv. 82. [x] Il. xxiv. 545.

demonstrable that the word in Homer sometimes means, not the strait, but the Archipelago. For Achilles, announcing his intention to sail home, says he will be seen passing Ἑλλήσποντον ἐπ᾽ ἰχθυόεντα[y], *over* the Hellespont, which, having his vessels already at the mouth of it, he clearly could not do if it meant the strait only. And, in truth, the etymology of the word speaks for itself: the Greeks never would have given the name πόντος at all to a narrow strip of water. The connection, which was thus established between this quarter and Greece through the medium of the name Helle, was recognised by the later Greeks: but they naturally altered its form, by keeping to their own country the honours of the fountain-head, while they made the eastward traces of the name to be secondary and derivative. In Apollonius, Phryxus and Helle are the children of Athamas, and grandchildren of Æolus: and they are carried from Thessaly on the back of a ram to the Troic sea, where she is dropped, and gives her name to it. This tradition is summed up in the argument to the Argonautica, and exhibits the belief of the Greeks in the early relationship of the countries.

All this marks the Helli not only as a people who had crossed the straits, but as one which had left its name associated with the northern coast of the Ægean, and moreover upon the country in the neighbourhood of the straits, up to the river Selleeis; a stream which we see must have been at a considerable distance beyond Troy, because all the rivers that descended from Mount Ida were employed in clearing away the Greek earthworks, and this one is not among them[z].

[y] Il. ix. 360.   [z] Il. xii. 19–23.

We find an insulated yet remarkable note of kin between the Dardan house and the Greeks in the case of Echepolus. He was a son of Anchises, and he resided in Sicyon. He was possessed of great wealth, and apparently he had also the fine breed of horses which was in his family: for he presented Agamemnon with the mare Αἴθη[a], as a consideration for not being required to follow him against Troy.

Now there was evidently at this time no commercial class formed in Greece. Echepolus must therefore have had a territorial fortune. To find a wealthy member of the Dardan house domesticated in Greece, and peacefully remaining there during the expedition, must excite some surprise. It seems to supply a new and strong presumption of the Hellic origin of the royal families of Troas. The name too, and the gift of a horse, are in remarkable conformity with the horse-rearing and horse-breaking pursuits of the highest Trojans.

We have already seen stray signs of the Pelasgic affinities between the two contending parties: but it would now appear, that there were affinities in the Hellic line also: and if so, then this institution of chieftaincy, standing above merely political supremacy, and indicated by the phrase ἄναξ ἀνδρῶν, may probably have subsisted among Trojans as well as Greeks.

The less warlike character of the Trojans, their more oriental manners, and their less multiform and imaginative religion, all point to considerable differences in the composition of the people. The Pelasgic ingredient was probably stronger in Troy: it appears to have had more influence over religion, manners, and institutions. But the circumstances mentioned above are tokens of an

[a] Il. xxiii. 293–9.

infusion of Hellic blood in the populations that inhabited Troas. Now this was nowhere so likely to be found as in the royal family; for we see the governing faculty everywhere accompanying the Hellic tribes through Greece, and asserting itself both by the acquisition of political power, and by the energetic use of it. Everywhere it rises, by a natural buoyancy, to the summit of society; and gives their first vent, in miniature, to those energies, which were afterwards to defy, or even to subdue the world.

At the same time, though it is in connection with the Hellic families alone that we find the ἄναξ ἀνδρῶν among the Greeks, we need not proceed so far as to deny the possibility that it might also have been a Pelasgic institution, and that its non-appearance, in connection with their name, might be sufficiently accounted for simply by their loss of political power. We have no reason to suppose the Pelasgi and Helli to have been families of mankind whose characters were in radical and absolute opposition to one another: the completeness of their fusion after a short period seems to prove, that, though with a different distribution of capacities and tendencies, they must have had many and important points of contact.

IV. *Case of Augeias.*

Let us take next the case of Augeias.

He appears in three passages of the Iliad.

1. The Epeans, who inhabited Elis, with Bouprasium and other towns enumerated in the Catalogue, and lying in the north-western corner of the Peloponnesus, sent to the Trojan war forty ships, in four divisions, under four separate leaders, and without any head over

the whole contingent. The fourth named of these is Polyxeinus, son of Agasthenes, himself a lord (ἄναξ), and the son of Augeias.

2. In the Eleventh Book, Nestor gives the curious history of the war of his boyhood or earliest youth, between the Elians (v. 671), called also Epeans (688), and the Pylians.

Neleus had sent to Elis a chariot with four horses to contend in the games, of which a tripod was the prize. The horses were detained by Augeias (v. 701).

τοὺς δ' αὖθι ἄναξ ἀνδρῶν Αὐγείας
κάσχεθε.

Nestor and the Pylians invaded Elis in return, and brought off an immense booty. The Elians then took arms and besieged Thryoessa (in the Catalogue Thryon), the border city of Pylos, at the ford of the Alpheus. Minerva brought the tidings to Pylos. The Pylian forces spent one night on the boundary river Minyeius, and marched to the Alpheus, beside which they spent a second night.

3. In the morning the battle was fought: the Epeans were defeated, and driven all the way to Bouprasium and the Olenian rock, upon the sea shore, in the western part of what was afterwards Achæa. There Pallas turned them back. The Pylians, who returned home, are called Achæans [a].

Nestor in the first fight had slain a warrior named Μούλιος. He was the son-in-law of Augeias, married to his eldest daughter Agamede, who was profoundly skilled in drugs (v. 741);

ἣ τόσα φάρμακα ᾔδη, ὅσα τρέφει εὐρεῖα χθών.

K. O. Müller (Orchomenus, p. 355) infers from the

[a] Il. xi. 759.

Catalogue, that Augeias was lord only of a fourth part of Elis. But this assumption seems quite gratuitous in connection with the passage in the Catalogue, and utterly in contradiction to the tenour of the history of the Pylian raid in B. xi. On the contrary, I infer with considerable confidence, from the acephalous state of the Elian division of the army, in which it differs from the other divisions, that there had been a revolution in that state since the time of Augeias; and if so, then indirectly the Catalogue confirms the Elian monarchy described in the Eleventh Book.

Thus then we find this ἄναξ ἀνδρῶν, Augeias, lord of Elis two generations before the Trojan war. He is neighbour to Achæans, whom we have already traced in Hellas: and he appears to have belonged to the same national origin with them, because they sent their chariots to run races at his games. Again, the fact of his holding these games at all, and at a place which subsequently contended for and obtained the superintendence of the great national assemblages celebrated at Olympia, testifies to his known connection with the cradle of the race whose custom it was to celebrate them; because these festivities had a religious and national character, and as such could not but have depended very greatly upon traditionary title. This race we have previously found to be the Hellenic race.

We may however find other indications of the descent of Augeias from a ruling Hellenic family, in local and personal notices which connect Elis, his own territory, with the north, and with Thessaly in particular.

For example: it was at the Alpheus in Elis that Thamyris suffered his calamity: and he was coming at

Notes of connection between Elis and the North. 503

the time from Œchalia[b], in the valley of the Upper Peneus, a part of the Homeric Thessaly or Hellas proper. (Il. ii. 730.)

The name Θρῆξ, too, which is applied to him, never seems to have spread farther southwards than the hills about Thessaly.

Further, he was coming from Eurytus of Œchalia, who is again named as the lord, apparently, of that city, in ii. 730. But the name Eurytus was one current among the descendants of Actor[c], for a descendant of Actor who bore it is named in the Catalogue a little below: and this latter Eurytus was an Epean chief: and the descendants of Actor are found in the Epean or Elian army of the Eleventh Book. (xi. 709, 739.)

Again, they are found in Thessaly or Phthiotis, for when Mercury had deflowered Polymele, the daughter of Phylas a Thessalian, Echecles, a descendant of Actor, married her; and yet again, they are found near Aspledon[d] and the Minyeian Orchomenos, between Bœotia and Phocis[e].

Again, the Pylian army halted, at a day's march from the Alpheus, on the Minyeius, a river evidently named from the Minyæ of Peloponnesus. But there was a Minya also in Thessaly[f], of which the site was not precisely known in historic times: and the northern Orchomenos was called Minyeius[g].

There is no part of Middle or of Southern Greece which so abounds in the local and personal notes of connection with Thessaly and the North as Elis and its neighbourhood. Some indications of it have already been given, and many more might be added. As for

---

[b] Il. ii. 592 et seqq. [c] Il. ii. 596, 621. [d] Il. xvi. 189.
[e] Il. ii. 513. [f] Cramer's Greece, i. 449. [g] Il. ii. 511.

example, there was an Enipeus[h], a river of Elis, so there was of Pieria and of Phthiotis. Doris, beneath Œta, is reflected or prefigured in the Homeric Dorium of the Pylian territories: the Thessalian Larissa in a Larissa, and a river Larissus, of Elis. The Thessalian name Œchalia is repeated in the district, over which Nestor ruled at the epoch of the *Troica;* and there is an Arcadian Orchomenos as well as a northern one. Cyparissus in Elis corresponds, again, with a Cyparissus in Phocis. Some other more doubtful indications may close the list. The Parrhasie of Arcadia may be from the same root with the Πύρασος[i] of the dominions of Protesilaus. Perhaps the Thessalian Helos and Pteleos may be akin to Alos in the country of Peleus[k]. The resemblance of names is not confined to the extremities of the line, but is scattered along the path of migration from north to south. It extends also to Laconia.

Nestor in his youth is summoned all the way from Pylos (τηλόθεν), to fight with Pirithous and others in Thessaly; (from whence Polypœtes, the son of Pirithous, led a division of the Greek army,) against the Φῆρες.

Thus far we find some presumptions as to the descent of Augeias, as to his connection with the Hellic institution of the games, and as to the relation between Elis, over which he reigned, and the line northwards into Thessaly; all tending, together with the evidently Hellic character of the Epeans, to shew that he was the representative of one of their ruling tribes.

But he also bears a distinct local mark, the nature of which I shall now endeavour to investigate.

The chieftainship of Agamemnon has been traced

---

[h] Thuc. iv. 76. Strabo, 356, 432. Cramer's Greece, i. 207, 399.
[i] Il. ii. 608, 695.   [k] Il. ii. 682.

and identified by means of his Achæan connection, without any assistance from local or territorial names connected with the abode of his family.

In such a case as his, we could not look for aid of that description: for his house had only been possessed for two generations of their dominions: we have no precise knowledge before that time of the place of their sojourn: and when they rose to power, it was in a territory, and in cities, which appear to have been already of historic fame. It was not therefore likely that their abodes should bear names such as, if they had come in the characters of founders and not of inheritors, they would probably have affixed to them.

In the case of the Dardan house, we have found, among other indications of their Hellic affinities, the two evidently Hellic names of the Hellespont and the River Selleeis.

There is another local name in Homer of paramount importance as a key to the question respecting the ruling Hellic tribes, the name of Ephyre ('Εφύρη).

Let us endeavour to collect the scattered lights which either the etymology, or the use and associations of the term in Homer, may supply.

And, first, we may notice in Homer a large cluster of names which are found running over Greece, and which are evidently in etymological association with one another: I will bring these together, before endeavouring to estimate their relation to the name Ephyre.

1. Φᾶρις, Il. ii. 582. In Lacedæmon.
2. Φεραὶ, Il. ii. 711. In Thessaly.
3. Φήρη, Il. v. 543. Between Pylus and Sparta.
4. Φήραι, Il. ix. 151, 293. Od. iii. 488. The same.

5. Φεαὶ, Od. xv. 296[1]. Otherwise read Φεραὶ, and, according to the Scholiast, the same with Φῆραι. The site is on the sea, between Pylus and Sparta.

6. Φεῖα, Il. vii. 135. On the Iardanus: and probably also on the Arcadian frontier towards Pylus: but, in the opinion of the Scholiast[m], the same with Φεαί.

Besides these names of places, we have also,

1. Φηρητιάδης, Il. ii. 763. xxiii. 376, the name of Eumelus; who was the son of Admetus, the lord of Φεραὶ in Il. ii. 711.

2. Φέρης, one of the sons of Cretheus, a Thessalian king, Od. xi. 259.

3. The Φῆρες, termed ὀρέσκῳοι in Il. i. 268, and λαχνήεντες in Il. ii. 743; the shaggy mountaineers, on whom Pirithous made war, when he was attended by Nestor.

With respect to the six local names, and the two first of the three personal names, there can be little doubt of their identity in root. It is directly probable from the text, that Φήρη and Φηραὶ were the same place. The name of Eumelus, who lives at Φεραὶ, and who is the grandson of Φέρης, yet is called Φηρητιάδης, clearly establishes the etymological relationship. This there is, again, no difficulty whatever in recognising between Φεραὶ and Φεαὶ, or again between Φεαὶ and Φεῖαι; and it is in the manner of Homer to give the name of the same country both in the singular and in the plural, as Μυκήνη, Il. iv. 52, and Μυκηναὶ, Il. ii. 569. Φᾶρις, the only remaining name, gives us the Doric or Æolic α for η, and an altered form of declension. This however is not at all incompatible with the manner of Homer, who not only uses Πηνελόπη and Πηνελόπεια, Ἀστυόχη and Ἀστυόχεια, Πηρείη (according to one reading), Il. ii. 766, and

---

[1] Strabo, b. viii. p. 351.
[m] Schol. Il. vii. 135. Od. xv. 297. Cramer, Geogr. Gr. iii. 87.

Πιερίη, Od. v. 50, but Ἑρμῆς and Ἑρμείας, Πατροκλέης and Πάτροκλος; and for towns, the Θρύον of Il. ii. 591 appears again as Θρυόεσσα in Il. xi. 711.

In general it is to be remembered that the instrument of language, at the time when Homer lived was as yet in a highly elastic state: it was in the state as it were of gristle; it had not yet hardened into bone, nor assumed the strict conventional forms which a formed literature requires. And for the same reasons that it has presented variations as between one time and another, it could not but do the like as between one place and another.

The very same causes which made change a law of language would give to that course of change in one place a greater, and in another a less velocity, older forms succumbing at a given time in one place, and yet surviving in another. Such a state of facts around him would give great liberty to a poet, independently of the exigencies of his verse; which appear indeed to have caused to such a man, and with such a language, little difficulty.

But we hardly require the benefit of these general considerations to cover the case of a varying declension for the name of a town. The true explanation probably is the very simple one, that in one declension it has been used substantively, and in the other adjectively. And this will be the more plain if we consider that the name of the town would usually be the representative of an idea, either in conjunction with a person, or directly. Thus θρύον is *a rush*, and θρυοείς *rushy*. The town Θρύον in the Catalogue is at the ford of the Alpheus, and in Il. xi. 711 it is τις Θρυόεσσα πόλις, αἰπεῖα κολώνη, which exhibits to us the adjective use in an actual example. So again by analogy we might have

Φῆρις from Φήρα or Φήρη, as πάτρις from πάτρα, ἀναλκὶς from ἄλκη.

We have a curious extra-Homeric remnant of geographical evidence with respect to this Pharis. Pausanias[n] relates to us, that the place where it was reported to have stood was in his time called Alesiæ, and that near it there was a river bearing the peculiar name of Phellias; which it seems most natural to regard as a corrupted form of the Homeric name Σελληείς. This connection of Pharis with Selleeis becomes in its turn an argument for relationship between Pharis and Ephyre, with which Selleeis is associated in the places where Homer mentions it as the name of a Greek river.

Nor are we without other traces, in this region, of that name which so often attends upon Ephyre: for Laconia had for its key on the north the town of Sellasia[o]. The Προσέληνοι of Arcadia should also here be borne in mind.

Thus then we appear to find the name of Ephyre according to one or other of its forms in Laconia, in Pylus, and in that part of Thessaly which was ruled by Admetus. The ruling race in the two former was Achæan, and therefore Hellic. Admetus was himself an ἄναξ ἀνδρῶν, and his Hellic origin will be shown presently. So far, therefore, we have a presumption established that the name of Ephyre signifies some peculiar connection with the Helli.

Etymologically it is obvious to connect these words with ἔρα as their root, and to suppose that they retain the prefix, which it had lost in the common Greek usage even before the days of Homer, as he employs ἔραζε without the digamma: and which prefix we find reproduced in the Latin *terra*.

[n] Paus. Lac. b. III. c. xx. 5, 3. [o] Cramer iii. 221.

Let us now pass on to the Φῆρες.

The Φῆρες of Homer are, like the Ἕλλοι, a mountain people, Il. i. 268, rude in manners (ii. 743), and aggressive upon the inhabitants of the plains; for the war in which Nestor engaged was evidently retributive, as the expression used is ἐτίσατο [P], Pirithous '*paid them off;*' and he was sovereign of a part of the plain country, called Pelasgic Argos. Nor does any adverse presumption arise from our finding a Hellic tribe (if such they were) of the mountains, making war on tribes of similar origin in the plain: any more than we are surprised at war between the Pylians and the Epeans, both apparently Hellic, though probably not both Achæan.

It may be well to remember, that the Dardans of Homer are often included in Trojans; as well as often separately designated: and that the Cephallenians are also apparently included among his Ἀχαιοί. Neither of these pairs of names are territorial: while in each pair one probably indicates a subdivision of the other.

The Φῆρες thus resembling the Ἕλλοι, we are led by their designation to another link between the name of Φῆραι with its cognates and the Hellic race. It seems thus far as if Φηραὶ were the appropriate name of a settlement formed by Φῆρες.

Having proceeded thus far, we may now observe the relation of the word Φὴρ,

1. To the Greek ἔρα, which evidently, from its passing into the Latin *terra*, had at one time a Greek prefix. With this we may probably associate the Greek ἔαρ, and the Latin *ver*.

2. To the Greek θὴρ, a wild beast.

3. To the Latin *fera*, with the same meaning.

4. To the Latin *terra*, meaning the earth.

[P] Il. ii. 743.

5. To the Italian *terra*, the old classical name, in that beautiful tongue, not for a district, but for an inclosed, walled, or fortified place. This word seems in Italian to be rarely, if at all, used for a district, but so generally for a town, that it is difficult to suppose the signification was derived in the same manner as Argos in Greek, from the tract of country in which it was situated. In Italian *terra* seems often to mean *tellus*, often *humus*, very rarely *ager*, constantly *oppidum* or *castrum*. Thus in Dante (Inferno, C., v. 97), ' Siede la terra, dove nata fui.'

This being so, it is natural to suppose that, while the correlative of the Greek ἔρα became in Latin *terra*, so as directly to signify *tellus* or *humus*, that of the Greek Φηρὰ became in Italian *terra*, so as to signify a walled place; or, in other words, that the original word, whatever it was, of the common mother language, which became Φηρὰ in Greek, in Italy became *terra* for this latter purpose. The exchange of θ for *t* we see in ἐσθὴς becoming *vestis*: and of *t* for $f\ (=\phi)$ in τρυγάω compared with *fruges*.

This sense of *terra* seems to have dropped altogether out of the Latin, and especially Pelasgian, branch of the old Italian tongue.

The relation between Φὴρ and θὴρ, the one applicable to men, and the other to wild beasts, appears evidently to throw us back upon that which the mountain tribes of men had in common with animals, namely, a wild and savage life, and the free possession of the earth. Thus the two stand in a common and near relation to the word ἔρα, the earth, and they seem to have ἐρ or ἠρ for their common root.

Before passing on to Ἐφύρη, I would remark that in this instance again we seem to derive light from Homer's unequalled point and precision in the use of epithets. His Φῆρες appear to be in fact the rude and uncombed mountaineers, who also have the name of Ἕλλοι in the same or other tribes. These Φῆρες are λαχνήεντες, shaggy. They come down to the plains, and acquire settled and civilised habits: from Φῆρες they are become Ἀχαιοὶ, but their long hair has not left them, and from λαχνήεντες, they are now καρηκομόωντες.

Now we find the word Ἐφύρη used many times in Homer: and once we have the name Ἔφυροι, applied to a people apparently Thessalian, on whom Mars[q], with his son Φόβος, makes war from out of Thrace.

Can we then presume an etymological connection between the word Ἐφύρη, and that group of words which we have been discussing, and which we have found to show marks of connection with the Helli?

For if so, then we shall be supported by various other reasons, which, as we shall find, connect the word Ephyre with the Hellic races in a very remarkable manner.

What we have here to consider is,
1. The prefix ε.
2. The change of ε or η for υ.

Dr. Donaldson[r] has given a list of Greek words which have, as prefixes unconnected with the root, sometimes the letter α, sometimes ε, sometimes ο.

Such in the second class are

ἐ-ρέφω, whence roof.
ἐ-λεύθερος, whence liber.
ἐ-ρυθρὸς, whence ruber, rufus.
ἐ-ρετμὸς, whence remus.

This point being disposed of, how are we to account for finding φυρη, instead of φερη or φηρη?

[q] Il. xiii. 301.   [r] New Cratylus iii. 1. p. 282, 286.

Can it be because, in cases of Greek syllabic augment, there is a tendency to avoid reduplication, as in ἀτιτάλλω for ἀτατάλλω? In but a small proportion of the cases given in Dr. Donaldson's table is the vowel prefix the same with the vowel following.

Can it be from that tendency of what we call comprehensively the digamma to lapse into the *v*, which Heyne has observed[s]?

Or, shall we found it on the principles laid down by Bopp[t], in his Comparative Grammar, that the *a* has a tendency to weaken itself into *v*, and that liquids having a preference for that latter vowel, influence the generation of it? the conditions of interchange between *a* and *v* resting, as he says, upon the laws of gravity or vocal equilibrium.

It must be observed that the original vowel of the root may, in this case, have been the *a* which we find in φᾶρις.

It is not only *a* that we may find supplanted by *v*. The ε suffers the same fate in the Italian *Siculus*, which appears as the representative of the Greek Σίκελος. Again we have, in the Latin, the kindred words *furo* and *fera*. Perhaps I am wrong in dealing thus scrupulously with the variation from ε to *v*, as if capable of affecting vitally the question of identity in the root. For in examining another root (that of κεφάλη), we have seen that its derivatives appear to include the whole, or nearly the whole range of the vowels of the alphabet.

Upon the whole it appears not unsafe, without pretending to any authoritative solution of a question fitted for philological scholars, among whom I cannot pretend to rank, to suppose that Ἐφύρη and Φηραὶ may

---

[s] Heyne Exc. iii. ad Hom. Il. xix. vol. vii. p. 770.
[t] Comp. Gram. sect. 490.

be drawn etymologically from the same root. If so, that root will be probably the same with that of ἔρα, and of φῆρ, of which we have ascertained that it is related to the Hellic races: and upon these suppositions we may already be prepared, I do not say to conclude, but to suspect that Ἐφύρη and Φεραὶ may properly denote, and may be the original and proper Hellic name for the *terre* (Ital.), or walled places, founded by the Hellic races; as Ἄργος signifies the open districts in which the Pelasgians were given to settling κωμηδὸν, for agricultural purposes.

I do not mean by this that the Pelasgian settlements contained no aggregations of houses, or that the Hellic were not connected with the cultivation of the soil. On the contrary, as the Pelasgians apparently built their Larissas for defence, so we seem to have indications connecting the name Ephyre with a fertile soil. When Homer represents the Ἔφυροι as objects of invasion by Mars from Thrace, he probably means by the name the inhabitants of a settled country in the plains, on whom predatory incursions were made by the Thracian highlanders. So that if we shall succeed in shewing a special connection between the local name Ephyre and the Hellic tribes, we may, by the reflected light of that conclusion, even venture to understand the word Ephyri as meaning Helli, who had come down into the low country, made settlements, and acquired something at least of the habits of civilized life.

Nor are we without further Homeric evidence to the effect that, wherever an Ephyre is found, there is usually an abundance of rich pasture and cultivable land, so that the name is well adapted to mark those spots which a conquering race would be apt to choose for its abodes.

For example, Elis has its Ephyre: and from the fact that Elis was the scene of the national chariot-races, we might at once conclude that it was famous for its horses, and if so, that it abounded in good soil and pasture, and in open country. Wherever in Homer we find the horse conspicuous, we find also good lands and opulence, whether it be in Troas, in the Thrace called ἐριβώλαξ[u], in Thessaly, or in Elis. For Homer gives us, as to the last, direct evidence of the fact, by his epithets εὐρύχορος, open, and ἱππόβοτος, horse-pasturing[v]. Elis, in fact, was most probably for Peloponnesus what Bœotia was for Middle Greece: the first halting place, from its fertile soil, of those who entered the region; the scene, accordingly, of rapid successions, and therefore frequent revolutions, but also the place bearing the strongest marks, through nomenclature, of the country from which the new-comers had proceeded.

Again, the Ephyre of the Odyssey is expressly called (Od. ii. 328), πίειραν ἄρουραν. And when Hercules took Astyoche from Ephyre (Il. ii. 659), after despoiling that with many other cities, we may clearly infer, that they were rich, and not poor places which he plundered, therefore that this Ephyre also was rich; and if so, rich in its soil, the only wealth, for regions, then known to Greece. Again, the Ephyre of Sisyphus (Il. vi. 152) became Corinth, and Corinth was even in Homer's time called ἀφνειός. This epithet is referred by some to its favourable position for commerce. But such an explanation is wholly unsuited to the age of Homer. For the commercial prominence of Corinth belongs to a later period; and we have nothing to support the idea, that commercial opulence existed in Greece at this period

---

[u] See Il. xi. 222. xx. 485. compared with x. 436, 545-7.
[v] Od. iv. 635; and xxi. 347.

at all. The natural explanation seems to be, the fertility of the soil of the plain between the rock of Corinth and Sicyon. This seems to have become, in after-time, the subject of a proverb. Hence the χρησμόλογος in the Aves of Aristophanes says (Av. 968),

ἀλλ' ὅταν οἰκήσωσι λύκοι πολιαί τε κορῶναι
ἐν ταυτῷ τὸ μεταξὺ Κορίνθου καὶ Σικυῶνος.

In the same sense as where Shakespeare says,

When Birnam wood shall move to Dunsinane.

The Scholiast gives two explanations, of which the best is εὔφορος γὰρ αὕτη ἡ χώρα.

Again, it is certainly confirmatory of the supposition that Ἐφύρη was the name of the primitive Hellic, as Ἄργος was of the Pelasgic settlement, when we find that the first, though clearly meaning a settled place, has etymologically no reference to agricultural labour, while the second is entirely based upon that idea; since these significations of the word chosen to denote settlement, in the two cases agree, in their reciprocal difference, with the different specific character of the Hellic and Pelasgic tribes, the former emerging from the mountains, predatory and poor, ardent, bold, and enterprising; the latter peaceful in their habits, and looking to nothing beyond the cultivation of the soil.

So much for the root of Ephyre and Pheræ, and for the relation between the two.

Now the Homeric testimony to the prevalence of these names is exactly such as most effectually establishes the connection between them on the one hand, and Thessaly with the Hellic races on the other.

First as to Ephyre.

1. Five generations before the Trojan war, Sisyphus, a son or descendant of Æolus, was settled, apparently as a subordinate prince or lord, in an Ephyre, which was

near the territory of Prœtus, and was situated μύχῳ Ἄργεος ἱπποβότοιο. Bellerophon, the grandson of Sisyphus, was driven out by Prœtus, king of the Argives; and was a ξεῖνος of Œneus, the ancestor of Diomed. These circumstances, combined with the tradition that attached the name of Ephyre to the site of Corinth, leave no doubt that Homer means to place Sisyphus in what was afterwards Corinth [w]. There was no other known Ephyre in a nook of Ἄργος, or what may be termed within reach of Prœtus and of Œneus: whereas this Ephyre lay upon the pass that communicated with the North from that part of the Peloponnesus.

But the line of Sisyphus had been displaced in the person of Bellerophon, two generations before the Trojan war. Together with this line the old name of Ephyre had disappeared: we hear of it in the Iliad only as Corinth, and as part of the Mycenian dominions. Now tradition connects the Æolid title particularly with Thessaly, the Æolids always having been recognised as one of the great primitive Greek races. And Homer gives us Æolids in Thessaly, as well as in Peloponnesus. In the time of Sisyphus then we see this Æolid name, which is Eteo-Hellenic, conjoined with the local name Ephyre: at the epoch of the Trojan war, both have disappeared from the spot.

The traditional name Ephyre remained, indeed, in many parts of Greece down to later times. Strabo (p. 338) reckons one in Elis, one in Thesprotia, and one in Thessaly, besides Corinth: and also five κωμαὶ of the name. But even in Homer's time, either these settlements had decayed, or else, which is more likely, the particular form Ἐφύρη had never acquired the pre-

[w] Compare Propertius, b. ii. El. v. 1.
Ephyreæ Laidos œdes.

cise force of a proper name, but remained rather in the category of a descriptive word: for otherwise it could hardly have happened, but that one or other of the Ephyres must have been named in the Catalogue of Homer. If a descriptive word, it was in all likelihood simply descriptive of primitive settlement for the Hellic race. Probably these Ἐφύραι were rude and small; and were, properly speaking, collections of a few buildings, rather than cities regularly formed.

2. That passage of the Thirteenth Iliad has already been mentioned, which places this name in the North. The Poet says, speaking of Mars and his son Φόβος,

τὼ μὲν ἄρ' ἐκ Θρῄκης Ἐφύρους μέτα θωρήσσεσθον,
ἠὲ μετὰ Φλέγυας μεγαλήτορας[x].

Two circumstances warrant our placing these Ἔφυροι in Thessaly: the first, that the name of Thrace does not extend farther southward: and the second, that here is the only known seat of the Phlegyæ.

3. It may be convenient next to take the Ephyre, which is mentioned twice in the Odyssey.

In the first of these passages Pallas, in the character of Mentes, Lord of the Taphians, remembers Ulysses in the days when he undertook other journeys before his Trojan one: remembers him,

ἐξ Ἐφύρης ἀνίοντα παρ' Ἴλου Μερμερίδαο.
ᾤχετο γὰρ καὶ κεῖσε θοῆς ἐπὶ νηὸς Ὀδυσσεὺς
φάρμακον ἀνδροφόνον διζήμενος[y].

And again, when the Suitors apprehend that Telemachus meditates mischief, they ask whether he will bring allies from Pylus, or even from Sparta (which was more remote).

ἤ τινας ἐκ Πύλου ἄξει ἀμύντορας ἠμαθόεντος
ἢ ὅγε καὶ Σπάρτηθεν, ἐπεί νύ περ ἵεται αἰνῶς·
ἠὲ καὶ εἰς Ἐφύρην ἐθέλει, πίειραν ἄρουραν·
ἐλθεῖν, ὄφρ' ἔνθεν θυμοφθόρα φάρμακ' ἐνείκῃ[z].

[x] Ver. 301.   [y] Od. i. 259.   [z] Od. ii. 326.

II. *Ethnology.*

For several reasons it appears probable that the Ephyre here meant was in Elis, and was therefore the Ephyre of Augeias.

1. Geographically it would appear likely to be in the Peloponnesus. Telemachus was little likely to make any more extended voyage. The intercourse of his family was generally with the Iasian Argos, or Western Peloponnesus. Hence it is said of Penelope[a], 'Could all the Achæans of Iasian Argos see thee.' And hence, in the Twenty-fourth Odyssey[b], the enemies of Ulysses anticipate that, unless prevented by them, he will resort either to Pylus or to Elis, where are the Epeans, for assistance. Hence, again, it is that, in the Second Odyssey, we find Ephyre joined with Pylus and Sparta (which last is mentioned as an extreme point, ἢ ὄγε καὶ Σπάρτηθεν,) as the quarters to which he might repair for aid. The names of Elis and the Epeans do not appear: and this of itself amounts nearly to a demonstration that Ephyre not only lay in, but actually stands in lieu of, Elis in this place.

We may however note one or two secondary points.

2. Corinth had now lost the name of Ephyre, that is to say, a new name had overshadowed the old one. But this Ephyre, if not Corinth, could only be the Elian Ephyre.

3. Post-Homeric tradition places an Ephyre in Elis.

We have already seen that Augeias was lord of Elis, that he ruled over an Hellenic race, that he is an ἄναξ ἀνδρῶν: was this Ephyre the seat of his empire?

Even from the bare fact of being in Elis, it stands in significant connection with Augeias: but more especially, it seems impossible not to connect the peculiar knowledge of drugs, preserved at the Ephyre to which Ulysses repaired, with the former fame of Agamede,

[a] Od. xviii. 245.   [b] Od. xxiv. 430.

the daughter of Augeias (Il. xi. 740), from whom it had, in all probability, been handed down to the next following generation.

It may be asked, what place had Ilus, the son of Mermerus[c], in an Ephyre, where Augeias had been king or lord? We can give at least this negative answer: the Catalogue shews that Elis, in the time of the Trojan war, was no longer patriarchally ruled; for the Epeans had four coordinate leaders; of whom the grandson of Augeias was but one. Therefore an Ilus may have been in the time of Ulysses possessed of the place, which belonged to Augeias in Nestor's boyhood: and we may observe, that no Epean or Elian chief, contemporary with the *Troica*, appears in Homer under the title of ἄναξ ἀνδρῶν.

Upon combining all these circumstances, we appear to have the strongest warrant for believing that Augeias was lord of Ephyre; that he was the head of one of the ruling families which derived themselves by a known and recorded lineage from Hellas and a Hellic tribe; and consequently that the archaic title of ἄναξ ἀνδρῶν was applied to him, not casually, but with a definite meaning, and in conformity to an established rule.

The following brief synopsis will, after what has been said, serve to indicate the chief presumptive grounds of the title of Augeias to ἄναξ ἀνδρῶν.

1. Augeias is connected with the φάρμακα, Il. xi. 739—41.
2. The φάρμακα with Ephyre, Od. i. 259.
3. Ephyre with Sisyphus, Il. vi. 152, 3.
4. Sisyphus is the son of Æolus, Il. vi. 154.
5. Æolus is Eteo-Hellenic, as the common ancestor

[c] Od. i. 251.

of several of the great Greek houses, and the lineal ancestor of at least one ἄναξ ἀνδρῶν[d].

6. Æolus is also of divine descent, for his descendant Bellerophon is θεοῦ γόνος, Il. vi. 191.

7. That is to say, he is a son of Jupiter; for θεὸς commonly means Jupiter, when there is no particular reference to any other deity in the context, and when a personal act or attribute is described.

The extra-Homeric tradition entirely supports this belief, for it makes Augeias the son of Salmoneus, and Salmoneus the son of Æolus.

And now, after we have considered so fully the term Ἐφύρη and its kindred words, we shall do well to notice that at least the dominions of Agamemnon are not void of some relation to this family of names; inasmuch as Φᾶρις, in the Catalogue, is one of the towns that provide his forces, and Φῆραι, in the Ninth Iliad, is one of the towns of which he promises to make Achilles lord. Of Phellias and Sellasia we have already treated.

V. *Case of Euphetes.*

I proceed to the case of Euphetes.

He is mentioned only once in the Homeric Poems. It is when, in the Fifteenth Iliad, Dolops strikes at Meges, son of Phyleus, who is saved by his stout breastplate: by that breastplate,

τόν ποτε Φύλευς
ἤγαγεν ἐξ Ἐφύρης, ποταμοῦ ἀπὸ Σελλήεντος.
ξεῖνος γάρ οἱ ἔδωκεν ἄναξ ἀνδρῶν Εὐφήτης[e].

This case, as it stands, is very simple. Euphetes is manifestly the king of Ephyre: the name of the place supplies the connection with the cradle of the Helle-

[d] Eumelus, sup. p. 428. [e] Il. xv. 530.

Case of Euphetes.

nes; the link is doubled by the name of the river Σελλήεις, and his rank presumably stamps him as of a ruling race in the country; for he is a ξεῖνος to a sovereign, and the xenial relation appears to have been always one between persons equal, or nearly so.

The passage, however, affords us no aid towards determining where this Ephyre lay; for it does not tell us where to look for the residence of Phyleus.

Was it the Ephyre of Elis, or was it another Ephyre, mentioned in a passage that we have not yet examined? To this passage let us now turn.

In the Greek Catalogue, Tlepolemus, the son of Hercules, commands nine ships from Rhodes, whither he had migrated, on account of having slain his grand uncle Licymnius. His birth is described as follows,—

ὃν τέκεν Ἀστυόχεια βίῃ Ἡρακληείῃ·
τὴν ἄγετ' ἐξ Ἐφύρης, ποταμοῦ ἀπὸ Σελλήεντος,
πέρσας ἄστεα πολλὰ Διοτρεφέων αἰζηῶν [f].

Hercules then led off Astyocheia from Ephyre beside Selleeis, after having devastated many cities. The opinion may perhaps be sustained from this passage, that the Ephyre mentioned in it is not the Ephyre of Elis, for the following reasons.

1. Tlepolemus[g] emigrates to Rhodes in consequence of homicide. He is more likely to have done this from Thessaly than Elis, for we see no signs of communication between western Peloponnesus and the islands of Asia Minor near the base of the Ægean.

2. If Astyocheia, the mother of Tlepolemus, was also the Astyoche who bore to Mars Ascalaphus and Ialmenus (Il. ii. 513), then he was more likely to be Thessalian than Elian; for Mars, dwelling in Thrace, bordered upon Thessaly, but is not heard of in Southern Greece;

[f] Il. ii. 658.   [g] Il. ii. 667.

and these princes ruled over the Minyeian Orchomenus, which is far from the Peloponnesus, but near Southern Thessaly.

3. Again, Nestor, in the Eleventh Book[h], where he sets forth the depression into which the Pylians had fallen, through the depredations of their neighbours the Elians, states that they had been unable to defend themselves against those ravages, because Hercules had devastated their country and slain their princes. Now he would hardly have said this, if the Elian Ephyre and its neighbourhood had likewise been devastated by Hercules, since his account would then have failed to explain the relative inferiority of the Pylians. But if it was not the Elian Ephyre, and since the situation of the Isthmus and its state make the passage inapplicable to the Corinthian Ephyre, then, still looking for some country known in connection with the exploits of Hercules, we must naturally take it to be the Ephyre of Thessaly, where the name Selleeis, as that of a neighbouring stream, would most naturally of all be looked for.

It is true that the geographers give us no record of a river Selleeis near the Thessalian Ephyre. But the fugitive character of the name Ephyre is manifest from the fact that, though there were several Ephyres in Homer's time, none of them was of sufficient importance to furnish a military contingent worth naming. If by Ephyre was meant the first site of a new colony, that name might naturally disappear, not only with a removal to a more secure or convenient spot, but even perhaps on the growth of a mere group of inclosed buildings into a walled town. It is therefore no wonder if the site of many of these towns has been

[h] Il. xi. 688–95.

forgotten, or if the neighbouring streams in consequence cannot be identified.

There is a tradition, external to Homer, but not at variance with him, that the Astyocheia whom Hercules carried off was the daughter of Phylas; and if so, Phylas was of course lord of the Ephyre, from which she was carried off. If we assume the veracity of this tradition, we can determine the seat of the Ephyre of Astyocheia to have been in Thessaly. For the five commanders under Achilles were of course all drawn from that country. But among them is Eudorus, the son of Polymele and grandson of Phylas[i].

It may here be asked, by the way, why is not this Eudorus an ἄναξ ἀνδρῶν? even his name is of the form to which the phrase is so well suited. The answer is that, though he was the son of Polymele, and the grandson of Phylas on the female side, his reputed father was Mercury, and he was therefore not descended in the male line from, and could not be called, the chieftain of a tribe.

If then Phylas was lord of the Thessalian Ephyre, and Euphetes was also lord of the Thessalian Ephyre, in what relation to one another are we to presume them to have stood as to time? There is here no appearance of discrepancy. Phyleus, as the father of Meges, was the ξεῖνος of Euphetes one generation before the Trojan war. Tlepolemus, contemporary of Meges, was by our supposition the grandson of Phylas. Phylas, lord of Ephyre, was therefore probably one generation earlier than Euphetes, and may have been his father.

Nor is it an objection to this reasoning, that Meges, son of Phyleus, was lord of Dulichium, and that we

[i] Il. xvi. 179.

cannot suppose Phyleus to have been the ξεῖνος of one dwelling so far off as the Thessalian Ephyre. For first, Nestor the Pylian had fought in Thessaly. And next, Meges had been a fugitive from his father's dwelling on account of a feud with him: which makes it even probable that he would remove to a distance, as we see that Tlepolemus went on a similar account from Thessaly, or at least from some part of Greece, to Rhodes.

If then Euphetes, who was an ἄναξ ἀνδρῶν, governed an Ephyre, and particularly if it was in Thessaly, the special seat of the Helli, we can have little difficulty in concluding that he bore the title as a patriarchal one, in right of his descent.

On the other hand, the Ephyre of Tlepolemus is certainly in the general opinion presumed to be the Ephyre of Elis. If this opinion be correct, it is still more easy to connect him with the title of ἄναξ ἀνδρῶν. Augeias lives two generations before the Trojan war, rules in Ephyre, and is ἄναξ ἀνδρῶν. Euphetes is contemporary with the father of Meges, who fights in the war; and he is therefore one generation after Augeias, while he rules in the same place, and bears the same title. If then the Ephyre of Euphetes was Elian, it seems impossible to escape the presumption that Euphetes was the son of Augeias.

This view as to the Ephyre of Euphetes on the whole will more completely satisfy the Homeric text. For we find Meges in the Thirteenth Book fighting at the head of Epean troops[k]. But the troops he led to Troy were from Dulichium and the Echinades[l]. So we can only conclude one of two things. Either Meges commanded the Epeans of Elis in virtue of the con-

[k] Il. xiii. 692.   [l] Il. ii. 625–30.

nection of his family with that country; or he commanded Epeans, whom his father Phyleus had taken with him from Elis across the Corinthian gulf. Either way a relation between Elis and the family of Meges is made good, which tends to place Euphetes, as the friend of that family, in the Ephyre of Elis.

There is yet another supposition open. Homer has told us that Phyleus was Διὶ φίλος,—a distinction he very rarely confers,—and that he migrated, as he implies rather than asserts, from Elis, on account of a quarrel with his father:

ὅς ποτε Δουλίχιόν δ' ἀπενάσσατο πατρὶ χολωθείς.

He does not mention the cause; but this abrupt allusion to the father of Phyleus implies that he was a person of note. Strabo[m] may therefore only be filling up a void in Homer, when he tells us, of course from some tradition, that Augeias was the father of Phyleus.

If this were so, we have to ask, why is not Phyleus an ἄναξ ἀνδρῶν? and who, upon this supposition, could Euphetes be?

As we must infer from the Catalogue that the Elian kingdom of Augeias was broken up at the epoch of the *Troica*, and as in consequence we do not find Polyxeinus, his grandson, called by the title in question, so neither need we expect it of Phyleus.

If Phyleus was the son of Augeias, Euphetes cannot have been sovereign of the Elian Ephyre, for they would in this case not have been ξεῖνοι, but brothers.

But he might still have been sovereign either of the Ephyre mentioned by Homer, μυχῷ Ἄργεος, which appears as Corinth in the Catalogue: or possibly of the Thesprotian Ephyre with which we become acquainted in Strabo.

[m] Strabo p. 459.

If Euphetes represented, with the title of ἄναξ ἀνδρῶν, one of the old Hellic chieftaincies at either of these places, nothing could be more natural than that the tie of hostship should subsist between him and Phyleus, the son of another Hellic chieftain of the same class.

In any case, though the Homeric evidence is palpably incomplete, yet by connecting the title of ἄναξ ἀνδρῶν with the highly characteristic local title of Ephyre, and the name of the river Selleeis, it unequivocally supports the interpretation of that title as one indicating an original and purely Hellic chieftaincy.

VI. *Case of Eumelus.*

It now only remains to consider the case of Eumelus, the last of the six persons to whom Homer gives the peculiar title of ἄναξ ἀνδρῶν.

He is introduced to us in the Catalogue as the φίλος παῖς[n] (φίλος meaning probably either the eldest or only son) of Admetus, who is never mentioned except in the oblique cases, and to whom therefore, consistently with his usage, Homer never applies the title ἄναξ ἀνδρῶν. He is in command of his father's forces; and, as Pheræ is the city first named in this list, we may infer that this was his principal city.

In the first place I would remark, that we have for this Pheræ a sign of wealth, which has been already noticed, the excellence, namely, of its breed of horses. There is also abundant evidence of the wealth and importance of Pheræ in the historic times[o]. This mark then accords with the hypothesis, that it was probably one of the primitive lowland settlements made by the Hellic race in Thessaly. In fact, Pheræ stands relatively

[n] Il. ii. 711–15.   [o] Cramer's Greece, vol. i. p. 392.

to Admetus, as Ephyre does relatively to Augeias, Euphetes, and the older Æolid, Sisyphus.

Through the medium of the name Pheræ we connect this family with Ἐφύρη, as its cognate name, and as the name which we have found, in the cases of Euphetes and Augeias, to be eminently characteristic of settlements under an ἄναξ ἀνδρῶν.

Next it appears, that the father or ancestor of Admetus took his name from the place which he inhabited, and was called Pheres, for says the poet,

Ἵπποι μὲν μέγ' ἄρισται ἔσαν Φηρητιάδαο,
τὰς Εὔμηλος ἔλαυνε [p].

The union between the names of the place and the person affords another sign of primitive settlement. Pheres was probably the founder of the town Φηραί.

Next, a passage in the Odyssey gives us an account of this Pheres[q]. He was the son of Cretheus, by Tyro:

τοὺς δ' ἑτέρους Κρηθῆϊ τέκεν βασίλεια γυναικῶν,
Αἴσονά τ' ἠδὲ Φέρητ' Ἀμυθάονά τ' ἱππιοχάρμην.

Now Cretheus was a son or descendant of Æolus:

Φῆ δὲ Κρηθῆος γυνὴ ἔμμεναι Αἰολίδαο [r].

And we have already seen the Æolids of Homer directly connected with the characteristic name of Ephyre in the person of Sisyphus (Il. vi. 152, 211). Outside the Homeric text, all tradition ascribes to the Æolians, not less than the Achæans, an Eteo-Hellenic origin. Again, we may observe, that among the Greek genealogies of Homer, the longest are those of the Æolids. From Æolus to Glaucus II, in the Sixth Iliad, are six generations: and here in like manner from Cretheus

[p] Il. ii. 763.   [q] Od. xi. 258.
[r] Ibid. xi. 237.

to Eumelus are four, which number will be increased to five or to six, according as we take Cretheus to be the son or the grandson of Æolus, or estimate the age of Eumelus. According to the Homeric force of the patronymic, he may be either. Eumelus, however, himself was, as we have seen, presumably not young at the time of the *Troica;* since he was wedded to Iphthime, the sister of Penelope, who must be taken to stand, with her husband Ulysses (Il. xxiii. 791), as above the average age of the army.

To sum up; it thus far appears,

1. That Eumelus was heir to Admetus, a reigning prince of Thessaly or Hellas.

2. That the capital of this prince bore testimony by its name to its primitive or Eteo-Hellenic character.

3. That Eumelus was a descendant in the male line from Æolus, of whose lineage several, according to Homer, seem to have possessed the character and borne the title of the ἄναξ ἀνδρῶν.

4. In virtue of his descent from Æolus, he is sprung from Jupiter.

To estimate fully the force of the evidence, it may be well to observe, that a great many Thessalian princes and leaders are noticed in the Catalogue besides Eumelus; to the last alone, however, the title of ἄναξ ἀνδρῶν is applied. But no one of the others bears any mark, personal or local, of the peculiar descent and social position to which this title appears to belong: although among them are found Podaleirius and Machaon, the sons of Asclepius; Polypœtes, the son of Pirithous, and grandson of Jupiter; Eurypylus, the distinguished warrior; Protesilaus and Philoctetes, each the subject of distinct historical notices.

Again, I would, from the case of Eumelus, illustrate the phrase ἄναξ ἀνδρῶν in another point of view.

He was descended by his mother Alcestis from Neptune. She was the daughter of Pelias, the son whom Tyro bore to the fabled ruler of the seas. This descent on the mother's side is mentioned in the Catalogue, where a total silence is observed as to his paternal lineage from Æolus and Cretheus.

Εὔμηλος, τὸν ὑπ' Ἀδμήτῳ τέκε δῖα γυναικῶν,
Ἄλκηστις, Πελίαο θυγατρῶν εἶδος ἀρίστη.

But it is plain that his descent from Jupiter by the father's side was more worthy of notice than his descent from Neptune through the bastard Pelias. Yet Homer has nowhere taken notice of the descent from Jupiter, in the case of Eumelus, unless it is implied in the meaning of the term ἄναξ ἀνδρῶν, though we know the descent as a fact: surely a strong proof that it is part of the meaning of the phrase ἄναξ ἀνδρῶν, and is a thing not only inseparable from it, but conveyed by it.

With regard to the divine descent of the Homeric chieftains bearing this title, our direct evidence from the Poet stands as follows:

1. That the Dardan line springs originally from Jupiter.

2. That Tyro, being called εὐπατέρεια in common with Helen only, is evidently meant to be described as sprung from that deity.

3. That Bellerophon, also an Æolid, is also θεοῦ γόνος, therefore himself a descendant of Jupiter.

4. And if so, then Eumelus, who was Æolid too, falls within the same description.

5. Augeias in like manner attains to the same honour by the Homeric presumptions which make him an Æolid, as well as by all extra-Homeric tradition.

6. With regard to Euphetes and Agamemnon, we have no direct evidence. But we have seen strong reason to suppose, that Euphetes was himself an Æolid: and no inconsiderable presumption that Tantalus was according to Homer what the later tradition makes him, a son of Jupiter, and that Agamemnon was descended from Tantalus.

Perhaps also, without venturing to attach any conclusive weight to such a sign, we may interpret the annexation of Διοτρεφὴς and Διογενὴς to Hellic kingship, as a sign that the earliest Hellic kingship, being also that which conveyed the title of ἄναξ ἀνδρῶν, was always associated with divine descent.

Among those who bear the title of ἄναξ ἀνδρῶν, we find no case of a descent from Jupiter reputed to be recent. The two lines in which the title is most clearly transmitted, those of Æolus and of Dardanus, are among the oldest genealogies in Homer. That of Agamemnon, apparently the shortest, interposes at the least four generations between Jupiter and him.

The line of Dardanus is apparently by one generation longer than any of the others belonging to an ἄναξ ἀνδρῶν. But nothing can be more natural: for any settlement, made by the Helli on the Hellespont during their eastward movement, would naturally precede by some time their descent from Olympus and the Thracian hills into Thessaly; so that the earlier date of the primary ancestor is a witness for, rather than against the relationship.

It cannot, however, be too carefully borne in mind, that the divine descent of the ἄναξ ἀνδρῶν from Jupiter is widely different from that of the more recent heroes, like Sarpedon or Hercules. We may suppose that in such cases as these the divine parent either screens the result of unlawful love, or perhaps indicates the sudden rise into eminence of a family previously obscure: with the ἄναξ ἀνδρῶν the case is quite distinct. The poetical meaning here is, that backward there lay nothing of family history beyond the ancestor from whom he claimed descent, whether it were Dardanus, or Æolus, or Tantalus: as if aiming at the effect legitimately produced by those words in the Gospel of St. Luke, with which the upward line of the genealogy given by him closes; 'which was the son of Adam, which was the son of God[s].' And the historic basis of the allegory may probably be this, that the person indicated was one of some ruling house, who, with his followers or kindred, separated from the migratory race of Helli as it swept westward along the hills, and founded a stable settlement, and a society more or less organized in orders and employments, in which his name became the symbol at once of sovereign rank, of the national point of origin, and of affinity in blood with a ruling race.

To conclude then: the notes of the ἄναξ ἀνδρῶν in Homer, probable or demonstrative, are these:

1. He must be born of Jupiter *ab antiquo*.

2. He must hold a sovereignty, either paramount or secondary, and either in whole, or, like Æneas, by devolution in part, over some given place or tribe.

3. His family must have held this sovereignty continuously from the time of the primary ancestor.

4. He must be the head of a ruling tribe or house of the original Hellenic stock: and must be connected with marks of the presence of Hellenic settlement. These marks may, as in the case of Agamemnon, be supplied by a race or tribe: or they may be territorial,

---

[s] St. Luke iii. 38.

such as those afforded by the name of the river Selleeis, and more especially by the name Ephyre, and the family of cognate words.

Now each of the six persons, to whom alone Homer gives the title ἄναξ ἀνδρῶν, partakes, by evidence either demonstrative or probable, of every one of these notes.

Among negative evidences that the title ἄναξ ἀνδρῶν conveys a peculiar sense, we may place the following:

1. The position of Priam in Troas, where he was the greatest man of North-western Asia, Il. xxiv. 543-6, and of Hector, or else Paris, as his heir, were such as called for the highest epithets of dignity. He had even a regular court of γέροντες, of whom it seems plain, that some at least, such as Antenor, were invested with some kind of sovereignty. Yet none of the Ilian family are called by the name of ἄναξ ἀνδρῶν.

2. Alcinous in the Odyssey affords another example of a lord over lords, who does not belong to the historical Greek stem, and who therefore is not called ἄναξ ἀνδρῶν. The example may appear weak, because of the divine descent of the Phæacians. But if this phrase had, like κρείων, been one of merely general ornament, why should it not have been applied to him as κρείων is, or to his brother Rhexenor, or his father Nausithous? If the divine descent of the Phæacians from Neptune renders the phrase inapplicable to them, this is of itself a proof of its very specific nature.

3. Again; it may be asked why Glaucus was not an ἄναξ ἀνδρῶν, as he was descended from an Æolid sovereign. The answer is, he was no longer the chieftain of any Hellenic clan. His grandfather Bellerophon had migrated simply as an individual fugitive into a South-Asian country, of which the people had no immediate

ties of race with him; and, while apart from his original tribe, he could not inherit a title as its head.

4. Sarpedon was under the same disqualification as Glaucus his brother king. Besides this, he was not descended in the male line from Æolus, but only through his mother Hippodamia.

5. Again, among the Greeks. Why, it may be asked, was not Peleus, or why was not Achilles an ἄναξ ἀνδρῶν? Here was a throne above thrones: for Patroclus was not only an ἄναξ, but was called Διογενής, which implies sovereignty; therefore Menœtius his father was the same: but Menœtius was in attendance at the court of Peleus. Phœnix again was tutor to that chief, though he ruled over the Dolopians by the gift of Peleus, as he tells us,

καί μ' ἀφνειὸν ἔθηκε, πολὺν δέ μοι ὤπασε λαόν,
ναῖον δ' ἐσχατίην Φθίης, Δολόπεσσιν ἀνάσσων[t].

Besides that he occupied a great position, and was of the highest descent, I think it is clear from the Catalogue that the Myrmidons, over whom Peleus reigned, were Achæans, and therefore a strictly Hellic race.

And again, the character of Achilles makes it quite clear that his family were from the Hellic stock. For it is in him that Homer has chosen to exhibit the prime and foremost pattern of the whole Greek nation: and he could surely never have chosen for such a purpose any family of foreign, or of doubtful blood.

It is not however in every Hellic race or family, but only among the known representatives by descent of the principal or senior branches, that we are justified in expecting to find the patriarchal title. And still less do we know whether the Myrmidons, even though Hellic and Achæan, were a principal tribe of that stock.

[t] Il. ix. 483.

The evidence as to the descent of Achilles may throw further light upon this part of the subject.

In those cases where a long line of ancestry purported to begin with Jupiter, as, for instance, the Trojan genealogy, it is doubtless natural to treat this as a sort of necessary introduction to a period, beyond which the memory of man, unaided as it was, did not run.

But when we find the paternity of a person contemporary with the Trojan war, or of some near ancestor of his, referred to Jupiter, the most proper interpretation of this legendary statement seems to be, that they were, so to speak, *novi homines*, who having come suddenly into the blaze of celebrity, and living among a nation accustomed to ask of every passing stranger who were his parents, yet having no parents to quote, or none worth quoting, gilded their origin by claiming some great deity for their father. I do not speak now of the distinct and yet cognate case, where a similar pretext was used to shield illegitimacy: as for example, not to travel from the line before us, in the instance of the son of Polydora[u], sister to Achilles himself. But the same principle applies to both: divine progenitorship was used to keep from view something that it was desirable to hide, whether this were the shame of a noble maiden, or the undistinguished ancestry of a great house or hero. Such a hero perhaps, according to this rule, was Hercules: such a house more clearly was that of the Æacids; for Æacus, grandfather of Achilles, was son of Jupiter[x]. He did not therefore represent a patriarchal family, and could not bear the title.

According to extra-Homeric tradition, the Myrmidons fled from Ægina to Thessaly under Peleus[y].

[u] Il. xvi. 175.   [x] Il. xxi. 189.   [y] Strabo ix. 5. p. 433.

6. Further examples may be taken from the Pelopid family. The Menelaus of the Iliad belongs to the highest order: he is more kingly than the other kings[z]. In the Odyssey he desires to transplant Ulysses to a portion of his dominions (Od. iv. 174). And Ægisthus actually occupies for years, during the exile of Orestes, the Pelopid throne: the name of either Menelaus or Ægisthus is of the metrical value most convenient for union with the ἄναξ ἀνδρῶν: but neither the one nor the other was the representative of the great Achæan house of Pelops, and accordingly neither the one nor the other receives the title.

7. Diomed is a Greek of the very highest descent: of him alone, among the kings before Troy, we may confidently say, that he was himself a hero, had a hero for his father, a hero for his uncle, and a hero for his grandfather. Œneus, Tydeus, Meleager, are three names not easily to be matched in early Greek story. They were likewise near the stock, as we may probably infer from the name of the founder of the race, Portheus, the Destroyer. He was father of Œneus and also of Ἄγριος the Rude, and Μέλας the Swarthy, all names indicating that the first stage of arrival within the precinct of civilization had not yet been passed. He commanded, too, one of the largest contingents: yet neither he nor his uncle Meleager, the Achilles of his day, is ever called ἄναξ ἀνδρῶν.

The reason doubtless is that, in the case of the Œneid family, there is no connection with a leading Greek ancestry. They are neither Æolid nor Pelopid; and they stand in no relation to the characteristic names of Ephyre and the Selleeis.

8. Let me notice, lastly, the case of Nestor. He

[z] Il. x. 239.

had been a warrior of the first class. His rich dominions supplied a contingent of ninety ships to the war; larger even than that of Diomed, or of any chief whatever, except Agamemnon, who had one hundred. His father, Neleus, was of great fame. He had actually more influence in council than any other chief, and always took the lead there. He was descended from Neptune, who indeed was but his grandfather: while his grandmother, Tyro, was probably, as we have found, a granddaughter of Æolus.

But he could not be ἄναξ ἀνδρῶν, because not in lineal male descent from the primary ancestor Æolus: nor was he the tribal head of the Hellenic race among which he ruled, which was an Achæan one (Il. xi. 759), since the Achæans owned the Pelopids for their chiefs. Also his father Neleus, apparently the younger twin, had migrated from the North, leaving Pelias the elder, as is probable, in possession. Thus Nestor presents none of the four notes of the ἄναξ ἀνδρῶν. Yet this title attached to an insignificant relative, Eumelus, his first cousin once removed, doubtless because he possessed them.

It is certainly true that there are a few cases where Homer has *not* applied the title of ἄναξ ἀνδρῶν to particular persons, to whom he might have given it consistently with the suppositions, as to its meaning, of which I have attempted to show the truth. They are, in one word, the ancestors of the persons to whom he has actually given the title. But all of these, such as Pelops and his line, Dardanus with his line as far as Tros, and the earlier descendants of Æolus, are persons mentioned in the poems for the most part but once, and rarely more than twice or thrice. Now, as Homer mentions frequently without the prefix, ἄναξ ἀνδρῶν, those to whom on other occasions he gives it, we are not entitled to require its application to all persons capable of bearing it, whom he mentions but once.

And again, if I am right in holding that this was strictly a title attaching to lineage, then it was wholly needless, when he had designated a particular person, as an ἄναξ ἀνδρῶν, to grace his predecessors also with the title, because, as a matter of course, inasmuch as they were his predecessors, it attached to them. No historic aim then was involved, and no purpose would have been gained if Admetus, for example, had been mentioned with this title as well as his son Eumelus.

But, I confess, it appears to me to afford no small confirmation to the arguments and the conclusions of these pages, when we remember that not only do the four rules for the sense of the phrase suit, as far as we can tell, all the six persons to whom it is applied, but that there is absolutely no other living person named in the poems, whom they would not effectually exclude, with the insignificant exceptions, first of Admetus, who has just been mentioned, and next of Orestes. In the Iliad, Orestes is only named in one single passage (twice repeated), of the Ninth Book[a]. In the Odyssey he is named several times, but the title of ἄναξ ἀνδρῶν is less suitable to the political state of Greece as it appears in this poem, and also to the subject. It never appears, except retrospectively.

A few words may perhaps be due to the case of Polyxeinus, grandson of Augeias, who, it is just possible, though unlikely, may have retained the position of his grandfather. It is just possible, because we are not assured of the contrary; but most unlikely, because Augeias appears as lord of the Epeans, Polyxeinus only

[a] Il. ix. 142, 284.

as commanding a division of them. Again, Polyxeinus is only once mentioned. It is also evident that the loss of his grandfather's throne, by a revolution in Elis, might naturally put an end to the application of the title in his particular case, by a process exactly the same with that to which its general and final extinction, now so speedily to arrive, was due.

It might indeed be of some interest to inquire why it is that, when Homer makes no practical or effective use of the phrase for any one except Agamemnon, he has notwithstanding been careful to register, as it were, a title to it on behalf of five other persons? Nor can I doubt that the just answer would be, that he did this because, with his historic aims, he may have deemed it a matter of national interest to record a title of such peculiar and primitive significance.

But of all the negative arguments that tend to show ἄναξ ἀνδρῶν not to have been a merely vague title, there is none on which I dwell with more confidence than its total disappearance with the Homeric age. For it was not so with the other less peculiar forms, βασιλεὺς, ἄναξ, and κρείων. Although they were supplanted in actual use by the term τύραννος, which became for the Greeks the type of supreme power in the hands of a single person, yet the idea of them was traditionally retained. Accordingly, even the name βασιλεὺς was applied by Greek writers to contemporary kings out of Greece, and to the old bygone Greek monarchies: and Thucydides has given it to them as a class, where he describes the πατρικαὶ βασιλεῖαι[b]. But the phrase ἄναξ ἀνδρῶν, the most specific of them all, disappears even from retrospective use: and the inference is, that its proper meaning had ceased to be

[b] Thuc. i. 13.

represented in the institutions either of Greece or of
the known world beyond the Greek borders; that it
had passed away with the archaic system, of which it
was the peculiar token.

Even independently of direct testimony, we might be
assured that the patriarchal and highland constitution
of society could not very long survive the multiplication
of settlements in the plains. For the wealth,
which these settlements created through the increased
efficiency of labour, the greater bounty of the earth, and
the augmented means of communication and exchange,
could not but bring with it at once new temptations,
and new sources of disturbance; whereas the art of controlling
these evils was but painfully and slowly, and
most incompletely learned. Among highland tribes,
there might be war and pillage with a view to immediate
wants: but stored wealth could not be stolen,
where, except in its simplest forms, it did not exist:
and men do not overturn hereditary power, or drag
society into revolutions, without an object.

But the Catalogue, as well as other parts of the
Homeric poems, show us how the causes thus indicated
had already worked. Of the Greek States comprised
in that invaluable enumeration, some were, as is plainly
asserted or implied, monarchically governed: for example,
the Mycenians, the Spartans, the Pylians, the
Myrmidons, the Arcadians, the Eubœans[c], and the
Ætolians. We may reasonably infer the same with
regard to the followers of those great chiefs, who are
treated as Βασιλεῖς in the body of the poems: the Salaminians
and Locrians, each under their Ajax, the
Cephallenians under Ulysses, the Cretans, or else a portion
of them, under Idomeneus, the Argives under

[c] Compare Il. ii. 540 with iv. 363.

Diomed. In each of these cases, either there is but a single leader, or, as in the two last, the text makes it obvious that the chief first named is supreme in rank. We may probably infer that monarchy prevailed in all the instances, including the Athenians, when only a single general appears. The expression δῆμος, applied to Athens, is perfectly compatible with kingship in Homer. But there remain six cases, where there are a plurality of leaders, apparently on an equal footing. These are the cases of

1. The Bœotians.
2. The people of Aspledon and the Minyeian Orchomenus; who are in fact a second Bœotian contingent.
3. The Phocians.
4. The Elians or Epeans: who differ from the others in being formally distributed into four divisions, under four leaders, and who are therefore strictly acephalous.
5. The Nisurians, &c.
6. The people of Tricce, Ithome, and Œchalia, under the sons of Asclepius.

It is observable with respect to the four first of these, that they were all in the comparatively open, and rich country; liable, therefore, to the influences which, as Thucydides observes[d], made Bœotia, Thessaly, and most of Peloponnesus peculiarly liable to revolutions; and whence doubtless it is, that Homer has been led to tell us that Amphion and Zethus built walls for Thebes, because they could not hold it without them.

With respect to the Nisurians, in stating that they were under Pheidippus and Antiphus, Homer adds that these were (Il. ii. 679)

Θεσσαλοῦ υἷε δύω Ἡρακλείδαο ἄνακτος.

On which we may observe

[d] Thuc. i. 2.

1. That the power divided between them had apparently been monarchical in the preceding generation.

2. That the name of their father points to his having been born in Thessaly[e], which from its richness was peculiarly open to revolutions.

3. That he was the son of Hercules, with whose name disturbance and convulsion are so much associated.

In the case of the sons of Asclepius, there is the same presumption that they divided a power which had been monarchical: and although the epithet κλωμακόεσσα given to Ithome, the site of which is unknown[f], may suggest rough and broken ground, yet the territory is within the limits of Thessaly[g], and on the river Peneus. Tricce was known in the historic times; and it is mentioned in Homer with the epithet ἱππόβοτος, indicating fertility.

Here, then, and particularly in the Bœotian and Elian cases, we have considerable signs of the weakening and gradual breaking up of the old highland institutions: I distinguish between those two and the rest, because where the division is only between two brothers, it may have implied little deviation from the monarchical form. Still that little might be the first stage of a deviation which was soon to grow indefinitely large.

There are other signs to the same effect, both in the Iliad, and to a greater extent in the Odyssey.

[e] The name of Thessaly is not found in Homer; and it is marked by Thucydides as modern: ἡ νῦν Θεσσαλία καλουμένη. May it not be reasonably conjectured, that when the great Dorian tribe had evacuated Hellas to reconquer the Peloponnesus, this Thessalid branch of the Heraclidæ, which had migrated to the south-east, went back thither, and imparted to it the name of their ancestor?

[f] Cramer i. 360.

[g] Il. iv. 202.

For example: the dynasty of the Œneids had disappeared among the Ætolians[h]: the dynasty of the Æolids, and the name Ephyre, from Corinth[i]: Polyxeinus, the grandson of Augeias, an ἄναξ ἀνδρῶν, is not described as an ἄναξ, or lord, at all: Hercules had laid waste the cities about Ephyre, and the cities about Pylos[k]: Tlepolemus, at war with his Heraclid relations, had been driven to emigrate to Rhodes: and all this since the family of the Perseids had disappeared before the Pelopids.

The changes observable in the Odyssey are such as connect themselves with a species of deluge, which had apparently overspread the face of the political society of Greece. They would merit a full examination, in connection with a view of the relation of that poem to the Iliad. Here it need only be observed, that the ἄναξ ἀνδρῶν appears nowhere in the action of the Odyssey: the phrase is used but twice, and then only with reference to the dead Agamemnon: and that the partial disappearance of the word from the later work of Homer evidently accompanies a great approach towards disorganisation of the old order of things and ideas in the political state of Greece.

I may now collect the results, as far as they are related to the present subject, of our whole ethnological inquiry.

1. From the Homeric text, the phrase ἄναξ ἀνδρῶν appears not to have belonged to political preeminence or power, or to personal heroism, or to the distinction of wealth, or to divine descent as such; but to the archaic form of sovereignty which united it continuously with the headship in blood of a ruling family

---

[h] Il. ii. 641.   [i] Il. vi. 152, compared with ii. 570.
[k] Il. ii. 659, 60, and xi. 689, 91.

or clan, inhabiting the country which was the reputed cradle of the nation, or able to trace lineally its derivation from that country. A tradition of original descent from Jupiter attached in all cases essentially to the possession of the title.

2. In each of the six instances where Homer employs it, he appears to do so in strict conformity with the rules thus indicated.

3. The immediate cradle of those Greek races, which possessed this primitive title and descent, was Thessaly; and of Thessaly Hellas was either a synonym, or a part.

4. The origin of the races thus ruling Hellas is to be sought among the Helli, who dwelt in the mountains around Dodona, apparently with those institutions which have ever been characteristic of mountaineers; and who represent, more faithfully than the inhabitants of lowlands, the earliest type of human society, cast at a time when its relationship to the family was still palpable and near.

5. The resemblances of the Helli and the Dardans afford, together with the probabilities of the case, strong evidence of their having some common affinity to the same branch of the great stem, from which a large part of Europe was peopled with its ruling race.

6. Finally, we may with reasonable grounds conjecture, that the patriarchal system denoted by the patriarchal chieftaincies, which had been shaken before the Trojan war, was further and violently disturbed by it, and by its direct and indirect political consequences; and that this system had vanished before the line of the post-Homeric Greek poets, to be reckoned from Hesiod, had begun. Thus, the basis of the title being

removed, the title itself naturally disappeared from literature as well as history; and if we find, that in later times the key to its meaning had been lost, it is but a new mark of the abruptness and width of the breach that lies between Homer and his successors, of the paucity of continuous traditions, and of the limited means possessed by the Greeks of the historic ages for research into the earlier periods of their national existence.

SECT. X.

On the connection of the Hellenes and Achæans with the East.

WE have reached the close of this inquiry, so far as it regards the origin, character, and pursuits of the Pelasgians; the character of the Hellenic tribes, and their relations to the Pelasgians; and the position of the Achæans among the Hellenes, as the first national representatives of the Hellenic stock. But who were these Achæans, and whence did they come? We have at present been able only to describe them by negatives. They were not the descendants of a legendary Achæus: they did not take their name from a Greek territory, nor from any pursuit that they followed; and the word has no apparent root in the etymology of the Greek tongue.

But we have seen manifest indications that the Hellic name did not first come into being on the western side of the Dardanelles: and if the Achæi were the first leaders of the Helli, why should we not trace them too beyond the Straits, and thus follow perhaps the Helli also, by their means, and as represented in them, up to a fountain-head?

At the same time, if I presume to affiliate the Hellic nation upon any Eastern parentage, and, again, to suggest relationships between that nation and others, which had also migrated from the first nurseries of man towards the West, it will, I hope, be understood, that all such propositions are asserted, not only as not demonstrable, but as likewise being, even within their own limits, those of merely probable truth, subject, by an admission tacitly carried all along, to every kind of qualification. The succession and intermixture of races, the combinations of language, the sympathetic and imitative communication of ideas and institutions, form a mass of phenomena complex enough, and difficult to describe, even by contemporaries; how much more so by the aid only of those faint and scattered rays that we can now find cast upon them.

Let us then proceed to consider what aid can be had from other sources in support of those presumptions, arising out of the text of Homer, which tend to connect the Hellenes of his day, and the Achæans as their leading tribe, with the East.

And here we may look first, as far as regards the general outlines of race and language, to the ethnological evidences afforded by the course of migration from Central Asia over Europe.

Next, to the evidence of those among ancient authors, who have taken notice of this diffusion in such a manner as in any degree to guide us towards the sources of the great factors of the Greek nation.

After that, we will inquire whether the names themselves, which are employed in Homer for the contemporary Greeks, can, by comparison with cognate names elsewhere, afford us any light.

And lastly, whether in the quarter to which these lines of information would lead us, we can discover any of those resemblances of manners and character with the Greeks which, if found, would afford the most satisfactory corroboration to the argument in favour of the derivation of one from the other.

The labours of ethnologists have associated together in one great family, at first called Indo-Germanic, and then Indo-European, but threatening to expand even beyond the scope of that comprehensive name, a mass of leading languages from the Celtic regions in the west to the plains of India in the east.

This great family, says Dr. Donaldson[a], divides itself into two groups. To these two groups respectively belong the Low German and the High German tongues: the former spoken in the plain countries to the north of Europe, the latter in the more mountainous countries to the south. The Low German languages contain evidence of greater antiquity, and those who speak them appear to have been driven onward in their migrations by the High Germans following them: the latter entering Europe by Asia Minor, the former to the north of the Euxine.

The distinction runs back to the earlier seat of the race in Ariana or Iran, a portion of Asia which may be loosely defined as lying between the Caspian and the Indian ocean to the north and south, the Indus and the Euphrates to the east and west. Within these limits are to be found two forms of language, holding the same relation to one another as that which subsists between the High German and Low German tongues; the first, corresponding with the High German, was spoken among the countries of the south-west, where lies Persia proper, and the other in its more northern and eastern portions, of which Media formed a central part. The population of this great tract issued forth in the direc-

[a] New Cratylus, ch. iv. p. 77.

tion of the south-east, over the northern parts of India; and again towards Asia Minor and Europe, in the direction of the north-west. Those who came first proceeded from Media, and supplied the base of what have been called, the Low German nations: Sarmatians, Saxons, Getæ (or Scythians or Goths). The language of these emigrants was that which, when it assumed an organized or classical form, and with due allowance for changes which the lapse of time must have introduced, became the tongue now best represented, at least as a literary language, by the Sanscrit.

The whole course of history seems to indicate a struggle of races in that quarter of the world, which may be used to illustrate the present inquiry. To a certain extent the scene of that struggle may be pointed out on the map. From the Caspian towards the south, and from the head of the Persian Gulf towards the north, the land soon rises to a great general elevation, but with marked and also highly diversified inequalities. Media would appear to have occupied the principal part of the great central space, defined by the mountains which form the outer line of this elevation. It corresponds with what is now the Province of Irak, and Ispahan is its principal city. Here, says Malcolm[b], we find the happiest climate that Persia can boast. To the south, near the Gulf, the summer heat is overpowering: as the country rises towards Shiraz the climate becomes temperate, and further improves as we advance northward, until we approach the hills that divide Irak from Mazenderan on the Caspian, where it deteriorates.

Immediately to the south of Irak, and touching the

[b] Hist. of Persia, ii. 507.

Persian gulf, a little to the east of the Karoon and Jerokh, which are the eastern tributaries of the great central rivers, Tigris and Euphrates, is the Province of Fars, which ascends the hills to its capital town Shiraz, and then extends in a north-easterly direction towards the sandy deserts. This is the province[c] where the Persian race is still to be found in its greatest purity; and from this tract the name of Persia, attached by Europeans to the empire of Iran, is supposed to be derived[d]. From Fars or Pars, for both forms are understood to exist, is drawn the name Parsee, borne by the fire-worshippers, who migrated for safety into India: and the same root appears to be clearly traceable in the great Persian tribe of Pasargadæ, named by Herodotus[e] as the leading tribe of the country. But though the province of Fars now embraces a considerable range of country and diversity of climate, all that is recorded of the ancient Persians would seem to connect them particularly with its ruder and more mountainous parts: for we have every reason to believe that Herodotus spoke truly when he described the Persians, properly so called, as poor, and their country as hard and barren in comparison with the rich valleys of Media, which at an early date attracted and repaid the labours of agriculture. It was inhabited, as Herodotus[f] says, κατὰ κώμας, that is, in the Pelasgian fashion, at the time when Dejoces acquired the throne.

The conflict of race between a bold highland people of superior energies, and the more advanced, but also more relaxed inhabitants of the more favoured district,

[c] Quart. Rev. vol. 101. p. 503.
[d] Malcolm's Hist. chap. i. p.
[e] Herod. i. 125.
[f] Ibid. 96.

is indicated even amidst the indistinctness of the earliest efforts of history. Ethnologically the general character of the movement is that of a pressure, to adopt the language of Dr. Donaldson[g], of the High upon the Low Iranians; I would be understood, however, to signify by the terms High and Low a distinction in language and not one in altitude of site. The overthrow of the Median empire by the Persians, related in different forms by Ctesias and Herodotus, and again in Holy Scripture, whatever be its chronological epoch, may be taken as a great crisis in the struggle, at which the High Iranians established themselves in the country of the Low, and in permanent political ascendancy among them. The Magian revolution, doubtless a great reaction against this ascendancy, was of short duration. The invasion of Media by the Scythians, which Herodotus has reported as proceeding from beyond the Euxine and the Palus Mæotis, but which was more probably from the east of the Caspian[h], indicates, it is probable, another form of this reaction. This invasion took place under Cyaxares, the grandson of Dejoces: and we may perhaps consider Media as having at this time received Persian influences, possibly by the immigration of groups of Persian families, before the general ascendancy of that race, just as we see the Æolid houses, and the family of Perseus, finding their way into Southern Greece before the days of the Achæan race, and of the general Hellenic ascendancy in the country.

The resemblance of the modern Persian to the modern High German language has been observed[i]: and

---

[g] New Cratylus, p. 86.
[h] Blakesley on Herod. i. 104.
[i] New Cratylus, chap. iv. as above.

it has even been thought probable, for reasons which will presently be considered, that the German name may have been derived from that quarter. The Hellic ingredient of the Greek tongue is referred to a similar origin. On the other hand, we are told that a traveller[k], taking a popular rather than a scientific view of language, has noticed the strong resemblance between the Latin and the modern Sclavonian forms. Again, the structure of the Latin language, from its repelling certain more modern tendencies of the Greek, is taken to indicate an antiquity beyond that of the Greek : and there is also an opinion that the older Greek forms, like the Latin, bear marks of correspondence with the Sclavonic. All this would tend to sustain the belief that the Pelasgians, who formed the older portion, and the basis, of the population of Italy and Greece, were offshoots from the old, or Low Iranian tribes: and that the more recent element was High Iranian or Persian.

Ethnological affinities, illustrative of what has here been advanced, have not escaped the attention of the Greek and Roman writers. What Strabo has said on this subject is particularly deserving of notice. His derivation of the German name from the Latin word *Germanus* may indeed be passed by as a notion which cannot be maintained, although it is supported by the opinion of Tacitus[1], that the name was recent: since even Roman inscriptions show, that it existed three hundred years before that historian. It is however very remarkable, that Strabo asserts the Germans and the Celts to have been nearly associated: μικρὸν ἐξαλλάττοντες τοῦ Κελτικοῦ φύλου τῷ τε πλεονασμῷ τῆς ἀγριό-

[k] New Cratylus, p. 92.   [1] Tac. Germ. c. 2. and Brotier's note.

II. Ethnology.

τητος, καὶ τοῦ μεγέθους, καὶ τῆς ξανθότητος, τἆλλα δὲ παραπλήσιοι καὶ μορφαῖς, καὶ ἤθεσι, καὶ βίοις ὄντες[m].

Now, the result of all that we have drawn from Homer thus far would be to connect the Celts with the Pelasgi, with Media, and with the Low Iranian countries: the 'Germans' with the Helli and with Persia. Observe, then, how the differences, noted by Strabo between Celts and 'Germans,' correspond with the Homeric differences between Helli and Pelasgi. First, as to ἀγριότης : let us call to mind the history of the name Ἀργεῖος; the use of Ἄγριος as an early Hellic proper name; the absence of names of this class among the Pelasgians; the rude manners of the Helli and the Pheres; the pacific habits, wealth, and advanced agriculture of the Pelasgian populations. Then as to stature: how this gift has Diana for its goddess, how it is a standing and essential element of beauty for women as well as men, how the Greek Chiefs in the Third Iliad are distinguished from the crowd by size,

ὥς μοι καὶ τόνδ' ἄνδρα πελώριον ἐξονομήνῃς,
ὅστις ὅδ' ἐστὶν Ἀχαιὸς ἀνὴρ ἠΰς τε μέγας τε[n],

and how Achilles, the bravest and mightiest chief of this army, was the first also in beauty and in size; for Ajax is always recorded as next to him, and at the same time as before all others[o]; except Nireus, who was beautiful, but who as a soldier was mere trash.

And, lastly, as to the auburn hair, which was with Homer in such esteem. Menelaus is ξανθός (*passim*); so is Meleager (Il. ii. 642); so is Rhadamanthus (Od. iv. 564); Agamede (Il. xi. 739); Ulysses (Od. xiii. 399, 431); lastly, Achilles (Il. i. 197). But never once, I

[m] Strabo vii. 2. p. 290.   [n] Il. iii. 166. cf. 226.
[o] Od. xi. 469.

think, does Homer bestow this epithet upon a Pelasgian name. None of the Trojan royal family, so renowned for beauty, are ξανθοί: none of the Chiefs, not even Euphorbus[p], of whose flowing hair the Poet has given us so beautiful and even so impassioned a description. Nothing Pelasgian, but Ceres[q], the καλλιπλόκαμος, is admitted to the honour of the epithet. It could hardly be denied to the goddess of the ruddy harvest:

> Excutit et flavas aurea terra comas[r].

Now Tacitus, describing the Germani, gives them *truces et cærulei oculi, rutilæ comæ, magna corpora*[s]. His treatise supplies many other points of comparison.

It is obvious, to compare the names of Scythæ, Getæ, Gothi, Massagetæ, Mœsi, Mysi, as carrying the marks of their own relationship; and the reader will find in Dr. Donaldson's New Cratylus[t] the various indications recorded by ancient writers of the extension of the Medians over Northern Egypt: namely, from Herodotus (v. 9), Pliny (Hist. Nat. vi. 7), and Diodorus (ii. 43). The last of these authors recognises the similarity of tongue between Greeks and Hyperboreans (ii. 47): and Clemens Alexandrinus, after reciting a series of inventions which the Greeks owed to the barbarians, records among them the saying of Anacharsis, whom some of the Greeks placed among their 'seven wise men,' and adds ἐμοὶ δὲ πάντες Ἕλληνες Σκυθίζουσι[u].

And again, Herodotus (i. 125) gives us a list of names belonging to the different tribes of Persia: the Persia, that is to say, of his own day. Six of these are settled or agricultural, and four nomad. Of the six,

[p] Il. xvii. 51.
[q] Il. v. 500.
[r] Propertius.
[s] Tac. Germ. i. 4.
[t] New Cratylus, p. 91.
[u] Clem. Alex. Strom. i. 299 C, and 308 A (Ed. Coloniæ 1688).

the Pasargadæ are the first. Then come the Μαράφιοι and Μάσπιοι. Three more follow, of whom one is named Γερμάνιοι. The precise correspondence of name immediately suggests that the modern Germans derive their appellation from this Persian tribe. But it is customary to derive that name from *wehr* and *man*, or from *heer* and *man*, thus giving it a military sense: and it is also observed[x] that, if it had borne this sense in the time of Herodotus, he would probably have assigned to it a higher place in his list. But he does not give us to understand, that he means to point out these tribal names as being the descriptive names of the various classes in one and the same homogeneous community, or as having, in any degree, the character of caste. To the first three, indeed, he assigns a political supremacy: for they were the tribes by whose means Cyrus effected his designs. But the idea of particular employments, and social duties, does not seem to belong even to these, and there is no sign of it with the others. It may have been that the Γερμάνιοι meant martial, as Κέφαλληνες seems to have meant Head or Chief Hellenes, and yet that, as the latter were not the chiefs of all the Hellenes, so the former were not the soldiery of all Persia. Again, as the Δωριέες of Homer lay undistinguished in the Hellenic mass, yet afterwards, and on the very same arena, attained to a long-lived supremacy, so, and yet more naturally, may it have happened that a tribe, secondary in Persia itself, may have taken or acquired the lead in a northward and westward migration from it, and may have given its name to the people, which afterwards coagulated (so to speak) around that migration.

There are not wanting either Homeric or post-Homeric traces of a connection between early Greece and

---

[x] Blakesley on Herod. i. 125.

Persia. In Homer, Perseus, father of a line of Peloponnesian kings, is the son of Jupiter and Danae[y]. A son of Nestor bears the same name[z]. We have also the name Περσεφόνεια, wife of Aidoneus or Pluto, and Perse, daughter of Oceanus, who bears Circe and Æetes to 'Ηέλιος, the Sun[a].

When Homer makes Perseus the son of Jupiter, he certainly implies of this sovereign, as of Minos, that he had no known paternal ancestry, and perhaps that he falsely claimed a maternal one, in the country where he attained to fame. But further, it very decidedly appears from the use of the word 'Αργεῖοι for the subjects of the Perseids, and from the intense attachment of the Homeric Juno to that family, that they were an Hellenic house, following upon the probably Egyptian dynasty of the Danaids. With them appears to begin what Homer esteems to be the really national history. Perseus therefore probably may have brought his name direct from among the Hellenes of the north. Why should it not have come to the Helli from Persia? Let it be recollected that we have two other links with the east supplied: one in Perse, daughter of the Eastern Oceanus, and bride of the Sun, the other in Persephoneia, whose ἄλσεα, as I hope to show in treating of the Outer Geography, are in the same quarter.

In Herodotus we find a tradition that Perseus visited Cepheus[b], the Persian king, at the period when the people were called by the Greeks Cephenes; that he married his daughter Andromeda, and had a son, Perses, who remained behind him, succeeded Cepheus, and gave his name to the country. This tale has the appearance of a palpable fiction, intended to cover what may have

[y] Il. xiv. 319. [a] Od. ix. 139.
[z] Od. iii. 414, 444. [b] Herod. vii. 61.

been a fact; that Perseus—who in Homer has himself all the appearance of an immigrant into Peloponnesus —was a stranger, and derived his name from that of the Persians. Now this was the version current among the Persians; who reported that Perseus, born one of themselves, became an Hellene, but that his ancestors had not been Hellenes. To this Persian account Herodotus appears to give his own adhesion: and he states that the Greeks reckoned Hellenic kings up to Perseus[c], but that before him they were Egyptian. This is in entire harmony with what can be gathered from the indirect, but consistent and converging, notices supplied by Homer. And again, the whole mass of the later reports concerning Perseus keep him in close relation with that outer circle of traditions, which I have designated as Phœnician; with the Gorgons of Hades, with Tartessus on the Ocean, with Æthiopia and Atlas. Lastly; the continuance of the name as a royal name, down to the very extinction of nationality in Greece—for the last Macedonian king was a Perseus—may probably be connected with a stream of tradition, that drew from Persia the oldest of the national monarchs.

Again, we find that the name 'Αχαιοὶ was the great descriptive name of the Hellic races in the Homeric age. Yet it is without any note of an Hellic or European origin. Let us therefore see, whether in the East we can find anything that stands, even though at first sight disguisedly, in affinity with it. Now Herodotus tells us, that in the leading tribe of Pasargadæ there was a family (φρήτρη), from which came the Persian kings; the family of the 'Αχαιμενίδαι. Even if it were not easy to trace the mode of the relationship, it would

[c] Herod. vi. 53, 4.

seem inevitable to recognise a connection between the name 'Αχαιμένης, or whatever is the proper Persian root of this Greek patronymic, and those 'Αχαιοὶ whom we find at the head of the Greek races. This connection receives a singular illustration from Strabo, who in describing the Asiatic country called Aria, which gives a name to the Arian race, states that it has three cities called after their founders, Artacaena, Alexandria, and Achaia. Artacaes was a distinguished Persian, of the army of Xerxes. The name of Alexander speaks for itself. With respect to either of these, Strabo may be understood to speak of what may, from the respective dates, have been genuine historical traditions. But he knew and could know nothing of a Persian Achæus, as the founder of the third city. And the Greek Achæus, if he existed at all, belonged to another country, and to a pre-historic antiquity. The real force of the tradition which reports that these cities bore the names of their founders, seems, however, to be pretty obvious. It must surely mean this: that they had borne the same names at all times within the memory of man. Thus we have the Achæan name thrown back, by a local testimony subsisting in Strabo's time, to a remote antiquity: there it finds a holding-ground in the Achæmenidæ of Herodotus: and both these authors become witnesses, I think, to the derivation of the 'Αχαιοὶ of Homer from Persia[c]. I do not mean that the Achæmenes, who, according to the Behistun Inscription, gave his name to the Achæmenidæ, was the father of the Achæans of the poems, for he appears to have lived only five generations before Darius. But the coincidence of name between the ruling family in Persia, and the dominant race in Greece, bears witness, in

[c] Strabo xi. 10. p. 516.

harmony with other testimonies, to a presumptive identity of origin.

It appears, too, that the name thus viewed may well have had its root in the ancient Arian language, if we judge from its extant forms. The word signifying 'friends,' according to Sir H. Rawlinson, is in Sanscrit *sakhá*, and in Persian *hakhá*.

"The name Achæmenes signifies 'friendly,' or 'possessing friends,' being formed of a Persian word *hakhá*, corresponding to the Sanscrit *sakhá*, and an attributive affix equivalent to the Sanscrit *mat*, which forms the nominative in *man*. H. R."[c]

The word, then, if we may rely on this high authority, undergoes no other change, on passing into the Greek tongue, than the loss of the initial aspirate, (while the second is retained in χ,) and the addition of the Greek termination ος or ιος. In this description of a ruling race by their common bond as associates, there is something that resembles the European and feudal name of peers.

There is indeed another name still existing in Persia, that of the Eelliats or itinerant tribes, the form of which, and the circumstances under which it appears, will shortly be noticed[d].

We have now obtained various lights, which point out to us the Persians as the probable ancestry of the Greeks. It still remains to learn, whether from the history of ancient Persia we can raise a presumption that there were, through resemblances subsisting there, marked signs of affinity between the two.

Herodotus has given us a remarkable, and apparently a careful, account of the ancient Persians, both as to religion and as to manners, which upon the whole both

[c] Rev. G. Rawlinson's Herodotus, vol. i. p. 264. note 5.
[d] Inf. p. 571.

exhibits striking points of resemblance to Greece, and likewise tends to attach that resemblance to the Hellic rather than the Pelasgian race.

In making the comparison, we must allow specially for two sources of error. The Hellic tribes of Homer's time had been probably for not less than eight or ten generations (since we trace the Dardanians on their own ground for seven generations, the Perseids and Æolids for six) detached from the parent stock, and might well have modified their character and customs, especially since they had mingled with the Pelasgians in the plains. And again, the account of Herodotus is later probably by 500 years or more, than the manners described in Homer. The Persians of his day had long been mixed with the Medes: and had, as he tells us[e], adopted their costume: probably much else along with it.

The Persians, says Herodotus[f], have no temples, altars, nor statues of the gods. Tacitus[g] gives a like account of the Germans. Of these Homer only enables us to trace altars with clearness as having been adopted by the Hellenic races at the period of the *Troica*. But the tendency to sacerdotal development among the Pelasgi may have had its counterpart in 'the symbolism and complicated ceremonial of Media[h].'

They worship Jupiter from high places. So did Hector. We have no reason to make the same assertion of the Trojans generally: but the place given to Jupiter on Ida, and the whole Olympian fabric, probably also the plan of scaling heaven by heaping mountains one on another, all belong to the same train of thought.

They, if we are to adopt the statement, call the

[e] vi. 54.   [f] Herod. i. 113.   [h] Blakesley's Herodotus, vol. i.
[g] Tac. Germ. c. 9.   428. Exc. on iii. 74.

II. *Ethnology.*

whole circuit of the heaven by the name of Jupiter. This same is the share of the universe, which, in the Homeric mythology, falls to the lot of Jupiter, and the name Ζεύς is said to be identical with the Sanscrit *Dyaus,* meaning 'the sky[i]:' a sense which we find in the *sub dio* and *sub Jove* of the Latin writers, belonging to the Augustan age. This elemental conception of him, however, is probably more Median than Persian.

They did not originally worship Venus (ἀρχῆθεν); but they learned the worship of her from others, apparently the Medes or Assyrians. This remarkably accords with the case of the Hellenes of Homer, who seem only to have been drawing towards, rather than to have accepted fully, the worship of Venus in his time[k].

They considered fire to be a god[l]: differing in this from the Egyptians, who held it to be an animal.

So we find that the worship of Vulcan appears to be Hellic more than Pelasgian, and that the fable of his origin distinctly points to what was for Homer the farthest east[m].

They paid a particular reverence to rivers[n]. Of this we have the amplest evidence in Homer among the Greeks as to Alpheus, Spercheus, and the River of Scheria: rivers, too, were honoured by a more distinct personification than was attributed to other natural objects. The Scamander is, indeed, similarly treated. But this is an exception to the general mode of representation: and no other Trojan River is actively personified[o]. Simois is addressed (Il. xxi. 308) by Scamander; but is himself a mute.

[i] Müller's Comparative Mythology, p. 45, in Oxford Essays for 1856.
[k] Inf. Religion and Morals, sect. 3.
[l] iii. 16.
[m] Il. xviii. 394, et seqq.
[n] i. 138.
[o] This subject will be resumed in treating of the Trojans.

The comparison as to religious belief. 561

These, however, are particular points: let us also consider more at large the general outline which Herodotus has given us of the Persian religion.

They did not, he says, consider as the Greeks did that the gods were (ἀνθρωποφυέας) anthropophuistic[p]. They called the entire circle of heaven by the name of Jupiter. They originally worshipped no gods except the sun, the moon, the earth, fire, water, and the winds. Afterwards they learned from the Assyrians and Arabians to worship Οὐρανίη under the name of Mitra.

I shall not attempt in this place to discuss the difficult subject of the Persian or Magian religions as they are in themselves; farther than to observe, that they appear to have been different. Here we have only to consider the relation, if any, between that system which the sketch by Herodotus describes, and the religion of heroic Greece.

It appears that the religion of the Persians[q], either as anterior to, or as independent of that of Zoroaster and the Magi, embraced, (1) the belief in one Supreme and incorporeal God, and (2) the worship of the host of heaven.

The sketch of Herodotus appears to be a representation of this religion: it contains no evidence of dualism, and fire-worship appears in it only as a subordinate characteristic. Only it would appear as if the historian had reflected upon Persia the leading idea of the Greek mythology, namely, that which invested Jupiter, as the supreme deity, especially with the charge of the sky and atmosphere: and that when he says the Persians call the heavens Jupiter, he probably means that they

---

[p] Herod. i. 131.   [q] Malcolm's Persia, vol. i. p. 185.

o o

consider the Supreme Being not to be circumscribed, but to pervade all space. The powers of outward Nature were doubtless worshipped by them, in the first instance, as organs of the Supreme Being.

In this sketch there is something to remind us of a primitive religion, or at least to suggest the traditional forms in which that religion was conveyed: it teaches the unity of God, and then steps only into the most natural and proximate form of deviation. It is well called by Dr. Döllinger 'a monotheism with polytheistic elements[r].'

It is unlike the Homeric religion, inasmuch as it does not contain any evidences of traditive derivation nearly so abundant or so specific as, I think, we shall find manifest in the Homeric system[s]. But then we must remember that it is junior, by many centuries, to the system of Homer: and that these evidences had become far less palpable, at the epoch when Herodotus lived, in the contemporary religion of Greece.

On the other hand, with respect to its human, inventive, and polytheistic element, it is evidently akin to the Homeric religion; under which Nature is everywhere animated and uplifted, and teems at every pore with some expression of divinity. The Greek scheme is indeed still more human, (for it takes everywhere the human dress,) more poetical and imaginative, than the Persian one; but the generative principle is one and the same, namely, the impersonation, though not necessarily in both cases alike under human conditions, of all powers observed and felt in outward nature. The whole group may well remind us, both in letter and in

---

[r] Döllinger's Heidenthum und Judenthum, vi. 2.
[s] See 'The Religion of the Homeric Age,' sect. ii.   [t] Il. iii. 276.

As to ritual and other resemblances. 563

spirit, of the invocation of Agamemnon, which after Jupiter enumerates the sun, the rivers, and the earth: though it also adds the infernal gods[t]. We find from another place in Herodotus, that he knew the Persians to believe in an infernal deity, to whom they offered human sacrifices[u].

If we conceive the Persians moving westward, and gathering mental and imaginative, as well as warlike and political energy, on their way, we shall see that they are only enlarging the scheme reported in Herodotus by a consistent application of its principles, and following them out in an imaginative and dramatic spirit to their results, when they people every meadow, wood, and fountain with deity, and when they construct the great Olympian court for heaven, with its several reflections; in the sea, around the throne of Nereus, and, in the nether world, under the gloomy sway of Aidoneus and Persephone.

Herodotus[x] also gives us a sketch of the Persian system as to ritual. Each person sacrificed for himself: without libation, music, garlands, or cakes: only in a becoming spot, and having the tiara wreathed usually with myrtle. When he had performed the essential part of the function, a *Magus* recited a religious chant; and no one could perform sacrifice except in presence of a *Magus*. It is plain that we see here, if not, as Mr. Blakesley thinks[y], the confusion, at any rate the combination, of the genuine Persian with the Median ritual. The presence of the Magian was required, or let us suppose that it was simply usual: yet he did not offer the sacrifice. This was perhaps the compromise between the sacerdotal system of the

[u] Herod. vii. 114.   [x] i. 132.   [y] In loc.

Pelasgians, and the independent or patriarchal principle of the Hellenes, who exhibit to us first ὑποφῆται, then μάντιες and θυοσκόοι, but who seem to know nothing, as among themselves, of priests.

Like the Hellic races, the Persians of old were remarkable for personal modesty. They did not practice any unnatural vice, until they learned it from Greece[z]. They placed an extremely high value on their own race, which they esteemed far before all others[a]. Different social relations among those who were intimate were marked by differences in the kiss[b]. Equals kissed with the mouths, unequals by the mouth of one on the cheek of the other: while persons greatly inferior fell prostrate. In the Odyssey, Ulysses kisses his son Telemachus (doubtless on the face) (Od. xvi. 190), and Penelope kisses Telemachus on the head and eyes (xvii. 39); but Ulysses kisses the king of Egypt, when he is a suppliant (xiv. 279) on the knees, and the slave Dolius on the hands (xxiv. 398): he kisses Eumæus and Philœtius on the head and hands, while they embrace, but do not kiss him (xxi. 224, 5). Dolius held the hand, and no more, of Ulysses. But the chief is kissed on the head and eyes by his grandmother (Od. xix. 417.)

Like the Greeks, the Persians shore the hair in mourning. They held lying to be the most disgraceful of all things. It was also disgraceful to be called a woman[c]. Again, the Persians in the time of Crœsus were highlanders[d], destitute of all the comforts of life, just as Achilles describes the Helli round Dodona. Like the καρηκομόωντες Ἀχαιοὶ, they wore their hair long[e].

[z] Herod i. 133, 135.
[a] Ibid. 134.
[b] Ibid.
[c] Il. ii. 235.
[d] Herod. i. 71, and ix. 122.
[e] Herod. vii. 19.

All these are points of similarity. Upon the other hand, there are two points of discrepancy, which may be noticed. The Persians had many wives and concubines: and they did not burn their dead. Upon the first of these points of discrepancy with the Greeks, the Persians were in harmony with, at least, the ruling race of Troas; and polygamy must always be an affair of ruling races, or of a select few.

A fragment of the old historian Xanthus[f] would lead us to suppose that they derived this habit from the Medes, who, according to that author, had no law of incest, and freely exchanged their wives.

On the second point, they differed from Troy: for the Trojans, like the Greeks, burned their dead.

It was also the Persian custom to introduce women to their banquets[g]. There is, however, a trace of this last-named practice at least in the Olympian banquets of Homer. And it is plain that Arete, the queen of Alcinous, was at the Phæacian banquet (Od. vii. 49, 50, 147, 8): but this may have been due to the unusual honour in which she was held (Od. vii. 67). More ordinarily the Greek women do not appear at meals with men.

Thus far we seem to be carried by the text of Herodotus standing alone. And it should be borne in mind, that Ctesias, as he is reported in Photius[h], though he condemns Herodotus as a teller of untruth, and contradicts him in his narrative, does not question his account of religion and manners.

But the discovery and deciphering by Rawlinson of the Behistun Inscription throws an additional light upon this question, and one highly confirmatory of the

[f] Rawlinson's Herodotus, Life, p. cxlviii. n.
[g] Herod. i. 135. iii. 16. v. 18.
[h] Photii Biblioth. Cod. lxxii.

general conclusions towards which we have tended. The Magian, called Smerdis[i] by Herodotus, appears in this Inscription under the name of Gomates: and it is now demonstrated, that the revolution which he wrought, or of which he took advantage, and which was reversed by Darius, was religious as well as political. For, says the Inscription, 'when Cambyses had proceeded to Egypt, the state became irreligious.' It is then related that Gomates obtained the empire. But, says Darius, 'I adored Ormuzd. Ormuzd brought me aid.' 'Then did I, with faithful men, slay Gomates the Magian ... By the grace of Ormuzd I became king. Ormuzd gave me the empire ..... The rites which Gomates the Magian had introduced I prohibited. I restored the chants, and the worship, to the State, and to those families, which Gomates the Magian had deprived of them.' Thus Darius represents in this great transaction the Persian party and its religion, as against the Medians and the Magi. Hence arises a direct presumption that the Magi were properly a Median class, and were adopted into the Persian system, only in consequence of the connection and political amalgamation of the Persians with the Medes.

Again, in a political point of view, we have the Persians clearly exhibited as standing in the same relation to the Medes, which the Helli held to the Pelasgi. The needy highlanders[k] come down upon and overpower the richer and more advanced inhabitants of the central valleys: under the Magian upstart, the latter take advantage of the absence of the sovereign to rebel, but they are, after a short interval, finally put down.

Darius, having obtained the throne, and established

[i] See Blakesley's Excursus on Herod. iii. 74.
[k] Herod. ix. 122.

the Persian supremacy, proceeded to organize the empire; and he appears to have displayed in this great sphere the same thoroughly political mind as the Hellenic races exhibited in their diminutive, but still extraordinary polities. He divided the empire by a cadastral system, under provincial governors; and he established everywhere fixed rates of tribute. These were great departures from the old Greek form of sovereignty: but we are now five centuries later than the heroic age: and, besides, we must remember that the paternal and everywhere fixed forms of government, which will suffice for very small states, are not always applicable to large ones. Yet, as we learn from Herodotus, the innovations of Darius were much resented by the Persians, who under Cyrus, and even under Cambyses, knew nothing of fixed rates of taxation, but offered benevolences (δῶρα) to the throne[1]; and a saying came into vogue, that Cyrus was a father, Cambyses an autocrat (δεσπότης), and Darius a tradesman (κάπηλος).

'Landlord of England art thou now, not King[m].'

We seem to have here an emphatic testimony to the original identity of the Persian and Hellic, or Hellenic ideas of government.

It is also worthy of remark, that in the case of Minos, who seems to have held a large and disjointed empire, we have traditional, and even Homeric indications of some proceeding not wholly unlike this of Darius. For this prince, according to Thucydides, governed the islands through his sons, that is, by a provincial organization under local officers[n]; in Homer we find Rhadamanthus acting at a distance, probably on his

[1] Herod. iii. 89. [m] Shakspeare's Richard II.
[n] Thuc. i. 4.

II. *Ethnology.*

behalf; and we may perhaps hence conceive, that there was truth in the tradition, afterwards so odious, that he imposed tribute upon the then **Pelasgian** Attica. Minos indeed was a reputed Phœnician: but in Homer the Phœnician and Persian traditions are closely combined, and the poet appears to have treated Phœnicia as the medium, perhaps even the symbol, of much that was Persian. Even geographically I believe that he placed the two countries in very close proximity.

It seems probable also, that we may consider the long continued application of the term Βασιλεὺς by the Greeks to the Persian kings, as having reference to an original identity of race and manners. It had been their own original name for a monarch. When the ancient monarchies passed away, so did the name from their usage; and the possessor of singlehanded power among the Greeks, having in all cases obtained it by the suppression of liberty, came to be called τύραννος; but the word Βασιλεὺς continued to be used with reference to Persia, where the chain of traditions had not been broken, and where monarchy had never ceased to prevail; so that there had been no reason for a change of usage, or for a deviation from the ancient respect and reverence towards the possessor of a throne. Again, the traditional throne of Lacedæmon continued to be held by Βασιλεῖς[o].

For the word Βασιλεὺς was one of no ordinary force; and down to a very late date it must have been surrounded with venerable recollections. It was borne by the emperors of Constantinople, and even at times stickled for by them, as a title distinguishing them from the emperors of the West. Though essentially Greek, it

[o] Ar. Pol. III. xiv. 3.

was also written in the Latin character. Unlike the word *Rex*, it appears never to have been applied to any ruler who exercised a merely derivative power. It travelled so far westward as to our own island: and King Edgar, in a charter, calls himself *Anglorum Basileus, omniumque Regum, Insularum, Oceanique Britanniam circumjacentis, cunctarumque nationum, quæ infra eam includuntur, Imperator et Dominus*[p].

Even now, after so many centuries of vicissitude, the Persian presents numerous points of resemblance, perhaps more than we can find in Modern Greece itself, to the primitive and heroic Greek of Homer. Upon the whole, without doubt, he stands upon a lower level. Lying, drunkenness, unnatural vice[q], the degradation of women, are all now rife in Persia. But such things were to be expected after so many ages of estrangement from the revealed knowledge of God, of moral contamination, and of political depression and misgovernment. But with allowance on these accounts, and on the score of the changes to Magianism and Mahometanism, the old features are still retained, and they present to our view abundant presumptions of identity.

The Persians[q] are still noted for hospitality and love of display: for highly refined manners and great personal beauty. They have still an intense love of poetry, of song, and also of music, while their practice of this art is rude and simple: they still associate poetry (sometimes licentious, as in the Eighth Odyssey) with

[p] Selden's Titles of Honour, chap. ii.
[q] Malcolm's Persia, ii. 585. 631, 6. Quarterly Review, vol. 101. p. 510.
[r] The traits mentioned in the text, where there is no special reference, are drawn from the three last chapters of Malcolm's Persia.

recitation and the banquet; and, when Malcolm wrote, printing was still unknown among the useful arts of the country. They are passionately fond of horses, much given to the chase and to the practice of horse-racing[r]. Men of letters are esteemed, and their society valued, even as in the Odyssey the Bard is among those whom men are accustomed to invite to dinner[s]. On the occasion of a marriage they celebrate prolonged feasts of three days for the poor, and from that up to thirty or forty days for the highest classes. Amidst great depravity, much of filial piety and of maternal influence remains[t]. It is observed that they do not usually allude to women by name[u]. There is an approach to this abstinence in the Homeric poems; where names of men, and likewise of goddesses, in the vocative are frequent, but I am not sure that we have any instances of a woman addressed by her proper name throughout the Iliad or Odyssey. But certainly one of the most curious notes of similarity is that, together with their high and refined politeness, they retain a liability, when under great excitement, to a sort of cannibal ferocity. A recent writer states[x] the following anecdotes. A few years ago, the chieftain of a tribe slew in a feud the chieftain of another. Shortly afterwards he was attacked while on a journey, taken after vigorous resistance, and put to death. His heart, if we may believe the recital, was then roasted, and was eaten by the mother of his former victim. And again; the husband of a beautiful young woman had been slain by a rival chief. The

[r] Malcolm's Persia, ii. 550, 558, 566, 611.
[s] Ibid. 576. Grote's History of Greece, P. I. c. xxi. vol. ii. p. 196 n.
[t] Ibid. 616, and Quart. Rev. p. 509.
[u] Quart. Rev. vol. 101. p. 509 n.
[x] Quart. Rev. vol. 101. p. 50.

widow, who had been much attached to the dead warrior, would minutely describe the incidents of the catastrophe, and then, lifting up her hands to heaven, would pray to Ali to deliver the murderer into her hands, 'that having cut out his heart, I may make it into kibabs, and eat it before I die.' These are certainly most pointed proofs that Homer has proceeded with his usual veracity, as an observer and chronicler of man, when he shocks us by making Achilles wish he could eat Hector, and Hecuba wish she could eat Achilles; nay, even when he yet further proves that this idea was familiar to his race and age, by making Jupiter tell Juno, she would, he believes, be well content to eat Priam and all his sons.

To appreciate fully, however, the resemblances of Greek and Persian, we must take the latter as he is found in the military tribes of the province of Pars or Fars. The members of these tribes are chiefly horsemen, all soldiers, and all brigands. But they abhor the name and character of thief; plunder is redeemed by violence in their eyes, and it is evidently accompanied with the practice of a generous and delicate hospitality. Elsewhere in Persia many degrading customs prevail, and women are regarded chiefly with a view to sensual use; but among these military tribes they are more highly valued, and are of remarkable modesty and chastity; yet they have an innocent freedom in their good offices to strangers[y], which at once recalls the Greek maidens of the Odyssey. Adultery is capitally punishable. Alexander the Great endeavoured to bring these tribes to settle, and to adopt agricultural habits; but they have defied his efforts, and still

[y] Malcolm, ii. 613.

remain like the old Helli of the hills, when they hung over the Pelasgians of the valleys. It is to be observed, that they are particularly mentioned in the Eteo-Persian province of Fars: and further, that they bear the name Eelleat[z], which at least presents a striking resemblance to that of the Helli. The aspirate would pass into the doubled ϵ, like ἥλιος into ἠέλιος, or ἕδνα into ἐέδνα. So Helli is the equivalent of Eelli.

In sum, the ancient Persians, like the Helli, were of Arian race, of highland character and habits, inhabitants of a rude country: apparently children of Japhet, akin closely to the Hellenes, and less palpably to the Osci and Umbri.

The Medians were *civilly* in a more advanced stage of social life, and were possessed of greater wealth, but endowed with inferior energies. They are presumed by many to have been of the race of Ham: to have peopled Egypt, and to be akin to the ancient Sicani, to the Basques, the Esthonians, the Lapps, and the Finns of modern Europe. For the purposes of this inquiry, they are to be regarded as in all likelihood the immediate fountain-head of the wide-spread Pelasgian races.

We began under the warning of Mr. Grote: and I fear that we end under the implied ban of another very able and recent writer, Dr. Latham[a]. He considers that we have been put in possession of no facts with respect to the Pelasgi more than those three, so slight and so incapable of effective combination, which are recognised by Mr. Grote[b]. But the principle he lays down is that, by which I wish to be tried. He says, the scholar finds a ποῦ στῶ in the *dictum* of this or

[z] Malcolm, i. 369. ii. 597, 634, 638.
[a] Latham's Man and his Migrations, pp. 33–6.
[b] History of Greece, vol. ii. p. 352.

that author, but the sound ethnologist 'on the last testified fact:' he demands for his basis 'the existing state of things as either known to ourselves, or known to contemporaries capable of learning them at the period nearest the time under consideration.' It appears to me that the text of Homer, so far as it goes, answers this demand: that his accounts of Pelasgian, Hellene, and Achæan, when we can get at them, and when we take into view his epoch and means of information, come clearly within the meaning of 'testified facts' in regard to that particular subject matter. I admit that, from their incidental and often unconscious nature, there is a great liability to error in the attempt to elicit them: but my assertion is, that the ground under foot is sound; and that, though we may go astray while travelling it, yet we are not attempting to tread upon a quicksand. As to the success with which this principle has here been applied, I am not too sanguine; but I contend earnestly for the principle itself, because I believe that it will, when admitted, legitimately work out its own results, and that they will make no unimportant addition to the primary facts of that great branch of philosophy, the history, and most of all the early history, of man.

ADDENDA.

Page 106. On the possible migration of the Dodonæan oracle, see below, p. 238.

P. 126. On the theory of Curtius respecting the Ionians, see p. 480.

P. 153. The wealth of Egyptian Thebes was known to Achilles; see Il. ix. 381.

P. 167. The Birth of Minos will be more fully discussed in connection with the Outer Geography of the Odyssey. On the ancient and extensive influence of Phœnicia upon Crete, see Höck's Creta, vol. i. pp. 68 and seqq.

P. 186. On the word *lupus*, see Müller's Dorians, II. vi. 8, 9, for its relation to λευκὸς, λυκὴ, λυκηγενὴς, or light-born, and *lux*.

P. 306. In general confirmation of what has been said above on the subject of language, I may refer to the *Römische Geschichte*[*] of Mommsen, which had not come under my eye when the Seventh Section went to press.

His conclusions are;

1. That the Greek and mid-Italian languages correspond, in what touches the rudiments of the material life of man.

2. That in the higher region of the mind, of religion, and of advanced polity, this correspondence wholly fails.

3. That the Græco-Italic agrees with the Sanscrit down to the pastoral stage of society only, and ceases with the commencement of the agricultural and settled stage.

4. That the abstract genius of the Roman religion bears a relation to the Greek anthropophuism, like that of the full-

---

[*] Leipsic, 1854, vol. i, ch. ii.

formed Indian mythology to the metaphysical scheme of the Zendavesta.

He appears to me to cast the balance overmuch on the Roman side: but his statement will well repay an attentive consideration.

He supplies the following words, which I would add to the lists I have given above. They generally corroborate the conclusions at which I have arrived.

χόρτος .... hortus.
κέγχρος .... cicer.
μελίνη .... milium.
πολτὸς .... puls.
μύλη .... mola.
ἄξων ⎱
ἄμ-αξα ⎰ ...... axis.
ποίνη .... pœna.
κρίνω, κρίμα ... crimen.
ταλάω .... talio.
χίτων .... tunica.

And, belonging to the higher domain—

σκύτος........... scutum (with an alteration, or progression of sense).
λόγχη............ lancea.
τέμενος .... templum.

Among these, the relationship of τέμενος and templum seems to require further proof.

I have to add the word κῆλον, which seems to be in nearer correspondence than βέλος is with *telum.* On the other side, I may note ἄορ, for *a sword*, and ὄχος, ὄχημα, for *a chariot*, as among the words not in correspondence.

P. 311. Add Φείδιππος. Il. ii. 768.

P. 313. The statement as to the persons slain by Hector and Mars is inaccurate. The seven first names are, so far as the text informs us, undistinguished, except Teuthras, who is called ἀντίθεος; and among these seven we have no name, which is clearly of Hellic etymology. But the nine others belong to a different part of the action (Il. xi. 301-4), and are expressly called ἡγεμόνες (or officers, Il. ii. 365): and among these, while we have four names of Hellic complexion, Dolops and Opheltius are the only two which can be positively assigned to the Pelasgian class.

P. 380. While I have stated the second sense of the word Ἄργος according to what appears to me to be the balance of the evidence, I admit it to be a doubtful point whether we ought rather, with Strabo (p. 365), to understand it preferably as capable of meaning the entire Peloponnesus.